Old Bird

The Irrepressible Mrs Hewlett

Old Bird

The Irrepressible Mrs Hewlett

Gail Hewlett

Matador
5 Weir Road
Kibworth Beauchamp
Leicester LE8 0LQ, UK
Tel: (+44) 116 279 2299
Fax: (+44) 116 279 2277
Email: books@troubador.co.uk
Web: www.troubador.co.uk/matador

ISBN 978-1848763-371

British Library Cataloguing in Publication Data.
A catalogue record for this book is available from the British Library.

Typeset in 11pt Book Antiqua by Troubador Publishing Ltd, Leicester, UK

Matador is an imprint of Troubador Publishing Ltd

To A,E, F and S

CONTENTS

PROLOGUE

To have paternal grandparents, one of whom had written historical romances and the other who had first flown their own aeroplane in 1911, was a powerful card to play in the early days of courtship and my husband-to-be played it along with his favourite records. And then he trumped it. It was not his grandfather who had been the early aviator, but his grandmother.

This reversal of what might generally be considered the conventional allocation of roles in the grandparental marriage, plus family speculation as to the exact nature of the extra-marital relationships of each grandparent, made them an intriguing pair. The autobiographical typescript, crisping and flaking at the edges left by the Old Bird, as Hilda B. Hewlett came to be known, was discretion itself and *The Letters of Maurice Hewlett*, published after his death, revealed little of a personal nature. If nothing else, it was going to be interesting find out how such an unlikely couple met and fared together.

Thus it was in 1991, one Friday in July – the 19th to be precise – I would have been found sitting in Leicester Square. I had just become the surprised and very proud possessor of a reading ticket for the British Museum. So proud, in fact, I had to keep taking it out of my pocket to look at it. And all thanks to our long-standing (and, in the event, critically and positively encouraging) friend, the actress and author, Barbara Ewing. Too busy herself to accept my husband's invitation to write up the Hewletts' story, she suggested that I might have the time and mind to undertake the task of researching and writing it. After discussing the potential for family sensibilities to be ruffled, we decided that, nevertheless, this 'outsider on the inside' should go ahead. Sitting in that July sunshine, almost brimming over with excitement – ready tears are such an embarrassment – I had not the smallest inkling of the amount of fun and work I was going to have. How could I? I was too busy coping with my awe at the thought of not only being allowed into the Reading Room at the British Museum, but of using it. Not until I was suitably calm, did I make my housewifely way home.

The British Museum, where the beautiful blue dome of the ceiling and the hush of the old Reading Room made entering it like stepping into an inner sanctum, seemed the very place to start looking for something, anything, on an author, once a 'name', who had slid into oblivion. But it was in the Manuscripts Department, then a mere foundling compared to its regeneration in the splendid British Library in St Pancras, where lay treasure: the typescript of Maurice Hewlett's diary from 1893-1923.

Simple! Hit upon the right resource and reap instant reward. Not so. Oh! The promise in that word diary! But, oh, the disappointment! It was neither a 'dear diary', a revelatory and personal journal, nor was it a series of engagement diaries chronicling all those family events and celebrations, appointments, meetings, dinners, concerts or plays, that provide the structure for the cladding of the subject's life and work. It was a hybrid: a chronological record of work in hand with a mere scattering of random personal entries and comments. However, as disappointing as it was on the first feverish gallop through its pages, on a soberer second reading it became, by its very unsatisfactory nature, more intriguing: after a third reading, questions were queuing for answers. And the first, who had arranged for the diary to be typed up and for a copy to be placed in the British Library?

Avid curiosity cheerfully displaces disappointment and the discovery that it was Mrs Gladys M.P. Welby-Everard (Hilda's youngest sister and always known as Gay) who was the depositor was a surprise, but perhaps not so great a one: after all, it was her name that was romantically linked with his. However, when a hardbacked, lined, foolscap book – the presumed original of the typescript – was confidently identified by one of Gay's daughters-in-law as being in Gay's hand, not Maurice Hewlett's, then the family rumours did not seem so improbable.

Similarly, Hilda B. Hewlett's reticence about her marriage, her family and her friends in her unpublished memoir raised more questions than answers. People came and went without introduction or farewell; some were significant forces in her life, like engineer and aviator Gustave Blondeau, while many mentioned were nameless. Of her five sisters, two remained anonymous, while the others appeared to go by anything other than their given name. She, herself, Hilda Beatrice (née Herbert) was only ever Billy to her family. And hence the problem of what to call her throughout this book. She might have signed herself Hilda B. Hewlett, but nowhere is there any proof that she was ever addressed as Hilda. Single, or married, her initials were HBH and initials are useful – they are easy to recognise visually and carry no emotional baggage. Williams, Maurice's affectionate twist on her family nickname, is charming, but Billy suits her well. It encompasses the childhood tomboy, the defiant teenager, and the energetic woman. Once she had taken to the air, her son and daughter affectionately dubbed her Old Bird, a name she cherished and used for the last third of her life, but as consistency is to be valued, she will begin and end as Billy, although Old Bird will be allowed to intrude. Her singular voice – recognisable for being in italics – will echo faintly throughout in snatches from her memoir.

Similarly, italics have been used for Maurice's personal comments from his so-called diary. And, as he was remarkable in his own if less unique way, and despite the bias of the title of this book in her favour, a genuine attempt has been made to give him as much of his due as his wife's life will allow. The nature of the man and his career are far from an irrelevancy in the story of his irrepressible wife. No one reads Maurice Hewlett's work now; not surprising, as his style – an acquired taste even in his day – is pretty indigestible. (Then again, no one reads his famous friend, J.M. Barrie: his name is principally kept alive by *Peter Pan* and an interest in his complex relationship with the Llewelyn Davies family.) To those interested in the early days of flying, the name of Hilda Hewlett and her place in the history of aviation is already known. What makes the Hewletts, each as singular as the other, so interesting is that together they were a reflection of the transition from the 19th to the 20th century. And, without each other, neither would have enjoyed the success they did. He as an author. She as an aviator.

For me, more homely calls on available time for research and writing than a professional writer would consider has not been without benefit. I began researching and writing before the advent of instant availability of data at the click of a computer mouse. However, the joy of the discovery of something new or pertinent in the reams skimmed or read closely was matchless. A sibilant "yessss", acknowledged with a grin by a stranger, and I was up there with explorers and seekers of truth. The extra time taken and the immersion in the papers, letters, journals and books directly or indirectly relevant to the Hewletts, allowed me more time for reflection. Both Maurice and Hilda became very much more admirable and very much nicer people than they had at first appeared. I hope I have served them well.

CHAPTER 1
EGYPT

The seeds of a wider and richer conception were sown

To say I enjoyed myself is underrating the effect it had on the rest of my life. I woke up from a narrow, conventional, stultifying childhood and first thought for myself. I believed till that time that I was ugly, ignorant, wicked and inferior.

So wrote Billy, looking back to fifty years earlier when she had visited Egypt in the company of her parents. To have reached nineteen and think so ill of herself suggested that Billy had been subjected to a childhood of horror. She had not, but life in the vicarage had certainly been repressive and any self-expression on Billy's part had too frequently been considered, fairly or otherwise, as trouble-making. Educated at home, apart from one term at boarding school – a brief concept of punishment she had enjoyed – Billy was more than ready to respond with a passion to what was new: its contrast to what she had so far experienced was thrilling beyond imagination. Attendance at the genteelly suitable classes for young ladies at the South Kensington Art School had already hinted that *something beautiful and big* could offer distraction from *the petty annoyances of life,* and her consequent vow *never to be without some object or interest of such importance that all discomfort, annoyance or temporary misery counted as of quite secondary consideration* had so far proved to be of considerable comfort. But it was a three-month trip to Egypt, in early1883, that sprang the locks of her childhood and released the Billy who would one day learn to fly: literally.

It has to be admitted, however, that if she had not been such an unruly member of her family, she might never have had her moment of glorious awakening. Her father, the Reverend George Herbert of St Peter's Vauxhall, his heart weakened by overwork and his ascetic lifestyle, had been ordered to rest for three months in a warm climate. Egypt promised the right weather; the Herberts had useful contacts among the English archeological fraternity in Cairo; and Cairo had an English church, where it was possible for Anglicans to take communion. To ensure that there would be peace at home in their absence, it had been decided that Billy should accompany them. Dora, the eldest of the family of seven and no friend to Billy, would be left in *loco parentis*, unprovoked and unchallenged: George, the only son, would be at Eton. Given that there were a number of relatives on whom Billy could have been foisted in their parents' absence, it is likely her fond father argued the educational benefits of the trip for his spirited daughter.

Perceived as more European than African – French being the first language after Arabic, and English the official language of the law courts and the administration – Egypt had barely re-stabilised after the failed revolution led by Arabi, 'El Wahid', the Only One and the idol of Egypt. *We went via Brindisi, then by boat to Alexandria. It was just after the bombardment, several bits of the town were destroyed and streets impassable.* In fact, Admiral Seymour had bombarded Alexandria towards the end of August 1882 before going on to crush Arabi's rebellion at Tel el-Kebir in September and so restoring the allies' (France and England) puppet Khedive Tewfik to his throne. *We came home via Suez and saw Tel-el Kebir strewn with skeletons and tins* was Billy's equally laconic reference to the end of that brief revolution. But it was not the effects of political upheaval that struck Billy – their's was the only dahabeah sailing up the Nile that Spring and so required a night-time guard when anchored near the bank – but the flood of sensory, intellectual and emotional experiences was what swept her away. From the moment she set eyes on Alexandria, exotic, dazzling white and green, set between a sea and sky of intense blue, she vowed to learn and experience all she could of Egypt and Arab life and art. She learnt some Arabic from their dragoman and was charmed by gifts of sugar-cane, fruit and the occasional piece of Ancient Egyptian pottery from the sailors; and when a sheikh took them on milk-white mules to one of the pyramids presented Billy with his own mule from Mecca and filled her head with Bedouin stories about stars, camels, date palms and desert life, it is a wonder she turned down his invitation to enter his harem.

In Cairo, Billy was gratified to be the recipient of unpatronising attention of both sexes and the miserably shy young woman began to blossom. But it was the particular kindness of Stanley Lane Poole, whose uncle was joint secretary of the recently formed Egypt Exploration Fund, who taught her how to look and learn as he went about collecting for the London museums, that set the caged bird free. *I was simply mad with delight and lived every moment in ecstasy. I fancy my Mother saw what a change travel had made, as she was constantly doing her best to keep the bonds of home teaching firmly tied all round me. I remember sitting still, in a dream of the East, while she preached original sin, my sins in particular, contrition and repentance. It was too late then; life had got me in her hurrying stream, there was no returning to stagnant water. I partly guessed there were no rigid standards of right and wrong. All passion of love and beauty could not be of the devil, and evil in consequence. The Sun and Earth were there for men to be happy in. Of course I didn't think it all out, but the seeds of a wider and richer conception were sown, the sowing time was a heaven of delight, so crammed with possibilities of learning that the brain was incapable of sorting, hardly capable of receiving all the new ideas for sheer enjoyment. No place, no travel, affected me so strongly again.*

Mrs Herbert's chief concern was for her daughter's Christian soul: her daughter's chief concern was to make *her own opportunities for enjoyment, some not conforming to the recognised proprieties.* Luckily, the fairly predictable outcome of this subversion, a love affair which taught Billy *a side of nature* of which she had been utterly ignorant, went undiscovered. Indeed, had it not been for the Herberts' timely departure from Cairo, Billy, as she coyly put it, would not have been saved *from the inevitable last experience,* although, as an afterthought, Billy censored her own typescript. She crossed out 'the inevitable last experience' and wrote in ink 'being found out and punished.'

Now that life had her in its 'hurrying stream' it is no surprise to learn that, on her return to London, Billy found art classes neither distracting nor absorptive, and longed to find fulfilment beyond the vicarage. Brought up to believe in service and duty and with the example of the women volunteers who taught and nursed the sick of her father's parish, nursing, she decided, would be an undeniably suitable key to release her from the restriction of home. In her account, Billy claimed that, at twenty, she was too young to become a nurse in England; her parents, on the other hand, might have been more concerned with the respectability of her choice: nursing in the 1880s was more on a par with domestic service. The Kaiserliche Augusta Hospital, however, founded in Berlin after the Franco-German war (1870-71) and staffed chiefly by women who had lost relatives in the conflict, promised an acceptable solution: it admitted only patients from *adelich* (noble, titled) families. Furthermore, there would be the added benefit of an opportunity for Billy to improve her smattering of German. Assured of the propriety of the arrangement, Mrs Herbert accompanied her daughter to Berlin for her interview with the stern Oberin (Billy translated her title as Mother Superior, although matron might be closer to the mark). Swayed perhaps by such august referees as E.W. Benson, the Archbishop of Canterbury, and Robert Gregory, the Dean of St Paul's and Billy's godfather, the Oberin agreed to take her on as a pupil nurse. If, as Billy claimed, her mother hoped that she would repent of her decision at the last minute and return home with her with promises of future good behaviour, it was a fruitless and expensive piece of brinkmanship on Mrs Herbert's part. *I had two days in which I could decide my own fate. I had made up my mind to do it and I never even thought of going back. It couldn't be worse than life at home. So I was left there, and I don't see now why I was expected to cry when my Mother never shed a tear. She was angry because I didn't care, and she didn't care herself. I did feel lonely, but wouldn't show it.* Billy did cry, but only once her mother had left.

After two months the Oberin wrote to the Herberts, refusing any more money for their daughter's training: Billy was proficient enough in German, she had attended her first operation without disgracing herself – just; and she was more than earning her keep. Billy was *enormously bucked that the vast, stern Oberin* considered the *hopeless fool and frivolous parasite that no one wanted* (ladling it on a little too thick here) worthy of promotion. Emboldened, it was not long before the most junior nurse on the women's surgical ward was once again kicking over the traces: the traces being the attitude of House Surgeon Schmidt. Tired of the needlessly daily task of mending the white apron he habitually ripped in his haste when taking it off, Billy asked the sister to ask him, politely, to use more care. Impossible, said the sister, it was never done to correct a doctor. So Billy mended the next rent very beautifully and strongly and, on the apron's bib, sewed a piece of paper that read in German, 'Please do not tear this apron anymore.' Next, she made herself scarce. Sister was furious. House Surgeon Schmidt was angry, but he never did tear his apron again. Round one to Billy.

Round two was fought over Dr Schmidt's habit of only prescribing sleeping drafts when he made his ward round between one or two in the morning. Billy, now promoted to night duty on two wards, thought this unnecessarily cruel to the patients and had the temerity to suggest that the prescriptions should be made up ready for her to administer when she came on duty at 10 o'clock at night. As Dr Schmidt ignored her suggestion, Billy warned him that unless he did his rounds earlier, or ordered up the drugs in the afternoon, she would undertake to dose any patient in need. The following night, Billy pretended that she had indeed dosed a woman, who happened to be sleeping peacefully. *"I shall report you and you will be taken from duty,"* was Dr Schmidt's calm reply. When she went off duty in the morning, Billy confessed the reasons for her little deception to the Oberin. To her astonishment, not only did the Oberin merely smile and sigh at her bravery, but Dr Schmidt forbore to report her and took to writing up his prescriptions for the sleeping draughts in the afternoon. Billy had *scored again*.

The discipline was very strict, the life tough, particularly in the summer, when the men's ward moved outside under canvas – all food and water had to be carried out and the cleaning was rough – but Billy regretted none of it. She had learnt how to keep her head when most needed, to be less defensive, more considerate of others and to have faith in herself and, most valuable of all, she had learnt that she could do anything if she tried hard enough. At the end of a year, fully expecting to return to the hospital as a sister, particular permission having been granted by the Empress Augusta, Billy went to stay in Wiesbaden with a great friend and fellow nurse. It was a wonderful holiday, with plenty of invitations and dances and Billy even quite enjoyed being a bridesmaid to an American girl, a former private patient. Her pleasure, however, was cut short by the sudden and awful appearance of her eldest sister. Billy was appalled. She had just been offered a most tempting position of paid companion/adopted daughter to a rich and very kind English woman living in Wiesbaden, but, unaccountably, she had written to her mother asking leave to accept. The answer, no, came with Dora to reinforce it. *I was twenty-one,* Billy wrote, *I can't think why I obeyed, but I did; it was my fault for asking for leave.*

Determined to salvage a measure of her hard-earned independence from the wreck of her hopes, Billy declined to be chaperoned by the family policeman, as she labelled Dora. She would make her own way home. Arriving when the vicarage was still dark and the family not yet awake, Billy bathed and changed and waited, unannounced, at the breakfast table. Expected as she was, her return to the fold could only be anticipated daily, but to appear, as if she had never been to Germany, had never been away for a year, appealed irresistibly to her sense of fun.

The jubilation of her father and four younger sisters exceeded anything the prodigal returned could have anticipated, as was the unexpected warmth of her mother. Billy felt quite suddenly that she was seen to be a young woman: gone was the tiresome child. And, as if further proof of her mother's change in attitude towards her most defiant daughter was needed, Billy found herself accompanying Mrs Herbert that very afternoon to the Westminster home of the influential, as yet unknighted, James Knowles. Still glowing from the warmth of her reception, Billy went without demur. Her reward for this unusually conciliatory attitude, the company for the whole afternoon of an arresting young man, with a piercing gaze and an abrupt manner of speaking. His marked attention, Billy noticed with mischievous glee, was much to the irritation of a far better-looking girl than herself: although, admittedly, even if she had appeared with a face like an old boot, Billy would still have been an object of enormous interest. A year spent nursing in Berlin distinguished her from any other young woman in her circle. But what further captivated the attentive nephew of their hosts (Billy did not learn his name, Maurice Hewlett, until their second meeting), was that the petite object of his curiosity should sparkle with vitality and ready laughter.

CHAPTER 2

A STERN UPBRINGING

Life in the Vicarage

Billy had been christened Hilda Beatrice Herbert. In a family much given to nicknames, it is likely the tomboy was called Billy from an early age. Born on February 17, 1864, in Cavendish House,[1] Clapham, the home of her paternal grandparents, she embarked on a childhood in which she didn't remember *ever being petted, called darling, pretty or good.* True, she admitted, she was none of those, but felt she might have tried for one or two such qualities, had she been so encouraged. For this she blamed her mother, whom she never remembered loving and whose *affection was like cold mutton on Wednesdays* and who *reaped lies, deceit and fear.* Louisa Herbert had been one month pregnant with her third child when her second daughter, Ethel Elizabeth, contracted whooping cough. The threat of contagion had required that the three-year-old be sent away to Brighton, where with her father, the Reverend Herbert, at her bedside she died. However, even without this grief to bear, it is unlikely Louisa Herbert would ever have had a happy relationship with her new daughter and their clash of personalities went a long way to making Billy the rebel she was. The Reverend George W. Herbert, on the other hand, was *a sport and a gentle man,* adored by all his children. Billy wished that his had been the greater influence at home and so much to their benefit, but Father Herbert, as he was known to his parishioners, devoted more energy to his parish than to his family.

Family lore had it that George W. Herbert built his own church. From the half-mocking Herbert family pride in the 'blood royal' and the odd piece of inherited monogrammed silver, the style of church suggested a solid, grey stone building in a comfortable parish. This cosy image of a respectable, mid-Victorian living is instantly dispelled upon seeing the church. Solid, large, dark, and built in brick on Kennington Lane, a road permanently forsworn by prosperity, the church and its environs also reflect on Father Herbert. Surely a more complicated man than the gentle sport of Billy's description, for it is no gentle church, nor is it set in a gentle place.

St Peter's, Vauxhall[2] owed its existence to the Reverend Robert Gregory,[3] vicar of the vast and crowded parish of St Mary the Less, Lambeth. Appalled by the poverty of the area, the future Dean of St Paul's first determined to reopen the existing church schools, previously shut for want of funds. He saw, too, that an art school would provide the draughtsmen, designers and artists, needed by a local engineering works and the Doulton pottery factory and when, in 1859, the once-glorious Vauxhall Gardens, now grown seedy and shabby, were broken up into lots and sold for development, he arranged for the purchase of land on which to build two parochial schools, one for boys and one for girls, plus a designated Art school. His friend, George Herbert, then curate at St Mary's Tothill Fields[4] (Vincent Square, Westminster) was made honorary secretary for the building fund and John L. Pearson was appointed as architect. A year later, in the first official public ceremony of his royal career, the Prince of Wales, in a suitably modest and manly manner, according to contemporary report, laid the foundation stone for the three schools. George Herbert led the prayers at the dedication ceremony but, in the way of Victorian illustrations, where everyone looks exactly the same as any other member of their own sex, he remains an anonymous figure among the clutch of clergy in the picture in the *Illustrated London News*.

Father Gregory also had the foresight to realise that a new parish with a new church should be carved out of his own huge parish in order to serve the influx of people attracted by the cheap housing of the Vauxhall Gardens development. It was never going to be a fashionable parish. Navvies working on the extension of the South Western Railway Line from Waterloo to Vauxhall had moved in, as had former slum dwellers, pushed south across the river by the clearances for the energetic development of Westminster. Of the local population of 15,000, only ninety persons (a quarter of whom were owners of public houses) could be assessed for income tax. However, when the developer who had sold the site for the art school generously donated its adjacent site for the proposed new church on condition that the seats in the church should be free, Father Gregory was more than happy: rented seating was a system that precluded the poor from being able to worship and one that he abhored.

Once again, John L. Pearson was the chosen architect and, it would seem, he was also responsible for transforming the former residence[5] of the manager of the Vauxhall Gardens on Miller's Lane (now St Oswald's Place) from an elegant Georgian house into something that would do tolerable duty as a Victorian parsonage. Happily, Pearson did not interfere with the original internal layout and the younger Herbert children invented wild and wonderful games, played in the interconnecting bedrooms that curved round the top of the central staircase. One particularly excellent game, the Siege of Plevna, involved the use of their parent's double bed, the mattress of which was rolled into a tunnel with the bedclothes covering each end and, while half the children stood guard on the bed, the other half attempted to crawl unobserved into the tunnel, burst it open and rout the enemy by attacking them furiously. Presumably, the absence of Father and Mrs Herbert and the *family policeman* were a necessary requirement, although they could not have failed to have been impressed by a game rooted in international current affairs: Plevna was a north Bulgarian town where the Turks had been besieged by the Russians for three months in 1877.

St. Peter's Church, Vauxhall, was considered to be the urban masterpiece of Pearson's middle period. His aim had been to build a church that filled those who entered it with a desire to worship God. Large, lofty, dark and awesome and much influenced by Italian Romanesque, St Peter's would indeed have sent its congregation to their knees. Built on the system of ratios known as the Golden Section, and as generously as money would allow for what had to be a cheap town church, St Peter's appears, if not exactly brutal, extremely powerful and muscular. Consecrated by the Bishop of Winchester in 1864 (its foundation stone had been laid by the Archbishop of Canterbury in 1863), St Peter's, like no other church, was a true testimony to George W. Herbert and his ministry. For thirty years until his death, Father Herbert laboured to make St Peter's as beautiful and as inspiring as he could for his flock, who lived hard lives in harsh conditions. His mission was to kindle in them the wholehearted devotion and commitment to God that he practised himself. 'Never be content,' he said, 'till you can give Him your whole heart, till you can say I love Him more than anything else.'[6]

Father Herbert's was a muscular faith, matched by the powerful new church. From out of the Preachers' Books and the Notices and printed addresses to parishioners comes a fighting voice. 'The object of a free Church is not to provide a subterfuge whereby the richer members may give less than they would pay for pews; but that the poorer being no longer treated as Paupers in Jerusalem, may have, as well as the richer, the privilege of presenting their Offering, each according to his ability, to Him, who gave HIMSELF for us ALL.'[7]

Family lore also had it that George Herbert's father-in-law had been 'something in stucco' and had 'drained the Grosvenor Basin' (no one knew quite what that might have been) but for which wealth, surely, would have been a necessity. Perhaps it had been Louisa Herbert's money that enabled her husband to build his church? To test this theory it was necessary to discover her maiden name. Standard procedure elicited that she was Louisa Mary, youngest of the sixteen children of Thomas Burn Hopgood, a silversmith in the city. Only the serendipitous discovery of *James Knowles. Victorian Editor and Architect* solved the money and the stucco question. It was not George's father-in-law but George's own father, William Herbert, a successful builder and developer and friend of Thomas Cubitt, who was associated with stucco and the Grosvenor Basin. First lesson learnt: family lore is not necessarily fact.

William Herbert played a part in the explosive expansion of London of the late-Regency, early-Victorian period, when ambitious craftsmen could advance from executing the designs of others into realising plans of their own. Originally from Leamington Hastings in Warwickshire and one of a family of eight, he rose from being a carpenter to become a builder and developer, first living at 1 Farm Street, near Berkley Square, before moving to the most fashionable and bosky suburb of Clapham. His path of advancement was very much the same as Cubitt's, the giant among developers, and that of James Knowles Snr, whose son was to feature in Maurice and Billy's story. In 1825, the Grosvenor Estate had completed the conversion of a series of reservoirs, once leased by the Chelsea Water Company, into the Grosvenor Canal and Grosvenor Basin. Lock gates controlled the tides of the Thames sufficiently to allow barges and small coasting vessels into the Basin. Wharves lined the basin and the canal, and engineers and builders, attracted by the easy access to the Grosvenor Estate, moved in for its development. William Herbert established a saw mill on the south of the Grosvenor Basin: the Herbert family's belief that their grandfather drained the Grosvenor Basin could have arisen from a confusion of the address of his saw mill with the later need for said Basin to be drained in order to create the site for the new railway terminus, Victoria Station. Whether that was a project he was associated with is not clear, but the osier beds of the three acres between the terminus and Vauxhall Bridge Road, which William Herbert had acquired for building development, did give him considerable drainage problems. Also, as the houses he built in Ecclestone Square bordered Thomas Cubitt's enormous Neathouse speculation, or stuccoville as it was nicknamed, owing to the favoured finish of the new houses, it would be reasonable to conclude that William Herbert had indeed been 'something in stucco'.

For the ex-carpenter from the country, possessed of status and fortune and a collection of pictures and sculpture of discernment, there was to be nothing but the best for his two children, and for his son it was to be Eton and Oxford, the education of a gentleman. When George announced his intention of going into the Church, after graduating from Exeter College, William Herbert's dismay was considerable. As George was still too young to be ordained, he continued to keep terms at Oxford, spending some time at Pershore as a layman in the parish. In the hope that a diversion of sufficient distraction might deflect George from his proposed ordination,[8] his father sent him in the long vacation on a Grand Tour, thus unwittingly promoting his son's burgeoning religious ideas, for it was in Italy that George soaked up all the ritual glory of Roman Catholicism, later reflected in his anglican ministry in Vauxhall.

Not content with defying his parents once, George added insult to injury by choosing a bride to whom they strongly objected.[9] This piece of information, courtesy of two of his daughters, is surprising to say the least, for Elizabeth Herbert, George's sister, had been married to James Hopgood, an older brother to Louisa, for some fifteen years. Either the

Herberts were ambitious for their son to marry upwards, possibly into a title, or they did not like Louisa. Had she been perceived to set her cap at George by encouraging him in his defiance of their wishes? Or maybe the redoubtable and uncomfortable qualities that were to make her such a zealot in her rescue and penitentiary work among 'the fallen', were already disconcertingly apparent. George was wealthy, he was good-looking, he had been given a gentleman's education; he was undoubtedly a catch, and Louisa caught him. They were married one early April day in 1856 in the Parish church of Hampstead, and after a brief spell in Pershore,[10] the newly-weds returned to London for George to take up his appointment as curate at St. Mary's, Tothill Fields, an area of Westminster that was slowly being reclaimed from the slums and stews of the Regency period. Herbert's calling was to work among the urban poor. When he crossed the river to Vauxhall, he realised his ambition.

According to Billy, her eldest sister, Dora, was the apple of her parents' eye and there she made sure to stay. Mary Louisa (b.1857) – only a long trawl through the Family Record office finally supplied the evidence of the true identity of the mysterious Dora – was seven years old when Billy was born. It was a gap in age sufficiently marked to disassociate Dora from the rest of *the children* – Hilda Beatrice (b.1864), George (b.1866), Grace Monica Patricia (Pat) (b. 1868), Olga Cecily (b. 1870), Verena Noelie (b.1872), Gwladys Muriel Petra (Gay) (b.1875): it always grated with Billy that her mother did not see them as individuals with potential, but lumped them together as *the children*. In effect, Billy became leader of this pack, subjected to *mass-education and organised duty*. Her soul mate and inseparable companion in all that was high-spirited and mischievous throughout their childhood was George: later he was to be her ally in her efforts to ensure that the younger girls suffered less than she had from their mother's repressive regime (his partial escape, if so seen, had been to Eton and Oxford). Mrs Herbert's iron hand bred a stoicism and fierce tribal loyalty: all were *to bear (their) punishments without tears, without any outward sign of pain or contrition and to never give in or sneak on each other.* A peer regime almost more terrifying than that of their mother's! Daring exploits that escaped detection were *de rigeur. To do something for the general welfare of the others, buy something that was forbidden but greatly needed* could turn walks with their governesses into team efforts of cunning and daring: a mission was deemed successful when the governess, all unaware, and her charges, once again at full strength, reached the vicarage doorstep together, thus avoiding trouble for either party.

Sundays were days of particular trial: *best clothes for breakfast, collect, epistle or gospel to be learned immediately afterwards, and said to Mother before church at 11 a.m. After church, Sunday dinner. If in London, there was nothing to do but loaf about till afternoon church, followed by high tea, then evening church. If you volunteered to wash up the tea things to let the servants go to the last service of the day, you were allowed, by this good deed, to change into weekday clothes.* Billy volunteered for this 'self-sacrificing' job as often as possible. Only religious books were to be read. Caught reading Dickens, Billy had the volume confiscated for a week; thenceforward, if she wanted to read any secular book on a Sunday, she was careful to have 'Stories of the Saints' to hand should a member of *the family police* enter the room. Who, beyond Dora, made up this force goes unrecorded. Games on a Sunday were deemed sinful and were forbidden, unless, quaintly, they could be played without preparation, or the use of the requisite implements; thus tennis, using hands in place of rackets but with tennis balls over the real net, or cricket, with a stick and non-cricket ball, were permissable. All knew instinctively what would or would not be allowed. A favourite Sunday game, inspired by a piece in the bible, Cities of Refuge,[11] was splendidly exciting. It began with a player killing a man, who had to fall down, the player then ran for a City of Refuge, hotly pursued by the Avengers. The rules were strict: the course was four times round the house, sticking to the paths, and the steps into the house was the City of Refuge. One Good Friday, when the children had been excused the three-hour church service, as they were still contagious with measles, they agreed that they should play a quiet Bible game and, given the day, Cities of Refuge was deemed the most appropriate as it began with a death. The day was warm and the windows of the church were open and, as the children sped silently round the garden, the sounds of the service carried to the Rectory garden. Suddenly, Pat broke the rules and ran across a flowerbed: the furious shouts and screams of the players only ceased when a black clad verger appeared from the church. *The rest of Good Friday was as sad a day as was befitting,* wrote Billy, *after boiled salt cod and hard, dry cold rice pudding, we were shut in the schoolroom with no toys or books.* Inventive as ever, they carved their desks and inlaid them with chewed paper, vividly coloured with different inks.

Monday was known as Black Monday as Mother's good resolutions to do her duty, made at church all Sunday, were put into immediate and drastic practice. We knew by the way she said family prayers before breakfast what was coming. Directly after prayers we were harried and chivvied, reproved and punished, reforms were instituted, things that had been conveniently lost were missed and had to be hunted for – our bodies and clothes were dirty or untidy, our conversation vulgar, frivolous or ungrammatical, our bedrooms slovenly (this was an adjective much overworked), our lessons neglected – in fact we seemed so bad that reform was impossible. We suffered equally with the governess, nurses and servants. There was nothing to do but wait for Tuesday, with resigned patience.

Duty, as Louisa Herbert believed, could only find expression for a woman in the home. Lecturing on 'Women's Responsibilities' in Rhyl in 1891, after thirty-five years of marriage, she said: 'Let us never fall into the fatal mistake of forgetting that the sphere of the rank and file of womanhood is *home*; that home duties, and home government, and home virtues are what the majority of us are to aim at, and by God's help to fit ourselves to fulfil.' 'A *stupid* mother is a thought to make one weep.' 'Stupidity is *sin*. My epitome of a girl's life is that she should have a full head and busy hands, and a heart anchored on that Divine Love which is the source and strength of all the precious human love she has to bestow.' There is a great deal in this vein – 'protesting' and 'too much' come to mind – but her closing sentence is the killer. 'Quiet, uneventful, monotonous your life may be, but if you are training up sons and daughters in the fear and admonition of the Lord, you are one of the makers of your country, and your children shall rise up to call you blessed.'

Louisa Herbert, herself, never intended to suffer the monotony of a quiet, uneventful life. She had married a man of wealth and with connections that could have promoted his steady rise through the ranks of the Church of England, but who opted to devote his entire life to one parish of grinding poverty. Her sense of womanly duty, perforce, grew increasingly rigid over the years that she bore him eight children at two-yearly intervals, but by expanding her role within and beyond the parish, she found an outlet for her formidable energy. Besides this, the cultivation of patrons and sponsors of charitable works brought her into contact with a higher and wealthier class of society than any to be found in Vauxhall.

As a good Christian it was her duty to support her husband in his parish. Acting as organist[12] and choirmaster until one could be employed was blessedly less humdrum than wifely duties, but running homes for fallen girls, whose babies were then placed in good Protestant homes, was the apotheosis of her creed. Cynical Billy claimed her mother was moved by sentiment rather than sympathy. One visitor to the Home in Gye Street[13] made the mistake of admiring a beautiful baby boy. She was severely rebuked: *No one can be proud of a child born in sin, we teach them to repent and sin no more, pride in the fruits of sin shows no true repentance.* 'Her rebukes,' wrote an anonymous correspondent, in a fit of myopic sentimentality on Mrs Herbert's death, 'were sometimes terrible, but her love always prevented the offender from feeling resentment. Her sympathy was both intelligent and unstinted, whether to women in Society who sought her advice, or to a poor girl rescued in one of the missions in which she worked.'[14] 'Poor girl rescued' sounds so much less grim than 'active in rescue and penitential[15] work', as described in the obituary in *The Times* of 1 June, 1915.

Billy also accused her mother of being a snob, although to be fair, if Louisa Herbert was to be active in raising funds for rescue and penitential work, then she would have to cultivate patrons with money and status. However, a child, resentful at being summoned from a perfectly excellent game in the outhouse where the boots were blacked and the chickens plucked, to be presented with her brother to a visiting marchioness, was unlikely to see it that way. The marchioness, by laughing out loud at the sight of the mortifyingly black and feathery couple and inviting them to play with her own children, thus avoided censure. Her children were deemed great sports by Billy, as they not only dared her to walk along the edge of a cattle drinking trough but, when she slipped in, took her frock, drawers and stockings to wash in a nearby stream. That the wearer had to go home with them wet fazed her not a bit.

The delights of the opposite sex which, for Billy and her sisters, had mostly taken the form of tormenting the poor curates – flour bombs from the rectory wall was part of their armoury – cost Billy her part in her mother's novel venture, a pageant about the Conversion of England. As she flirted with a fellow actor, the Secretary to her Queen, she missed her entrance. He was too good an actor to sack, but she was deposed by a girl of whom Mrs Herbert's comment became a family catch phrase:

'*She may not be clever, but she is a regular communicant.*' Discovery of Billy in what she referred to as her *first love affair* precipitated her into what she considered the worst ten days of her life at home. Locked in a room before pre-breakfast prayers until she should show contrition, Billy felt she had no other recourse but to escape out the window: unfortunately, with no clear idea as to where she would go. Conspicuous with neither hat nor coat, she was soon caught and returned home. *Mother treated me as one of her fallen girls, and the first thing necessary was what she called a 'conviction of sin,' followed by confession and repentance.* Isolated from the family, forbidden books, lessons, work and exercise, in order that she might be free to consider and repent, Billy grew desperately bored. She feigned illness and refused to get up, but her hearty appetite gave her away. More extreme measures on her part were called for and she began to babble nonsense when alone, adding the odd bit of raving and tearing of clothes. This gained her the right to go out for a daily walk and to eat with the family. Finally, the still unrepentant Billy was sent away to a boarding school in the north. *I was glad to get away and showed it, though I remember sending secret messages to George and the other children saying how much I should miss them. I was not allowed even to say goodbye, but did so at night quite successfully.* This school Billy rather enjoyed and soon acquired a reputation for daring, which she felt obliged to maintain. Her fellow pupils were *silly cowards and most inferior beings. At the end of the term I returned home in no way reformed. I'm sure the school was glad to be rid of me.*

Whether Father Herbert was aware of how oppressive his daughters found life at home is debatable. His dutiful wife took care to shield him from cares that had no bearing on his work and his work absorbed him, body and soul. The children knew he was too busy to be disturbed and they never went to his study unless sent there when they had been particularly wicked: a punishment more awful than any other. *He never jawed us, but after gently pointing out our fault, he would suddenly kneel down and pray – we had to kneel beside him. I hated it more than smacks with a hair brush on the bare behind from Mother.* To his uniformly high-spirited and healthy children, he was an awesome, if beloved, presence who, according to Veena, seemed 'surrounded by a holy atmosphere, which prevented one from doing anything unworthy in his presence, in thought, word or deed. He loved the poor, and every morning at Vauxhall, for an hour after breakfast, they could come to the Parsonage and tell him their needs. They sat on a bench in the hall and we children were taught to find out what they wanted and report to him, and he told us that, by waiting on them, we were waiting on Our Lord Himself.' Holiness might command admiration, but it was when Father Herbert became father, the man who refused to disturb the cat and her litter in the knee-hole of his desk, who let his parrot on his shoulder sip from his coffee-cup, who smiled when the children confessed to teaching the new French maid that "Kiss me quick, my little darling"was the English for Bon Jour, who romped with them and *let them be natural and high spirited* on holiday in Cromer, that he won his children's love and affection.

A modest man, who hated publicity and never put notices in the *Church Times*, as he had no desire to make his church fashionable, George Herbert became a very wealthy man on his father's death in 1863. Besides providing very comfortably for his large family, he also spent large sums annually on his parish, upholding all its charities, supplementing the stipends of the Assistant Clergy (four in all) and providing for the monetary deficiencies of its schools.[16] A man of interesting contradictions – a rich man who practised such economies as writing notes for his sermons on the backs of old envelopes – he expected even the poorest of his parishioners to contribute their mite to their church and its adornment. He was a High Churchman, a Ritualist of the Ritualists of whom it was said, 'No Primitive Methodist could preach a simpler gospel than he preached, or be more definite in his desire to bring about the conversion of souls.'[17] Father Herbert's evangelical, Anglo-Catholicism positively crackles through the Preacher's Books, parish accounts, printed sermons and church notices and that, combined with his self-effacement, his asceticism, his zeal, and his energy in carrying out the more temporal duties of a vicar, endeared him to his parishioners and endowed him with authority. A former choirboy remembered Father Herbert asking them, in a charming manner, not to frighten a stray cat they were chasing from the church: a request obeyed willingly by the tough little choirboys, who thought nothing of doing battle royal with their counterparts from the Catholic church if they met on the street. And two of his daughters, Olga and Verena, were witnesses when, disturbed by a man and his drunken wife brawling under his study window as he was preparing a sermon, their father quietly joined the throng, picked up the woman's bonnet which had fallen into the mud, wiped it clean and said: 'I think I'd put it on now, if I were you.' Without a word, the woman took her hat and the couple and onlookers drifted away.

When Father Herbert had first arrived in his grimy, impoverished and densely populated parish, where the air was laden with the smell of the gas works and the smoke from the pottery factory, and cholera, smallpox and typhus were rife, he began to preach wearing a surplice: twenty years earlier and there would have been a riot. Determined to reach out to his parishioners in a way that was demanding and beguiling, he slowly introduced music and colour and ornament to services and when St Peter's church was eventually built and consecrated in the summer of 1864, the *Morning Advertiser* observed that the vastly impressive service of consecration was reminiscent of High Mass (mass was a term not used in the Anglican Church until early 20th century). At the time, the Ritual controversy was strong and bitter and Father Herbert was dangerously close to prosecution, although he prudently abandoned his plan for altar lights in view of the Privy council's judgement of 1863 (they did not become legal until 1890). However, his unswerving belief in the power and value of ritual was born out by the number of communicants increasing from nineteen to one hundred and forty-six within the first four years.

St Peter's might have been for the poor of the parish, but first they had to be educated and converted in order that they might use their church. Classes, prayer meetings and annual parochial missions were set up to consolidate all the good evangelical work done, but it was not enough simply to save souls, those souls needed practical help and encouragement to remain saved. To give each member of the congregation his own special obligations and place in Church life, a system of Guilds[18] was established; members were obliged to attend certain services and a monthly ward meeting, the last made more palatable by the provision of a Tea. Thus a loyalty and pride in their church was fostered among the parishioners, who were more than a match for those intent on disrupting a service. Zealous followers of J. Kensit, founder of the fundamentalist evangelical Protestant Truth Society that abhorred high church Anglicanism, were routed when a group of cinder-yard women quietly surrounded the young men. Proximity to women as filthy as those who sorted through the rubbish heaps on Thames-side was more than the Kensitites could endure: defeated, they slunk one by one from the church.

Volunteers, many of whom were women from affluent families from outside the parish, assisted in such parochial responsibilities as supplying food, clothing, nursing and education to the needy. Out of the desire of two women to form a sisterhood, St Peter's Mission Sisterhood was founded by Father Herbert with the intention that a group of dedicated women might work in the parish, but follow a religious code of discipline, a Rule. Its development and expansion, beyond the bounds of St Peter's, to become The Community of the Mission Sisters of the Holy Name of Jesus (1876) was done with his encouragement and concrete aid in the form of a mission house which he had built at 331 Kennington Lane. When, eleven years later, the Community acquired their own home and moved to the Convent of the Holy Name in Malvern Link, he would have regretted the loss of a core of valued workers. He would, however, have been comforted and humbly proud to know that, over a hundred years later, the Convent of the Holy Name would continue to thrive in Oakwood, Derbyshire.

It was inevitable that a life run so hard, should be short. Father Herbert's death, three days after suffering a heart attack while preaching at Sunday Evensong, was to produce scenes of such mourning that comment was not confined to the religious press. 'Rarely, if ever – save in the case, perhaps, of a Czar of Russia – have some thirty offices for the dead been said in the presence of a dead body which has remained for five days in the chancel of a parish church. Such has happened within a mile of the Houses of Parliament at St. Peter's Vauxhall where the Rev. George William Herbert has lain since Wednesday.'[19] As one paper remarked, the death of the vicar of an obscure London parish would normally be covered in a couple of lines in the daily paper, but the column inches devoted to describing the funeral procession were as noteworthy as the length of the procession itself. Three hundred of the congregation made their way on foot behind the surpliced priests and choir, the cross-bearer and acolytes, the file of veiled sisters, and the bands of guilds, as they processed solemnly down Kennington Lane to Westminster Bridge Road towards the Necropolis Station of the London and South-Western Railway, bound for the Woking cemetery. Eager and solemn crowds of working men and women thronged the roadway with even the roughest doffing their hats in respect as the coffin of their 'stay-at-home priest' was borne past. So remarkable was the behaviour of the onlookers that one astonished commentator was moved to observe that the 'behaviour of the poor cabbies on the route was excellent, many of them uncovering and maintaining that reverential attitude until the procession passed.'[20]

When Verena married the Rev Douglas Raymond Pelly in St Peter's church four years after her father's death, the obverse of such an outpouring of grief again astonished all who witnessed it. Invited guests had difficulty in reaching and entering the church for the numbers of spectators who thronged the streets, leant from windows and even took to the roofs for a better view. Also, according to the eminently useful purveyor of respectable and mild gossip, the *Malvern Gazette*,[21] the two pages were clad in matching reseda green suits with old French brocade waistcoats and green velvet caps: one was, Dora's son, Ivor McClure, the other, Francis, the son of Mr and Mrs Maurice Hewlett.

CHAPTER 3

AN INCALCULABLE FITFUL CREATURE

As Maurice Saw Himself

Maurice Hewlett, after his utterly delightful afternoon of flirtation, on the day Miss Hilda Herbert returned from Germany, had left his aunt and uncle Knowles'[1] splendid new home, Queen Anne's Lodge, and returned to his lodgings in happy anticipation of further enjoying the company of the diminutive charmer. He guessed it would be days, rather than weeks, before he could see her again, as Mrs Herbert would be taking her daughters out and about in society – husbands were required to be found – and his uncle was an hospitable man and very much 'in society'.

As the romantic lead in Billy's story, it has to be admitted that Maurice did not start out promisingly, if what he wrote of himself as a boy in *Lore of Proserpine* was true. 'Moody, irresolute and hatefully reserved, I lived a thronged and busy life, a secret life, full of terror, triumph, wonder, frantic enterprise, a noble and gallant figure among my peers, while to my parents, brothers and sisters I was an incalculable, fitful creature, often lethargic and often in the sulks.' This confession, however, was made when he had acquired a considerable reputation as a romantic novelist. Better, perhaps, to portray oneself thus, than to admit to being the loved and loving member of the family that his younger brother, Edward, remembered.

Born on January 22, 1861, Maurice was the first born son of Henry Gay and Emmeline Mary Hewlett. Henry Hewlett, a poet by inclination, a lawyer by training, and a civil servant by profession, was also a man determined to sleep in pure air and wake to the sound of the birds, even though it meant a daily commute to London. Therefore, he whisked his young bride, the twenty-one year old sister of his greatest friend, James Knowles, off to Oatlands Park, Surrey, where, over the next eight years, she bore him six children, before they moved to West Molesey in 1868. After four years, the family was once more on the move, this time to Farningham, Kent. When Mr Hewlett moved his family for the last time, ten years later, it had increased by two and Shaw House, Addington, provided the necessary extra accommodation.

Raised in a predominantly female household, Henry Hewlett was the only son and eldest of a family of six, which, coupled with the example of his own father's exquisite courtesy, might have gone some way to explaining his over-protective attitude towards his impulsive, generous and extravagant little wife, whom he treated with a chivalry beyond commonsense. She, before her marriage, had known the luxury of a large house, extensive grounds, four carriages and the requisite number of servants to make life comfortable. As her husband so shielded her from the cares and concerns of household management, she was to know nothing of banks and cheques, nor how to run a household – least of all in the straitened circumstances in which she was eventually to find herself upon his death after nearly forty years of marriage.

A solicitor in partnership in the firm established by his grandfather, Hewlett acquired a great deal of experience in the one field of expertise in which the firm practised, Antiquarian Law. As Antiquarian experts were rare, it was inevitable that the Civil Service should snap him up and, in 1865, the Lords Commissioners of Her Majesty's Treasury, appointed Henry G. Hewlett as Keeper of His Majesty's Lands, Revenues, Records and Enrolments, in the sylvan setting of the department of Woods and Forests. Once established as a member of a Treasury department and, hence, a government official, Maurice's father was required to be conveyed to and from his home and the London train in a style commensurate with the dignity of his post. Thus, armoured by a less than acute sense of the ridiculous and dressed in full city fig of top hat and frock coat, he was driven by the very grumpy gardener, pressed into service as coachman complete with cockade, in the family wagonette drawn by Biddy the very fat mare.

A reserved man who never raised his voice, Henry G. Hewlett was a devoted husband and fond father, although he and Maurice only found common ground in their love of poetry,[2] once Maurice had moved away from home. A deeply religious man, Hewlett had, in his search for the truth, moved from the rigid creed of his evangelical upbringing through agnosticism to end as a committed Unitarian. 'Rejoicing in his own freedom from conventional religion, he gave free rein to his children, but yet felt intensely their return to the orthodoxy which he had abjured; and most of them did so return, as they came to years of discretion.' So wrote Edward, himself ordained into the Church of England in 1898, a year after his father's death. Maurice's 'years of discretion' were twenty-four when, for an unfathomable reason, he decided to be baptised and then confirmed. His mother, in reply to his letter in which he broke the news, could only regret that her dearest Mos had not given her greater warning: they had dinner guests the Saturday before the Sunday of his confirmation. This precipitate decision on Maurice's part is indicative of his lifelong ambivalence concerning a Christian faith. He was to tell Edward that he accepted the Christian Articles of Faith as poetic truths, but Edward, who thought his brother in later life might have been described as a Pantheistic Christian, wrote in the introductory memoir to *The Letters of Maurice Hewlett*: 'A Christian, at all events, he was in practice and no man ever had higher ideals or strove harder to live up to them than he.'

Maurice's mother had been the youngest of her family. In her flashing wit and vivacious manner, she resembled her eldest brother but, unlike James, she did not share her husband's intellectual pursuits, nor his religious beliefs. Nevertheless, Emmeline's marriage to the tall and ungainly Henry was happy. She had no favourites among her children, ruling by her love for and faith in them with, in Edward's view, greater success than if she had used more Spartan methods. In others' eyes, she was indulgent to a fault. A spoiled girl to the end of her life, who never lost her youthful outlook, she had an unconventional disregard of worldly opinion. Indeed some of the remarks she made were absurd, but it was always felt she knew what she said; she liked to amuse.

Maurice, with Edward, spent a good part of the school holidays with one or other set of grandparents in Clapham. Friday Grove, with grandmother Knowles, whose shrewd tongue and sharp thrusts were much appreciated by Maurice, was their favourite, but not solely for its material comforts: at Friday Grove there was Uncle George. Admired excessively for his eccentric and unique form of dress, whose company for a day at Crystal Palace was rated the best treat of all, Uncle George was a talented painter and musician and could sing like Caruso – as long as he first removed his teeth! He was endowed with a truly amazing memory that, in the opinion of George's youngest nephew, must have been 'without parallel at any period subsequent to the Homeric age.' He could recite word for word a number of Shakespeare's plays, including the less well-known, and would individualize each character with his voice. So eccentric did this uncle eventually become that he took to getting up later and later 'until at last he was breakfasting at eleven o'clock at night. This necessitated the serving of dinner at seven o'clock in the morning,' the same awed nephew recounted, 'and to these hours he finally adhered. But perhaps the most extraordinary thing about him was that he retained his cook.' How happy for Uncle George that he was in a position and blessed with sufficient means to allow him to be eccentric, rather than fall by the label of a less forgiving condition.

In contrast, the household of the Hewlett grandparents was simpler and more austere: treats were of an educational nature, such as excursions to the British Museum or the Egyptian Hall of Mysteries. Grandfather Hewlett was a man of innate courtesy and regular habits. In the early years of his move to Clapham, he would ride his sturdy grey cob from the countryside of Acre Lane to his office in Grays Inn. As the clock struck ten, he would be passing Whitehall and another horseman, identically mounted, would be approaching his office. 'Good morning, Mr Hewlett,' the Duke of Wellington would gravely remark, and 'Good morning, your Grace,' would be the equally grave response: it was a warm, if limited, acquaintanceship. Although Maurice and Edward were always shown great kindess and they enjoyed staying with their Hewlett grandparents, they were rather more subdued at Acre Lane than they were wont to be elsewhere. Maurice remembered how his grandfather would put his hand on his head and murmur, '… as if to himself, "My boy, my boy,"' in such a way that I felt in leaving him, as perhaps Jacob did with Isaac, that it would be impossible ever to do anything wrong again and betray such noble affection.'

According to the available copy of the family tree, bringing up the rear of Maurice's siblings was this venerable gentleman's namesake and there he might have remained, unresearched, but for the mention of a raffish brother of Maurice Hewlett in Andro Linklater's biography of Compton Mackenzie. This part-time actor and alleged bisexual – although introducing the young Compton Mackenzie to recognised homosexual haunts hardly rates as proof positive that he was bisexual – going by the name of Dick (there was certainly no Richard in the family tree) demanded to be traced, if for no other reason than that the Hewletts had, so far, been models of rectitude and decorum. Run to ground in the index of the first four volumes of Mackenzie's autobiographical Octavos, Dick, Mackenzie's engaging and impecunious friend of his late teens, proved to be none other than Hewlett, Henry William (Dick). The rewards of further investigation over time were to prove as bountiful as they were unexpected.

Maurice's family, in his daughter's opinion,[3] could be divided into two groups: round-faced, cheerful, un-neurotic, or thin, pale-complexioned, dark-haired, and nervy. Members of the first group were but two: Edward and, as thoroughly good as he, shy Edith (Edie) who became a hospital nurse and died aged forty. Eleanor (Nellie), Cecily (Cissie), and Julia (Eppie), were in the same mould as Dick (Willie to his family) and Maurice: all had inherited the nervy intensity of their mother. This nervy intensity had found conscious form in art in Maurice; in Cissie, religious dedication; in Eppie, a complete refusal to take part in life. Only Nellie had been endowed with a practical streak and it was she who kept the hens, minded the store room and undertook the daily task of trimming and filling the paraffin lamps rather than relying on the maids to keep them from smell or smoke. When their father died, Nellie felt that she could not leave her mother, which Billy thought absolutely idiotic, but, eventually, in her mid-forties, Nellie did marry and lived very contentedly with her cousin and faithful suitor of many years, Bertie Roxby. A tea-taster, who travelled every year to India, he was a giant of a man, over six and a half feet tall. To accommodate his great height, the drawing room floor in their house in Addington had to be lowered by a foot and the bedroom ceiling removed altogether; in the hall, half-moon shaped pieces were cut out of the beams of the ceiling.

Eppie, evidently, was so farouche that even talking to a tradesman was an ordeal and, even if she did, she would have no idea what she was talking about. Long allowed to indulge in her various neuroses and inhibitions – Eppie never went anywhere except to the village or church – she always wore a black blouse (in the summer the blouse was black and white striped) buttoned up to the neck, with a pinned on small gold cross, and a black skirt. As she undertook all the parish work normally undertaken by the vicar's wife, Maurice always suspected that Eppie was in love with the vicar, a man he could not stand who swore and drank. Mrs Guise, the vicar's wife, was far too interested in hunting and being fashionably dressed to mind one way or the other.

But what of Dick, the marvelous uncle, beloved by all children, and trial to his family? How to trace him and his deeds? Hewlett cousins seemed the only possible source of information: but where to find them? As a man of the cloth, whose career could be traced in Crockfords, the Reverend Edward Hewlett seemed the only promising start point and if, as it did not seem unreasonable to suppose, one of his three sons had followed him into the church, he too would feature in Crockfords. And he did.

The Reverend Michael Hewlett (Edward's eldest was called Michael) was of the right age and living a mere ten miles distant. A letter, as the politer approach, was abandoned as being too slow in the face of so exciting a discovery. One telephone call later and my husband found himself the surprised and shaken beneficiary of a family of which he had hitherto been entirely ignorant and the recipient of an invitation to the impending celebration of his cousin Michael's 80th birthday. Not only that, the son and daughter of great-uncle Dick would also be there and it was they who generously made available a copy of their father's typescript, his unpublished *A Spade's a Spade. An Experiment in Autobiography*. An experiment, it has to be said, that was like his brother's partial autobiography, *Lore of Proserpine,* short on the gossipy detail that flatters or dismays a family member, helps a researcher, and generally spices things up for a reader.

The spade dug up few weeds and planted no seedlings, but there were one or two flowers for the plucking: anecdotes relevant to his brother's life and a sincere and constructive review of Maurice's disconcerting dissertation on fairies. The racketty sociable London of Willie or Dick (however he preferred to be known) was far removed from the London of the '90's that the married Hewletts knew. 'Squalid vicious congested uncomfortable adorable London! She was unique. There was no city in the least like her anywhere in the world, no city with an appeal so subtle, so elusive, so irresistible; no city whose grasp on the affections was so intimate, so human ....' 'Who that has heard it can forget the jingle of a hansom cab passing the window at dead of night? Who that has waged it can ever forget that desperate struggle for the coveted 'outside' on the last southbound bus – 1.00 a.m. from Piccadilly Circus: the electrifying (not electric) ting-ting of the conductor's bell – the answering plunge of the horses – the wild rock and sway down Haymarket – the breathless canter along deserted Whitehall – the freshening breeze that caught you as you swept up and over Westminster Bridge – the perilous jolts and swerves that told you when the tram-lines were reached – the rush and rattle of Kennington Road?' After not graduating in Classics from St Andrews university, Dick had joined the family law firm, where 'the teeth-on-edge quality of those rolls of parchment' and 'the odour that rose from them, an odour that seemed impregnated with the very spirit and essence of Eld' soon drove him away. With but the ten shillings a week allowance from his family – and, given their financial circumstances on the recent death of his father, it is likely that it came from Maurice's pocket – to tide him over until he gained alternative employment, Dick found himself posing as a young man of independent means. Three months later, before he quite sank below the poverty line, his family redeemed his pawned clothes and possessions and packed him off to Berlin to study music. Dick found the musical life of that city immeasurably exciting and claimed he devoted a great deal of time to his studies: of this his family were not so certain. He also discovered it was possible to enjoy a life of gaiety on very little money. Dick's life, financially, was either feast or famine. Good-looking, charming, he appeared utterly without ambition and invariably 'fell' into doing things: he was, in his time, actor, concert party artist, songwriter,[4] author of several novels, schoolmaster, private tutor and revue sketch writer. Like Maurice he developed a strong personal morality and pronounced views on sex and religion, and if either of them had found their vocation, as Edward had in organised religion, they would both have been enthusiastic and persuasive preachers.

Between Maurice and Dick there was a gap of seventeen years; between Maurice and Edward, or Ted, a gap of three years. Charming, outgoing and kindly and one of the few naturally holy persons that Maurice had ever known, Ted, a perfect foil for his introspective and intellectual older brother, was closest of all to Maurice throughout their childhood. Any similarity between their companionship and that of Billy and her brother George rests merely in their being the eldest two of a group of six. Not for Maurice and Ted the excitement of subversion and rebellion: life in the Hewlett household was gentle, non-confrontational. Collective solidarity in the face of parental rule was not a family requisite. Rather, theirs were the shared pleasures of visiting the grandparents, or learning fly-fishing: a sport which Maurice loved and pursued throughout his life from the chalk streams of Wiltshire to the rivers and lakes of Scotland and, arguably, the only skill that he was to teach his son. And when – rather exhaustingly for the rest of the family – they *became* the knights of Malory's Arthurian Legends, it was a rare occasion when Ted was able to share with his brother something of the world in which Maurice preferred to dwell: books.

The eldest, naturally shy and reserved, with a precocious ability to read from a very early age, Maurice 'found in every book an open door, and went in and dwelt in its world,' alone and apart. His taste was Catholic, his appetite voracious and from nine years old he could count the company of Nelson, Napoleon, Galahad, Tristram, Socrates, Don Quixote or Tom Jones, as more real to him than that of his schoolfellows. And if the people of his books stepped out and inhabited him, he, in a strange reversal, would confer on the characters of his imaginary games the looks or qualities of the schoolmates that he never wished for as playmates. In a world of his own imagining, Maurice felt himself 'alone in a household of a dozen friendly persons,' while at school he was content to be a cipher among his schoolmates, whom he watched, heard, judged and studied intently. Few penetrated his detachment; a repulsive bully with 'a lickerous tongue and a taste for sweet things,' had to be faced; 'a furtive, nail-bitten pick-nose wretch with an unholy hunger for ink, earth-worms and the like' to be pitied; and lastly an older school-fellow, Harkness, who 'had he known the way in, would have been at home in the Garden of Priapus.' The 'precocious, affectionate, and philoprogenitive Harkness' had taken a liking to the younger boy and undertook to instruct him on his favourite subject, women and love. And it was as they lounged under a great oak, one summer evening, that

Maurice 'saw' his first spirit: a dryad bathing in the warmth of the evening sun. As Harkness 'rehearsed the progress of his amours with his mother's housemaid', Maurice, roused, translated the eroticism of Harkness's talk and the beauty of the languorous golden evening into a poetic image. In retrospect, he realised that the precocious child had begun his transition to manhood; he also realised that the taboos of society were in conflict with what his body wanted him to do. 'I discovered that there were two ways of looking at a young woman, and two ways of thinking about her. I discovered that it was lawful to have some kinds of appetite, and to take pleasure in food, exercise, sleep, warmth, cold water, hot water, the smell of flowers, and quite unlawful so much as to think of, or to admit to myself the existence of other kinds of appetite. I discovered, in fact, that love was a shameful thing, that if one was in love, one concealed it from the world, and, above all the world, from the object of one's love. The conviction was probably instinctive, for one is not the descendant of puritans for nothing; but the discovery of it is another matter.'

Tractable, 'being, in fact, too little interested in the world as it was, to resent any duties cast upon' him, Maurice nevertheless was a trial and a problem to his father. In fact, he suspected that his father could not have born their regular Sunday walks if it had not been for the company of Edward, who was alert to what there was to be seen and appreciated; he, on the other hand, found himself filled with such intense spiritual fatigue he 'felt like some chained slave going to the hulks.' Reciprocal Sunday misery was reduced for father and eldest son when Maurice, aged thirteen, went as a boarder to the Palace School, Enfield. Happy there, Maurice was then dismayed to be transported a year later, along with brother Ted, to the International College at Spring Grove, Isleworth; a college established in the belief that education of boys of all nationalities together would lead to universal brotherhood.[5]

'It may be true that all men are brothers,' Maurice wrote, 'but it is not logical to infer from that that all brothers are better for each other's society.' Ted, 'an ideal schoolboy, diligent, brisk, lovable, abounding in friendships, good at his work and excellent at his play,' deserved his own happy triumph there. Maurice, on the other hand, was not popular and he knew it; he neither played football nor cricket and his brief moment of glory on the track – he won the 300 Yards Open Handicap and, according to the legend engraved on his silver tankard, within 36 seconds with a 15 yards handicap – did nothing to prevent him from being 'negligible and neglected'. He loathed his time at Spring Grove. 'The cruel, dull, false gods of English convention (for thought it is not) held me fast; masters and pupils alike were gaolers to me. I ate and drank of their provision and can recall still with nausea the sour, stale taste, and still choke with the memory of the chaff and grit of its quality.' 'The English boarding-school system is that of the straw-yard where colts are broken by routine, and again of the farmyard where pups are walked. Drill in school, *laissez-faire* out of it.'

Salvaged from this wreck was Maurice's lifelong admiration for Homer and Plato. 'The surging music and tremendous themes of the poet, the sweet persuasion of the sophist were a wonder and delight. I remember even now the thrill with which I heard my form-master translate for us the prayer with which the Phaedrus closes: 'Beloved Pan, and all ye other gods who haunt this place ...' Beloved Pan! My knowledge of Pan was of the vaguest, and yet more than once or twice did I utter that prayer wandering alone the playing field, or watching the evening mist roll down the Thames Valley and blot up the elm trees, thick and white, clinging to the day like a fleece.' The books of Homer became Maurice's Bible and the Greek deities became more real to him than the deities of his own land. He had taken to them instantly. 'I seemed to breathe the air of their breath; they appealed to my reason; I knew that they had existed and did still exist.' 'Mythology was one of the few subjects I diligently read at school, and all I got out of it was pure profit ...' Oreads, dryads, nymphs and fauns became as real as the trees and streams and forests that they represented to the Ancient Greeks.

With a brief and idyllic attachment to a fellow pupil – very fervent, very romantic, entirely his own and very beautiful, of which nothing remained 'but the fragrance of it, and its dream-like quality' – Maurice's schooldays ended. He never blamed his father for sending him to the College, for he realised he had been an unknown quantity to both his parents; besides, he suspected that it had been no worse than any other large boarding-school and that his experiences had been very much those of others. For that reason, and that reason alone, he had taken the trouble to articulate them.

Christmas, 1878, and Henry G. Hewlett wrote a careful and close-written letter to his cousin, William O. Hewlett.[6] It was time to negotiate the terms on which Maurice should begin his career in the family law firm. Reminding W.O. Hewlett, with some delicacy, of how it had been to his long-term financial benefit to have inherited the family law firm, once he himself had moved to the Civil Service, Maurice's father suggested that, if only on moral grounds, this should be taken into account when admitting his son. After some resistance – W.O. Hewlett could foresee that taking on his young cousin would complicate the issue of ownership of the practice should a son of his own join the firm – agreement was reached. And in February of 1879, he sought special permission for the under-age Maurice to visit the British Library.[7] So began at one and the same time, Maurice's career as a legal antiquary and his productive association with the British Museum, where he broadened his knowledge of matters classical, as well as those antiquarian, and formed the habit of research: roots of his future in writing.

At first, Maurice lived at home and commuted daily to London like his father, but by the time the family had moved to Addington, which entailed a longer journey, he decided to share digs in Albert Street, Camden, with an old school friend, then 'walking the hospitals.' Freed from the stress of a restrictive routine, Maurice took pleasure in certain aspects of his work, his leisure time and even, surprisingly, dancing. His visits home, in the company of friends of 'assured manner and deportment who filled the house with their worldly laughter,' were to convince the very young Dick that London was a place of 'romance, mystery, knowledge, business and pleasure.'

London, where Maurice developed 'from a lad of inarticulate mind and unexpressed desires into a sentient and self-conscious being' also, literally, gave him the space to sublimate his natural and physical urges in waking visions, much as he had done when he watched the dryad as his school friend spoke of sex. 'More or less of a man, not only adventurous but bold in the pursuit of adventure,' the solitary Maurice, not the convival one who liked to go dancing, frequently spent the hours between work and midnight reading, after which he would set out to walk London, west to east, north to south. An overactive imagination, well-nourished by Greek mythology and Spenser's Faerie Queen and stimulated by exercise and lack of sleep, feverishly peopled the darkness, that other world of Persephone (Proserpine) for Maurice. One moonlit

April night, he 'saw' a radiant, shimmering version of a young woman, whom he watched daily from his office window, appear quite suddenly among the sheep grazing on Parliament Hill; this fairy being was then joined, at her soft, piercing call, by others of the fairy kind, male and female, to play without a hint of sexuality but with a 'zest for mere irresponsible movement.'

The term 'fairy kind' is difficult and unsatisfactory: it brings to mind too readily Conan Doyle and the infamous photographic fakes, or fancy dress outfits with wings and wands dear to little, and even not so little, girls. The fairies of which Maurice wrote were neither ghosts of the dead, nor spirits: they were other beings, from another, co-existent world who, for some reason, had come to live in the human world and whom he saw with his inner self. 'We may believe ourselves to be two persons, at least, in one, and I fancy that one at least of them is a constant.' For Maurice, his inner self had either not grown up at all, unlike the visible 'forsensic creature of senses, passions, ambitions and self-indulgences, the eating, sleeping, vainglorious, assertive male of common experience,' or it had been 'born whole and in a flash.' Seeing the radiant fairy version of the shameless 'pale-faced, curling-papered, half-bodiced, unwashed drab of a girl,' with a 'smile as pure as a seraph's,' that he watched from his office window, was rather like a grown-up version of his childhood games in which players in his daydreams had taken on the features of his schoolfriends.

Maurice's fairies transformed the commonplace, the dirty and troubling, into something beautiful and elevating. When, in his fifties, Maurice wrote his semi-autobiography, *Lore of Proserpine*, it was a time when he was driven by the need to find some form of public expression of a turbulent and private emotion. Significantly, rather than continue with his startlingly honest account of himself as a boy growing into manhood, he stopped at London and the brink of his love life. He was unable to touch upon his marriage, children, friends, career, anything too close to the man he had become. Instead, he devoted the last two-thirds of *Lore of Proserpine* to the experience, his and others', of seeing spirit or fairy-beings. Was this a different form of courage, or was it foolhardiness? His disturbing account, witnessed, he claimed, when he was twelve, of the lascivious torture by near-throttling of a rabbit by another being – 'a boy in the wood' – was so vivid he risked condemnation (might in reality it have been he who was the boy in the wood), or mockery. But his thesis, which he somehow combined with the myth of Demeter and Persephone and the Socratean idea that every soul is made up of at least three persons, on a parallel world whirling with other beings, was a true extension of his young and introspective self. 'I hope nobody will ask me whether the things in this book are true, for it will then be my humiliating duty to reply that I don't know.' Of what he did know to be true, he could not or would not write.

For the young Maurice, mercifully, there had been his aunt and uncle Knowles to provide him with less rarefied and more worldly conviviality and entertainment. James Knowles, deeply involved in all that was humming on the metaphysical, literary and political scene and fast moving up in society had, in 1884, moved from fashionable Clapham to be closer to the heart of things; his splendid new home, with its garden down to Birdcage Walk, was part of the major gentrification of the area and within a short walk of Whitehall. There, the sociable and astute Knowles created in No 1, Queen Square Place, a mini *salon* frequented by anybody who was somebody. Maurice's father was a regular dinner guest, along with the likes of Gladstone, Huxley, Tennyson and Wilde; Maurice, a contemporary of his cousin, Arthur Knowles,[8] was made to feel very much at home at Queen Anne's Lodge. Which was precisely what Hilda Herbert, his wife-to-be, had noted the first time she met him.

CHAPTER 4

BETROTHAL

M and his Darling Girl

Billy's second encounter with Maurice Hewlett was again *chez* Knowles: at a Shakespeare reading. It is a measure of how desperately bored she must have been at home that she even went to it. But, there was the sinewy graceful young man, who smiled at her warmly and patted the seat he had saved next to him: it was delightfully flattering. Her third encounter with the smitten Maurice was, yet again, at Queen Anne's Lodge, at a ball attended by the Prince of Wales. *Why I was taken I can't conceive*, wrote Billy, *but I enjoyed it, thanks to M, who hid the Prince's cigarettes under a chair for me, found a secluded seat in the garden and danced quite well.* By the end of the evening, more for her own diversion than any overwhelming need to see Maurice over the summer, Billy had contrived for Mrs Herbert to invite him to take the opportunity, when his work in Antiquarian law took him for a spell to South Wales, to call upon them at their country house in Malvern Link.

In fact, Mr Hewlett received an invitation for a weekend and Billy, the only member of the family skilled enough to drive the phaeton, met him off the train one Saturday. Together, they ate a late luncheon and as they sat chatting in deckchairs in the garden, the watching Dora remarked injudiciously to the governess that Mr Hewlett seemed too intelligent to be interested in Billy's silly conversation: an observation the governess, *no fool*, made sure to pass on. Mr Hewlett, far from finding Billy wanting in conversational skills, found her desirable in all possible attributes. Before the weekend was out, he had proposed to her. Billy, not at all sure that she wanted to be engaged, although she liked him quite well, asked for a week in which to make up her mind.

Three days before that unforgivably long week was up, Maurice sent a telegram, begging Billy to say yes, to an effect beyond anything he could have anticipated. Mr Hewlett's intentions, not unexpectedly, were already a matter of interested family speculation, so when Mrs Herbert learnt of Billy's wire and, upon her insistence, its contents, her fury was twofold. Not only had Billy kept the proposal a secret, but, shockingly, she had allowed what was *sacred and the subject of prayer* to have been the subject of a telegram. She scolded her daughter bitterly, called her flippant and a flirt – the last Billy mentally acknowledged to be true – and said she would never forgive her for treating a man's love in such a worldly manner. Billy refused to discuss the matter with her mother; she said nothing to her sisters. Only after she had returned from the post office, later that day, did they learn that she had telegraphed her reply: yes. There was nothing for Mrs Herbert to do but invite her future son-in-law to stay the following weekend. *After that*, wrote Billy, *mother was quite decent to M for a time, and also to me*. In *The Letters of Maurice Hewlett*, September was the stated month in which they became engaged; Billy remembered it as being July; the method of proposal and acceptance, however, is consistent with both their personalities.

That first summer, given whatever time Antiquarian law would allow, Maurice spent with the Herbert familing, riding, boating, playing tennis, or idling away Sunday afternoons in a spinney by a stream. And to Billy's delight, he became *great pals* with her beloved brother, George. George, by dint of manipulating his unique status within the family and making the most preposterous demands on his sisters, had established himself as the charmer to be adored by all. Once, laid up with a sore knee, the pipe he had demanded had to be smoked by its bearer – he was too crippled to smoke it himself; the apple he longed for, but had no appetite to eat, had to be eaten for him. He was utterly unselfconscious and had made life worth living for Billy, when he was at home. They *never quarreled or fought and were so entirely one in aim and in sin that unity was an absolute necessity*. As children they were uncontrollable, unrepentant and scornful of punishment. It was not that they were deliberately naughty; it was just that adventures had a habit of becoming escapades, such as when one summer in Malvern, Billy had been required *to accompany Mother to a County Archery Meeting. I resented it*, she remembered, *as an undeserved punishment. Sulkily I dressed in my best clothes and was taken in the carriage. I endured about one hour of horrid boredom, then I told Mother I didn't feel well, and couldn't eat any tea and nature called me loudly to retire. She looked very concerned and worried, but I explained that I could walk home by the fields and be sick if I had to. She reluctantly let me go.* Billy's route took her through an orchard, where she discovered George and one of her younger sisters. Mistletoe in a tree exerted a strong appeal and soon Billy, with her best dress discarded, was gathering bunches from the trees. Unfortunately, the local policeman happened to spot them. With a breathtaking rapidity of invention, and instructions in French to her brother and sister, Billy engineered for the policeman to cease to think of them as thieves and for the farmer to be happy for her to take some mistletoe for *the poor suffering people in a London hospital.* Legging it home, *sans* dress, Billy then *reclined languidly on the lawn in a hammock* in time for her mother's return. George, who never knew when to end a joke, *almost overdid it, as he wanted to put a basin and a glass of water by* [her] *side and be found holding her head.*

Maurice, swept up by the audacious high spirits of the family, entered willingly into their pranks; another factor that worked powerfully in his favour in the eyes of his fiancée. On the day that George's behaviour was truly outrageous and Billy, on impulse, drove the phaeton through the lodge gates of a County Lunatic Asylum, it was Maurice who explained to the attendant that they had a most trying case for admittance. The trying case, for his part, acted with such realism the resident doctor had to be hurriedly fetched. To him Billy confided, when the case became violent and abusive on being told to get out of the phaeton, that if they made as if to turn for home, George would calm down. She drove slowly through the gates and headed for home at a spanking pace.

In fact, Billy began to wonder at the extreme of her brother's behaviour, as he swung between bouts of violent energy and periods of indolence and slackness. Home from Oxford, after nearly being sent down for writing New College in plates on the lawn and singing Gregorian chants from the window of his rooms, he would stay in bed until lunch, unmoved by any attempts to get him up, even those of his mother. And, in her view, a severe bout of scarlet fever when he was twenty-eight, which prevented him from attending the funeral of his dearly-loved father, tipped the balance against George. He was then a curate in Lower Gornal, he had been ordained in 1890, and although he moved on to St

Mary Magdalene, Munster Square, London, Crockfords has nothing to relate as to the rest of his ecclesiastical career. By 1912 he was living at 61 Preston Road, Brighton and well on the way to becoming the eccentric recluse that he could afford to be. He replaced all the plate glass of the windows with Georgian panes and all electric light fittings with candelabra and lived in just two rooms, richly decorated. He lost all his splendid vitality, ate and drank spasmodically and unwisely, and spent all winter in bed. His devoted landlady tolerated his foibles, which was as well for him, for as he grew older and his life narrowed down to his two fields of expertise, plain-song and Roman remains, he also shunned family contact. By then, Billy had *no pleasure in seeing George.*

In the summer of 1886, however, he was still her glorious co-conspirator of childhood. George, who prided himself on his most beautiful handwriting, small, exact and scholarly, would often insist on writing out the letters of his sisters and he even wrote many of Billy's love letters to Maurice, as he declared the poor man wanted to know about her and couldn't read what she wrote. That she did not know what to write in her firm, round hand might have been more accurate. Billy had begun her engagement to Maurice more out of contrariness than conviction. However, by the time the Herbert family went back to town at the end of summer, Billy *loved M, lived for him, and never altered for sixteen years.*

Left to labour in Wales, Maurice grumbled: 'My Darling Girl: '... I have been these two days tracing out what one man did with his property... I shall go down to my grave (and so must you) cursing the name of Joseph Duffield. May he stew, and boil and grill!' Again, he wrote from Hell (Pontypool). 'Your Mater said in her letter to me that "the discipline of a little separation is very good for both of you". I for my part don't see it. It neither tends to a profitable nor happy Sunday. But I know that some people have the idea that the more miserable you make this life, the happier the next one will be, and I think your Mother is one of these. It is a revival of the old system of hair shirts and peas in your shoes. If you ask me, I prefer the peas boiled.'

Maurice, all things considered, was an acceptable, if not hugely eligible, suitor. He dressed with care, was intelligent and, although his expectations working in Antiquarian law were hardly dazzling, he was following an honourable profession in an established family firm. True, his family might be of modest means, but it had no taint of trade in its background, which could not be said of the comfortably off Herbert/Hopgood alliance. And true his father was a Unitarian, which did not march happily with George Herbert's Anglo-Catholicism, but that hardly made Maurice an unacceptable influence on their daughter. On the Hewlett side there seems to have been no dissent to the proposed union. Maurice's father was fond of Billy, who bore a superficial resemblance to his wife, tiny, quick and loved to laugh, but there the similarity ended. Billy never showed any likelihood of becoming a retiring wife and mother.

Until marriage took her from the family home, the happy and confident Billy determined to make the vicarage *full of life, fun and individuality* and enlisted George to help protect their younger sisters, ranging from eleven to eighteen years of age, from the grimmer aspects of the regime they had known. So effective were their methods and so co-operative were the four girls, Billy's *poor worried parents* were left with the acute problem of what to do with the ringleader of disobedience. As she was engaged and over twenty-one, it is a puzzle as to why they did not seize the golden opportunity of being shot of such a stormy member by allowing her to marry without delay. Perhaps they were waiting for Dora, the eldest, to do the right thing and marry first, or perhaps they had stipulated that Maurice should first pass his exam for the Bar before marrying Billy. Either way, their attempt at bribing her to return to Germany and the lady desirous of her company by promising to pay her regular allowance to accumulate for her return to London, failed. A year without seeing M. was unthinkable to Billy.

Eager, loving and ready to learn, equally as when, under the wing of the intellectual set in Egypt as an impressionable eighteen-year old, she was ready to be as avid as Maurice in exploring such subjects as philosophy that questioned the imperatives of her upbringing. As Maurice slogged away in 'Hell – with the door shut again', or The Drain or La Slum (22 Old Buildings, Lincoln's Inn), the prospect of tackling 'a translation (2/6!) of Kant's "Kritik der Reinen Vernunft"' when they next saw each other, was positively romantic. Even so, her fiancé was careful not to be too schoolmasterly. 'Did you read Roderick Hudson? I wonder if you like it. ... If not chuck the thing away and tell me not to find you such indigestible stuff any more ...' And when he wrote that friends of

Mrs Herbert, 'a Lady — — with a Mrs — — and a very subdued daughter who looks as if she was whipped every day,' gave him 'the blues every time I meet them. They look so starved and proper, so tied up in conventionalities and proprieties!' Billy would have rejoiced at what he had to say. 'If only some of these good people knew what fun it was to be natural – and not to care whether one is *outré* or not, the world would be a very different place. As it is, what precious few people dare enjoy themselves! After all it doesn't very much matter if your hat is the same shape, or your pills the same prescription as everybody else's. The result is the great point.'

Billy did not name the *interfering uncle who wrote to her mother and made some remark about M's future being a poor outlook for her daughter*, but both John and James Hopgood, Mrs Herbert's brothers and solicitors, who were right-hand men to Thomas Cubitt and James Knowles, are likely candidates. From their point of view, the prospects offered by practising Antiquarian law, chiefly on behalf of the Civil Service, were too narrow: they knew how modestly Maurice's father lived in comparison to themselves. It was an opinion with which Mrs Herbert justified what she did next. With a dispiriting lack of commonsense, she wrote secretly to Maurice informing him that the engagement was at an end. Shocked, but honourable, Maurice replied that he could not withdraw his offer of marriage unless it was Billy's particular wish that he did so. Her underhand meddling thus exposed, Mrs Herbert was confronted by a furious Billy, who threatened to *leave home at once, marry and live in a workman's flat and go out as a nurse*. Providentially, an unavoidable invitation to a garden party at Lambeth Palace intervened between threat and consequent action; but once home and changed out of her best into her oldest clothes, Billy *wrote a telegram to M, telling him to take a workman's flat in Chelsea,* for they were to marry at once. She showed it to her mother. That very evening, Billy's intended accepted an invitation to dine. No doubt grateful he had not immediately been required to buy a special licence and live in a workman's cottage in Chelsea with his Darling Girl, Maurice remained engaged to Billy and continued to battle on with his exams for the Bar.

Father Herbert, it would seem, was ignorant of this drama, or else, out of love and loyalty, Billy could not bear to admit he played any part. However, it is more likely that Louisa Herbert acted on her own for, even if she had been aware that her husband harboured faint reservations as to his future son-in-law's suitability, she would have known they had more to do with Maurice's beliefs than modest pecuniary prospects. After all, did her husband not love the poor, and had he not married her, despite parental disapproval?

As the day of their wedding approached, Maurice wrote to his 'sweet love'. 'I am no believer in St. Paul's dictum "wives submit yourselves to your husbands" as a hard and fast rule. I think, if anything, it ought to be the other way. But certainly I should never wish you to do anything I ask because I ask it, but because you love me and like to please me. If you didn't feel any pleasure in pleasing me (which you do) I would much rather you pleased yourself. But I don't see why "obedience" should follow "loving" and "honouring" in the Marriage Service at all. Where true love is, honour and respect must be – the rest follows equally of course.'

Three days into the New Year, 1888, Maurice and Billy were married. On Tuesday, January 3rd, the Preacher's Book of St Peter's recorded that Father Herbert took the early morning service and the evening service; in between, at 2.00 p.m., he assisted at his daughter's wedding. A note to the effect that the Tower door of St. Peter's was not sufficient to admit large numbers[1] is the sole, extant reference to their wedding. The first of the Herbert girls to marry was going to notch up a few more firsts in her time.

CHAPTER 5

EARLY MARRIED LIFE

Necessaries and treats

The first and one of the most useful of his wife's talents that Maurice was to appreciate was her ability to create with few resources, but plenty of imagination, a decor both exotic and economic for their flat in Colville Mansions, Bayswater. There, snugly unbound by conventionalities, they lounged in a quasi-Eastern manner on piles of cushions in a decor that reflected the designs and warmth and colours of the east that had so ravished Billy on her trip to Egypt. It also reflected their comparative poverty: they might dine *sparingly off Nankeen china plates* (a wedding present), but could not afford the chairs on which to sit to dine. For Billy, whose inventive use of paint and fabric was unlimited – she even fashioned tiles out of cardboard which she then varnished – it was a blessing in disguise. Her friend from Egypt gave them a plaque inscribed with a welcome in Arabic from the Koran and his uncle, Dr Reginald Stuart Poole, Keeper of Coins and Medals in the British Museum, arranged for Billy to be given a student's ticket for the Reading Room, which she used to great effect researching Arab art. To her the Stuart Pooles were the *most darling, kind and unselfish friends* and Billy loved being invited round for lunch or tea in their home situated inside the gates of the British Museum or, as she referred to it, the *holy precincts*. She had a particularly soft spot for the famously absent-minded Mrs Poole who, once, when she forgot the name of a lady on whom she was calling, pressed half-a-crown into the palm of the puzzled butler when he opened the door, murmured "thank you" and walked away.

Her husband, as Billy soon learnt, was never to be of robust health.

A year into their marriage, he was ordered to take three months complete rest and her father, who had destroyed his own health by overwork, gave the young couple sufficient money with which to seek rest and sunshine away from London's winter. Billy was eager that her M should experience something of the wonder she had known in Egypt and she felt that, *in a modified way,* their choice of the French colony of Algeria, *woke in him new ideas.*

'Wet and chill day all wrapped up,' Maurice scribbled in his sketch-book among drawings as unpromising as that February day. But the weather improved, the sky lightened, and the accumulative burden of family expectations, the grind of work since he was seventeen, the stress of studying for the Bar, and the strain of the first year of marriage, all became as remote as the cold and fogs of London. His sketches dwindled away to nothing and Maurice, abroad for the first time in his twenty-eight years, began to enjoy a freedom hitherto unimaginable. Wrapped in the warmth and light of Chercel, with his rudely healthy, vivacious little wife at his side, he uncoiled. There was nothing else to do but loaf about and enjoy what was on offer – their hotel, a large Moorish house built round a courtyard filled with palms and fruit trees and run by a French couple who fed them like fighting cocks for five shillings a day. Additionally, the company of an amusing English couple, there also for the husband's health; the excursions by donkey into the countryside; the fishing trips led by a convivial Parisian and the chef of their hotel; even the disastrously enthusiastic hospitality of the local baker, were all enjoyed. Maurice wrote of it in his *Last Essays.* 'A baker in his covered cart was taking us to see some sight or other; and along the sea-front held his course magnificently indifferent to everything but the speed and joy of it all – aided not a little thereto by the fine afternoon, the business of the road, and the café tables hemming it, dense with customers. For it was the hour of absinthe. The trams flashed past us, coming or going, but little cared he for that. His object was to pass them, and he did pass one or two. Presently, however, at a curve he flogged his horse to pass one, on the wrong side, and just as he drew level, behold, another bearing swiftly down up on us! I confess that I blenched – but he did not; rather held on his way, and not until the last tick of our last minute on earth did it strike him that he must do something. And what did he do? He gave a wild shout and turned his horse sharply to the left. On his left was the overflow of a café – tin tables, bentwood chairs, syphons, opal-brimmed glasses, citizens in straw hats, with straws to their mouths, with cigars or newspapers – as thick as a flock of sheep. Into the midst of this, as once Don Quixote hurled himself, we plunged, horse, cart and passengers. Tables flew right and left, citizens were upset, glasses shivered, waiters wrung their hands. You never saw such a sight.' In the midst of the chaos, Maurice and Billy clung to each other helpless with laughter.

Carefree and happy and with Billy's enthusiastic support and encouragement, Maurice began to allow himself to dream for the future and when it came time to leave Algeria, the single most important thing he took home was his resolve to become a writer; preferably, and more audaciously, a poet.[1] Not that noble aspirations dictated that the Hewletts – *We would rather have bare white walls than one ugly thing to hurt the eye: the result being that we cheerfully denied ourselves many necessaries to buy one thing of beauty – be it useful or not* – went home empty-handed. Serious, if eccentric, souvenir hunters of taste and resourcefulness, they were accompanied, on trains and steamers back to London and reality, by Roman remains found in the local ruins, quantities of pottery, a nargile (a hookah) and an ancient door.

Further informed on Arabic art, the two of them wrote, illustrated and delivered lectures in private homes on the subject; Maurice also continued to earn a little extra by giving a series of lectures on subjects that interested him, one being early frescoes in English churches. As was his habit, he read exhaustively in his spare time on anything ranging from religion to philosophy, history to Italian art. Billy, meanwhile, discovered she could earn a good wage with her art beyond the amateur circuit of private homes; by creating, as well as executing her own designs, she received considerably more than those merely employed to do decorative work for a large (annoyingly unspecified) London firm. Regrettably, her parents were not impressed; shocked to think that their daughter might continue to disgrace them by being what they called a shop girl, they threatened to stop her personal allowance . As her allowance outstripped her earnings, Billy reluctantly agreed to give up what had so enjoyably and productively filled her time.

When work required, Maurice spent days at a time in places as far afield as Chester or Holt, Glasgow or Manchester, and daily letters were looked for by each. Years later, after his death, Billy still had in her keeping a number from the first fifteen years of their marriage: hers to Maurice went the way of all his papers. Wherever he went, Maurice always had some writing in hand, the progress of which he regularly reported. Recuperating from a bad attack of 'flu, one lonely week in Winchelsea, Maurice wrote from his private sitting room, whence he had been forced to retire by the trippers from Hastings – 'You know the style,' he had written to his sweetest Chick, 'cigars and fat women with ear-rings' – who filled the hotel's very small coffee room. 'I have finished with Michelangelo, I hope for ever. He will travel up to town to-night and I wish I were going with him. He is very bad I think, – worse than usual. He will probably be rejected without thanks; which will give me a valuable lesson.' But he stoutly refused to be too downhearted. 'I like failing sometimes, – it does one lots of good you know, and only makes me determined to 'arrive' one day.'

Notwithstanding his lack of literary success, Maurice and Billy continued very happy in the superiority of their modest lifestyle. 'Has she bored you to death with her eternal trivialities, her dog-maunder, her dull gossip and helplessness,' Maurice had raged to Billy staying with a wealthy family friend. 'Have the two long, idle men dizzied you as they dizzied me with the unspeakable emptiness of such a life? Really I *cannot* tell you how sick and ashamed I felt that two huge, strapping men *with souls* should devote themselves to brushing my coat and handing me from silver dishes things wherewith to feed my belly!' Happily, good friends such as the Stuart Pooles offered less ostentatious entertainment both in London and the country house they took each summer. With them, after-dinner entertainment, such as charades, were to be enjoyed unaffectedly. Maurice was a memorable hit as Cromwell, with a tennis ball for the infamous wart attached to his nose by a net over his head, and Billy relished the occasion when a certain Mrs Cockpen unknowingly marked the spot where Lot's wife turned to a pillar of salt. This lady, *who greatly revered her family tree,* (had) *held forth on modern democracy with hatred and scorn, saying, 'You never know who you are shaking hands with nowadays, it may be your butcher or your dressmaker.'* Billy, who knew she should have held her tongue, but it was ever an unruly member, blurted out that she could not see that it hurt to shake hands with anyone. Mrs Cockpen, if that truly was her name, hoped frostily that Billy, with no experience of life, might gain it without sorrow.

Feeling *more angry than squashed*, Billy said no more, but when it came time for all to retire to bed, instead of shaking hands with the lady seated in state in a large armchair, as did all the family and other guests, Billy curtseyed deeply, bowed her head and murmured good-night. When the *grande dame* put out her hand, Billy refused it: *'I don't know if my ancestors were shop-keepers, and I may have to earn my living, so you may not wish to know me.'* Two grandfathers, one a silversmith, the other a builder and speculator, were never so Trade-ish as *shop-keepers*, but the remark about earning her own living was later proved not to have been so outlandish. Gently reproved by her hostess the following morning, Billy readily apologised to Mrs Cockpen who, thenceforward, treated her as though she *was a poor working-class person she had hurt.*

In the quiet country lanes of Addington, where Maurice's family lived, the Hewletts learnt to ride a penny-farthing and once mounting and dismounting the contraption had been mastered without a disabling casualty, no mean feat for the diminutive Billy, they were overtaken by cycling fever. Swiftly advancing to a safety bicycle – one with wheels of equal size – the Hewletts were foremost in all that the newest craze offered. They joined a private club; they rode through the city at midnight; they cut a dash with the Herbert sisters all in their cycling bloomers as they sped round Hyde Park, although Billy, it would appear, eschewed such "rational dress" until she took up skiing; they explored the countryside on expeditions lasting several days. Once they took what they called an arm and leg holiday: they cycled to Oxford and returned to London by a double outrigged skiff. As for so many others of their age and status unable to afford a horse and carriage, the freedom of movement for the price of two bicycles was intoxicating. Billy, particularly, loved the feeling of independence and the sensation of speed, and, whereas her husband lacked all mechanical aptitude – he had been known to leave his bicycle in the ditch rather than mend the chain – she was quite the reverse.

Three years to the month they were married, Billy gave birth to her adored son, 'the life she loved longest and first,' as Maurice wrote. Breaking with Herbert and Hewlett tradition, she and M avoided combinations of the names Henry, William and George for their firstborn and plumped instead for Francis Esme Theodore,[2] who, because his father was in the grip of a new and significant passion, the Italian Renaissance, was known from his very beginning as Cecco (pronounced Checko), the diminutive of Francesco, the Italian form of Francis. Maurice's fascination with Tuscany and the Italian Renaissance dominated his reading and imagination and was to inspire and inform a great deal of his writing, whether poetry, essays, travel books or novels. Early in the morning, before he left for work and home again in the evening, he read Petrarch, Politian and Dante; he absorbed their humanism, essayed lyric poetry in their mould, and identified strongly with the ideals of the lovers of Laura, Beatrice and Simonetta. He researched the bellicose Guelphs and Ghibellines and he anthropomorphized and feminized the cities of Tuscany and Emilia; Florence, the pale Queen crowned with olive; Pisa, a winsome maid-of-honour to the lady of the land; Prato, a brown country girl; Pistoia, ruddy-haired and ample; Siena, a lovely black-eyed wretch, as keen as a hawk; Lucca, dove-like. Indeed, it was a relief to discover that he could find time for the living and his family: the artist A.S. Hartrick remarked on how 'high before the fireplace' his friend had tossed his little son, the future airman.

In Rome, rather than belabour his brains with Baedeker and marble, Maurice preferred 'to loaf about the Forum and tread the very pavements of old Rome, still in their places.' Billy preferred to poke around in the markets and shops. From the flat roof of the villa lent to them one autumn, Maurice gazed over the Vatican. From the same flat roof, Billy witnessed the resident dog, with its resident fleas that resisted her most energetic efforts to dislodge them, chase a rat over the edge. Thankfully, the hound survived the fall: confessing to the loss of their kindly friends' pet would have been too distressing. Dealing with more mundane hazards, such as the too frequent and too careless spitting occuring on the trams, was, on the other hand, more of an occasion for mirth. When a fat man beside her spat on her shoe, Billy first made sure to silence her horrified husband with a steely look, after which she casually wiped the gobbet of spittle on to the man's trouser leg, while turning away as if unaware of what she had done. The man could only glare. Mute, Maurice feigned obliviousness. Not until they had alighted did the Hewletts allow themselves the luxury of laughter and they could very well have still been laughing when they reached their destination: certainly, Billy was known for her laughter. The Italian servant of great devotion and fidelity to the notable English hostess, Janet Ross[3] had her own way of announcing English and other foreign visitors. *An artist who wore goloshes was 'Il signor with slippers'. A lady who wore a most unusual and remarkable hat was 'the signora with the lamp-shade'. Another with a deep voice was 'the lady who talks like a man'.* Billy was *'the small lady who laughs.'* It can only be regretted that Billy either did not choose, or could not recall, how Maurice was announced. It could have been illuminating.

That trip to Rome had also included a far greater irritant than the dog's fleas; Maurice's sister, Cicely. Cissie in her mid-twenties, suffering a severe emotional crisis, which manifested itself in a lot of crying and very little eating, had been sent to stay with the Hewletts, in the hope that life in London would provide sufficient distraction to effect a cure. Uncured, she had then accompanied them to Italy, where she continued to weep and refrain from eating, which tested her sister-in-law's patience to the limit. However, the outcome of her trip was to be happy for Cissie, shocking for her father, the Unitarian, and a blessed relief for her brother and his wife. Back in London, Cissie began to seek out Catholic churches and, eventually, electrified her family by converting to Roman Catholicism and joining the Order of St. Catherine of Siena, in which she spent a long and useful life teaching dancing and music in a school run by the Order.

The trials of Cissie did not make it to Maurice's diary, but that was not so extraordinary for it was, in essence, a log of his work in hand. Begun in 1893 as enthusiastically as many diaries are, the torrent of its entries eased up over the years to barely a trickle on those occasions when personal matters outweighed his flagging inspiration. But in 1893, when he was 32 and brimful of of determined optimism and energy, he filled every spare moment, reworking poems and stories, reviewing for the *Academy*, lecturing, taking Italian lessons, reading Keats and Browning out loud to Billy. She, willing as she had been to be instructed by her M in a subject of which she had little knowledge, nevertheless found greater pleasure in her arts and crafts. Left on her own, when Antiquarian Law required Maurice to visit courts around the country and when he retreated to his reading and writing, Billy's natural independence made it easier for her to fill her time than a wife inflicted with a conscientious attitude to household duties. After five years, the Hewletts' marriage had settled into a loving and companiable relationship: its sixth year was to bring sorrow to Billy. It was also to usher in a crisis for Maurice.

CHAPTER 6

TO STRATFORD WITH GAY

Guilt and inspiration

Classical Greece vied with Renaissance Italy as the focus for Maurice's poetry in 1894, but to his disappointment the publishing partnership of Elkin Mathews and John Lane declined to publish his piece on Theseus and Ariadne. As he had found Robert Bridges' newly published *Milton's Prosody* most useful, Maurice decided to seek Bridge's advice. The doctor-turned-poet warned that he would only advise and criticise on metrical form and charmingly claimed that he was 'naturally stupid about allegory'.[1] Once he had read the poem, he admitted he could not quite understand Mr Hewlett's drift, but if Mr Hewlett would like to stay with him in order to talk the matter over – Mr Hewlett would indeed – Mr Hewlett would be most welcome. A visit was arranged for mid-September, once the Hewletts had returned from holidaying in Scotland.

It had been a very happy month in Pittenweem and there Maurice had written *The Chamber Idyll*. Read without any reference to its inspiration – Edward Calvert's ravishing engraving of that name – the object of the poet's love is clearly not a wife of six years. However, once it is understood that Calvert represented a honeymoon night, the final verse:

See, we are side to side,
Virgin in deed and name -
Come, for love will not be denied,
Tarry not, have no shame:
Are we not man and bride!

makes sense. And when Maurice and his Williams parted, he for London and she for Malvern Link, Billy was four weeks pregnant with their second child.

'Darling Williams, Your postcard has made me comfortable; a letter will be still more welcome, for I am in a chastened mood," Maurice wrote from London four days after they had left Pittenweem. 'You will be sorry to hear that your praiseworthy schemes to have me picturesque at Bridges' will be partially destroyed. I am frustrated: my grey flannel trousers – two large oily blotches on the rump; two on the thighs; two on the shins – two on the calves.' Happily, Maurice's reception in Yattenden was not affected. 'Here I am and very well treated. B. and his wife are awfully kind to me, and I *think* R.B. thinks I am some good. I learn this much from him – I may call myself a poet, which I have never dared do before. I must say I am enjoying myself.'

No wonder Maurice enjoyed himself; Bridges had liked Theseus, if *not its arrangement*. Praise, even qualified praise, from a man he so respected was unspeakably exciting and in his letter of fervent thanks written to Mrs Bridges in his very best and tidiest handwriting, Maurice declared that his proposed solitary walking tour held no pleasures for him after the kindness he had been shown. He would join his family in Malvern.

To abandon his solitary walking tour, in exchange for the pleasure of sharing with his Darling Little Williams how indebted he felt to Bridges for his stimulating encouragement, would seem natural and unremarkable. But, in view of what happened next, the possibility that Maurice, in the first place, might have had a reason for engineering an acceptable excuse for not joining his family in Malvern is not too far-fetched. Of course, he could genuinely have preferred his own company to that of the Herbert family *en masse* – walking tours were very much 'the thing' for men – but he might have had an uneasy feeling that he should keep his distance. Whatever his reasons, his change of plan and his heightened emotional state made him particularly vulnerable to what, anyway, might well have been unavoidable He arrived in the Herbert household keyed-up, brimful of poetic aspirations, afire with joyous dedication, and in a state of exaltation; more than a little trying, no doubt, for a wife suffering the early weeks of pregnancy. Billy, despite their initial hopes in the early days of their marriage, had been unable to gambol in the Elysian fields of poetic inspiration with her Maurie; a good story was what she preferred. But Gay, a wayward, noisy dear of nineteen, was there to be dazzled by her charismatic brother-in-law, with his talk of poetry, Greek classics and Italian art. And how natural it was to accompany him on outings which held little appeal for her sister; worshipping at Shakespeare's birthplace was not a top priority with Billy.

In a diary, remarkable for its dearth of personal entries, where Maurice appeared to move through life for the most part unaccompanied, his *To Stratford on Avon with Gay* first seemed an innocuous anomaly. Its significance only became apparent when a letter came to light that Maurice had written to his friend, the poet Harold Monro, many, many years later. Replying to something that had made rueful reading, Maurice, in surprise and dismay, repudiated the notion that there was anything between himself and Alida Klemtaski, Monro's assistant and future second wife. Not only was Alida the same age as his own daughter, but he thought Monro knew very well who had been the keeper of his heart for nearly twenty years. The trip to Stratford with Gay had been in September 1894. Maurice's letter to Monro had been written in 1915. Monro could not have failed to have known of whom Maurice was speaking: Gay had been Maurice's regular companion since 1910. Suddenly and blazingly, that modest diary entry, *To Stratford on Avon with Gay*, mocked the long-held belief by later generations of the Hewlett/Herbert circle that Maurice had fallen in love with Gay the year Billy left him for aviation. But two oblique references twenty years apart is flimsy proof for a new and startling theory. If Maurice had indeed fallen in love with Gay fifteen years earlier than previously understood, concrete evidence was required. But where to find it?

His so-called Diary contained so little of a personal matter that, on the face of it, it was hard not to suspect that it had been subjected to censorship. As the typescript had been deposited in the British Library by Gay, who had first undertaken the laborious task of copying out thirty years' worth of journal in long-hand in a hardbacked, lined, foolscap book, she must be a prime suspect. But why, in the first instance had she copied out the journal? Had it been for the benefit of Laurence Binyon with his task of collating and editing *The Letters of Maurice Hewlett*? It could not have been out of pity for a typist, for as terrible as his writing was, no typist had failed to cope with Maurice's manuscripts. Perhaps the so-called diary had been compiled from more than one source. By bequeathing Gay all his account books, letters (whether written by or to him), diaries, papers, memoranda and unpublished manuscripts of every description with the request that she examine and destroy 'such as she shall in her uncontrolled discretion consider ought not to be preserved,' Maurice Hewlett had, in effect, entrusted her with his posthumous reputation. Gay might also have found that 'uncontrolled discretion' was required to preserve her own reputation. Judicious editing of his diaries and subsequent destruction of the originals might have been a necessity. Immediately upon her mother's death, her daughter, Penelope, had made a bonfire of all Gay's papers, notebooks, diaries and letters. Anyone who has tried to burn something as slight as a heap of receipts will appreciate what a massive fire it had to have been. The fury with which Penelope was seen to fling, at the last, a beautiful silk kimono dressing-gown onto the pyre, is an expression of a more than pious execution of her mother's final wishes.

So, with whatever real proof that might have existed of what happened between Maurice and Gay long gone-up in smoke and no living witness to question, there remained only Maurice's writing as a possible repository of the truth. And there it was. With Gay in mind, close reading of the Artemesian sonnets that streamed from his pen after their visit to Stratford on Avon, reveals Maurice's thraldom. He addresses the object of his unrequitable passion as Artemis, sometimes as Hymnia, the softer alternative – a future and frequent dedicatee of his work. Steeped in Greek mythology, Maurice had chosen the most apposite of all the Greek goddesses to represent the object of his worship. Artemis, a complex character, was the goddess of the chase and chastity; twin sister to Apollo and the obverse of the sun god's coin, Artemis was a divinity of light, the moon. A slim and supple virgin, unmoved by love, she imposed strict laws of chastity on her companions, Oceanids and Nymphs. Depicted either as a huntress, clad in a short tunic, with a bow and arrow and a spear, or in flowing robes and veiled face as goddess of the moon, she had a dark and vindictive side to her character and punished any slight or insolence, but was benevolent to those who honoured her.

Bound to his unsuspecting wife by love as much as loyalty, waylaid by an emotion that was as acute as it was forbidden, Maurice found, as he had as a boy, greater reality in literature. In his love for Gay, Maurice could find parallels with Dante's unrequited love for his beautiful muse, Beatrice. It was natural, therefore, his imagination swollen with Classicism, that Maurice should find a safe and necessary emotional outlet in poetry and, in the guise of retold classical Greek myths, he wrote reams of longing and desire, loss and grief. The avuncular and shrewd Bridges, with whom he continued to correspond, recognised a hectic quality in the work of the highly-strung young man and he warned Maurice against saying too much about himself in his verses, which seemed excited with too little reserve. However, Maurice's decision to delay publication of much of what he wrote over the next three years probably owed more to personal reasons than Bridges' criticism: the majority of the sonnets of 1894, and early 1895, remained unpublished until years later, when they were included in a privately printed limited edition of poetry entitled *The Wreath. 1894-1914*.[2] Once, practising a certain amount of self-deception, Maurice had remarked to his friend, Stephen Gwynn,[3] that he could never, like Gwynn, expose himself in his poetry. In the Artemisian sonnets he did, but only to those in the know.

Canon law would have forbidden his marriage to Gay, even if Maurice had wished to divorce Billy, which he did not; to hurt her so terribly was unthinkable, besides he had not ceased to love Billy because he had had the dubious pleasure of acquiring an additional love. And now, with Billy pregnant with their second child, it was even more imperative that his secret should be locked in his unseen poetry. Outwardly, he would remain the affectionate older brother of Gay, whom he had known since she was eleven years old and to whom he would be careful not to confess his love for fear of frightening her. Imagination, suppression and the realisation that in Gay he had found a more like-minded companion than her sister, whom she closely resembled in many ways, did nothing to cool his ardour. It was only at Gay's bidding, some two years later, that Maurice was resolutely to suppress his romantic, unrequitable ardour, but not before he had succumbed to the temptation of confessing his love to his chaste Artemis, when he became aware that she was not unmoved by him.

For Gay, the pleasure the husband of her admired elder sister took in her company had to have been flattering, thrilling and troubling. He was singular in appearance and manner, with an engaging smile that cracked through the wary reserve that deterred those who did not know him; a bit of a dandy with a touch of bohemianism, he was anything but a desiccated Antiquarian lawyer: a married man, forbidden fruit, made heroically attractive by his suppressed desire. But how much had Gay loved him? 'Here lies Love, murder'd at the Call Of one who dar'd not love at all.' Maurice had written bitterly and with a touch of self-pity that only spurned lovers are allowed. 'As sobbing on my Floor he lay; I slew and cast the Child away And tore his broken Feathers off.' Christmas, 1896, and the secret affair, unconsummated even by a kiss, if the poem speaks the truth, had to end. Maurice's love was an unwelcome and heavy burden for Gay. She was a devout Christian; she was a young woman; and she was of an age when she should find a husband: she needed to feel free and guiltless. *In a Church* with Maurice, she prayed.

HE: You bow your head the Rood to kiss:
        And I have never kiss'd your sorrowful face.
        Speak! Do you know I love you?
SHE: It is sin.
        You must not love me. That is why I pray.
HE: That I should cease to love you?
SHE: That you win
        Enough of grace to dare to go away.
HE: You are my Saint!
SHE: Alas! no Saint am I
HE: Why do you hold your heart so close?
SHE: It aches.
HE: And I must leave you aching?
SHE: Yes. Good-bye.
HE: Why do you hold your heart?
SHE: For fear it breaks.

CHAPTER 7

SOME MATERIAL ADVANCEMENT

Some personal loss

At the end of its second year, an emotionally charged Maurice had written in his diary: *1894 has been a momentous year for me; the first year of partial attainment, a year of moral awakening, of mental struggle, of some sorrow but much compensation, of hope to begin another ...* In conclusion of what was the first, longest and most detailed of all his annual retrospectives, when he summed up his work and the tenure of his life, he declared himself *dedicated to Poetry.* He dared *not any more be unfaithful to the Image of Beauty and Immortal Truth, which it* (had) *been permitted* (him) *to approach.* The sudden death of Father Herbert in the November could only have added to his inner turmoil over Gay. As guilt mingled with sorrow and pity for the desolation and loss felt particularly by Billy, it is small wonder he couched his thoughts in devotional language. *My dear wife has been my constant companion in happiness and trouble. I can never say what I owe her from first to last. I solemnly purpose to work for her and our little son (and, if God grant it, yet another child we have good hopes of) until the end.*

It was a mercy that Maurice had Billy to save him from immolation on the sacrificial pyre of poetry. With his family on the increase and intent on honouring his pledge to his *dear wife*, Maurice had first to apply himself to the necessary task of finding roomier accommodation. At the same time, the Herbert family uprooted from the vicarage was settling-in to a new development just across the river from Vauxhall, Eccleston Square. It is not impossible that it was suggested that the Hewletts should take one of the stucco-fronted houses – in time, numbers 9, 39, 73, 80 and 82 were to be occupied by various members of Billy's family – but even if, from the terms of Father Herbert's will,[1] Billy was due to receive a greater annual sum than that of her allowance, thus improving the Hewletts' finances, affordable proximity to her mother and sisters would not necessarily have been to her liking. She and Maurice had, from the start, enjoyed a certain degree of independence by choosing to live north of Hyde Park. The discovery just round the corner from them of no. 53 Colville Gardens, a large, upstairs flat (or, as Billy described it, *a staircase with rooms off it, being the top part of a house*) with a balcony that was tree-top high, saw the Hewletts moving in within ten days of beginning house-hunting.

February 1895 was a terrible month and London was a cliché of Victorian cold and fog. It was also the month of Billy's birthday and the arrival of her birthday present, Graffiacane. 'A rat-like sight indeed – nothing but a nose on 4 legs,' Maurice wrote in a chatty letter to Gay, who had been whisked off to Rome in the company of the *family policeman*, Dora. Dora was a practised chaperone: seven years earlier, she had taken her enthusiastic eighteen-year old sister, Olga, on a tour sketching and studying Normandy cathedrals and churches from roof to crypt. 'At present he bids fair to be an exorbitant anxiety,' Maurice grumbled on to Gay, 'perpetually wanting to be watered or fed; perpetually watering and feeding himself in the wrong places and at impossible times. I have got to crawl out into a raw fog with the glass below zero to exercise the animal. Oh, why in the name of glory did we buy a dawg?'

Further misery was to follow: within days of their move, four-year old Cecco fell seriously ill. For over a fortnight Billy, Maurice and Cecco's nanny, Julia Sparkes, took it in turns to share the round-the-clock watch over him. Not until he was convalescing in Worthing in the care of the Family Jewel, or Jule as Julia was affectionately known, did 'many dogs, painters, paperers, plasterers and their familiars' descend on the Hewletts. Then Billy, despite being six months pregnant, threw herself into painting beams for the ceiling and carving panels for the walls. Maurice took a hand as well, but, as he wrote to Gay: 'I don't know that there is much chance of any pomes being worked off. Nevertheless I try to be cheerful and when I consider Williams who suffereth long and is kind, in spite of it all, I feel very much ashamed.' Graffiacane, regrettably, had little of his short life left and added further to their trials by being 'very ill through swallowing quantities of coals.'

Earthwork in boards. I got the first copy today. Maurice's first book, *Earthwork in Tuscany*, was published at the end of March. His daughter, born two months later, on 14 May, 1895, registered as Simonetta Gay,[2] christened Barbara Freda, only ever called Pia, later described it as a collection of essays, rather preciously written. Her father's claimed intention had been to express the inner secret of Italian life, which could 'be read, not in painting alone, nor poem alone, but in the swift sun, in the streets and shrouded lanes …' But, although the book enjoyed a *succès d'estime* among highbrows and the artistic, it baffled the majority of its readers; one man's essence of Tuscany is another man's useless guide book. In many ways, it was an adventurous book; Maurice used essays, stories and dramatic scenes, with characters real and imaginary, to convey his vision of Tuscany. James Knowles, who enjoyed philosophical or challenging ideas was particularly impressed by the chapter, 'A Sacrifice at Prato'. In it 'a cultivated Pagan of the Empire' who had journeyed in Time and Space to the cathedral of Pistoia, at first tried to equate what he witnessed of the Christian religion with the gods of his own. Given the images of saints, such as Catherine on her wheel, and Sebastian stuck with his arrows, he first assumed that the divinity must be Bacchus/Dionysus – one god, two names, a variety of attributes and worshippers given to violent frenzy. The icons of the Virgin Mary were clearly those of bounteous Venus, but the agonised figure of the man on the cross, the sacrifice, puzzled him. After conversation with a worshipper, he concluded that the figure on the cross must needs be, according to Plato's version of Love, 'the Divine Eros'.

The Hewletts arranged for their children to be christened but, apart from that, laid little emphasis on them conforming to organised religion. Maurice struggled to reconcile his doubts about Christianity with his need for some form of spirituality in his life. Billy maintained that she had heard enough sermons as a child to last her a lifetime and saw absolutely no need to go to church to set anyone a good example; out of the Herbert clan, she and Pat (Grace Monica), were the only two who never actively or publicly confirmed their faith.[3]

For some reason the Hewletts arranged for Pia to be christened in Addington (Pia, accompanied by Jule, an Addington girl, was to stay there regularly throughout her childhood). Although Billy got on well with her father-in-law, she considered her mother-in-law to be spoilt and her relationship with her sisters-in-law was fragile, to say the least. The unfortunate Nellie once dared, in the heat of the moment, to tell Billy that she was unfit to have children – it was over some incident concerning little Cecco. 'God knows what Old Bird must have said,' Pia wrote of the incident, 'but she never forgave her and never forgot it and never went to the house again.' Billy held very decided views on the right way to raise children and no one, but no one, was going to criticise her methods, least of all a stay-at-home spinster, a year her junior. Way back, in her *sock and strap-shoe age*, Billy had vowed that her children would be loved and spoilt. As an adult, she vowed that fear would never be part of the armoury to command respect, a word which she hated, it *wore so badly and was such a broken reed to build on.*

As customary for the age, when they were very little, Cecco and Pia spent more time in the care of the nursemaid than their parents, although, as they grew older they were encouraged to participate in certain adult social occasions. It was a policy that carried a certain amount of risk for potential embarrassment to the hostess; small ears and innocent minds could lead to awkward questions. Summer holidays were always family holidays, usually in Scotland, but as soon as finances allowed, the children accompanied their parents on foreign holidays. Never overtly demonstrative towards her children, Billy nevertheless considered they were spoiled, but as they were popular, natural to a fault and told her everything without fear of incurring her anger, her bracing and un-censorious mothering obviously worked. Indeed, years later Maurice was ungallant enough to tell Hilaire Belloc's sister, Marie Belloc Lowndes, that he thought Billy had been a much better mother than she. The one thing that did irritate him was when Billy, infected by the children's *laughter at nothing at all*, had to join in. Cecco and Pia learnt to trade on their mother's happy fallibility. One much later Christmas, when Pia was home from boarding school and Cecco was on leave from Dartmouth, Billy took them shopping for clothes at the Army and Navy Stores. *Perfectly weak with laughter and joy*, Billy allowed herself to be held on either side – the Stores were so full and she so small she might get lost – while her irrepressible children found every reason for buying nothing and teased her unmercifully, repeatedly calling her Ma, a title Billy loathed.

The close of 1895 saw the publication of Maurice's verse lament for the passing of the Renaissance glory of Florence: *Masque for Dead Florentines*, a less than gripping read. Dedicated to Billy, his 'proved companion of Florentine days and other seasons of fair and foul weather' it is debatable that it was to her taste. Maurice had once ruefully admitted, after reading aloud an excerpt from his poem, 'Hippolytus', to his dutifully listening wife, that that class of writing was not in her line. Possibly more to her taste was his patriotic poem published in the *Pall Mall Gazette*, after Maurice had suffered a rush of blood to the head and joined the Inns of Court Rifle Volunteers in the New Year of 1896. It has to be assumed that it was news of the Jameson Raid (Billy admired the *great man*) that prompted his bellicose reaction. The thought of Maurice subjecting himself to the discipline of about-turning at someone else's command is laughable but, as he immediately considered it to be a *damn nuisance* to have to attend his first drill, his career as a volunteer was destined to be short: four days and three war poems later, he declared *no more*; mercifully. Less than fifteen years later he was fiercely anti-war.

When ill health forced Henry G. Hewlett to retire as Keeper at the Land Revenue Records Office, Maurice was appointed his father's successor (August of 1896). As a Government employee, Maurice could expect material advancement, some honour, regular hours, lighter work, a salary, and a pension;[4] a hitherto unforeseen career path. His father's resignation was, thus, to Maurice's financial benefit; his father's death, the following year, unleashed more than the expected grief. The threat to the family home, hinted at but unspecified, on his father's resignation, proved to have been rooted in financial difficulties. More devastating, however, was the resultant rift, never to be repaired, between Maurice and his Uncle James.

Knowles in '96, Maurice particularly noted, had been very kind and encouraging; he had also undertaken to interest Henry Irving in Maurice's play, *Pan and the Young Shepherd*. Regrettably, in the following January, *Pan came back: no go*, but Maurice had snatched a crumb of comfort in his uncle's prophesy that he would one day *do something great*. Now, barely two months later and stricken by the loss of his *dear father*,[5] whose death seemed *to have been a signal for family differences*, Maurice *quarreled inevitably with J. Knowles*: the reason for the inevitable quarrel possibly lay in the fact that Maurice had been forced to judge his beloved Mother. Acknowledging that Emmeline Mary could not bring herself to face mental or moral trouble, an inherited fault he indiscriminately and unfairly ascribed to all her children, was a *miserable business*. Nevertheless, as head of the family, Maurice felt a responsibility for his mother and siblings left in straitened circumstances. Criticism from one equally as proud and touchy as himself, and as close to the subject of their quarrel, would have had him mounted and spurred on his high horse, flashing past the finishing post of no return. Maurice had been in the habit of actively seeking the advice and opinion of Knowles, ever a kind and generous friend to the young Hewletts. It is, therefore, ironic and sad that their quarrel should follow the death of a man so dear to them both.[6] Maurice had not only lost his father, but also the friendly and valued patronage of a very influential man.

In June, Maurice's constitution crumpled under the strain of the previous months; not for him watching the Queen's Diamond Jubilee celebrations from the balcony of the Land Revenue Record office. However, Pittenweem in August was the effective restorative and within ten days of their arrival there, Billy and Maurice had sailed for Rotterdam and thence to Germany for two weeks and the Bayreuth Festival, leaving the children holidaying in the care of the Family Jewel. It was madly fashionable to go to Wagner's operas and Billy had enjoyed their sorties, complete with a hamper of sustenance as they queued for gallery seats at Covent Garden, but Wagner's approach to the dramatic retelling of myths and legends struck a chord with Maurice. 'Nor shall I deny that Wagner's method in opera has seemed to me entirely applicable to poetical drama. Wagner's libretti were written on a strict metrical system; but his music was not. In my plays I have followed faithfully, I believe, the music which I have certainly heard, but am incapable of rendering otherwise than by rhythm.' Maurice's sense of rhythm, judging by some of his verse, goes some way to explaining Billy's verdict that he danced only *quite well.*

Left in Pittenweem, when her husband returned to the office in September, Billy took comfort from his letters. 'My Dearest Love,' Maurice wrote, 'I know what you are feeling only too well – I have been very low at the thought of so dear and small a creature beginning to shift for himself. All these things are hateful, but they all have to be. Parents don't have a very good time ever, unless it is good to love something very much and very truly.' The small creature who was about to shift for himself? Cecco.

Surprisingly, it was Billy who initiated the wrenching separation. *When Cecco was seven years old, he had a bad attack of bronchitis, he was very weak and pulled down after it, London did not seem to agree with him. With the advice of our lady doctor, I took him to Pittenweem for the summer. He recovered so wonderfully that I thought it a pity to take him back to London. During our stay there we made friends with the English clergyman and his wife. He tutored men for the 'Varsity, but found it hard work to keep up with all the examiners required. I asked Mrs. Lloyd, his kind, practical wife, if she would look after Cecco for a winter.*

Winter was to become nearly a year and, as happy-natured and interested in all things as Maurice declared Cecco to be, it was drastic medicine for one so young. And Maurice's heartsearching about principles and lack of moral fibre, consequent upon his father's death, appear to have clouded his judgment as to what a child of less than seven might be taught. 'The next thing to teach him (it seems to me),' he wrote to Billy, 'is that it is a duty in him as well as a privilege to be a gentleman of good descent. You know I am not a snob, and glorious over a long pedigree; but I do think it will help him, as it has helped me to remember that his forefathers have not been able to afford low amusements, or grossness to women, or cruelty, or to think meanly of people in other stations of life.' Maurice was hardly less realistic about what his son could assimilate of religion, although, in the light of his own growing doubts about Christianity, what he asked seems reasonable. 'Along with this I always put the love of God, as I see God in a fine action, a noble thought, a beautiful person, place or thing, or in good love. I should like Mr. L. to teach him the New Testament as it is, and the Old Testament as he would teach him the stories in the Odyssey.'

Having to leave *Cecco so far away hung over me like a black cloud. When the day came, I took him to their house, Mrs. Lloyd was so kind and sympathetic, still I was miserable and had to bear it alone, as M had already gone back to London.* Poor little Cecco. He coped and never fussed. When he travelled to and fro for the holidays, Mr. Lloyd would put him on the express at Edinburgh and Billy and Maurice would meet him at Kings Cross. On the return journey, they would take him to Kings Cross, undress him, and put him to bed; in the morning the guard took him some tea, made sure he was dressed before the train arrived in Edinburgh and handed him over to Mr Lloyd. Who would dare to do that today? *However much he enjoyed his holidays, he never minded going back*, claimed Billy, but Cecco never forgot the desolation of being left so alone, so far from home.

During that September, while Billy lingered in Scotland with Cecco, Maurice devoted the greater part of his writing time to his newest and most ambitious work so far: his first novel. Inspired by a cycling trip to the New Forest and conceived on the day they had got lost, *The Forest Lovers* had Maurice writing four times within five days to his Williams about them. 'A new character has turned up and I don't quite know what to do with the woman.... I wish she had gone to the devil rather than come just now. She's like an uninvited guest who drops in and finds you with a dinner party on your hands.' 'Meantime I am getting on very well with my Lovers, in whose fortunes I am getting entirely absorbed. I know much more than I did about them, when I wrote down what I read to you. I am beginning to like Prosper as much as I do the girl. We have become excellent friends. He is one of those active out-of-door natures (very unlike my own by the way) to which it never occurs to need love. The girl is very still outwardly, but hot inside and a born lover. The problem is, how love gets into the man. Through pity and respect I think, and not until he has gone through the stages of indifference and the tempest of animal desire which good living and idleness might give him. ... The style is unequal, but better than when you heard it. I am trying to maintain simplicity with fullness and realism with romance. So, you see, I have my work cut out, and am entertained with my own wit.

'I am so glad you like my preface, as I hoped you would. I knew it was very good as I wrote it straight down, and one always is at one's best under those circumstances. As to the Lovers, you will see, I think it will come out all right enough. I must talk to you about it. The point is this – if it stands as it was when you heard it, it can only be at the best a happy bit of imitation of a medieval story, very pretty and as successful as you like BUT imitation and not far removed from Wardour Street.[7]

If, on the other hand, it arrives anywhere near my present notion, it will be a piece of myself – neither modern nor antique, but a queer composite, rather bewildering to those who love to classify and label what they read – but interesting I hope, and occasionally strong. This week I really cannot dine out. I must stick to my novel.'

Maurice wrote on at a furious pace throughout September and October, no doubt much in the style described by the *New York Daily Tribune*. 'He has an eccentric method of his own which suits his temperament. He writes morning and evening with great rapidity, warming up to his work as soon as the pen is in his hand and dashing off page after page of manuscript without stopping for revision or deliberate study. When the manuscript is finished he looks it over carelessly and either tears it up or casts it aside. Making a fresh start, he writes his story a second time without reference to the first effort, dashing it off page by page and writing always with his imagination at white heat. When the second manuscript is completed, he surveys his work critically and either flings the copy into the waste basket or lays it aside where he cannot refer to it. He makes a third, and possibly a fourth attempt on the same lines, and finally succeeds in finishing his story to his satisfaction.'

Two days after the Hewletts' tenth wedding anniversary, the manuscript of *The Forest Lovers* was sent off to be typed. But then what? Finding a publisher to consider a novel was very different to submitting a poem to a magazine and with Uncle James no longer being available for advice, Maurice needed help.

CHAPTER 8

THE FOREST LOVERS

The Hewletts taste success

It was Billy who, ever in the interest of promoting her man, had first approached their near neighbour, Mrs Clifford,[1] with whom the Hewletts *lived as relations very soon afterwards, only nice and dear relations, not those you have to see and do not want to.* 'Long ago,' Mrs Clifford wrote, 'they (the Hewletts) lived opposite our house – he and his little wife, who was as clever as she could stick, and as unconventional as himself. One afternoon, to my surprise, Mrs. Hewlett appeared, and explained that they had read a book of mine; her husband wrote poetry, we were neighbours – and – and would we know them? We did, and much delight grew out of it.' Mrs Clifford, a novelist, whose weekly if slightly old fashioned and dowdy salon attracted young writers and poets, had, as a regular contributor to the *Standard*, generously put Maurice in the way of reviewing novels for that paper. She was, therefore, the obvious person for Maurice to turn to, but the burden of reading a friend's first novel was onerous, as Mrs Clifford recalled. 'Charming and apologetic, he (Maurice) arrived with a brown paper parcel under his arm. He had written a novel, didn't know if it was any good, probably not, would I read it and if necessary be brutally truthful? Of course I would; and he left it. That brown paper parcel sat on a side table and worried me for days – in which he carefully avoided me, but went up and down the road on his bicycle, till it was like the flick of a whip. When I could bear it no longer, late one evening, I undid the string and found – *The Forest Lovers*. I read it all night and could have danced for joy, probably did. I insisted on its going to the Macmillans, wrote to them, or went to them. They agreed to read it, but they had it a long time without making a sign: and again Maurice Hewlett went up and down on his bicycle, with his head turned my way this time. I pretended not to see him. One afternoon at a party I met Sir Frederick (then Mr) Macmillan. He shook his head: "Our readers have tackled it," he said, "but I am afraid your friend's book won't do." I called his readers a bad name or two, and begged him to go home and read it himself.'

Macmillan takes The Forest Lovers, Maurice wrote in his diary against March 5. And with it, Frederick Macmillan took a terrific chance. His trusted readers had both been perplexed to find themselves mildly entertained by the book, but felt that the reading public, despite the pretty bits, would not go for something so puzzlingly fantastic. Macmillan, as ambivalent as they, having read the book for himself, nevertheless, decided to be swayed by Mrs Clifford's enthusiasm, but he confessed to Maurice that he would be more sorry than surprised should the circulating library public not care for the outlandishness of the story. As the tyro novelist shared Macmillan's opinion, his offer of ten per cent royalties on the first 500 copies sold and fifteen per cent on all thereafter, with 4d on New York and Colonial Library editions seemed more than handsome.

In early April, 'hot', as he was fond of saying, with ideas for stories to be researched, Maurice departed for Italy, taking with him the remaining unrevised proofs of *The Forest Lovers*. He arrived in Milan on the Sunday, finished and dispatched the proofs and proceeded to Ferrara, an exciting venue for a future story; Verona, the most beautiful town he had ever been in and Venice, where, as he exclaimed to his Darling Little Girl: 'I never thought to be reduced again to saying "Oh!" when I saw a place – but I said it when I got to Venice.' The weather made him glad that he had his ulster with him; he nearly died of a Pontifical High Mass at St Mark's; and he was enchanted by the strangeness and colours of the city and its sea, grey, pink, bright green, dark blue, coral, and french grey.

Reunited with his wife and the routine of the office, Maurice awaited the imminent publication of his first novel with a mixture of apprehension and excitement. Would his style be considered as previously affected and disagreeable? Would his Lovers be charming enough to be received kindly? Within the space of five weeks after publication, in which Maurice had ideas for five novels, Billy's sister, Verena, married the Reverend Douglas Pelly,[2] Edward Burne-Jones died and the Hewletts went to three Wagner operas, the buying public decided *The Forest Lovers* fate and, ultimately, Maurice's. The book was a wild success and after years of hopeful endeavour, Maurice Hewlett suddenly found himself the writer of the moment. And it unnnerved him. In fact, it unnerved him so much, he did something very unusual: he commented on it in the body of his diary. *Chiefly I am boomed for the Forest Lovers and don't like the sensation,* he wrote in July.

Billy, as may be imagined, loved it. She was fearfully proud of her own M, as she had every right to be, for without her forbearance and encouragement, Maurice might never have believed in himself enough to keep plugging away at his writing. Stephen Gwynn[3] remembered how Billy, who had first impressed him as being like 'the jolliest kind of terrier, with her nose a little cocked in the air, and all tingling with friendly vitality,' had laughed with him about 'her comical and lovable little swagger.' 'Whenever I go into a room,' Billy had said, 'I look at the other women and I say to myself, *Your* husband hasn't written *The Forest Lovers.*'[4]

A romance – an historical romance, set in no particular place, in no particular time, a pre-Raphaelite picture in prose spiced with refreshing flashes of sardonic humour. Blended from a mixture of ingredients that included Mallory's King Arthur, Renaissance Italy, and the New Forest, slow-baked in Medieval Latin and the Norman French of the antique legalities of Crown Lands, it was a grown-ups' faery tale about an impossibly chaste, but passionate, heroine and an insouciant hero. Isoult la Desirous and Prosper Le Gai – for such are the Lovers called; she pale, drooping and a child of the forest; he a bit of a lad with class; she with moral and physical courage; he yet to acquire the moral courage; the two who find love in the end. Written with dash and verve, informed by all the knowledge acquired in his research into land records, sprinkled with names fabricated to sound as though they could have come over with the Normans, coloured by his expertise in heraldry and his strong visual sense, it is truly Maurice's most spontaneous work, in that it had been well-brewed but written comparatively quickly. Later he was to dismiss it as tushery, but for the present he was content to concede that his forté appeared *to be the humorous enunciation of certain fundamental truths.*

If the fundamental truths were that the reading public liked a good romantic story, then he had got it in one. They did not mind the preciosity that some critics saw in it and loved the sheer escapism of the story so poetically told. And, if *The Forest Lovers* was quite unlike any other historical romance, so was the author. Stephen Gwynn doubted if anyone so picturesque had taken the town by storm since Byron's day: not a comparison Maurice would have found complimentary, he disliked Byron intensely. 'Maurice Hewlett with his crisp dark hair and strongly lined face was always the Englishman Italianate, and he had one feature which gave a romantic and slightly formidable suggestion that he might easily be also the devil incarnate of old saying. This was his mouth, with the queer twist in the upper lip that only just escaped deformity, but, escaping it, gave a notable emphasis to the face.' And from the description of his friend by E.V. Lucas, it is possible to picture some of the dashing uncomformity that must have been so appealing to Billy in the early days of their courtship, but which the photographs of the time fail utterly to capture. Lucas thought Maurice a wilful aristocrat with a personality so vivid that in company he was the most noticeable: his clothes were distinguished, his eyes sparkled in his finely modelled head and his dark moustache and imperial framed his crooked mouth. Enthusiastic or sardonic, Maurice spoke with resonance and, when he laughed, he laughed without reservation. Denis Mackail, in his biography of J.M. Barrie, reckoned that Maurice played up his Mephistophelian looks – true, the sandals he liked to wear were devilishly out of character – but Maurice's looks and manner of speaking were deceptive. Below the surface lay a warmth and sweetness revealed on greater acquaintance; Maurice, in Mackail's opinion, was one of the kindest people ever. The sandal-wearing, incidentally, most likely came later in his career, once he was comfortably established as a man of letters and could afford those eccentricities denied a Treasury solicitor. Compton Mackenzie remembered his astonishment in 1912, noting that Maurice wore sandals with a tail suit at a dinner at the Poets Club in honour of the Italian Futurist poet, Marinetti. At least he didn't wear socks with the sandals.

Suddenly, it seemed, everyone wanted a piece of this new romantic star, magazine editors, publishers and the literary agent, A.P. Watt. And Maurice, astonished by the glowing cuttings from the American papers that Macmillan sent him, was more than happy to assure his publisher that any future work would go his way. How short the distance between application and benefaction!

Carried on such a high wave that (he felt) *stranded in the ebb,* the author for whom longed-for recognition brought pleasure as well as trepidation, still had the office grind to be ground. From a wintry Newcastle, a place he hated the more each hour he stayed there, he wrote to his dearest Soul. 'Last night the High Sheriff gave a ball; the place was up to the neck, – which was more than the ladies were, I assure you. This morning I went for a walk about the greasy streets; all the same, the view of chimneys and smoke and dirty water from the Tyne Bridge is not without points. Two poor old black churches and a shabby castle look scared – as if they were wondering still where on earth they were.' Work then took him on to Corbridge and he again wrote to Billy, this time about the *Song of Renny,* a project he would shortly set aside for over a decade. 'Renny last night was a great success. Hermia grows to be the image of you – a cross between you and Gay perhaps, but more like you every stroke I put on her. I am awfully in love with the little Lady (as perhaps you will allow me to be) and as is right and proper I like her all the more for the wrong things she does – all lovers do that. I don't know whether it applies to women. I fancy you like me less for my faults; but I certainly like you better for yours. Droll!'

In gratitude, Maurice had dedicated *The Forest Lovers* 'To Mrs W.K. Clifford with the author's homage.' In gratitude to Billy, who had seen her man through illness, nervous exhaustion and ten years unremitting labour, he had said it all in his dedication of *Pan and the Young Shepherd*: 'In all love and honour to HBH. What I have is yours; What I do is through you. Take you the best of me, To hearten the rest of me.' In recognition of her part in the success of *The Forest Lovers,* M gave his Williams *an old enamelled and jewelled order, converted into a necklace, with a bit of paper inside more beautiful than the jewel, as it made (her) a partner of his success and his work – 'From one Forest Lover to the Other'*

CHAPTER 9

HOT WITH IDEAS

Maurice the historical romancer

In addition to Billy, Maurice had acquired another champion and flatteringly so; Frederic Harrison.[1] To him he confessed that his collection of stories, the product of his solo trip to Italy, were 'a little Boccaccian – meaning by that that they were intended as entertainment ... and dealt with real men and women as opposed to dummies.' In *Little Novels of Italy* he had taken a different city for his five variations on a theme of love in which, however dire the peril, the 'clean-hearted' young women triumph, their honour intact. Clement Shorter, editor of the *Illustrated London News*, was deeply offended by 'The Madonna of the Peach Tree' in which an innocent girl, stoned out of Verona for alleged adultery, was thrice mistaken for a vision of the Virgin Mary with wondrous result. He accused Maurice of being an immoral writer. 'The moral of that particular story was beyond cavil, and it would *not* have been without the treatment,' Maurice had defended himself to Shorter. 'You cannot show a thing white unless you show something else black.' Frederic Harrison, on the other hand, held it to be 'as perfect a short story' of the time, full of 'humour, poetry, pathos, mystery, imaginative history, and a pure humanity.'

Of the five, Billy's favourite was 'Ippolita in the Hills'.[2] The humour of its first half, when the ravishingly beautiful heroine, Ippolita, born in the poorest quarter of Padua, becomes the exasperated focus for the ecstatic devotion of a poet and his friends, is enjoyably sly. When Ippolita, disguised as a boy, takes to the hills and is accepted by a group of goatherds, the roughest of whom she falls in love with, plausibility is strained and the zest of the story is muted, but the final scene when it is so engineered that the two boys kiss, one, of course, ignorant until that moment of the other's true sex, is neatly done. Alfred Sutro[3] liked it too and he collaborated with Maurice on its dramatisation.

The Sutros were very good friends of the Hewletts and would even look after, when required, the playful and self-willed Bedlington terrier Maurice had given Billy. Such was Peachem's charm, however, it was no great chore. A dog of cunning and character, he had been observed jumping from rug to rug in the hall – his claws would clatter so on the wooden floor – in his effort to reach the open front door, unheard. When he died, the Hewletts had to send a telegram to their hosts for dinner that evening: *Lost great friend, too miserable to come.*

The Sutros also, in Billy's opinion, had *a flair for getting together the right people and letting them do as they liked.* The young Harry Irving, Sir Henry's son, Laurence Housman and George Frampton, the sculptor of Peter Pan in Kensington Gardens, were often among their house guests. One lovely summer night, when staying with the Sutros in Dorset, Billy wished to sleep out of doors. She undressed in her bedroom and slipped out over the dewy lawn to her improvised bed of hammock, rugs and cushions. A roar of laughter, when she said *a very common word* as it collapsed under her, alerted Billy to Irving and Housman, watching the fun from their bedroom window, but, as gentlemen should, they re-set the hammock. Harry Irving bought the rights to the dramatised 'Ippolita,' but it never reached the stage.

Here ends a year of prosperity, praised be God, and much content, Maurice had been able to write at the end of 1899. *I have made friends and lost none; if I have done no new work, I have pushed my standard, as it should be, a little out of my reach. There is no other way of living so far as I can see. My total earnings by Literature this year have been I see £1,163.18s. 3d. and I venture to take pride in the thought that all the stuff that represents has been as good as I can make it, honestly expressive that is.*

Prosperity and praise bring unexpected pressures; the need to maintain a more expensive but enjoyable standard of living and to match, if not exceed, the success of his work so far. As the new century began, Maurice struggled to finish the first draft of his romance about Richard Coeur de Lion; he found writing a romance true to its historical hero in essence far trickier than writing complete fiction. *I can make it a piece of life, but not yet a work of Art – and my conscience won't let me work upon it failing that.* His conscience, too, would remind him that he had been paid a princely advance of £1,000 on the book by Macmillan,[4] who, in a neat money-go-round, agreed to sell the thirty year lease on his home in Maida Vale to Maurice; Maurice signed the contract in January, but the purchase was not to be completed until Michaelmas.

Not unexpectedly, the expansion of the Hewletts circle of friends had a marked literary bias. One of their newest friends was Edmund Gosse with whom Maurice had much in common. Each was a civil servant and had aspired to be a poet,[5] each had left school at seventeen and acquired a further education by their own endeavours and each liked to sprinkle their correspondence with a variety of foreign phrases, as evidence of their familiarity with Latin and Greek, French, German and Italian, even once a smattering of Scandinavian. Each was kindly but with a tendency to asperity. When they met, Gosse was something of an elder statesman in the world of literature, but mutual admiration and flattery oil the wheels of friendship; the playful tone of many of Maurice's letters reveal the genuine warmth of his affection for Gosse. As for Nellie, Gosse's self-effacing and kindly wife, with whom she shared an artistic talent and an independence of spirit, Billy thought her *a perfect dear.* And it was the Gosses who recommended Norway as the ideal location in which Maurice should recuperate in the summer of 1900, when the burden of work, the agony of producing a revised and final version of his novel about King Richard, compounded by a full social calendar and the imminent upheaval of their move to Northwick Terrace had taken their toll. *Fell ill – horribly ill – damnably ill*, Maurice wrote in his diary. 'I have been in the nethermost pit,' he wrote to Gosse, who had kindly called to enquire after him, 'only pulled out by morphia. Better now, but to appearance a cause of derision to mine enemies.'[6] His optimism was premature, for that same night he suffered from tic, as he described it, of the most dolorous description, but well enough, ten days later, he and his family set sail for Norway.

Jule and both children were very seasick on the way to Bergen. M and I, Billy remembered, *felt unhappy certainly, but were capable of helping those that were in extremis.* Disembarked and faced with breakfast which *was all brown: brown bread, brown coffee, brown cheese*, M and Billy did their best, *but both children ate of the 'browns' with enormous appetites.* (A note of maternal pride there, surely.)

Once ensconced in the tiny village on the Hardangar Fjord, Maurice wrote joyfully to his friend. 'Oh, my dear Gosse, not the Eulogies in front of a windy fiction can express my debt to you for putting me upon the line of this place! These wicked black mountains, the play of light on them – the forests, the sky, the smell of the moss! If it weren't for the rheumatics I would kneel to praise your name.'[7]

Their lodging was in a brand new and sparsely furnished pine house; company, entertainment and daily meals were provided by the local hotel; and swimming, boating and fishing was provided by the fjord. Within two weeks he had dispatched *Richard* to Macmillan. Billy and Maurice fished together – Billy had been highly amused when her eminent husband, struggling in flapping cape to get a hook on his line one wet and windy day, forgot himself and swore *a real good, long, partly old-world swear* – and they became prodigious walkers; *26 miles; 15 miles; 5 hrs up 3 hrs down; over Folgefonna- 5,300 ft – couldn't get off – back again 12 hrs on ice 35 miles. Came to Jondal and then home late. Glorious weather. Hard work.*

That last, laconic diary entry in no way hints at the extreme physical discomfort of an outing that Maurice embellished to dramatic effect sixteen years later in his *Love and Lucy*. And, if it had not been for Billy's own gleefully detailed account of events, the connection between fact and fiction would never have come to light. Accompanying the Hewletts were three others, including, quite possibly Geoffrey Hope Hawkins, brother to Antony, and his Norwegian wife.[8]

The plan was for them to be ferried across the fjord, to break the walk to Folgefonna with an overnight stop, which turned out to be spartan in the extreme – a bed in a hut, a morning wash in an icy mountain stream and a cup of tea for breakfast – climb up and over the ice-field on to Odda, whence they would travel, presumably by road, to Jondal and take the boat back to base. Walking through soft snow and mist, the party only moved into sunlight once they reached the edge of the deep blue lake of ice, Folgefonna. By then they were tired, footsore and extremely hungry, and were keen to press on to Odda, but their guide, uncertain as to the route, went off to recce. As they stood and waited for his return, they fantasised about dinner: champagne, yes; salmon trout, no, they had dined on salmon trout too frequently; red and bloody beef, definitely. Just as they had moved onto the sweet course, their guide returned. There was no way forward, they must turn back.

M and the two young men turned quite nasty with that guide, wrote Billy. *They said things in English, not knowing his language (which was lucky), while they held their sticks very tightly. The other lady and I grinned. We were pleased that the guide should be blamed. M calmed down first, he spoke the words of riper wisdom to the younger men, till imagination overcame anger.* Turning, they followed the guide who set a punishing pace: the temperature would drop to freezing point after sunset. It was in silent agony that the exhausted and ravenously hungry group staggered back to Jondal, where they had landed the previous day. They roused the boatman from his bed and, as they lay like so many dead fish in the bottom of his boat, he rowed them back to the opposite shore. They blessed his wife for the loan of warm, thick socks for their frozen and blistered feet, but for days they were lame and for weeks they were unable to wear boots.

For *The Life and Death of Richard Yea and Nay* (hardly a snappy title), Maurice had read everything about King Richard in English, French and Arabic as he could. He believed that he had got the whole man, but in order to do so he invented a heroine – Jehane – of heroically improbable nobility of spirit, denied long-lasting bliss in the arms of her lover by historical fact. To the admirers of the novel, Maurice's Richard was a believable personality in all his contradictions, whose character was delineated with a modern, psychological sensibility, through a vividly convincing evocation of the time. 'At last we have a fine writer of romance – of historical romance in the old meaning of that somewhat languishing art,' trumpeted Frederic Harrison in *The Fortnightly*. 'Such historic imagination, such glowing colour, such crashing speed, set forth in such pregnant form,' carried him away spell-bound. The *Daily Telegraph* was in hot pursuit. 'The story carries us along as though throughout we were galloping on strong horses. There is a rush and fervour about it all which sweeps us off our feet till the end is reached, and the tale is done. It is very clever, very spirited.'

Not all reviews were so enthusiastic, nor friends and family so impressed. Calvin, as George Herbert now rather alarmingly signed himself, wrote a snippy letter to his brother-in-law, the Revd Edmund McClure: 'My dearest Luther. Yes, the *Standard* is down on M's book, which I have not read, but which Mother is reading. I don't want to judge him, but we always thought alike about him.' Heavens! What was it they always thought alike about Maurice? And was it 'Calvin' and 'Luther' who were as one in the matter, or George and his mother? Mrs Herbert might well have understood that Maurice could not afford to be squeamish when dealing with momentous themes in *Richard Yea and Nay*, but appreciating the nobility of the fictitious heroine, Jehane, bearer of the king's illegitimate child, however, was another matter. Jehane saved the Lionheart's life by ransoming herself to the Lord of the Assassins,[9] but subsequently was shameless enough to become the Lord's favourite wife and bear him a number of sons! It is safe to say, however, that Maurice would not have cared one jot what Mrs Herbert, 'Calvin', 'Luther' and his wife, Dora, who now unaccountably signed herself 'Brave', thought; he didn't, God help him, 'write to tickle ears.' But he might have wondered why the son and son-in-law of the anglo-catholic Father Herbert should choose the pseudonyms Calvin and Luther. Had they undergone their own mini-Reformation? Diet, worms and turning are in there somewhere.

CHAPTER 10

NEVER TO PLAY BRIDGE

One resolution bred of literary success

To be able to afford, from the wagging of his pen, to write a cheque for £2,500 for the 30 year lease on 7, Northwick Terrace, Maida Vale, was a matter of pride and wonder to Maurice. To Billy, the large house with its well-established garden was composed of three wonders and she could not decide which was the greatest: the studio, the garage, or the brass door knob, letter box and knocker for the front door. Lady Macmillan, concerned the Hewletts *were so poor [they] could not afford to keep them clean*, had offered to replace the door furniture with bronze ones. *I said*, wrote Billy, *that the glory was so great that I would clean them myself everyday*. That the Macmillans should be shaken at the thought of her trim small self standing on the front doorstep with Brasso and rags, she could only put down to their lack of a sense of humour. One friend, however, had some sympathy for Lady Macmillan, who dreaded what the lavish use of poker work might do to her London drawing-room. Her fears were unrealised, but Maurice's dressing room would have been a revelation. Billy, mischievously acting upon his tongue in cheek suggestion for a decor *all pink and roses like a bride*, arranged exactly that. Returning from a week's research into Mary Queen of Scots, he found pink curtains, pink carpet and a briar rose, twining and curling upwards, painted by Billy on a sheet of pink linen hanging between the two windows. Maurice really liked it and assured Billy, when she hinted that pink was not her colour, that his next bride would be chosen to suit the pink roses.

The studio, a large room beyond the garage and with a good top light,

Billy called her mess-room and allowed no one in to tidy or clean. Embroidery, leatherwork, wood carving, or repoussé work, Billy could turn her hand to any of these. Interested in the technique of inlaying, she once, bored by a rather sticky literary party at Kensington Palace, took the opportunity to study the furniture. Despite taking cover behind a stout lady, Billy was spotted kneeling down in order to get a closer look at a bureau; after the Princess had ascertained from her lady-in-waiting what it was that Billy was seemingly praying to, she gave her a guided tour of the best pieces in the room.

Billy was friends with Holman Hunt's daughter, Gladys, and the gesso and gilt *cassone* (an Italian bride chest) that Billy had made and Gladys painted a panel for, was exhibited in the New Gallery. Next to the tiny Billy, Gladys Hunt would have looked even taller than she was; her niece, Diana Holman Hunt, called her Big Aunt, for she was the biggest aunt she'd ever seen. In 1900, Holman Hunt, old and with failing sight, began a copy of his most famous painting 'The Light of the World', although by the time it was finished in 1903, the greater part of this larger version had been painted by Frederick Stephens. Billy undertook to make the frame; *a work of months of patience, not only because it was a very long job, and though Holman Hunt knew what he wanted, his sight was not good, his sketches were too vague for words: no – not for words, but for carving.* Once Billy had drawn what she interpreted as the artist's wishes, she began to carve the frame and Holman Hunt would check her work for mistakes by feeling it all over. *He was pleased at the end. The picture travelled all over the world for exhibition,*[1] *finally resting in St. Paul's Cathedral.* Whether it was a matter of relevance, or coincidence, it is interesting, nevertheless, to note that Robert Gregory (Billy's Godfather) was Dean of St Paul's Cathedral at the time.

But it was the garage at Northwick Terrace that was probably the greatest glory. Bicycles had served the Hewletts very well, but the joy of being able to afford to keep and run an automobile was heaven for Billy. She loved the driving and she was undaunted by the mechanical aspects. She would watch the chauffeur replace spare parts or dismantle the engine for servicing, and soon learnt enough to undertake some of the satisfyingly grimy tasks herself. Motoring was to afford Billy an unconventional amount of personal freedom. A High Court judge and fellow dinner guest had been deeply shocked to learn that, bowing to personal whim or clemency of weather, Billy might go for a spin in her car; she, in turn, had been deeply depressed by his iron routine and reliance on finding his wife at home every day. She offered up thanks for Maurice who hated the drudgery of routine as much as she and understood her need to be occupied outside the social round.

To save themselves from the tyranny of the social round that expanded alongside Maurice's success and to give him time to write, the Hewletts established certain rules for themselves; never to go out more than three nights a week, never to play bridge, the new social craze, and to be sure to leave London at least every Sunday, if not for the whole weekend. Billy also drew up her own rules which, as admirable as they were, were never going to earn her a sparkling reputation in society: *A. Never to break bread or even drink tea with any people I did not like – and intended to say what I thought about. B. Never to criticise any friends or acquaintances whose hospitality I had partaken of – nor allow it in my hearing. C. If I wished to criticise anyone, never to pretend to like them, confine myself to the merest conventional greetings when obliged to do so in society.* As she remarked: *These precepts sound so very obvious and universal among 'nice' people, that I hardly like to say what trouble they got me into.* A *conceited aspiring woman and a snob* were some of the names she was called: inaccurate insults both. Now, if she had been called an inverted snob …!

Despite these strictures there was plenty to amuse Billy in society, although her imposed anonymity on the objects of her entertainment could be very frustrating. *I met the "Purple Cow" the first time at a friend's house. He was eating his tea sitting on the hearthrug, and made a place for my cup and saucer beside his. I shared his rug, consequently he saw me home, and later spent many evenings with us. M thought him rather footling, but amusing. One night M was dining out alone, I had a lonely girl to dine with me. As she poured out her troubles, the maid announced that a "man" wished to see me, but refused to give his name. I sent word to say that I was engaged and would he please tell me what he wanted. Up came a card on which was drawn a "goop". I recognised it at once. A small man in tattered trousers, a torn coat, a huge dark muffler, and a cap over his eyes, the P. Cow came in. He had been seeing London as a hooligan. He sat at the table as he was, cap and all, and illustrated his night out with "goops" and stories. The dull girl forgot all her troubles and she laughed enough for a month – so did I.* Who could this handy man have been? The puzzle was intriguing, but a dim recollection of something about goops and soup led to Gelett Burgess[2] and thence to a "poem" about a purple cow, which sealed his identity.

If Mark Twain was introduced to Billy as Sam Clemens, she didn't say, but what she did recall was how once they had been introduced – Twain had been detailed to take her in to dinner at a large party on one of his visits to London, – he immediately launched into a long story, which concerned two old maids, a shared double bed in a reputedly haunted house and a sleep-walking butler who laid up their bed for dinner, with them in it awake and quaking. Just as the procession of guests assembled, ready to move into the dining room, her escort embarked on another tale, which ended with the room nearly empty and the last couple, Twain and her small self, impatiently awaited by their hostess. Billy finally won her struggle to hustle the robust American into the dining room, but not before he was half way through his third story.

Another American, the painter James Whistler, was far less jovial company, but nobody, Billy felt, could take offence at his rude, conceited remarks, as they were witty and deliberately studied for effect. Pressed by the hostess to attend a dinner party, despite Maurice being in Italy at the time, Billy arrived rather late to find a dapper man, not much taller than herself, waiting to be let in. Expressing her relief at finding she was not the last, she was surprised to be told that *'No one can ever be last where I dine.'* As she later learnt, Whistler, for it was he, made sure always to arrive late – sometimes very late. Throughout dinner, Whistler held court on subjects ranging from his Ashbee designed house in Cheyne Walk, which he described as *'consisting of raw wood, made into the most uncomfortable contortions and called furniture,'* to the Boer War, then still in progress. As a fervent admirer of Dr Jameson – Billy had once sat next to him at a dinner – she found herself quite unable to counter Whistler's pro-Boer arguments, and was finally reduced to saying: *'We are fighting, we had better win.'* At this Whistler looked at her with amused scepticism and drawled, *'How interesting to hear the views of the middle-class.'*

Why can't people be just natural – if they are vulgar, they can't hide it. I am vulgar and cheeky, and I know it will out, I do try to hide my 'worser' faults, not so visible to others – but the lesser faults haven't had their turn for repression yet, wrote Billy, brushing chips from her shoulders with pride. Pretension and conspicuous display, another bugbear, certainly brought out the cheekiness in her. *Once at a very large party, where riches were more displayed than brains, the ladies were not provided with cigarettes at dessert, but had to wait until coffee and cigarettes were served in the drawing room* (the feminine equivalent of the masculine port and cigars?) *A very beautiful woman, wife of a famous writer and the public's darling of the moment, didn't choose to wait. She had her own smoke, struck her match on the sole of her shoe, and walked about enjoying it.* As you may imagine, Billy was highly amused by the silent disapproval positively steaming from the seated ladies. When the cigarettes at last arrived, she took one, positioned herself in the middle of the room, collected as many shocked eyes as she could, grinned and struck a match on the sole of her shoe. There was sudden and general laughter and Billy returned to her corner to enjoy her smoke.

When it was her turn to organise a dinner party, Billy never entertained more than twelve at a time, nor did she have any food or servant assistance from outside. She liked to throw *convention to the winds, before dinner, if possible* (if only she had explained how), she *banned music and was careful to collect friends who would like to meet each other.* The Sunday evening suppers, *hot soup, and then all cold food, and no servants,* as per the custom of many of their friends, were a different matter. *They were freer, the talk was more personal and far more brilliant, no one roared, all were just there to listen as well as talk – they mostly played with ideas and let imagination run riot. Literature at play, they were called.* One such evening, of remembered delight, was when the celebrated Loie Fuller[3] was guest of honour. Young and un-censorious friends were particularly invited, but when the Goddess of Light arrived with a Catholic priest in tow, Billy feared the evening would be a *frost.* Quite the contrary. It was the young Jesuit, with his *merry eye and bulgy front,* who entertained the company non-stop with racy stories of missionary life in wild parts. How he came to accompany Loie Fuller, Billy never discovered.

Arguably, Billy's starriest piece of entertaining was the day Sarah Bernhardt came to tea. The Hewletts had met the ageing but still great French actress at a supper party given for her by Antony Hope Hawkins at the Piccadilly restaurant after her performance in 'L'Aiglon' at her Majesty's Theatre. Israel Zangwill,[4] grumpy, in Billy's view, that he sat neither on the right nor the left of the guest of honour, had leant over in the middle of the meal and in perfect French, but with an accent that could be cut with a knife, had asked her how it was that she had made herself look so thin in L'Aiglon. 'Monsieur, ce n'est pas moi, c'est l'Art,' had been the divine Bernhardt's put down. Her answer in response to an elderly spinster at the Hewletts' who had quavered in hesitant French, *'Madame, you are married, as you have a son whom you have just mentioned called Maurice?'* was gentler. *'Non, ca – ce n'est rien, ce n'est qu'un accident d'amour.'* Naturally, Billy had had to break all her rules and invite all her friends to the tea party, otherwise she would never have been forgiven. For himself, Maurice took the opportunity to capitalise on their mini social coup by inviting Thomas Hardy: 'If you know her already, she will certainly be glad to meet you; and if you don't, I think you will like her.'[5] The party *was a horrid squash* but *Sarah was at her most charmingest, Pia presented her with a bouquet. Everyone spoke French, as it should not be spoken.* Unquestionably, a social triumph.

The year of the tea party was the year that Maurice took the momentous step of abandoning security and casting himself into the billows of writing full-time. Writing in his diary at the close of 1900, he looked back over the year with satisfaction and forward to the next with sombre daring. *This year goes out weeping, and I sit alone; but, God be praised, I believe all is well with those I love at this hour. They are all at Salcombe with Veena and her husband. … There is a busy year before me, and (possibly) a great change and venture in our life; I know very well what I want to do, and am fixed in my resolve to do it. I pray God to keep me fixed in courage and honour; and I thank Him here for giving me so noble and brave and true a wife, and such dear children – God bless us all. Amen.* After staying with a clergyman and his family, it is perhaps not surprising Maurice used such language: he always considered himself something of a sponge, although sponges can also be wrung dry.

From his office, on New Year's Eve, he wrote to Billy.

'My Dearest Wife,

Here we are at the end of 1900 and who knows what may be before us? It will be a momentous year for me if I decide to give this place the go by and live on my wits. We shall want courage and a good deal of strength of mind; but I don't doubt of you, and I hope you don't doubt of me. Whatever may happen let us be openly true to one another and (if necessary) defy the world to do its worst.

I hope I have a good deal of work before me – indeed I hope that my name will be known, if known at all, as of a man who led the

20th Century, rather than one who came at the end of the 19th. I like to look on what I have done so far as a beginning; but if I die next year it is a beginning which I hope will count for something. Whether I live or die, I hope it will be as a baddish man, trying to be better, and as a writer taking his art seriously ...

I hope Fate will be kind to us next year; but I am sure he will not be unless we try to deserve it. I mean to go straight ahead, doing what I believe I am meant to do, – trying to do rather more than I am able to do. Please Fate, I shall have you by my side and our darling children for us both to work for.

There is no reason why I should give you all this solemnity now, of course, except that the day marks a period of time, and that I am in rather a solemn mood.

God bless you, my dearest Love, and make a better husband and father – Pray for me.

Yours, M'

CHAPTER 11

THE OLD RECTORY

A poet's paradise

George P.Brett, President of Macmillan, New York (who was later to animadvert on the greed of authors) with his offer of £1,000 for the American Royalties of *Richard Yea and Nay* might, without his knowing it, have dealt the final card in Maurice's game of shall I, shan't I. On 7 March, the day he learnt of Brett's offer, Maurice tendered his resignation and, citing the state of his health and the urgency of private affairs, he was able to declare himself a *Free Man* a month later. The man, who at heart felt himself to be a Victorian, now ventured into the new as the Edwardian era began.

Shortly before his freedom, Mary Stuart made her first appearance in Maurice's diary. Andrew Lang,[1] who had suggested Mary as a subject, exhorted Maurice to *be brave,* to which Maurice had retorted *I intend to be,* but on whose behalf, the queen's or his own, he did not make clear. Certainly he was going to have to show fortitude; he knew how terribly he had been taxed, physically and emotionally, on his first historical novel. And he could not afford to jeopardise the faith Billy had shown in him. Few of his circle were in the same situation and E.V. Lucas, in hindsight, thought Maurice would have been happier if he had retained his Record Office work and continued to write in his spare time. Gosse, too, who was never without the safety line of a salaried post, thought that Maurice's over-impetuous nature needed the drag of a monotonous and routine employment against which to write. But only Maurice knew what a grind he had found his post at the LRRO and, prone as he was to debilitating attacks of influenza, bronchitis and migraine, he must have hoped that his health would improve without the pressure of running two careers concurrently. He could not have foreseen that earning his living by his pen alone would prove as hard as it did, nor that his initial success and wealth would subtly weaken the very underpinnings – aspiration, great endeavour and little money – that had strengthened a marriage begun in love and affection and mutual respect. Greater spending power was to allow Maurice and Billy greater freedom each to follow their nose, and there were signs their noses were beginning to point in different directions.

Unsettled by his so-called freedom, Maurice suffered a passing regret for the loss of his little room in St Stephens House and his old regime. Billy, more than likely, did so too. It must have been trying to have underfoot one who now had his wish – more time in which to write – but was unable to use it. However, when the Scottish queen beckoned and Maurice was unable to follow, visits to friends offered excellent diversion. By now good friends with the Barries, the Hewletts stayed with them more than once. Their children had not had the same inspirational qualities for J.M.Barrie as the Llewelyn Davies boys, but the day Cecco lost a penny when walking with Barrie in Kensington Gardens was commemorated on the map on the inside cover of Barrie's *The Little White Bird*. Cecco's Tree marked the spot where the day after he had lost his precious penny he returned, on Barrie's insistence, and found instead a threepenny bit. Later, it amused Barrie to name one of the pirates in *Peter Pan* after Cecco; at the time, Cecco was a thirteen year old cadet, undergoing a rigorous education at the Royal Naval College, Osborne.

If you were a friend of Barrie, then you played for his literary cricket team. The first match in which Maurice played for the Allahakbarries had been against Edwin Abbey's team of artists at 1, Denmark Hill the previous year. Being a bit of a dandy, Maurice had gone on to the field looking splendidly right for the part, to score nil (not out); happily, a fellow member of the team, A.E.W. Mason,[2] of the booming laugh and a reasonable claim to some form of athleticism – he was a keen alpine climber – fared no better. This year, the match was played at the Barries'country cottage, Black Lake, near Farnham. Barrie was a charming and amusing host and Billy, good friends with Mary Barrie, enjoyed the houseparty as much as her husband; Barrie's peculiar game of golf-croquet, played on the Sunday by all, not just the men, was exactly the sort of fun she enjoyed.

By the time the Hewletts were due to travel northwards for their family holiday, Maurice was getting to grips with the Scottish queen, the peace and quiet of Bowerhope on the edge of St Mary's Loch promising. The *Glasgow Herald*, in its Casual Column, ran a little piece shortly after Maurice's death, which claimed that 'Hewlett was not popular among the sparse inhabitants of that wildly beautiful district; but this was no doubt as much to his retired habits and absorption in his work as to indifference to his fellow creatures outside his own family.' The *Glasgow Herald* also had Maurice writing the greater part of *Queen's Quair* in Bowerhope in 1903. Maurice did not stay in Bowerhope in 1903, and he only toyed with the Queen there in 1901.

The journey there, including the train to Moffat and a fifteen-mile ride by carrier to the Tibbie Shiels Inn at the southern end of the Loch took twelve hours. The family and Jule arrived in darkness and in darkness they and their luggage, including bicycles and fishing gear, were divided between two boats to be rowed by the two brothers of Miss Laidlaw, who awaited the exhausted party at the farm further up the loch. Billy, Jule and six year old Pia went with Alec, who, it transpired, was the black sheep of Messrs Laidlaw; sobriety conferred anonymity on his brother. Alec started off steadily enough, but then he began to sing and row powerfully but erratically across the pitch black loch, until they lost audible contact with the other boat. Billy, despite her natural anxiety for the safety of Pia, quite enjoyed the adventure and decided that the only thing to do was to sit tight and hope that the effort of rowing would work off the effects of alcohol. At last, an hour later, they touched shore, made their way towards a light and were gathered up into the warm kitchen of Miss Laidlaw, *a woman with refined manners and a very sad face*. Loyally, she defended Alec against Billy's wrath: Alec *knew his way better than many a sober man* (a confidence sadly misplaced as he was years later to meet a watery end in the dark when returning home drunk). Miss Laidlaw never scolded Alec, not even when he wrung the neck of her prize cockerel. Returning home roaring drunk one dawn, Alec had settled himself down in the small room adjacent to the henhouse, where the two brothers slept while there were paying guests in the farmhouse, but, just as he did so, the cock began to crow. Alec stumbled out, grabbed the bird, wrung its neck, hung it on the door latch and returned to bed. *Poor Miss Laidlaw!* How she cried, she was upset for days. Cecco and Pia, on the other hand, were inspired to gory illustration and dramatic embellishment in a re-enactment of the sorry episode.

It is beyond imagination to clad the family in lycra shorts and anoraks, but it is not so impossible to believe that they might have enjoyed lightweight mountain bikes. Expeditions invariably required shouldering their heavy bikes and wading barefoot across the narrowest point of the loch so that they might cycle to the main road, or pushing their bikes through the braes until they reached a rideable track. As the stones surrounding the loch were sharp and made daily bathing hard on the feet – one pink and portly relative, clad in a moth-eaten and inadequate blue bathing suit, had been forced to reach the water on all fours, much to the family's unseemly mirth – the Hewletts clearly were a hardy bunch. A Norwegian canoe, nick-named the Butter Dish, was hired so that mail might be collected, washing might be delivered to the carrier, half a lamb might be fetched from the Rodono Hotel, people carried, or trout trolled for in the loch. Famously calm one minute, the loch could be whipped up by sudden shifts in the wind into waves and foam. One *very strong, decided character*, who insisted *that she was an expert boatwoman and would enjoy the pull*, ignored all Billy's protestations as to the inadvisability of the venture, particularly in the bad weather and the waterproof that she had donned: not only did they fail to make the meeting point with the carrier, but *the big salmon boat* was required to rescue them. For Billy, such ignominy was made all the worse by being scolded for *risking the life of (her) friend and guest!* Fishing was far less hazardous, although there was a certain thrill to fishing on a Sunday, which was forbidden. With their rods folded to look like walking sticks, they would leave the farm, little Pia clinging to Billy's back like a monkey, until they found a suitable spot quite out of sight; any fish that were caught were cached by the stream until they could be collected the next day. *Bower-hope was a lonely, lovely spot, plenty of burns within reach of boat or bicycle, which led into valleys amongst heather hills, tumbling water, deep pools under waterfalls, and the green-pink beds of moss. We were very happy there*, Billy recalled.

A very happy holiday, and an amicable settlement with Macmillan over the Mary Queen of Scots book, had Maurice in high spirits. He had a 'perfect griping plot' for *The Queen's Quair*, as it would be called and with what he had to say, he anticipated either a Baronetcy, or banishment from all decent drawing rooms. 'My Darling Williams, (he wrote from Whittingame, where he was staying with the future Prime Minister, Arthur Balfour), Here I am in the Seats of the Mighty just after tea, writing by my own Fire in my own room. There are lots of things to see here, and A.J.B. asked me to stay till Friday, so that he can take me round.' One of the downsides to his visiting the key sites of his subject's story was that Maurice had to revise his image of Bothwell: 'A fine animal he must have been, but quite different from all my ideas and fancies. However, there it is, one must make the best of him, but in some ways, I am sorry I saw it. I had made up a much better Bothwell of my own, and he must go.'

E.V.Lucas maintained that Maurice wore himself out gathering material for his two royal subjects, which, up to a point was true, but what Maurice found even more taxing was using that material in such a way as to produce *imaginative history*; it brought on the tic douloreux and the terrible headaches. In *Richard Yay and Nay*, adopting a practice frowned upon by pure historical biographers, Maurice had invented fictitious characters through whom he could present what he saw as the essence, the truth, of his subject. With Mary Queen of Scots, he had first resolved that there should be no such invention, but struggle as he might, he could neither feel the story nor see its people. Once he had invented a page and confidant of the Queen, whom Maurice claimed was forced upon him *by the need of one honest man – not to be found in the history of the time*, the task became easier. It still took him four drafts before he could write against July 17, 1903, *Q.Q. finished*, his relief made more eloquent by his emphasis on the time, *10.30 a.m.*, than by any row of exclamation marks[3].

A family bolt-hole in the country, away from the noise, dirt and demands of London became an increasingly attractive idea to Billy and Maurice. Cycling forays into the New Forest, as splendid as they were, meant finding suitable accommodation; not always easy, particularly if they wished to take the children during school holidays. So, with money in the bank and bare necessities packed into a mackintosh parcel fastened to the carriers on their bicycles, the two of them set out for Wiltshire one weekend in May, 1903. Discovering that their hoped-for dream house, complete with chalk stream, had just been let, they cycled on to Broad Chalke, some two miles further on, to view a suggested alternative owned by King's College, Cambridge.

There, next to the church and opposite the village post office-cum-general store – of which *the smell inside was the most provoking sensation, cheese, soap, boots, oil, etc. all entangled* – was the Old Rectory. All they could initially see was a long, high, grey, stone wall flush with the village street with but two windows. A screen of pollarded lime trees ran along the wall and ended at double doors, in which was set a tiny studded door. Intrigued by this unusual and stern exterior, they pulled on the iron bell rod. As the door was opened they *saw a courtyard, then a sloping grass bank leading to a soft mossy lawn.* Beyond the lawn was a gin-clear, trout-full chalk stream that ran through the extensive, but overgrown grounds. On the left were outhouses, on the right was the shabby Old Rectory,[4] its two and a half feet thick walls and stone-mullioned windows barely visible for ivy and Virginia creeper. Behind the solid oak front door studded with iron nails lay the house, decaying and fusty, neglected, burdened by ugly Victorian improvements and hideous furniture. It was not until they were well on their way home and had flung down their bikes in a field of cowslips, so that they might rest, did the Hewletts confer. *"Did you see what they had done, mended the floor with sardine tins and tintacks?"* Billy asked in scorn. But her romantic husband was way ahead of her. *"I see that place in a few years, you and I can make it like my vision, you've got to love it and do everything to make it beautiful."*

They signed a three-month rental agreement, but by the autumn Billy *was mad to get to work.* Maurice politely sounded out Macmillan on the possibility of an advance on the projected sales of *The Queen's Quair*, as he was purchasing the freehold of the Old Rectory. As the Hewletts were soon ripping out the Victorian atrocities, removing the crumbling wood panelling, repairing the rotten floors, tearing down the flimsy partition dividing the grand old hall, stripping out the wallpapers, painting white all that they should, restoring the original fireplaces and chestnut staircase, and transforming the mistreated old building into a beautiful and friendly home, Macmillan had clearly obliged.

The large garden of their London home, with its mature trees and drifts of snowdrops in early Spring, was an urban pleasure, but it was the challenge of the long neglected grounds of the Old Rectory that awoke in Maurice a real passion for gardening. With the aid and advice of their friend, Charles Marillier,[5] Maurice built two bridges over the river and along its banks he made grass walks. He made fruit walls with an overhanging tiled coping in the traditional Wiltshire way with chalk and straw, and along these walls he grew peaches and nectarines, figs and grapes. Where the chalk for the walls had been dug out of the ground, he made a rockery with a double pool. He made yew walks, planted pleached beech and hornbeam hedges and also created a hedge of blue delphiniums; apples and pears grew in arches, forming a tunnel in the kitchen garden.

Pleased to help Maurice in the reformation were Parrott and Morgan Emm, both hefty labouring men nicknamed the Giants by the family. No longer in regular work, they took odd jobs locally, helping out where and when extra hands were needed. They would arrive together, on the dot, the same time every morning. If they failed to do so, a reason, if rather quaint, was always given for their non-appearance. 'I've a bin cutting some other little man's corns,' was one that first puzzled then long appealed to Maurice. Impressed by their sturdy attitude to life, he delighted in their conversation as they worked and, as he listened, he learnt about the ways of the country labourer. The seed for Hodge, the hero of his future epic, *The Song of the Plow,* was sown.

The Old Rectory was a poet's paradise to Maurice. His study, where he wrote often standing at a lectern, had once been the monks' chapel from whence, if he needed a break, he could dash outside with his rod and try a few casts from the bridge for his 'trouts'. However, as much as he rejoiced in the peace and quiet in which to work, the poet neither wished for, nor expected total solitude in his paradise, for it was a family home. There were relations, his and Billy's; friends, his, hers and the childrens', journalists, playwrights, actors, doctors, and artists, all to be invited to enjoy the easy hospitality on offer at the Old Rectory. Celia Newbolt once voiced her preference for Maurice Hewlett's country house over those with butlers and footmen and her father reflected, dryly, that it was more likely the presence of a son, rather than the absence of staff, that attracted her.

The romance of the Old Rectory was lost on the urbane E.V.Lucas, who had a morbid horror of draughts and a conviction that his friend, Maurice, did not dislike discomfort. The Hewletts were less concerned with creature comforts than most, but they had no hesitation in installing the latest in central heating and gas lighting to make the Rectory habitable all year round. In one of the outhouses, an acetylene gas generator was installed, fed by water drawn up from the river by a purpose-built waterwheel. The cost of the plant was considerable, and the piping to the house had to be made of the highest quality brass, but the purity and hygiene of the light provided by acetylene gas, as compared to that of paraffin, made it worthwhile. Fortunately, certain early drawbacks in the manufacture of acetylene gas (it readily exploded) had by then been eliminated. What had not been eliminated was the need to clean out the greasy sediment at the bottom of the tank, a task which Cecco always remembered as one of the dirtiest, smelliest and most tiresome imaginable.

Billy and Maurice both enjoyed sleeping out of doors. A tent under the old cedar tree on the lawn beside the stream doubled as summer bedroom and a changing room for those among their houseguests who liked to bathe. A visiting bishop, due to preach at evensong in the local church, had been much shaken when he called on the Hewletts under the misapprehension he would find Mrs Herbert staying with them, to discover instead her daughter with wet hair, bare feet and the lawn strewn with wet bathing clothes and towels. Even given the eminent physician, Sir Nestor Tirard,[6] calmly sketched the house from the river bank and his wife, Lady Helen, chatted idly with her host in the shade of the cedar tree, the pleasurable warmth of the summer afternoon in an instant turned oppressive. As the bishop sat stiffly and partook of tea, even the loquacious Billy was left without an adequate response when he departed with the awesome: "*I may see you again after the service.*" To their relief, he did not.

For those who neither wished to fish nor swim, the river could be enjoyed by canoe though remaining dry, however, was not a certainty. To Billy's mortification, the esteemed Dr Hagberg Wright,[7] a dear and popular guest, suffered an unexpected ducking when he missed his footing as he stepped from canoe to land, after she had entertained him, in Maurice's absence, to a watery tour of the garden. Luckily, his sense of humour matched his erudition.

Certain summer visitors were less than welcome to Cecco, although they, the tutors, were not unknown to provide amusement for the rest of the household. The first, a young mathematics undergraduate from a very academic Cambridge family, had seen fit to enquire what it was that Barrie did for a living – heaven knows what he thought his employer did – when he found the discussion between Barrie and Maurice over dinner quite incomprehensible. *"Oh,* he replied on being enlightened, *"I had no idea you made money by writing those kinds of books, I thought you made a little by educational books, but that novels and plays were only for recreation."* The second was a raw and painfully literal Lutheran pastor, recommended to them by Elizabeth von Arnim to help brush up Cecco's German; fluent themselves, Maurice and Billy were keen for their children to follow suit. As a holiday time concession, Herr Steinweg, proud possessor of a top hat (cylindrical hat, as he called it), was not expected to give formal lessons, but to chat with Cecco in German whenever possible. Unfortunately, the only topic for conversation he could think of with the reluctant boy was Cecco's pet water snake; almost hourly he would ask what the snake was doing and since the snake never moved, or ate, when anyone was looking and Cecco answered 'Nichts' every time, it hardly served the purpose of fostering conversation. However, the children's much-loved Uncle Ted came to stay and to the household's utter delight began a theological discussion with Herr Steinweg, which lasted ten days, on and off. Reverend Hewlett had not a word of German, Herr Steinweg only poor English, but each disputant fervently believed in the efficacy of shouting for putting across their point of view and the din of their argument reduced even the maids to fits of giggles.

The impact of acquiring the Old Rectory was to have a long-term effect on both Maurice the poet, and Maurice the man. For Billy, the Rectory afforded more immediate pleasures, such as when the whole household decamped from London for the school holidays. Then they tried out skis on the wintry downs – the Hewletts were once again among the earliest enthusiastic participators in a new and sporting recreation. Years later, Billy was to negotiate a most satisfactory deal with Henry Lunn: she would lecture on aviation and her involvement to fellow guests in exchange for a week's skiing holiday for herself, Cecco and Pia in Wengen.

Summer sports included fishing, or following the otter hunt, but, on the whole, were of a less bloodthirsty nature – watching rather than catching the wildlife, or picnicing, quite modestly, judging by Billy's reaction to her experience holidaying in Algiers with Mary Barrie. Then, rather than partake of the iced champagne, pâté de foie gras, and four or five courses provided for lunch on their long drives into the foothills, she had begged just a little food and wandered off to enjoy the local scenery and plants.

Billy also appreciated the admirable housing for the motors provided by the rectory's stables and coach houses; Albert, their chauffeur, on the other hand, was distressed that they also provided shelter for a family of swallows, who would leave, as he delicately put it, *trace de pigeon* on his metal charges. One metal charge was the Coffin, so named by the family as it was more often dead than alive. It was the car that Billy would frequently use to drive herself to and from London and, to break the journey, she would often stop by the roadside to eat her lunch and have a cigarette. One day she was joined by a woman from a nearby cottage who, as they sat and smoked, poured out her life story. It seemed the woman was very lonely, as she only saw her husband, a railwayman, every ten days and, possibly seeing in Billy a kindred spirit, wondered whether she too had a husband who worked on the railway. On subsequent trips, Billy looked out for the woman, but the cottage was empty. M, she thought, would have made such a very bad railway official.

CHAPTER 12

THE MOTOR

HB's beloved

So early did I start driving a car that it came under the red flag in front law. If that was so, whose motor did Billy drive? The red flag act was repealed in the Locomotives on Highways Act of 1896, before her husband was earning a fortune. If it had been her own car, Maurice was either very indulgent, or Billy had sufficient personal funds to cover the cost of a vehicle and its garaging, as well as a chauffeur. *Numbers and licences were not invented.* Now, that sounds more likely. They *'were not invented'* until 1903, in the Motor Car Act of that year, when the speed limit was also raised to 20 mph. By then, Maurice had been earning undreamt of amounts of money from his books for at least five years. Whenever she began to drive, it was inevitable the gauntlet of a speed limit was one to be picked up and run with by Billy. She loved motoring jaunts with friends when *an amateur race would enliven the driving,* after which they sat about *without (their) best frocks and behaviour to match, while the clever ones re-arranged the universe,* but being caught regularly in a speed-trap did have a dampening effect. Turning the tables and becoming a trap-hunter, however, provided excellent sport.[1,2]

As the trap very often consisted of one policeman hiding behind hedge, wall, pig-stye, or barn, who then had to leap out and wave and whistle furiously to his mate similarly hidden further up the road, the odds would seem to have been stacked in favour of the motorists, particularly when some of the trappers did not understand how to use a stop-watch. *One asked us to show him. We did, as we thought it fairer for our side. They often made mistakes more through ignorance than meaning to cheat.*

Typically, as with any new enthusiasm, Billy threw herself wholeheartedly into every aspect of motoring, in races, rallies, trials, as participant or spectator; with equipment and engines, as driver or mechanic. Nellie Gosse had been amused, but not shocked or surprised, to witness Billy driving up Netherhall Gardens, an excellent steep hill well-known among the motoring fraternity for testing purposes, on a box roped onto a chassis bare of body and mudguards, in the teeming rain. Billy was trying out a new chassis. Her only concession to the proper ladylike and done thing was not to drive herself to dinner parties, otherwise Billy drove herself wherever she could.

In speed and trial circles, affordable only to wealthy amateurs, the small percentage of women drivers were accepted and not so grudgingly as might have been assumed. Billy acquired a reputation for skilful driving and good mechanical skills, which elicited an invitation from Miss Muriel Hind, a noted motor-cyclist, to act as her mechanic and working passenger in two trials, one after the other, the Annual London to Edinburgh Trial, organised by the Motor Cycling Club and the Land's End to John o'Groats Reliability Trial promoted by the Auto-Cycle Club. They would drive a 2-cylinder, 9 h.p. Singer Tri-car. Tri-cars were half-way between a motor cycle and a motor car, the driver's seat looked very much like a car seat of the time, but placed over the single back wheel. The passenger's seat was between the two front wheels with a sort of scoop out front for the passenger's legs. Rather like a human windshield, the passenger bore the brunt of the elements and anything that the unsealed roads might throw up. A driving coat, a hat tied firmly under the chin with a wide scarf, goggles and a tarpaulin up to the armpits, was barely protection enough. At ten o'clock on the cold first night of June, 1906, the start of the London-Edinburgh trial, now open to all 'types of motor pleasure vehicles' was watched by a tremendous crowd at the top of Highgate Hill. 'Miss Hind on a Singer, who pluckily went through with a lady passenger, received quite an ovation from the sporting crowd.' 'Their courage,' gushed the *Motor*, 'was commendable, in view of the long drive in front of them and the keenness of the north-east wind which they would have to face.' Among the finalists to reach Edinburgh within the twenty-four hour time limit were two all-women vehicles, one lady-laden car and the tri-car with Miss Hind and Billy.

Ten days later, they were off again, this time from Land's End in the reliability trial for Auto Cycles. Six days, 889 miles later, at a basic minimum speed of 15 miles per hour and maximum speed of 20 miles per hour, they arrived at John o' Groat's, where a large crowd of spectators had gathered. Particular enthusiasm was displayed on the arrival of 'Miss Hind and her lady passenger, who were to be congratulated upon their plucky performance.' Pluck was obviously a highly-rated commodity. The *Motor* printed a photograph of 'The plucky lady driver, Miss Muriel Hind, signing check card at Gloucester.' Her anonymous passenger thought *Miss Hind deserved her medal* (a special one awarded by The Motor Cycle for Private Owners in the Passenger Class), which was generous of her, as it was Billy who, beyond taking the wheel once or twice during the Trial, had had to wrestle with the chain. *From my experience on that occasion I never wanted to see a chain again and the vile roads* had been enough *to try their endurance and tempers.* [3,4]

Teresina,[5] a fashionable and successful palmist, recommended by a friend and daughter-in-law of George Meredith (a writer with whom Maurice was frequently compared, to his disgust), lamented that Billy favoured mechanics over art. Billy, who had consulted Teresina more in the interest of exposing her as a fraud than to receive advice – she had hoped to be anonymous and unrecognisable in old clothes and without a wedding ring on her dirtied hands – had been impressed by Teresina's uncannily intimate knowledge of her background. But not so impressed that she ever abandoned mechanics.

As much as Billy enjoyed motoring, none of her enthusiasm rubbed off on Maurice. He knew his limitations, for compared to the mechanical problems of a bicycle, those of a car were insuperable. He was content to be driven by their chauffeur, or Billy. When he was commissioned to write his idiosyncratic travel book *The Road in Tuscany*, his preferred method of learning the ways of a country 'by keeping to its ways' by Shanks's pony was impractically slow and he employed the next best thing, a horse-drawn carriage. Two years later, the book still not finished and further research necessary, Billy agreed to join him again, but on one condition and one condition only, that they travelled by car. Their first trip in 1902 had been branded on her memory with a single word, misery.

When Billy joined Maurice in Siena in May 1902, Maurice had already been in Tuscany for a month and had written to her nearly every day; his description of the two *dizgrazia* he experienced at the hands of a Florentine cabman should, perhaps, have forewarned her of the potential hazards of travelling in hired transport in Italy. On the first occasion, he had been en route to Settignano after a dinner in the city. His cabman, for want of a proper lamp, had fashioned a makeshift light from a candle, some paper and a piece of string. Naturally, the candle was extinguished by the merest movement and the cabman had to stop and make great play of lighting his lamp each time he saw a gendarme. But that was not the *dizgrazia*. That was when the horse fell down on the Ponte Vecchio, broke its harness, which had to be mended with the ubiquitous string, and was urged to its feet with the aid of an onlooker's coat and the prayers of the cabman and the swelling crowd. Possibly mellow after a good dinner, Maurice had merely commented: 'They are a happy set of people, but so slipshod.' He was less than forbearing, however, when he, his friend James Kerr-Lawson,[6] and a picture dealer had the misfortune to have the same cabman a day or two later, and the whole cab went over in the middle of the street, just as it was turning a corner. Maurice, who felt it going, wrote: 'In that extraordinary cool way one has, when one knows a thing must happen, I sat still and waited, while I rolled gently in the gutter.' Lawson rolled on top of him, and the picture dealer, who had been on the box beside the driver, now rated by Maurice as 'a mere pig', escaped death between the horses hooves by sheer luck.

The choice of collaborative illustrator for *The Road in Tuscany* had, to Maurice's disappointment, been 'the dog Pennell', whom he thought would be the devil to work with. Joseph Pennell[7] had not been over the moon either. A Quaker, good friends with James Whistler, a man of strong convictions and fierce pride in his own ability, Pennell had arrived in England in 1885. Never one to mince his words, his withering comments were as revealing of himself, as of the authors with whom he collaborated. He did not hesitate in *The Adventures of an Illustrator* to boast that he paid little attention to what Hewlett had to say and credited him with 'always having a definite idea where he was going, and then never going there.' Somehow they both survived the ordeal, no doubt by frequently going their separate ways – Pennell alone, Maurice in the company of Kerr-Lawson and his wife, Cassie. Old friends – it is not inconceivable that they had introduced the Hewletts to Pittenweem – the Kerr-Lawsons had a house in Corbignano that had once belonged to Boccacio's father.

Pennell waspishly reckoned Hewlett's Italian had more or less stopped short with the Cinquecento period; Maurice had thrice been taken for an Italian on the Milan train. Pennell also claimed, enjoying artistic licence, that Hewlett had hired the coachman because he had killed more people than there were left in Tuscany. It was true, Trombino had killed, but just the once, and it had been a pre-emptive strike of self-preservation against the man he had been cuckolding. Fleeing his home town and retribution, Trombino had taken to the road. Maurice, enjoying even greater poetic licence than Pennell, likened Trombino to a Roman senator who wrote a history of Alexander the Great: 'Good soul, with exactly the same words and act he would have obeyed me though the Chimaera had stood fire-belching in his road. Nay, had the earth yawned and discovered him a pit of blackness, *Avanti* from me had made a Quintus Curtius of him.' For travellers carrying more money than many locals would earn in a lifetime, it was comforting having a loyal ruffian of a coachman, as there was still a danger of brigands: Pennell had had great difficulty finding accommodation in Lucca because of the trial of a famous and feared brigand by the name of Mussolini, no relation, it is believed, of Il Duce.

Happily, Billy was spared one misery, the overnight stay in Volterra. On the alert, when 'Trombino drooped, the whip drooped, the horses crawled like lice,' as they wound up the road to that city – a 'snarling wolf that can never be tamed to turn a spit'- the travellers, neverthless, had been taken aback by their chilly reception at their inn. It then transpired that there was no landlord to greet them, warmly or otherwise, for he was in the process of dying of typhoid. As the horses were exhausted, darkness was falling and there was nowhere else within a radius of twenty kilometers they could stay, they had no option but to stop the night. Even after so grim an adventure, Maurice still managed to put a romantic spin, of sorts, on the city. 'To woo a bride from Volterra would be to adventure among the Scythians. You would have to fight with your chosen maid – it would be an affair of muscles, tussles, and hard knocks. Having grassed her, you would throw her over your shoulder, like a dead stag, or a Lapith haled home by a Centaur, and so bear her to your house.' Golly!

Unprepared as she was for the discomfort she was to endure, Billy might have found the torture of travelling in the overloaded *diligence* less extreme, if she could but have shared her companions' enthusiasm for visiting ancient churches, ancient cathedrals, ancient towns. The back seat for two was tolerable, but the front seat, on which she regularly sat, was but nine inches deep and the iron bar of the driver's seat cut into her neck, unless she sat bolt upright at all times. There was also an ever-present danger of being poked in the eye by one of the spokes of a large green umbrella, doubling up as a sunshade, secured by four pieces of string to any available point in the carriage.

The Kerr-Lawsons, anonymous in Billy's typescript but *darling people and good travellers, if one made allowance for certain peculiarities,* sorely tried her patience, particularly he of *the delicate artistic temperament* who could not bear one square inch of sun to rest upon his body and who went to considerable lengths to prevent *some form of sun-fever. Consequently when the sun smote upon his elbow or knee, it must be shaded immediately. He held his sketch-book above the place, or his wife's parasol, his hat or his shoes.* His feet had to be kept at a regulated temperature, which necessitated *shoes and sandals loose on the carriage floor, so that when too hot, he removed the socks and put on shoes. If the temperature still continued to mount, he took off the shoes and wore sandals. On the slightest change to rain or coolness, he put on socks and sandals.* It did not help that mixed up with the footwear in the bottom of the carriage were bottles of drinking water, which had a distressing tendency to break. Nor did Trombino, whose trousers were worn so low and so loose that his passengers were in a permanent state of anxiety for his decency, improve matters by frequently clambering down from the still moving carriage to gather wildflowers for Billy. She had let slip how much she loved them, but she had wished rather that he had extended his thoughtfulness to his disgracefully overworked horses. Billy remembered nothing *of pleasure or interest from that journey, only the dust, dirty inns, stinking lavatories, which required no indication as to their situation by signs, rain in torrents, umbrella points, and neck and back bruises.*

In April 1904, Maurice bought, in Billy's words, *a wonderful De Dietrich.* In the first week of May, with Albert the chauffeur at the wheel, they drove to Southampton. There the precious new vehicle was hoisted in a sling aboard the Le Havre ferry for the start of the twelve day journey down through France to Cannes and on to Florence, the springboard for Tuscany. They would visit remote villages never before visited by an English woman, let alone a motorcar. Billy chattered happily of the adventure ahead. Maurice groaned at the slog of taking notes over the miles they were to cover, for his American publisher was growing impatient and *The Road in Tuscany* had to be finished.

No *diligence*, certainly, but the De Dietrich was only marginally more comfortable. Without windscreen or hood for protection, Albert and his employers were either choked, if it was dry, by the eighteen-inch thick dust that swirled up from the road, or soaked if it rained. Caught unprepared by a fearful thunderstorm as the car laboured over a mountain pass, Albert (*for once our dear chauffeur was furious*) had had to fling off his goggles so that he could see better, before he wrenched the wheel from Billy's hands in order to steer straight on through the hail. The storm left them with flotsam swilling about in the mud on the floor of the car and Albert with eyes were so swollen and bloodshot he could barely see; Billy had to bathe them in Hazeline, her sovereign remedy for many ills. Other hazards they encountered were the cattle, sheep or goats, whose herdsmen took as much fright as did their beasts at the novel and outlandish conveyance, and the hills' inhabitants, who hurled insults and stones as the car bumped over the twisting roads. Nor was it unusual to be stared at very long and very hard, when they stopped for a break. Only once the curiosity of the locals had been satisfied were they served with food or drink

Billy's fervent hope that she might not be in the permanent company of a man *who suffered from sunspot fever or toe temperature*, was realised. However, there was one brief expedition with the Kerr-Lawsons which was not without event. *En route* for Massa Maritima, the De Dietrich ran out of petrol. *There was nothing to do but pull the car by the side of the road and consider the situation. The artist and wife were, as usual, very reluctant to walk two or three miles in dust and heat. I offered to walk into the town and see what I could do – so I started off walking. Even I found it most unpleasant.* But why did Billy go on her own? The whole arrangement was very odd. Evidently, Albert had to mind the motor: perhaps his Italian and his legs were not up to the task of finding petrol. But why did Maurice neither accompany his wife nor go in her place, the expected common courtesy of a gentleman, which he was? With instructions as to where to look and what to fetch, his Italian and his legs would have carried him through. It is possible that he had been feeling unwell. It is also possible that there had been a deep and personal reason for the unaccountability of their actions, which three decades later Billy chose to conceal, an argument perhaps. Whether memory failure, or memory suppression coloured Billy's account, we know not, but what is certain is that kicking her heels and hoping for help from a passer-by would not have been her favourite option. Decision made, Billy was an unstoppable force, as her husband knew.

So, Billy walked and when a horse-drawn vehicle passed her, she rashly hailed it. The vehicle, such as it was, consisted of two large wheels with a bit of canvas stretched between them for a seat, on which sat two men, the whole drawn by a skittish young horse. Billy spoke very bad Italian, but she managed to explain that she needed a lift to Massa Maritima and the fatter of the men got down, lifted her up onto the cart, climbed up beside her and put her on his knee. *It was all most unpleasant,* she remarked dryly. Held far too firmly and squeezed even tighter when the horse shied or broke into a canter, Billy sat as still as she could, understood more than she let on and only divulged that she had a husband and two friends in an auto. To her relief, as they entered the town, she spied a chemist shop with, providentially, a policeman close-by. With a sudden huge effort she grabbed the harness and leapt down from the vehicle. Safely on the ground, she thanked the men profusely, gave them her hand and dashed into the chemist shop. There she bought a two-foot high glass jar of petrol, which she proudly bore back to the stranded motor, travelling, this time, in a carriage licensed for hire. Surprised to find Albert alone – Maurice and the Kerr-Lawsons had been given a lift onwards to the town – she helped him carefully fill up the tank with petrol with the aid of a small saucepan (standard issue for motorists in those days?) and, as they drove to Massa Maritima, listened to his adventure of the afternoon. While he had been waiting at the roadside, a horse, pulling a cart similar to the one on which Billy had hitched a lift, had taken fright at the stationary car and shied, tipping its two passengers onto the road. Albert had caught the horse, led it past the car, retied the piece of netting forming the seat, dusted the men down and waved them goodbye as they trotted on their way, safely remounted.

Once reunited with her party, Billy recounted over dinner the two adventures, her's and Albert's. Suddenly, commotion, as three policemen and two men strode into the dining room. They sought the Inglesi whose auto had run into and damaged a cart, rendering one passenger unconcious and injuring the hand of the other. The Inglesi would not be allowed to leave until they had paid compensation to the injured parties. Instant consternation, for without any other witnesses to back him up, what was the word of a mere chauffeur against that of the two men? No amount of indignation, explanation or gesticulation was going to impress the Caribinieri. They were obdurate. Impasse. It was one of *two beautiful Italian officers*, which is how they must have seemed, for Billy corrected this Freudian slip to *two beautifully dressed Italian officers,* at an adjacent table, who rose to their rescue. Springing to attention, he bowed smartly and addressed the English party: *'I have heard the story the small lady has told, allow me to deal with the Carabineri.'* And he did. Coffee and liqueurs and much laughter celebrated the rout of the enemy.

At last, the working trip was over and the De Dietrich was pointed north. The higher they twisted and turned from Turin, the cooler the temperature and the hotter the engine, but the De Dietrich battled bravely on. Once over the Mont Cenis pass, Billy *went quite mad with joy, got off the car and just revelled in seeing and loving the alpine flowers. M wanted to hurry on,* but Billy revolted. She *had looked at churches, pictures, museums and towers for months with him.* At last, flower-worship over, the engine, obedient to the swing of the starting handle, was re-started and Albert slipped the car into gear, but, panting and willing, it was unable to move. There are no details as to who gave the car a starting push, nor how they got back into it as it set off downhill, but *when the hill ended, so did* (their) *run.* Miraculously, no one was hurt and they were able to borrow the horse of a baker homeward-bound to pull the car into St. Jean de Maurienne, the three of them following on foot.

The smash, as he called it, was the final straw for Maurice. It had been a long and taxing trip, and ahead of him loomed the grind of writing up two months' worth of copious notes. He had had enough of heat, flies, cars and, no doubt, as she admitted, of Billy. The thought of having to stay in the one, small, fly-blown inn in what was the middle of nowhere for an indefinite period until they would clamber back into the car, made even more cramped by *quantitites of Roman earthenware and six wild cat skins* (from which Billy intended to make a rug), was more than he could bear. It was to their mutual relief, therefore, that Billy waved M off the following day on the through train to Paris. She was perfectly content; there were walks to enjoy, wild tulip bulbs to be collected and friends to be made with the mechanic. He, providentially, for such an isolated spot, proved to be a first class workman under Albert's direction. Within three days they were on the road again.

If, as had been suggested, Billy had been one of the very few women to take part in the races across Europe, banned eventually for being too dangerous, then, in a fit of uncharacteristic modesty, she forbore to mention it. The only time she admitted to a race beyond the English Channel was the impromptu one in which she and Albert found themselves as they shared the drive home, two hours on, two hours off. Roused by an English car overtaking them, they returned the compliment, but a burst back tyre, which required that Billy and Albert *changed cover and tube,* allowed their rivals to flash past them and reach Le Havre and the queue for the midnight ferry ahead of the De Dietrich. In the booking office, the *North-country people, kind, full of life and friendliness,* introduced themselves to Billy and invited her to *dine with them and play about till the boat departed,* which she did to her great enjoyment.

So ended the second trip to Italy – which blotted out the sad remembrance of the first. That's as may be, but reading between the lines of Billy's account, it also reflected where the fault lines lay in the Hewlett marriage. Each had disparate interests and incompatible priorities and with little to share, except their love for their children, it was not surprising that Billy and Maurice should be drifting apart. The requirement for a writer to shut himself away – an unintentional snub by exclusion – can well encourage independence in their partner. As Maurice researched and wrote and grew more successful, so Billy had the greater licence to pursue what pleased her. For solitary entertainment she had her art and craft work; for companionable entertainment there was motoring. In motoring she discovered her own abilities in the company of likeminded sporting people, who relished rather than bemoaned its novelty and promise. However, the cost of sustaining what his success had brought the Hewletts put considerable pressure on Maurice. *At present there is a necessity to earn money, which is the deuce. Broadchalke (my beloved) and the motor (HB's beloved) are costing too much.* In addition, he had another stick with which to belabour himself, that of maintaining his perceived status as a writer. The year before the motor trip to Italy he had written: *Barrie and I, it is commonly said, are at the top of Literature now. I believe it, but don't like to confess it, even here.* At the end of the year of the trip, 1904, after publication of the two works of hard labour, *The Queen's Quair* and *The*

Road in Tuscany, he wrote: *It is not hard to do well when it matters nothing what you do – but to do well, when it is a question of default if you don't is serious.*

This sombre mood was made even darker by something too personal to allow elaboration, but too painful for Maurice to ignore. *The year closed in a Swiss train – my three near me, most asleep. It has been a year of hard work for me and some sadness and trouble – which I record merely. What can't be mended must be endured. God be thanked for long and great happiness in spite of all. My dear Chicks are well and growing. Cecco is still at Osborne, but is not certain of stopping yet.[8] Pia has gone to school.[9] It was splendid to see how happy they were under the frosty edges of winter in Switzerland.* Of his Williams, his dearest wife, there was no mention.

Billy, when she had first written of Maurice and the summer of their engagement had said: *By the time the family went back to town, I loved M, lived for him, and never altered for sixteen years.*[10]

Such precision has to be taken seriously. Sixteen years from 1886 takes her up to 1902. If she had ceased to love him by then, the misery of the first Tuscan research trip had to have been tenfold. However, in the light of Maurice's enigmatic *some sadness and trouble,* sixteen years after they were married, 1904 could have been the year when Billy ceased to love and live for M. As there is no way of knowing whether it had been a slow, or sudden process, it does not seem too absurd to propose that friction, unavoidable on the gruelling car trip to Italy, had brought matters to a head. In the heat of the moment, dormant thoughts catch light. Had Maurice let slip his earlier love for her sister? Infidelity, in thought rather than in deed, would seem as great a betrayal. A cause for Billy to cease to love him so suddenly? Or had Billy come to realise what she had been slow to acknowledge: that M was no longer the focus of her life? He had become what he had wanted to be. She had helped him. There was nothing further she could do. She might even have become a little bored of him. Conjecture. Conjecture. All most unsatisfactory and likely to remain so. Neither party would ever have made personal intimacies matters of public concern. *God be thanked for long and great happiness in spite of all,* Maurice had written, as though acknowledging that theirs had been an unlikely union, with as much chance of success as failure. With their love for their children, their only common ground, marriage became a lonelier place for each. *What cant be mended must be endured*: to echo Maurice.

CHAPTER 13

THE MODERN TACK

The beginning of the end

Whatever the understanding between them, it did not preclude Billy accompanying Maurice in his quest for local colour for his romance, *The Spanish Jade*,[1] which included a fatal stabbing, unrequited love and a noble beauty from the gutter. As he wrote *Thank God* against the dates they returned to London via Paris, it may be assumed that Spain did not greatly appeal. Certainly, Maurice despised this novel to the end. Billy, on the other hand, was inspired to create two curtains that were copies of old Cordova leather and exhibited them at an Arts and Crafts Exhibition the following year. The dearth of entries in Maurice's diary and the fact that he ended the year 1905 in September forecasting the end of his *novel-writing epoch* and was *puzzled to say why,* is some indication of his emotional state. Another is that he had such a severe bout of what he called rheumatics, that he missed the family holiday and spent it in a London nursing home. He was, however, able to joke to Gosse about the masseur, the puncher who pummeled him after puncheon.

Happily, for the Hewlett coffers, Maurice's romantic romp, *The Fool Errant*, earnt him *much money*. Unhappily, it also precipitated a row and the eventual severance of his ties with Macmillan New York. The row was over advance payments and royalties and it was a measure of his anger and concern that Maurice should turn to Frederick Macmillan to intercede on his behalf, even though the New York office was independent of the London office.

Diplomat, master and servant, successfully all three, Frederick

Macmillan had a gentle way of chiding without offending. Maybe the vulnerable and self-defensive Maurice with his fitful way of working – raging enthusiasm at the start of a project that crumbled into doubt and struggle before the book was whipped into shape – was no more demanding of Macmillan than many other authors, who expected their dues or generous advances and fussed that their books were not sufficiently well promoted. Macmillan oversaw the publication of Hewlett fact and fiction, romance and poetry up until 1916, when the gentlemanly working relationship, gratefully and appreciatively acknowledged by Maurice, came to an end. By then Macmillan's one-time money-spinner had turned to epic poetry and Icelandic sagas, neither of which were in his line, and the disruption and shortages of war had drastically affected publishing.

It is disappointing that, in her memoir with the accent very much on the me with a long e, Billy mentioned but one piece of M's writing, when 'From one Forest Lover to the Other' he gave her a necklace. The occasion, when *Pan and the Young Shepherd* was included in the 1906 season of Vedrenne-Barker Matinees[2] at the Royal Court Theatre,[3] would surely have been worthy of note. But then again, given its reception by the critics, perhaps she was more wise than indifferent. *Pan produced,* Maurice wrote, W (Williams?) *assures me with great success. Rapture of yesterday much modified. Critics are howling – but Barker is satisfied and I ought to be. Many people were really pleased.* Howling among the critics was Desmond Macarthy of *The Speaker*. According to him, Mr Hewlett had done nearly all that was possible to unpoeticise Pan by being too preoccupied with sex, for his hot and swollen style ill suited the contentment of the woods of Arcadia.

Dick Hewlett who, by a supreme effort of will, composed the music for the production – *some hundred and eighty pages of 'incidental', several songs and choruses, two preludes and an entracte* – credited *the high prestige of the Court Theatre* with attracting a splendid cast, more than half of whom, he knew, accepted less than their usual fee. The handsome Henry Ainley of the rich voice, played Neanias, the hero. Grace Lane was *a not impossible Aglae – interesting looking, slim and innocent,* necessary, as the heroine was dumb for the greater part of the play. Granville Barker's wife, Lilla McCarthy, played Erotion and Suzanne Sheldon, Ainley's wife, had the dubious privilege of playing a feisty character called Merla. 'The head of a snake, the neck of a drake backed like a beam and sided like a bream,' was how Pan, a dreadful goaty old man, was moved to describe this cowherdess of Champney Valtort.

Merla – a name Dick so liked he chose it for his first born – was hardly the epitome of desirable femininity, being as lusty as a steer, capable of killing a pig and looking better when 'drest for church'. She was also much given to violent, if plucky, exclamation. 'Sakes alive is this a place for a decent girl? Well I never did. I'll Merl 'em. What now, you tearsheets? What now, you shameless rompstalls?' she cried, on being abandoned in the stormy dark. 'D'ye see my arm? I've dizzied a mad cow with un before this.' All in all, her determination to bring her 'shag-haired'suitor, the god Pan, to the altar steps was commendable. And somehow, Suzanne Sheldon managed to trip without mishap through such tongue-twisting, snigger-threatening lines as: 'Seek! I'll tell you what I seek in a snack, you saucy missies. I seek a stick, I seek a stiff stick.'

Dick felt, as Maurice did, that the parts of the 'earth-spirits' attendant on Pan might have been more effectively played with less sophistication, but reading between the critics' lines, it is doubtful whether some 'slight gaucherie' would have made such scenes any less risible, nor saved the production from the drubbing it received. 'There is no use blinking the fact that Mr. Maurice Hewlett has no real instinct for the stage, and one can only wonder that such shrewd men of business as the Court managers should have thought of presenting so essentially literary a drama ...' (It gets no better.) 'Half masque, half Shakesperian imitation, this "pastoral comedy", which with its curious mixture of heathen mythology and Christian faith, of rude village clowns and queenly earth-nymphs, affords very pretty reading in the study, makes but puzzling and dull entertainment in the playhouse because there is no grip or development in the story, no logical necessity for its very capricious action. The one genuine piece of drama in the play is the not too pleasant scene in which the village maiden, Merla, surrenders herself to the amorous earth-god, Pan, and so bribes him to allow the hapless nymph, Aglae, to return to her boy lover.' (Oh dear!) 'As for the dancing of the nymphs, it is made in the Court representation too reminiscent altogether of musical comedy; while their courtship of Neanias (a character interpreted very pleasingly by Mr. Ainley) simply provokes ill-natured merriment.' What could they have been doing?

It was years before Maurice was seriously tempted to try to write for the commercial theatre again, although he and Barrie had fleetingly considered collaborating on a play about a woman jester at a medieval court. It has been suggested that Barrie, who would have known *Pan and the Young Shepherd* when it was first published in 1898, could have been subconsciously influenced by the opening words of the piece – "Boy, boy wilt thou be a boy forever?" – when his character David from *The Little White Bird* metamorphosed into the famous *Peter Pan*. If so, a tiny fragment remains of a piece written in all sincerity and adapted for the stage in all seriousness: a piece that now, unfortunately, resembles nothing so much as a plum of a vehicle for a rip-roaring send-up of an amateur production of cod Shakespeare.

Work on two novels had been disrupted by the thoroughly enjoyable rehearsal period and it was a struggle and a bore for Maurice to return to his desk, but gardening and Broad Chalke were blessed distractions. Billy was busy motoring round the country and, interestingly, a trip to the Pyrennees and Pont du Gard – all in the interests of background material for a book – left the Hewletts ready to introduce the children to wider horizons, by car. Midges and fishing were to be exchanged for the alpine meadows of Switzerland. Except they weren't.

Their practice, as they drove through France, Maurice, ever the snappy dresser, in the flat cap he wore for motoring, Billy in her long red leather driving coat, wide hat anchored with a huge bow under her chin, was to buy provisions for a picnic lunch which they took wherever their fancy dictated. On the third day, having left their shopping until too late, the family lunched at an inn. Arriving that evening at Chaumont, *Maurie did not eat anything and went to bed as soon as he could.* Billy, rather than disturb him, shared the larger of their two rooms with the children. During the night all three were taken ill with a range of symptoms from extreme giddiness, a wildly irritable scarlet rash and severe stomach pains. In the morning, Billy, near to fainting, answered a knock at the door and in response to the urgent message that he needed her, went in to Maurice who had been wracked by diarrhoea and sickness all night. Too ill to be able to help him, she had to leave him. *That day was sheer misery,* Billy remembered. *None of us could eat anything, always giddy and faint, but towards evening the children had some milk. I changed rooms so as to be with M, the children in another room opening out of his. He had another bad night, so I sent for a doctor the next morning.* He diagnosed summer diarrhoea and said it would pass in three days. The raucous jollity of a fair blared outside the hotel windows and the heat grew ever more oppressive. All night Billy fanned Maurice in a frantic effort to cool him. In the morning, aware that her own nursing skills were inadequate and lacking confidence in the local man, she telegraphed two Parisian doctors, but they were both on holiday. Maurice, now delirious, raged to get dressed to leave in the car, at once. Billy had to struggle to hold him down and warned Cecco that she might call him in the night. Surprised, at midnight, to find Cecco still awake, she asked him if he could not sleep. *He said he was afraid I might call him and he would not come quickly enough.* By now, Billy thought to prepare Cecco for the unthinkable: *"Your Dada is very ill, I don't know what to do, he may die." "You can't let him die, you must think of something and I'll do it." It just wanted those words,* Billy wrote, *to pull me together.*

She telegraphed Alfred Sutro and asked him to find a doctor in London who would come instantly to Chaumont, as she suspected M had ptomaine poisoning. Next, she sent a telegram to General Joseph Bonus, Pia's godfather.[4] Then she waited. Maurice, no longer delirious, was now growing weaker and his pulse was so feeble that Billy, ignoring the local doctor's orders, took it upon herself to administer a little brandy with the white of egg. Exhausted, from lack of sleep and food, feeling desperately lonely, she maintained her watchful vigil in a frenzy of anxiety and impatience for the arrival of help.

It arrived the following day in the form of the London doctor, who at once confirmed ptomaine poisoning. He gave Maurice an injection. *M fainted while it was in progress so it had to be given at intervals. He looked so grey that I thought he would not come to.* Only when the doctor promised not to leave his patient did Billy obey orders to go to bed. Dead to the world and the mighty thunderstorm that broke the sultry weather, Billy slept the day through and awoke to learn that the crisis was over. Maurice, kept alive by her doses of brandy, would recover. On the heels of this good news came *the dear General, the truest friend, who always did the best thing and said very little.* Billy flung herself into his arms and wept on his shoulder. *It was lovely to have a big, strong character to lean on and help one.* General Bonus, living up to his commendable reputation said: *"I'll take those children of yours home, you are better without them."* He said *a few words to M, stayed a night and went off in the car with the children.*

The doctor, despite Maurice wanting only Billy to nurse him, found a nun of beauty and gentleness, whose calm in repose, with her hands folded in her sleeves, soothed the impatient patient. After a week, he was strong enough to travel home by train in the ambulance organised by Billy. Dressing him ready for the journey, she was shocked to find him like a skeleton. *Humorous as ever, he said, 'Economical in trousers, both my legs can get into half a pair.'*

'A ghost inhabiting a bag of bones' lay under the great cedar tree in the Old Rectory garden and wrote to thank his true and good friend, Gosse, for a letter that had touched him greatly. Believing himself to be better morally as well as physically, he felt as though his arrogant heart had been drained of all evil by the experience. He hoped he would remain as humble as he now felt. Introspection, a not unexpected reaction to a near-death experience, had set Maurice off on what he called *the modern tack.* His sort of literature at the beginning of his career – *poetry with inspiration behind it* – was at an end with him. Now he wished to preach an idealistic philosophy of life. And as he opened a new door, he quietly and pensively closed an old one behind him; he never again wrote his annual review.

I was as near death as a man can be this autumn – saved by the devotion and skill of my dear and noble wife. I learnt much from that illness. The children have grown in grace and strength – any parent must be proud of such a pair. They are never out of my thoughts and I can't reproach myself in their regard, at least. In whose regard, other than theirs, might he reproach himself, his noble wife's? And why did he think his wife noble, as well as dear? Had her nobility lain in the way she had coped and saved his life and nursed him so devotedly? Or, was it because she had done so, despite no longer loving him as a wife?

That terrifying experience and the way that Billy wrote it up, testifies to the well of affection that was the Hewletts and which enabled them to jog along for the next three years quite comfortably together. 'I escape from this cess-pit of triviality and over-eating in a week,' Maurice had written one summer from the Wells House Hotel in the spa town of Ilkley.[5] 'Then I go with my Williams adventuring in Devon to see Cecco at Torbay. And together with Pia, they visited Cecco serving as a Midshipman on HMS *Canopus* in the Mediterranean and Home Fleets and stationed in

Malta. It was 1909. Billy wrote: *I was given good advice which I did not follow, and which, I suppose, every mother of one son cannot take. It was, never to follow your son in the navy to any port.* Predictably, they *had the usual disappointment. The first five days were sheer joy. Drives, invitations, tennis, theatres, with charming people.* On the sixth day, with night blanketing the April sky, they watched as HMS *Canopus glided out like a grey monster on a dark sea* for the earthquake ruined Messina. *Very impressive, very inevitable to us. Such a tiny thing on that ship held our hearts.* (Tiny thing? Cecco was eighteen, had survived a rigorous naval education and had been to sea since the age of sixteen). *He was ours, yet he had to go.* Hereon, it is difficult to know whether to believe Billy's account of what the *Canopus* and her crew did next, or the official version. Billy's version, the product of remembered regret and events possibly fractured and re-arranged by memory, had the crew *helping to dig out buried people. Cecco young as he was, had to help. He saw the most dreadful sights.* The official version allowed the *Canopus* only a small role in the huge relief effort – that of delivering flour and medical supplies to the stricken city. Evidently, no man went ashore and, thereby, not one of the ship's company was awarded the Messina Earthquake Commemorative Medal.

Duty having deprived the Hewletts of Cecco's company, there was nothing to keep them in Malta and they embarked on a round trip to Naples, Pompei and Vesuvius, before returning to Malta and their journey home. The likelihood of this having been part of the original plan is high: it would have been a wasted opportunity of visiting ancient classical sites otherwise. As their trip entailed travelling via Syracuse and Messina, they glimpsed very briefly a little of the horror of Messina three months after the quake. Men were still dragging out what they could find from heaps of rubble, robbery and looting was still rife and flies rose, when disturbed, in swirling clouds over the ruined city.

Back in England, school awaited Pia, the Society of Authors awaited Maurice, whose chairmanship of the Management Committee[6] was to embroil him in literary politics over the next two years and for Billy? What awaited Billy was a future as unimaginable as any she might, if she had been prone to dream, have aspired to.

St Peter's Church, Vauxhall

The future Mr and Mrs Maurice Hewlett

Cecco Hewlett by James Kerr-Lawson

The Hewletts with their host J.M. Barrie

The Hewletts with unidentified holiday guests at Bowerhope 1901

*The Old Rectory,
Broad Chalke*

Sleeping out at the Old Rectory

*1904 postcard to her co-driver
from Miss Hind*

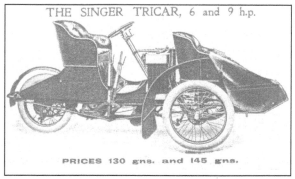

THE SINGER TRICAR, 6 and 9 h.p.

PRICES 130 gns. and 145 gns.

*What the plucky two drove,
London-Edinburgh trial 1906*

Gustave Blondeau flying at Mourmelon

Menu.

Consomme International.
Cobblehaugh Cream.

Clyde Salmon.
Dunsyre Sauce.

Cutlets and Hangar Sauce.

Roast Lamb and Pylon Sauce.

Cross Country Chickens
and Chips.

Cobbinshaw Cream.
Altitude Jelly.

Aggregate Cheese Straws.

Oranges.

Cafe Aviation.

CLYDESDALE HOTEL,
LANARK,
13th August, 1910.

Commemorative dinner, Aviation Meeting, Lanark 1910

*Tuning up the two Hewlett and Blondeau machines
outside their shed at Brooklands*

*Pashley Brothers' Hewlett & Blondeau Farman at Shoreham, 1913.
Photo courtesy Philip Jarrett*

Grace Bird no longer

Suitably attired for a flying celebrity

The First

*Mrs Maurice Hewlett flying
at Brooklands*

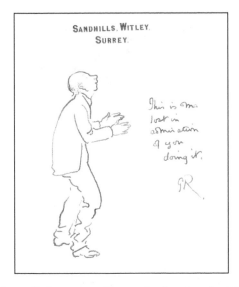

SANDHILLS. WITLEY.
SURREY.

This is me
lost in
admiration
of you
doing it.

W. Graham Robertson who made the sign for The Limit

FLIGHT

MESSRS. HEWLETT AND BLONDEAU'S WORKS AT CLAPHAM JUNCTION.—Above, the main assembly shop; in the centre, to the left, where the wings are made, covered, and doped; to the right, a section of the metal working shop. Below, a section of the works, showing the pattern shop and the store.

Hewlett & Blondeau Ltd, Omnia Works, Vardens Road, Battersea

CHAPTER 14

AN AEROPLANE

HB's most desired

We stood in the mud and waited. A great white thing was slowly pushed out of a shed, so big and strange. Paulhan[1] climbed up somehow, men twisted something round and round behind, when suddenly there was a roar which got louder and louder. The white thing moved – slowly – then faster and faster, till as it passed in front of me I saw one foot of space between it and the dirty muddy grass. That one foot of space which grew more and more made everything within me stop still. I wanted to cry, or laugh, but I could not move or think, I could only look with all my other faculties dead and useless. Something inside me felt it must burst. I had seen a reality as big as a storm at sea, or Vesuvius throwing up fire and rocks – it made more impression than either of these. There seemed to be no limit to its future. I was rooted to the spot in thick mud and wonder and did not want to move. I wanted to feel that power under my own hand and understand about why and how. The whole trend of life seemed altered, somehow, lots of important things were forgotten, a new future of vague wonder and power was opened.

Billy was standing in a rain sodden field in Blackpool, the venue for Britain's first international flying meeting.[2] It was October, 1909, and at her side was Gustave Blondeau, a Frenchman who suddenly and mysteriously appears in her memoir, without introduction or explanation. Edwardian *entente cordiale* and the easy and regular commerce between certain French and English circles, particularly those of the motoring world, no doubt provided the opportunity for Billy to meet this civil engineer, working as a draughtsman for a car engine firm. Blondeau had tested his own two-stroke engine in the Circuit des Ardennes in 1903; he was acquainted with Henri Farman, a competitive motorist who had abandoned the sport after a serious accident to become a very early record-breaking pilot before joining his two brothers in the development and manufacture of aircraft;[3] and he had helped in some early trials on propellors. It was inevitable, therefore, that conversation between Billy and Blondeau should move from cars to heavier-than-air-craft, the latest and most exciting development in man's desire to become airborne. That Blondeau spoke very little English was no hindrance; years of education at the hands of French governesses had made fluent French speakers of all the Herbert girls.

Billy would have us believe that the reason for Blondeau accompanying her to the flying meeting had everything to do with Maurice and an invitation for him to stay with Lord Balfour in connection with his research for *The Queen's Quair*. Since that book had been published five years earlier, this explanation is clearly flawed. Either Maurice had found the prospect of standing in a field to watch some flimsy machines do something of no interest whatsoever to himself quite deadly, or Billy had never intended that he should accompany her in the first place. She then claimed that her decision to drive herself to Blackpool, rather than take the big car plus chauffeur, worried Maurice, for he did not like her travelling alone, especially in the Coffin. Evidently, he had *said he did not mind who (she) took, as long as he did not have to think of (her) sitting alone in a ditch while he was comfortably in bed.* Billy *suggested taking Mr Blondeau.* How neat!

Gustave, as Billy called him from the start, soberly dressed and with a heavy moustache, could have been taken for her chauffeur, as it was, his company proved a godsend. *I should not only have been in many ditches,* wrote Billy, *but most probably drowned in the Coffin if I had not been with a very competent driver and mechanic. Three times in a fortnight the car broke down, it gave every sort of trouble imaginable, both usual and very unusual.* On day two of their expedition, Billy had to leave the poor man somewhere deep in the countryside while she took a faulty coil back to London to be repaired. Her exchange with the porter, as she waited on the lonely branch line station for the London train, was so memorable she was compelled to record it. It had begun because of her impatience for the train to arrive.

"You've asked me three times, now you stay quiet and I'll fetch you when the train comes. I'm going by it myself."

"How kind of you," I said. "I'm sorry that I didn't notice that I had asked you before."

"All right, all right, ma'am. I'm accustomed to ladies who don't travel much, they always worry about trains. Now I travel twice a day and spend my time with trains, so I don't think much about them."

Glad to talk to anyone on any subject but coils and cars, I said, "Are you the porter here?"

He explained, "Well, I'm that and I'm more. I just am the station from 3.30 a.hem. to 3.30 p.hem."

"Oh, how early! Then are you going home now?"

"I am. I live two stations up the line and I take the same train every day."

"What do you do when you get home?"

"I 'as a wash, I 'as me tea with me wife, and I goes to the pub till bedtime."

"I suppose you go for a walk sometimes" I said, rather shocked that he spent his whole time away from his wife.

"No, I don't. What do you think I want to walk about the bloody fields for? I 'ave enough of this bloody station. I want to sit down and drink me beer."

I had such a fit of laughter that I turned to fetch my coil. My new friend took it from me and said it was heavy. I told him it was part of a car.

"Uncertain things, they are, you give 'em the go-by and travel by train. I see they ain't doing you any good, see how you worry about this train."

As if to seal their amicable interchange, once they had boarded the train in a third-class carriage, the porter instantly fell asleep. Although he leant heavily against her, Billy let him be. She thought he must have been very tired.

Her mission accomplished, Billy returned to the waiting Gustave some time later that evening and held the lamp as he installed the repaired coil. A *wretched bed and a more wretched breakfast* later, they set off again. Although this unscheduled stop had delayed them, Billy was still keen to call on an old friend, Walter Cadby.[4]

He and his first wife, who died tragically early, had been friends with the Hewletts and although he moved out of London to the country, they had never lost touch. Now he and his second wife and their son, Thompson, were living, until the house they were building was completed, in two or three huts surrounded by a fence of up-ended railway sleepers. Cadby's eccentricities delighted Billy; his numerous chopping blocks covered with inverted enamel bowls to keep them from rotting dotted the garden like giant mushrooms; coats, short and long, male and female, in the process of being waterproofed with several coats of linseed oil covered the bushes; undergarments soaking in a tin bath, a strange daily ritual to prevent rheumatism. In the summer, when the weather allowed, the Cadbys felt free to dispense with all their clothes, but even their stockade could not ensure their modesty. Once, Mrs Cadby, clad only in an apron and called from the kitchen by the clang of the dinner bell at the gate, had been shaken to find the local parson who had come to call (always a serious mistake, in Billy's view). Showing great presence of mind and as little of anything else as she could, she had walked backwards up the path to the hut, lowered herself into a chair, indicated one for the vicar, and thus saved his blushes. It had been with regret that Billy and Blondeau declined the Cadbys' warm invitation to stay overnight. Courteously, Cadby, with the two-year old Thompson strapped firmly rather like a dog into a basket on the front of his motorcycle, escorted his guests back to the main road.

For absolutely unadulterated vile weather this trip held the record. At some point, as they neared their destination, the coastal road, normally separated from the sea by a marsh, was so flooded they could not see it; watching their wake to make sure they drove in a straight line, as there were no helpful telegraph posts to mark the way, they inched along. Once safely through and frisking along on dry road, they were jerked to a halt when a pin sheered between the double fly-wheel. They pushed the car to a garage and Gustave explained in broken English and fluent hand language what had happened. Leaving the car in the garage while they enjoyed a badly needed lunch, Billy was taken aside on their return by the foreman. In his opinion, her French friend knew very little about cars, whereas he himself was an expert and would be able to effect the repair with good mechanics and tools by six o'clock the following evening. Billy thanked him and said she would consider his advice, but her friend would have *just to see* first, at which she and Gustave donned overalls, took out the tools they carried *always in readiness for the coffin's death struggles,* and set to. The garage hands watched; they were not going to miss the fun. When he had finished, Gustave took off his overall, washed his hands, pushed the Coffin out onto the road. Billy paid the bill and filled up with petrol. Gustave handed her in to the car, put on his hat and bent to turn the starting handle. *By that time the hands of the garage were ready for a real joke and did not intend to miss the first point. Nor did Gustave. I never saw keener expectation from an audience, nor more cool confidence from an actor. The coffin gave no trouble. I must own Gustave was very deliberate in arranging everything, looking as if he was trying to remember if he had a clean pocket handkerchief and gloves before he let in his first speed, then looked at his watch and said in English, "It is five o'clock." "Yes,"* Billy had said, *"we'll have tea soon."*

Quite what her hosts for the week of the Blackpool flying meeting made of Billy travelling with a single, younger man is hard to imagine. Douglas Pelly, as vicar of Buckley, had his position to consider but it must be assumed that he did not feel too compromised by his sister-in-law, as he and his wife, Veena, twice joined the many that suffered the tedium of waiting for something, anything, to happen in the mud that immobilised cars, as the rain converted the ground round the aeroplane sheds into a lake. However, despite the Saturday programme being washed out and the meeting coming to a premature and soggy end, it was deemed overall to have been a success. Of the English contestants, only A.V. Roe succeeded in leaving the ground in 'one or two short jumps' and the few Germans were no match for the French: so Farman, Rougier, Paulhan and Latham shared the generous prize money of £4,150. The reporter for the magazine *Flight* waxed lyrical. 'There is an exhilaration about the start, a fascination about the caressing separation of wheels and soil, as the machine almost imperceptibly takes wing, a grandeur about its stately progress through the open air which is well-nigh irresistible.'

Not all onlookers were so enthusiastic. One probably spoke for the majority, there simply to see the latest sporting craze: 'The first circuit you see done is a marvel beyond the power of words to describe, yet it is so natural and seemingly effortless that after seeing a man do three rounds you say: "Come away, and let's have a drink."' The *Flight* reporter, however, had been determined to take matters seriously; for him there was 'nothing equal to its educational value to ocular demonstration.'

For Billy, 'ocular demonstration' had been more than educational, it had been inspirational. It was not in her nature to use such terms, but an epiphany, and comparison of a field near Blackpool with the road to Damascus might have come close to describing the effect the sight of flight had on her. Who flew, in what and when at that Blackpool meeting were trivia, irrelevant incidentals to the one thrilling moment when she watched Paulhan take flight and soar in a Henri Farman[5] biplane against the grey of the weather, above the mud of the field. For Billy, there was nothing to match that moment. Latham's[6] daring and skilful flight in a half gale in a plane more beautiful than Paulhan's might lift the spirits of the patient spectators, suffering from too much weather and too little flying, but it was Paulhan's flight that had filled Billy with wonder and awe and changed her life for ever. *That one foot of space which grew more and more between his plane and the dirty muddy grass* had filled her with a longing as shattering as if she had fallen in love with the pilot and eloped with him there and then.

Consumed by her desire to own and fly a heavier-than-air craft, Billy returned to London and the *banalities of life*. M, glad no disaster had befallen his wife was, nevertheless, flabbergasted by the turn of events. The danger, the expense, the logistics of Billy realising such a preposterous dream were far beyond anything that becoming a motorist had entailed. He thought her not a little mad, as, indeed, so did she. It was an impossible and ridiculous idea. She would forget it. In a determined effort to do so, Billy plunged into a round of teas, dinners, and visits to the theatre. She embarked on a project to inlay a large piece of furniture, but distraction, like the good counsel of her friends, was to no avail. M promised her a bigger and better car of her choice. She was not even tempted to consider such an offer. Everything she did seemed temporary, *as if it had to be got through as quickly as possible to be ready for something else*.

Eventually, it was a kindness to a friend that led to a resolution. Maurice had been one of the signatories to the letter asking the Press to grant J.M.Barrie privacy over his divorce. Nevertheless, deep in his trilogy dealing with sex, love and modern marriage, he thought Barrie's behaviour towards Mary Barrie nothing short of ungentlemanly and expressed himself, no doubt too emphatically, on the matter. The result was the severance of a friendship of which he had once been very proud. (Years later, after Maurice's death, Barrie was to write that he thought Maurice 'one of the most sympathetic as well as remarkable men (he) had known.')[7] Mary Barrie, raw from the recent divorce and the discovery in the process that her lover, Gilbert Cannon, was not as steadfast as herself, had turned to Billy for company one weekend. She poured her heart out to her friend and cried: *'You have all you want, you can't understand my troubles.'* Billy, hoping to persuade Mrs Barrie that others, even apparently blessed and happy others, suffered, told her of the *mad and unreasonable longing* that beset her. *'Either,'* said Mrs Barrie, *it was there for some good, or else it was hysteria: the best thing was to prove it one way or t'other.'* The decidedly unhysterical Billy returned home, determined to put herself to the test.

Not unexpectedly, she began with Blondeau, who had been keeping her *au courant* with developments in aviation. He, it would appear, was seriously considering giving up his current job and going into aviation, but lacked the necessary funds, so he was going to have to begin by working for a firm in Paris. *I asked him if he would join me in making a start at aviation if I could collect some money to buy a machine.* In that one cool sentence of a myriad implications, Billy changed her life.

Writing in retrospect in her sixties, Billy neither justified her decision, nor enlarged upon what her proposal meant to herself or her family at the time, or what it came to mean in the future. In any light, it was an audacious proposal, but coming from a married woman to a single man, coming from a woman his elder by some ten years and of no great personal wealth to a man of no wealth at all, it was a particularly audacious proposal. It was also touched by ambiguity. *Join me in making a start at aviation.* Did that mean it was solely intended as an invitation to join her in learning to fly, after which they would go their separate ways? Or did it mean that she had something more long-term in mind, beyond the immediate gratification of becoming an owner/pilot? A hazy, unformulated future, dangerous and exciting?

As spontaneous an act as Billy made it seem, it had to have been long considered. The purpose of the days spent in each other's company at Blackpool had been to make the most of an opportunity to see the pioneer greats of aviation; the weather, however vile, would not have been their chief topic of conversation. For enthusiasts such as themselves, Billy and Blondeau, could not have forborne to wonder 'what if' and 'how'. The Blackpool flying meeting had ended in the last week of October; then followed the period of unsuccessful distractions that culminated in Billy visiting Mary Barrie, which, she alleged, did not happen until close to Christmas. It is impressive, therefore, that by the third week in January,

Billy was already across the Channel and in the company of Blondeau. Even if the eager Blondeau – he had accepted Billy's proposal – had embarked immediately for France *to gain information and report results,* Billy had still to raise what she estimated was needed to acquire a machine and pay for lessons. Raising money can take time, especially when it is one thousand pounds.

Good, sound, conservative cousin Cecil Dowson, the family lawyer, who administered the Herbert family trust, had not been encouraging. The capital of the trust from which Billy received an allowance could not be touched, nor would the sale of some inherited property realise more than a third of what she needed. With only three hundred pounds to her name and in the hope of frightening Cousin Cecil into somehow finding seven hundred pounds for her, Billy threatened to *go to the Jews.* Too gentlemanly to ask the reason for her urgent need for so large a sum, he drily observed that she would be required to insure her life to borrow money. Despite it having been a hollow threat, as Billy had *no idea how you went to 'the Jews', or who the Jews were you went to,* this last was a *stumper:* flying was neither a profession nor a pastime for which there would be any cover. At this point, misinterpreting Billy's desire for secrecy and reluctance to approach any of her friends for a loan, Mr Dowson gently laid his hand on her arm and begged: *"Don't elope, you may be sorry afterwards."* His face, when Billy cried that it was not an elopement she wanted so badly, but an aeroplane, was a study. An erring wife, Billy felt, he could have dealt with, *but a woman who had a husband, two children, a house in town and in the country, two cars, who lacked neither friends, society or interests – wanting an aeroplane! No – it was beyond him.* Nevertheless, he promised to do his best and curiously enough, he did. With a final total of eight hundred pounds and the proceeds from the sale of the Coffin to add to the kitty, Billy *thought it good enough.*

For anyone wishing to learn to fly, as opposed to developing their own flying machine, France was the only place to go. Even a course on aerostatics, which Billy had considered but then rejected because of the requirement to pass an exam in advanced mathematics, was in France. She had been left with but one option, to buy a French machine and thus, automatically, become eligible for flying lessons at the manufacturer's school. France, an early investor in heavier-than-air craft, had the machines and the flying schools; the first ever international aviation meeting at Rheims in August 1909 had been dominated by French machines and pilots. Britain lagged behind France much as it had done in the earliest days of motoring, despite the *Daily Mail's* energetic promotion of aviation; despite public interest – it had been estimated that 120,000 Londoners flocked to see Bleriot's famous plane displayed as a publicity stunt in the ground-breaking new department store, Selfridges; and despite the enthusiasm of a small group of visionaries. 'Why are not aeroplanists more encouraged at Brooklands?' the *Autocar* had asked in July 1908, for aeroplanists, even those uncertain to get airborne, were a potential draw for spectators for whom the novelty of motor-racing had worn thin.

Choosing which French plane and thus which school to apply to had been easy for Billy. At the moment when, as she said, everything within her stopped still as she watched the space between the ground and Paulhan grow and grow, Paulhan had been flying a Henri Farman. So a Henri Farman it had to be, no other plane would do. Once the money was raised, Billy had telegraphed the go-ahead to Blondeau in France. He ordered an aircraft, secured himself a place in the Farman flying school at Mourmelon, and arranged an interview for his generous sponsor with Dick, the third Farman brother, who ran the business side of things in Paris.

CHAPTER 15

LEARNING PATIENCE

Mrs Bird goes to France

Billy left me – dreadful day. Ill. That pencilled entry, against 22 January, 1910, is the sole, extant contemporary reaction to mark the end of the Hewletts' married life as they had known it. And if one black, pocket engagement diary had not somehow slipped the net of Gay's control, Maurice's desolation when Billy became Mrs Grace Bird – her pseudonym – would have gone unremarked. It was Maurice's forty-ninth birthday, but the tears that Billy confessed to shedding all the way from London to Paris – *I cried like a baby all the way there* – had had, so she implied, more to do with anxiety and the denial to Mrs Grace Bird of the privileges normally enjoyed by Mrs Maurice Hewlett than remorse. She wrote not a word of anything so drastic as leaving her husband. Similarly, if Maurice's journal was to have been believed, he had suffered no convulsion in his life whatsoever. He *spoke well* at Leicester on the fifteenth of January (he had been drawn to politics and socialism) and went to Brighton for a week on the ninth of February. It was as if his wife – so different to one of his fictional heroines who invariably found happiness in the arms of a poet – had never gone to find her own happiness in danger and a muddy field in France. That one rogue appointment diary was the chink through which some of the anguish of that day could be glimpsed. *Billy left me – dreadful day. Ill.* Maurice was left to face a sad truth. Billy, once his own sweet Williams, had found the next big thing in her life. She had no need of him.

I called myself Mrs Grace Bird, as M objected to his name being used in what he thought was a silly and passing escapade. Some time later, Billy credited M with a little more than mere pomposity for she pinned a handwritten amendment to her typescript. *My husband did not believe in the future of flying, he had made his name by writing, he considered the ridicule of the press would be welcome to neither of us. I quite agreed, and welcomed the idea as I wanted to do my test on my own and not as the wife of a man of note.* All very commendable, but she was joining another man in this 'test'; the least known about that, the better. Her frequent absences from home had already been the subject of gleefully malicious comment and she would have had no more desire than Maurice to feed gossip. It suited them both for Mrs Hewlett to go adventuring under an alias, although even that is intriguing. If only Maurice had written Billy's memoirs. Psychology and the use of precisely the right word for the occasion informed all his writing: he would have explained how Mrs Maurice Hewlett lit upon Grace Bird as a charming *nom de guerre*. In the context of her actions, Bird is naturally aspirational, but with the forename of Grace, Mrs Bird's initials matched those of Gustave Blondeau: was that intentional, or merely coincidental?

Autobiographies, or contemporary biographies of writers such as Antony Hawkins, E.V.Lucas, Henry Newbolt, Alfred Sutro, all in the Hewletts' circle, are remarkable for the absence of personal detail; private correspondence, if quoted, is done so with circumspection, and wives and mistresses are marginalised. Printing and thus underlining what discretionary tolerance had confined to hearsay would have seemed ill-mannered and shocking, which is perhaps why Billy did not enlarge upon her skeletal remark: *I went to Paris in January.* Whether, during the years preceding her departure, she had been hurt, angry, jealous or indifferent, whether she expected it to be a temporary episode, or the first step to a permanent separation, or whether her motives for joining up with Blondeau were not solely to do with flying, the terms on which she and Maurice parted was nobody else's business but their own. According to their lights, our curiosity would appear undignified and presumptuous. However, if Stephen Gwynn's comment is anything to go by, there would have been little in the way of self-pity or reproach on either side: 'Gallant people were these two; life with them was a spirited and courageous business.' Billy had the courage to exchange the security of her married home for the risk of the unknown. Maurice had the courage to abide by his principles and accept her going.

Billy's first experience, as the independent Mrs Grace Bird, was a mournful one and the tears she shed all the way to Paris were reflected in the floods that met her there. Heavy rain had swollen the Seine to overflowing, the metro was practically at a standstill, there were major power cuts and all the clocks had stopped at twelve. Sandbags were piled alongside the Seine and, in order to prevent the bridges being washed away by the pressure, men hung over them with grappling hooks guiding the masses of floating furniture, wash-houses and general flotsam through the arches. At the Jardin des Plantes the brown bears were rescued from drowning and the polar bears were given a raft. Turned out of her *measly hotel near the Gare S. Lazare* due to the threat of imminent flooding early in the morning of her second day, Billy was forced to take the only accommodation available in what turned out to be an hotel of dubious repute. *Mrs Grace Bird didn't seem to be having such a nice time as Mrs Maurice Hewlett was used to.* Her pre-arranged visit to the Gnome works, where the engines that powered the Farman planes were made, was a wash out; the works were flooded and inaccessible, something she did not discover until after a train journey from Paris and a two mile walk in a snowstorm. That, and her eventual interview with Dick Farman, which was more a lecture on the need for patience, never one of her virtues, made her even more woeful. However, before her enthusiasm was quite extinguished, Farman's permission for her to join Blondeau in Mourmelon and the diverting exchange between her own cab driver with another, after a mild accident on the way to the station, were enough to raise her flagging spirits.

As soon as she arrived at Mourmelon-le-Grand, Mrs Grace Bird checked in at an hotel, blessed with but one virtue – its proximity to the Camp de Mourmelon, where the major construction firms had their flying schools.[1] Setting off for the aviation ground with Blondeau, Billy was so excited to see an aeroplane a mile in the distance, she began to run. Gustave, rather dampingly, pointed out that it was hardly necessary to do so, as she would soon see so many. Billy was introduced to Henri Farman and the great man himself showed them over his hangars and gave them permission to study and work in the constructing shops. He could not, unfortunately, give them a date for the completion of their machine, nor permit more than one pupil per machine ordered to have flying lessons. This was a shocking blow. Gustave was unwilling to learn before Billy, but from what he had already seen, the Farman school was *far from being a nursery, it was a battle for first come first served: it would be wiser and better for him to learn first.* Billy, swallowing her bitter disappointment, rallied and agreed with Gustave for his eventual participation in flying trials and competitions would be their only means of recouping their investment. *So began five months of learning patience, and incidentally and spasmodically, flying.*

Mourmelon was a mushroom village sprung to life as a camp parasite. A series of shacks, no drainage, no order, no inhabitants except what hung around for soldiers' and officers' welfare and money. The French government had lent a bit of this huge Camp de Mourmelon for use as an aviation ground – it was about two miles from the collection of dwellings called Mourmelon le Grand. No shack for Billy but the relative comfort of an hotel – no word of Blondeau's whereabouts – *a curious place, as it provided no meals, chiefly being a lodging house for officers who were attached to the Camp de Mourmelon; each regiment having their own mess, they did not dine there.* Apart from being treated as interlopers by the military, the civilian aviators had to be tough to survive the cold, the shortage of food and the battle for flying lessons when the vagaries of wind and weather allowed. Many dropped out, but those that remained were *a small and most truly wondrous company, representing the most daring, adventurous, don't-care, brave and idealistic youth of Europe. Some had money and went in for the thing as sport. Some were sent by learned Societies who had ordered a machine and were training a pilot to use it for research in aerostatics. Others were racers on cycles, motor-cycles, autos and boats. Two women were there to learn for shows. One had been an acrobat and had a diamond set between her front teeth.* Stoical, obsessed with flying, they talked nothing but 'shop'; they even watched the flag in between mouthfuls as they ate, in case it indicated that the direction and strength of the wind was propitious for flying. Sunrise or sunset were the choicest times to fly and there would a terrible clangor of claxons' calls, hooters and bells, as the aviators called each other in the dash to the flying ground. Billy could never understand why the wretched inhabitants of Mourmelon put up with the din, nor, if it came to that, how it was they endured the open cesspool and dumping pit, a disgusting, stinking, festering mass of filth, in the middle of the town. But, despite her fears and much to her surprise, neither she nor anyone else became ill as a result of proximity to it.

Generally critical of her compatriots – all were invariably found guilty of chauvinism or class-consciousness – Billy, superior in her fluency in French, was particularly down on one large, new owner of a Farman aircraft, in which he determined to prove that his English engine was as good as the French Gnome. She spent days watching as his French mechanic, who was utterly devoted to the man, assisted in the struggle to install the engine and tried in vain to guess to which tool his *patron* referred in his vile French: *'Ou a ma narto'* or *'Donna moi le screwdriver vit'*. As often as not, the little mechanic would offer up the whole bag of tools. After days of prodigious work, the plane was wheeled out and the motor started, *the tail refused to lift, the plane ran over a ditch, the undercarriage broke and the Englishman landed up under one wing. The dear mechanic,* crying, *'Quel desastre, quel desastre, bon Dieu! O la, la, la'* ran nearly a mile to reach the crash: there he found the pilot, unharmed and cursing for all he was worth.

Snobbery for Billy was, of course, unforgivable. Fierce in her convictions, biased in her attitude, Billy's reliability as to the accuracy of her recall cannot always be taken for granted but, perhaps, her conclusion, drawn from her account of two French brothers and their lady friends, may have, in essence, been correct. Evidently, the brothers, each constructing machines independently of the other at Mourmelon, although rarely at the same time, would regularly be accompanied by a lady friend and the lady, whatever her class or estate in life, became, temporarily, *la Duchesse* or *la Baronne*. It happened that Brother One appeared with *La Baronne de la R…* who had the ill luck to break her leg when the aircraft, in which she was a passenger, crashed. Sceptical Billy, the sole woman among her compatriots, did not believe that the lady friend was truly a Baronne; the Englishmen, however, sent flowers, fruit, sweets and pretty messages, and were received charmingly in La Baronne's bedroom. Presently, Brother Two arrived with La Duchesse, who was a little jealous of the first titled lady. One evening, when La Baronne was favoured for some reason over her, La Duchesse displayed her own fine sense of class superiority. *'She is only a chimneysweep's daughter,'* she blurted, furiously, *'I am a milliner from Paris.'* The joke, according to Billy, was not appreciated by the Englishmen. *Snobs at heart they forgave any irregularities for a title, but the title gone, they sniffed and turned virtuous.*[2]

Amours, farcical, successful or disastrous, were hardly private in such a small community with little else to do but wait to fly. One young Englishman had the misfortune to discover the shoes of his lover, a

Parisian dancer, in the company of those of a Russian flyer outside the door of his amour's hotel room: a discovery all the more painful as he was sincerely in love with the girl and paying for the room. Pitying the poor boy, Billy let him pour his heart out to her. To the journalist, paid by his Marseilles newspaper to learn to fly, she lent a different ear. *A never ceasing joke, at times a treasure to the fretted nerves of impatient ones*, he was a great one for the ladies, but a poor pilot. He also showed a want of judgment when he took a perfectly ghastly shack in a bit of muddy field for his beautiful wife, whom he had invited to stay. Having washed it out, added a bed and chair and one or two other comforts, he put in a paraffin stove and lamp which, because the mud under the floor was still damp, he lit in the hope that it would dry out the hut while he went to Rheims to meet his wife. Unfortunately, the Marseilles' train was delayed and to while away the time Monsieur Cheret and a rather showy lady, from one of the Mourmelon flying schools, repaired to the only local restaurant for some refreshment. When Mme Cheret eventually arrived and found no one on the windswept platform to greet her, she too decided to find somewhere more comfortable to wait and repaired to the same restaurant. When Cheret eventually caught up with his wife in the hotel in Mourmelon, relations were strained to say the least. Trusting in his own charm and that of his alternative accommodation to restore marital harmony, Cheret eventually persuaded the gallant Mme Cheret to follow him, in her high heels, across the muddy field to the shack. As he flung wide the door with a dramatic flourish, out rolled a stinking black cloud of damp and paraffin: the lamp had flared. Mme Cheret returned to the Mourmelon hotel that night and Marseilles the next morning. Cheret shrugged, as he ended his tale at the Aero Bar: "*C'est dommage, c'est chic cette petite cabine.*" (It is a pity. It is a smart little hut.)

The Aero Bar was *a dark and dirty shanty on the camp kept by a vast old Frenchman in shirt sleeves*. It was not a place Billy chose to go after early morning flying, she preferred to buy hot rolls at the bakery and to make her own coffee, but for the rest of the day it was a place of education (she *learnt a great deal about life in the rough and aviation in the future*), as well as of amusement. On the walls were advertisements for blacking, drinks, aeroplanes etc. and on very wet or windy days, when everyone was bored to death, the benches were stacked against the wall and billiards, improvised athletic sports, and dancing to the wind-up gramophone helped pass the time. On this gramophone *'old fat shirt sleeves '* played Rule Britannia and even went as far as to provide a blue, if dirty, tablecloth and real milk the day Mrs Bird entertained an English couple of whom, most wondrously, she approved; they *entered into the spirit of the Aero Bar*. Without revealing her true identity, Billy established that she and this couple, who had dropped by in the hope of seeing some flying, had mutual friends in London. This was not surprising, as he was a Master in Chancery and the Hewletts had moved in legal circles before literary ones. Blondeau, whom they watched fly that afternoon, cherished for the rest of his life the silver St Christopher medal given to him by the judge's wife.

Occasionally, after days and days of no flying endured in cheerless conditions, the need for diversion and a meal that was not disgusting drove as many as sixteen would-be aviators to visit a village some ten kilometres distant, where they could get a large room with a piano and a perfect dinner with champagne for five francs. How lovely those evenings seemed to Billy. The dreary Camp de Mourmelon was forgotten for a few hours in conversation of polyglot inanities, and songs and recitations too improper for a drawing room – but then, as she made sure to emphasise, they were neither in English, nor were they in England. Merry, rather than really drunk, they would pile out at *any old hour* for the return journey, climbing into, onto, or hanging from whatever cars had been mustered. It didn't pay to be too befuddled, though. A driver of an old two-seater found his car going backwards when his friends, for a joke, pulled rather than pushed to get him started. *The driver got out, tried hard to think, and finally decided it was best to leave the car. His friends got in and drove off leaving him absolutely mystified. He took a seat on someone's bonnet* and the convoy, led by the only car with lights, rolled homewards.

Mistakes and accidents – there were plenty of smashes and broken limbs but, happily, no fatalities – were as instructive as any teaching. Yet as dutiful a spectator as she was, Billy longed and longed to climb on – for there was no cockpit, or fuselage to climb into, no belts for security – to one of the flimsy machines and feel what it was like to fly. That was what had brought her to a cold, muddy flying field in France. That was why she had endured weeks of discomfort and boredom. With her savings nearly gone and her future uncertain, she needed more than ever to experience what had so exhilarated her when she saw Paulhan at Blackpool. She had to fly.

At last, in April, she had her opportunity. Efimoff (M. Yefimov), a large, childlike and good natured Ukrainian, offered to take her up as a passenger in his new Henri Farman biplane. As he was a natural flyer and she was anxious to learn as much as she could from him, Billy decided to watch his every move from her position behind him, where he sat in a bucket seat between the wings and the wheels, with the control stick between his legs and his feet on the rudder bar. She was so intent watching over his shoulder as he taxied and took to the air, she did not notice how very high they climbed. When she did, her heart stood still. It was all she could do to resist her *first impulse to put her hand on his shoulder and yell in his ear*. They appeared to be suspended, immobile. No grass, trees or roads raced beneath her feet. Only when she realised that the motor was roaring beautifully and the wind was singing in the wires was the eerie illusion broken. She was flying and it was glorious, utterly, utterly glorious. Eventually, miles later, Efimoff turned for home; as they neared the base, he cut the engine and in a whisper the Farman glided back to the flying ground. Drunk with elation, Billy could only shake and shake Efimoff's hand in thanks, as they each, in their own tongue, shared their joy in flying.

'Efimoff having obtained delivery of his new Henry Farman machine, was trying it on Saturday and carried out some splendid flights over the country surrounding Chalons and the following day he flew with two lady passengers, Miss Bird and Miss Franck.' That must surely be our bird and her first recorded flight. Madame Franck, with the advantage over Billy of having a plane to herself, was a competent pupil and took Miss Bird up as a passenger. And the American, C.T. Weymann, not to be confused with the authorial Prince of Romance, Stanley Weymann, was another who helped make all the discomforts endured worthwhile.

The practice of those who had already acquired both machine and certificate to take up fellow pupils – for a consideration – arose because the numbers of schools' machines and instructors were too few for the numbers of pupils; a situation made more difficult by the wind and weather and regular damage. Blondeau, whose patience after two months had worn as thin as Billy's, was offered lessons by a Belgian trick cyclist from a circus, who had learnt to fly at his employer's expense and in his employer's machine. Incompetent and reluctant to fly in anything other than near calm conditions, he was not a tutor Gustave was prepared to accept, let alone tip for the favour of the lessons. 'I could fly myself without any teaching,' Blondeau boasted to the future pilot, Vedrines,[3] then a mechanic for Henri

Farman, but there was one problem: getting the tricky Gnome engine to start up. Some fifty years later, in his expressive, if idiosyncratic, English, Blondeau recalled what happened. While all the pupils including the Belgian were passing the time in the Aero Club waiting for the wind to drop, 'Vedrines said: "Get in the seat of the pilot's seat" and while I get up there, he pass underneath. There was long bar holding the tail of the plane and then he turns the engine 2/3 times without switch on. "Now you can switch," say (sic) Vedrines. Then he pulled propeller and brrrrr – contact – and we started at once. All the people inside came along, but I did not wait and then I ran with the plane – and then – oop, I felt it leaving the ground. Well, I raise a good bit. Not very high. There was a group of trees in the middle of the flying ground there. Well there was plenty of room round it for me. I said, in case, I will fly so that I can clear the trees and then I raise and raise, like that, and then I make my turn, like that, and come back where I started, you see. I sort of shoosh in like that. Then I landed nicely.'[4] Farman then came up and asked why Gustave had stopped. 'I saw all agitated people there,' laughed Gustave, but Farman bade him continue and Gustave took the plane up again for another twenty minutes.[5]

At last, Blondeau was close to taking his ticket and their plane was close to completion. With Spring came optimism: but their hopes were to be shattered. Early one morning, a hurricane-like wind swept through the camp; it ripped the sheets of corrugated iron from the roofs of the workships, and tossed the flimsy planes under construction one against the other: torn canvas, wooden ribs, tangled wires and struts were strewn over half a square mile of mud in the drenching rain. Every plane under construction was destroyed. To occupy himself profitably until their plane was replaced, Blondeau preferred to study the Gnome engine in its Paris workshops. Billy remained at the camp, but patience hadn't done with teaching them a lesson. In May, the new aeroplane was ready, but, horror of horrors, Gustave crashed it soon afterwards. *I cried like a waterspout,* wrote Billy, *and I fancy he did too. It was no fault of his, just an accident, a tragedy no less.* This time, Billy decided to keep her frustration in check by spending some time at home preparing for when they should return to England. Just as Maurice had taken a radical step in the first month of the accession of a new king, so did Billy. But although Edward VII had just died, his era was to linger on almost until the war, by which time Mrs Hewlett was established in English aviation history.

CHAPTER 16

ENTER SENHOUSE

The gentleman gypsy has much to say about marriage

I flew at Mourmelon.[1] A surprising, no, possibly the most surprising sentence in Maurice's diary. Maurice, who had thought Billy was indulging in *a passing and silly escapade*, Maurice who never learnt to drive a car, Maurice, who had shown a certain stoicism but little enthusiasm for physical thrills, had gone to see Billy in Mourmelon and had dared to accept a ride with Charles Weymann. Quite possibly it was the first passenger flight ever to be made by a celebrated author. And how came it about that he was there, shortly before Billy returned home with Blondeau and the Blue Bird in tow?

Given his grief the day Billy set off for France, and given that he had been prepared to buy her the car of her choice as a consoling distraction in the face of her insane desire to fly, it would seem reasonable to assume that he had never wished to dismantle his marriage; in fact he had been content to continue with Billy in whatever form their relationship had taken and under whatever constraints that implied. Arranging to travel on the Continent for a month in the company of his extra-marital love would have been a destabilising wish too far. But, in May 1910, that is just what he did, licensed by Billy who, in her flight to France, had dared so much. And that was how he came to call in on Mourmelon at the end of his trip with Gay.

For how long Gay had been an extra element in his marriage may be divined, once again, from the change in Maurice's writing in 1906, when he embarked on what developed into a trio of contemporary novels in which he explored themes of sex, marriage and property. Sympathetic towards the needs of his Williams to express herself in a world as alien as his literary world was to her, Maurice was also fine-tuned to pick up on the frustration felt by his Artemis in her marriage to Everard Welby-Everard, a respectable barrister and a solid, kindly man. For Gay, the conduit to the pleasure and stimulation of the artistic world was her successful brother-in-law. The inevitability of meeting at family gatherings and the more leisurely time spent together when the Hewletts visited the large house that her husband, Evvie, had inherited in Gosberton, only served to foster the belief that Maurice and Gay had found their soulmate in each other.

And now, after twelve years of marriage, Evvie, saintly, or put-upon – marriage to any one of the Herbert girls required a degree of robustness in a husband – found himself in the galling position of learning that his wife proposed to accompany his wretched brother-in-law on a month-long Continental tour. Evvie was left with no other recourse but to refer to Maurice, a mite bitterly, as Gay's lover. The family jury, some of whom harboured skeletons of indiscretion of their own, no doubt knew whether by "lover" Evvie meant tiresome admirer, or something more carnal. Two generations later, the family jury has not reached a verdict. The older generation, of which there are now none, adhered to the it-was-nothing-like-that school but the younger generation, in the light of contemporary mores, find that hard to believe.

However, before Gay and her "lover" embarked for the continent, there was one crucial hurdle to clear, which took the form of Mrs Herbert, arch enemy of impropriety and champion of wifely duty to husband and hearth. Approached but three days before their departure, Mrs Herbert could only accept, if not approve, the arrangement. However, as Billy was the only one of her offspring not to receive a personal bequest in her will, it is to be wondered whether Mrs Herbert's sympathies did not already lie with Maurice. Either she had been grimly confirmed in her opinion that, even at the advanced age of forty-six, Billy was hoydenish and wilful, which predisposed Mrs Herbert to feel abnormally kindly towards Maurice, or the play of his trump card, his fifteen year old daughter, had won the trick. For what better chaperone on an educational trip for Pia than her Aunt Gay, for whom, after bearing her third child some six months earlier, the sights and art of Italy would be welcome refreshment? The chaperone would be chaperoned by her charge. Happy respectability. *The wonderful journey* took the three of them south down through the once Roman-occupied France on into Italy via Alassio and thus to Tuscany. For Maurice, the joy of unguarded companionship with his love was inexpressible and to share his delight and knowledge of the more than fifteen towns and villages he and his willing co-tourists visited, made the parting of their ways before he alone went on to Mourmelon very hard. To return to a country in mourning for its recently deceased king suited his mood.

1910 was a year that gave Maurice *more happiness and more misery than any one (he) could remember*. It closed with him giving evidence to the 1910 Divorce Commission; his invitation to do so prompted, no doubt, by his so-called modern trilogy: a trilogy which at first, if I am honest, had seemed nothing more than a confusion. The books were neither written nor published in chronological order and had appeared, disappeared and reappeared in his Diary over three years. However, from what he wrote of them to his publisher and his friends, it became necessary to pay close attention to them. Skimming, or the yet more dishonourable method of relying on reviews, would not suffice: *Open Country, Halfway House,* and *Rest Harrow* had to be read and taken as a whole, as advocated by Stephen Gwynn.

Halfway House, the second in the trilogy, but written first, seemed the logical starting point. Its opening scene, delineated without the mannerisms which so appealed to the artist in him but which Maurice himself recognised were a snare, was positively Austen-like (perhaps he had just finished reading that lady, she was a favourite author of his) and gave hope that the promise of its sub-title, 'a comedy of degrees,' would be delivered. Discovering why Maurice should write a prequel and a sequel might not, after all, prove too taxing. It soon transpired that his message on religion, property, love and sex, in the delivery of which Maurice made his characters suffer as much angst as they did surprising turns of the plot, had proved too big for one book. And although he sub-titled each book in turn a 'Comedy – 'of Degree', 'with a Sting' and 'of Resolution' – and true, the dictionary might define a comedy as 'a serious composition depicting human existence or portraying truth, and ending happily', they were hardly a bundle of laughs.

Maurice had invented for his mouthpiece – 'I feel that I can't go wrong with this person. I know him by heart – and ought to, as he is very largely my poor self' – a gentleman gipsy called Senhouse. A drop-out who, 'on a certain May morning in the year 1885 rose as usual, dressed as usual in grey flannel trousers, white sweater, and pair of nailed boots; breakfasted as usual upon an egg and some coffee, and walked out of his rooms, out of his college, out of Cambridge, never to return.' Son of a respectable alderman, Senhouse turned his back on all that his father and his family business had to offer and took to travelling. As he went, he collected languages and plants: an acquisitiveness shared by his creator. As Senhouse grew older 'and his passion for naturalising foreign plants grew with him,' all England became his garden; he stuffed the cracks in the rocks of Land's End with alpine plants and planted swathes of irises, crocuses, and peonies on the moors of Devon and Cumberland. Maurice prudently confined the planting of the bulbs and roots he dug up on his travels to his garden. Senhouse, the beneficent gardener and amateur poet, earnt a crust by selling the odd watercolour, and tinkering. 'To supply his wants, which were simple, he lived in a tent of his own stitching, which he carried about in a tilt-cart drawn by a lean horse named Rosinante. Everything he owned was in this cart.' Theoretically, this peripatetic style of living would have appealed to Maurice, though practically, its inherent, routine chores would have bored him to distraction. Senhouse 'was a noticeable fellow, unlike anybody else, very thin, very dark, saturnine, looking taller than he really was' – shades of Maurice here – but he had 'the look of a wild animal which seems friendly and assured, but is ready at any instant to dart into hiding. They used to call him the Faun, and tease to be shown his ears.'[2]

Senhouse, the gentleman gipsy, the philosopher, who had renounced society because he wanted to get back to health and the laws of nature; who wore sandals – something which Maurice liked to do; and his hair long – not something that his creator liked to do; and who talked secrets with the plants – something that Maurice might have been tempted to do – sounds more hippy, or new age traveller, than faun. His role in *Halfway House* is chiefly to be the witness for the prosecution of the marriage contract, a contract in which women become property. Along the way, he makes sure to broadcast a variety of his philosophical seeds. 'You are property – and that's the Bible's doing,' Senhouse lectured the heroine. 'Why – why look at the Ten Commandments – His wife, servant, maid, ox, ass – everything that is his! … If men are to buy and hoard women, it's quite clear that women mayn't have souls of their own. The whole social system depends upon their having none. It is really too degrading.' The heroine in question, a young governess of modest family background, attracted by and pursued by a less than honourable young man, has married a gentleman Rector, superior to her in class and twice her age, with predictable and melancholy effect. She ends the book as a young widow, willed by her deceased husband to be wealthy only if she remains chaste and unmarried. Senhouse, who refuses to bind her by marriage, offers her love and the freedom of the road: they go off hand in hand to the Black Forest.

If *Halfway House* had been intended as a one-off, the wildly romantic Senhouse hijacked that scheme. From America – 'marvellous nation' – Maurice received a commission which required that he set aside the sequel he had begun. *Letters to Sanchia*[3] duly delivered, Maurice realised that, with judicious recycling, he could convert it into a full-length novel, which would, in effect, be a prequel to *Halfway House* and should be called *Open Country*. His plans for *Rest Harrow,* the novel he perforce had to set aside to undertake the American commission, would have to be altered. If this all seems dreadfully confusing, Maurice's resume for a Mr E.L. Burlinghame, who proposed to serialise *Rest Harrow,* the projected final book in what had now grown to be a trilogy, is a model of clarity.

'Lands End (original name for *Open Country* and to be considered the first of the trilogy). Early life of J. Senhouse. His love affair with a very young lady, Miss Percival. He objects to marriage and dares not offer her anything less; so renounces his pretensions and takes himself off. Miss Percival – partly influenced by his theories of life and partly by other honourable motives – accepts the proposals of Mr. N. Ingram – a gentleman unhappily married and separated from his wife – and becomes, let us say, his morganatic wife. (Period 1894-1900)

Halfway House. Mr. Senhouse, as you know, consoles himself with Mrs. Germain. (Period 1904)

Rest Harrow. Miss Percival's difficulties in her irregular position with Mr. Ingram. Mr Senhouse's difficulties in his equally irregular one with Mrs. Germain. Exact details are wanting, but the end will be that Mrs Germain will regularise herself by marrying Mr. Duplessis (see *Halfway House*) and that Miss Percival and Mr. Senhouse will be made happy.'

Mr Burlingame, mindful of the morganatic marriage of Miss Percival in *Open Country*, was not a little concerned on this final point. Maurice reassured him: '*Rest Harrow* will almost certainly end in the triumph of the old order – in this case, of the marriage law. I don't bind myself, of course – for who can foresee how an unfinished novel will finish? But as it is entirely sketched out I am able to say there will be nothing polemical about its tendency. It will be the last of three novels – and its end will be harmonious, restful and final.'

Stephen Gwynn wrote: 'We have in these books his [Maurice's] philosophy of love; but it is a philosophy for the leisured classes. Marriage for the leisured classes in England is presumed to be based on sex-attraction, and Senhouse argues, or asserts, with great eloquence that a union so based should not be legally enforced. He repudiates the idea of ownership: it is contrary to freedom; and he repudiates it in the interest of woman, not of man.' Maurice may have started out with this theme in mind, but once he had devoted *Halfway House* exclusively to it, it is clear from the rapidity of the disappearance of its heroine, Mary Germain, from the plot of her sequel, *Rest Harrow*, that a more potent element had entered Maurice's philosophical story telling. With Sanchia Percival, conceived to receive Senhouse's letters, it had become personal: Gay was the model for Sanchia. Not that *Open Country* or *Rest Harrow* bore any semblance to the lives of Maurice or Gay, but they were testimony to Maurice's love for Gay, frustrated now not by his own marriage, but by Gay's marriage to Evvie.

Sanchia is twenty when Senhouse first sees her, with her skirt tucked up higher than her knees and about to wade into a forest pool. 'Not Artemis, high-girt for the chase, could have bared finer or dared more,' thinks Senhouse. And as the artist in him 'admired, and the man was stirred,' Senhouse dated his subjection from that moment. Maurice uses, in his prose, the imagery of his sonnets of 'Artemis Hymnia.' This time, however, the object of Senhouse's adoration is considerably more down to earth. '… she ravished him quite; she was like a wood-nymph half-tame, meek in a stiff gown and belt, her quick feet in little narrow shoes and stockings; her wild hair knotted behind her head, her quick eyes recollected, her nimble movements always curbed. And yet below bodice and belt you could sense the heart beat faster for the wild kiss of the wind on the cheek; and you could well believe that in woods, on airy summits of hills, in meadows by streams, in ploughlands after rain, she was living a double life – within, the ears of her heart alert to secret strains, magic calls, and incitations to be free; outwardly, all her beautiful body staidly disposed to the common world's observances.'

As the heroine concealed a freer being than her outward attire belied, so the two books in which the hero, Senhouse, and the heroine, Sanchia, do-si-do'd in the square dance of Maurice's calling, hid a sub-text: a letter of love and longing to Gay and, perhaps, an admission to Billy. She, over whom Maurice had never claimed ownership, could not have failed to recognise the original of a character bleakly described by Senhouse: 'His children grew up and went into the world; his wife tired of him and went her ways also.'

Interestingly, by the conclusion of *Rest Harrow*, Senhouse had meekly come to realise that his liberalising philosophies had caused more grief than good for those who strove to live by them. And Maurice, whether he actually believed that or not, managed to contrive a happy ending to his love story, without seeming to compromise Senhouse and his principles on marriage, or offending the sensibilities of the readers of Mr Burlingame's journal. In a splendidly ambiguous final chapter, Sanchia and Senhouse, who had taken 'their wild joy' (without the punctuation of a suggestive string of dots), busied themselves preparing their supper over the camp fire, under a starlit sky. As, for some unexplained reason, they could not be married for a week – time, no doubt, for those disposed to wish it, for the couple to procure a marriage licence – Senhouse declared that his house (which he had built himself there on the Wiltshire downs) should be Sanchia's and the stars would see her wed. As there was no further elucidation, an unconventional wedding ceremony has to be imagined, after which: 'Very early on the morning after the night when, as has been foretold, she was made a wife under the stars, Senhouse came back to her bedside and put a little flower into her hand.' 'Glozed and dewy' from her dreams, Sanchia looked at it. 'In grey-green leafage, dewy and downy, lay a little blossom of delicate pink, chalice-shaped, with a lip of flushed white.' It was a Rest Harrow.[4]

Gwynn is quite clear as to what Maurice meant. 'There is no legal marriage here; but we are told with emphasis that children are to come of it. For once a shade less than outspoken, Hewlett nowhere comments on the fact that Sanchia's first venture[5] of defiance had no such result. But out of all this finespun, highflown poetising about love and marriage, one thing stands out clear. To Hewlett, love in its sexual form came to mean one thing necessarily: fertilisation. To disregard that was for human natures to disregard the law of their being; it was to neglect what in one of his *Wiltshire Essays* he called 'The Great Affair'.'[6]

Had Gwynn, in that paragraph, confirmed what family members closest to Gay always insisted, namely, that "nothing had happened" and that "it wasn't like that" between Maurice and Gay? Gwynn was writing after Maurice's death and fifteen years after the books were published; his phrase 'came to mean' could be read as an indication that Maurice had not started out with that philosophy. Might there ever have been a window of opportunity, however tiny, for Maurice and Gay to have let "something happen"? When had he developed this strong conviction, that procreation, rather than the institution of marriage, blessed sex: before, during, or after his marriage ended? And why? Both he and Billy knew what it was to be one of seven children and, given their natures, a large family would have held little appeal for either of them. But Maurice was a sensual man. Abstinence from the pleasures of the flesh, the most effective form of contraception, would have been easier to bear if given an idealistic gloss. Or had guilt when, as a married man of seven years with a second child on the way, he had fallen violently in love with the unobtainable and devout Gay, driven him to fashion, out of the necessary suppression of his physical desire, the positive philosophy that procreation was the object of sex?

If so, whatever subsequent love affair Maurice might embark on would surely have been platonic, if unusually so in his circle. However, the image of Gay's daughter, Penelope, feeding the vast bonfire with her mother's personal papers will intrude, as do the puzzling blanks in Maurice's "official" diary and the destruction of all but one of his engagement diaries, wherein indecipherable symbols appear against certain dates during *the wonderful journey* of 1910. And, although speculation about the paternity of any of Gay's children, in the light of Maurice's wild poetic celebration of his love for her, does seem rather grubby, there was the matter of his will. In it, he had bequeathed his watch, which he had inherited from his own father, to his Godson, Gay's youngest; he also made the provision that 'should his own son and daughter both predecease him without leaving issue who survived him, then his freehold property and residuary estate should pass to Gay to be held for her son, Christopher Earle Welby-Everard, until his twenty first birthday. Admittedly, hardly proof of Maurice's paternity, particularly as Christopher was pure Welby-Everard to look at, but it is puzzling as to why Maurice should single him out, when there were other and certainly needier nephews and nieces of his own who might have been very grateful for a share of his small estate.

The revelation, courtesy of a close and reliable source, that Evvie never saw his wife naked – she would summon him by her little handbell to her bedroom only when she was ready and willing, firmly buttoned up to her chin in her nightie – leads to the conclusion that Gay was neither an impulsive nor a sensual woman. But perhaps, in the line of marital duty, Gay had never had the opportunity to explore the possibilities outlined in Marie Stopes's *Married Love*. At a guess, Maurice could have helped her: he had thought the book contained exceedingly good doctrine, as he told Stopes, who had begun a correspondence with him when she had fallen for his hero, Senhouse. 'The intelligent, I should say, coloro che sanno, or at any rate those who have 'intelletto d'amore,' have made your discoveries for themselves – but it is proper that all men should be plainly told what are women's dues in such a matter.' Good man. However, three years later, he was to disappoint Stopes most horribly when he returned her proof sent for his approval. Maurice in language rather more bald than his friend's, confirmed what Gwynn had written: 'I am sorry to say that I can't support you in the project. I thought you knew that I do not believe in birth control; I have never disguised my opinion.'[7]

Artemis is a strange choice of simile for one's beloved, for the goddess possessed few redeeming features. A virgin huntress, who punished cruelly any negligence in their observance by her worshippers, or any transgression among her followers – although a nightie buttoned to the chin is a happier substitute for having he who saw her naked transformed into a deer and hunted to death by hounds – Artemis would not have made for easy loving. On reflection, Maurice's choice was probably apposite. His most extreme and most romantic love affair with Gay was thrilling; it was cruel; it was celebrated in poetry and prose; and it was most likely never consummated. Only Senhouse and his Artemis Hymnia,

Sanchia, who, after years knowing and loving each other intellectually and platonically, are allowed to unite in passionate and sacrosanct love at the end of *Rest Harrow*.

Maurice was never a lady's man, ever on the flirt, but from the early days and his love for his mother and pleasure in his paternal grandmother's astringent wit, he had enjoyed women's company. In his *Wiltshire Essays* he confessed to being struck dumb by two things, one 'the blind blundering of man, the other the inexhaustible bounty of woman.' Of Ella Coltman, the Newbolts' lifelong friend, he wrote: 'She's a generous creature if ever there was one. But she's a woman, so it's of course.' If only his ingrained chivalry towards women, learnt from his father, combined with his predisposition to worship had not constantly been at war with his sensual nature, he might have found an object for his love who possessed an inexhaustible bounty of the sort to save him from a lot of frustration: and from writing passages such as the following:

'Out of the warm brown soil, sheltered by the eaves, the iris clump made a brave show. Its leaves like grey scimitars, its great flower-stems like spears. Stiffly they reared, erect, smooth, well-rounded, and each was crowned with the swollen bud of promise. She displayed them proudly, she counted them, made him check her counting. She glowed over them, fascinated by their virile pride. Struan watched her more than her treasures. he was pale still, and bit his lip; had nothing to say.

'She knelt and took one of the great stalks tenderly in her hand. A kind of rapture was upon her, a mystic's ecstasy. She passed her closed hand up and down, feeling the stiff smoothness; she clasped and pressed the bursting bud. "Feel it, Struan, feel it," she said. "It's alive." He turned, shaking away.

' "They say," she went on, caressing the bud, '"that this is really the Lily of the Annunciation. It's a symbol, I've read. Gabriel held one in his hand when he stood before Our Lady. Did you know that?"'[8]

Poor Struan, hapless tool (Oh dear! Innuendo breeds innuendo), did he suffer for the advancement of the plot of *Rest Harrow* the sort of teasing flirtation Maurice enjoyed at the hands of Gay? Rather that Maurice included such a scene, that sits so oddly in a book so thoroughly earnest, out of mischief than from a lack of judgment or, worse still, a poor sense of the ridiculous. When accused of belonging to the 'fleshly' school of writing, Maurice was unrepentant. 'As to the Flesh: we are clothed in it, don't want to be without it, and cannot conceive of life divested of it. ... The characters of my novels are men and women, and when I see them doing things which men and women do – kissing and mating, as well as praying and fighting, I say so and make no bones. I have never in my life been 'suggestive' for the sake of lust, and never prurient. But I don't see why I should leave out half of life, when I am writing for men and women who are alive.' He had not then written of the trembling Struan.

Unfortunately, the men and women to whom Maurice wanted to preach – he had been willing to take a modest share of the risk of publication with Macmillan – did not like being drenched with Senhouse's meditations. Maurice had not been entirely blind to such a danger and had had the grace to make Senhouse call himself a bit of a prig, with a fatal inclination for instructing the young. The books did not sell well and came in for some harsh criticism: nauseating twaddle; inane frippery; more reality in his romances than in this set of novels; unwholesome. Maurice was thus convinced that when he gave his testimony to Lord Gorell's Divorce Commission, it would be the end of him. For advice he turned to his most admired male confidante, his dear friend Harry, for Newbolt was not only a kindred spirit in the field of literature, but he too had found love outside marriage: although each managed it differently. Maurice, in fact, so trusted Newbolt he was to beg his 'pious and benevolent watchfulness' over a bequest in a will later made redundant: a bequest, no doubt, that related to Gay. After the two men had hammered out the arguments for and against late into the night, Maurice knew that he should not and would not back away.

In the event, Maurice was thanked for the 'sincerity and highmindedness with which he had given his evidence' by Lord Gorell, the President of the Probate Divorce and Admiralty Division of the Supreme Court[9] and censure only came later, in 1912. *The Quarterly Review*, in its commentary on the publication of all five volumes of the Minutes of Evidence, singled him out for 'crank' evidence. 'Perhaps the most flagrant instance is that of Mr Maurice Hewlett. He produced a memorandum the object of which was to insist that, sexual desire being part of the essence of marriage, its cessation ought to be a sufficient ground for divorce. It is a repulsive attempt to disguise selfish lust by describing it in high-sounding words, so that lechery becomes, for those who possess what Mr Hewlett calls 'higher natures', merely a transfer of 'bodily desire and spiritual intention' from one partner to another, which the law ought to facilitate and public opinion to sanction.' There were in all some 246 witnesses called over the weeks of the Commission, less than a quarter of whom were reported: the views of a successful author would, not unexpectedly, provide copy for the papers. *The Times* was a model of restraint and unbiased in its reportage. 'Mr Maurice Hewlett said that the Commission did not seem to have considered what must be called the psychical welfare of the married. He urged, among other proposals, that marriage should be voidable by agreement of the parties and evidence from one of them that desire or intention were absent or elsewhere engaged, saving always the interests of the children. In all cases of divorce the Court ought to be assisted by two lay assessors – one male and one female.'[10]

It is hard now to realise how radical he was being. At that time, if a husband could prove a single act of infidelity by his wife, he could obtain a divorce; she, poor soul, could not divorce however adulterous a husband, unless she had proof positive that he was also cruel, or had committed sodomy, rape, incest or bigamy. Women were not equal partners in marriage, but here Maurice was proposing that they should have as much right as a man to say that their 'desire or intention were absent or elsewhere engaged.' Personal circumstances, observation of the experiences of friends and family, and an innate sympathy for people, honed his convictions and he abhorred 'the tendency of hypocritical public opinion to preserve in all events what are called the outward decencies of life.' His confidante and, pleasingly and consequently a good friend of Gay's, Marie Belloc Lowndes found everything that her friend said worthy of consideration, despite, as a Roman Catholic, being fiercely opposed to divorce. She agreed with him that, 'to serious minds, marriage is one of the most serious acts of life; to the frivolous it may be an episode; to the base a means of base gratification' and she was very 'pleased that he stood up for the equality of the sexes, and also for the equal right of working people to the relief which was then denied to those who could not afford the cost of divorce.'[11]

So no martyrdom, only castigation in an emotive piece a couple of years after the event. Yet, however profoundly Maurice believed in the need for a different attitude to marriage and divorce, a change in the law would have made little difference to himself. The Deceased Wife's Sister's

Marriage Act, in which it became legal for a widower to marry his wife's sister, had only been passed in 1907. The liberalisation of attitudes to remarriage certainly did not extend to divorcees. To marry the divorced sister of one's divorced wife would have been too unpleasantly scandalous. Not that either Maurice, or Gay would ever have been in such a situation. Gay's marriage, if not fulfilling, was comfortable; she had three children, and her religious beliefs forbade divorce. Her faithful lover, fourteen years her senior, frequently suffered from nervous exhaustion, bronchitis aggravated by heavy smoking, and tic douloureux; he afforded her an entrée to a world that suited her perfectly, but his income was as erratic as his religious belief. Constancy, and ardour in verbal torrents from a distance, add piquancy to a sensible marriage, but do not promise security or comfort outside it. Gay's love for Maurice was never put to the test and he never had to face possible rejection, which is something to be glad about. Far better that he loved Gay passionately, but chastely, his celibacy either enforced by, or sanctioned by, his own obverse code of birth control: no sex unless for conception.

CHAPTER 17

SIMPLY MAD WITH DELIGHT

Patience rewarded

In London, with a white elephant and no elephant house, a pilot and no ground – and no money. That was Billy, home in the summer of 1910, after six months of grinding tedium in harsh conditions, still in pursuit of a dream potent with danger and heartbreak. Crated, her beautiful Blue Bird, named with Maeterlink's express permission, was indeed a white elephant, but the provision of temporary storage facilities by her brother-in-law and ever a friend in need, David Milne-Watson of the Gas Light and Coke Company, relieved Billy of one burden. All she had to do next was find an aerodrome with a hangar to rent: the problem of the money would have to wait.

As Mrs Hilda B. Hewlett she had already applied and been accepted for membership of the Royal Aero Club along with her dear friend and Pia's Godmother, the exotic-sounding, Jersey de Knoop. The Club's flying ground was at Eastchurch and was Billy's first choice,[1] but it had developed from an outpost for keen aviation amateurs into a somewhat exclusive club for wealthy flyers and, as the bridge *en route* had insufficient clearance for the great packing cases, Billy declared it *a washout*.

Blondeau favoured Brooklands. It was not far from London, close to a railway line, had hangars to rent and offered prizes for flying. Initially, the proprietors of the new purpose-built motor-racing track had been disinclined to countenance Brooklands for any other use, but George H. Thomas, newspaper magnate and passionate believer in the future of aviation, had influenced their grudging change of heart by persuading them to engage Paulhan to demonstrate his skill on the large area of pasture and waste ground encircled by the track. The size of the crowds drawn to watch Paulhan impressed the committee, who conceded that a regular added attraction of flying would be to the benefit of the Brooklands Motor Course, and they duly saw to it that trees were cleared, the rough ground levelled and hangars were erected. Among the first of the aspiring aviators to avail themselves of such facilities was A.V. Roe, who despite having been given short shrift by the Brooklands' Club some two years earlier, appreciated the potential of the place.

In the persona of Mrs Grace Bird, Billy called on the Secretary of the Brooklands Club. She introduced herself as someone who had flown a great deal over the past six months, albeit as a passenger, who intended to take her certificate as soon as possible; she had a Farman aircraft and was looking for an available hangar and somewhere to fly; her partner was a qualified pilot, a trained engineer and a Frenchman. The Secretary, evidently, laughed. *'We shall perhaps see your Frenchman fly. I've not much confidence in Frenchmen myself, and as for your future in flying, it is certainly unlikely and not to be taken into consideration at all. I will rent you a hangar at £10 a month, or your French pilot can contract to fly, or 'try to fly', at the next race meeting, in which case you could have a hangar free of charge for a month.'* Even if the Secretary's response to a small, middle-aged woman had not been quite so rude, the sentiment, however expressed, gave her every justification in reporting it as such. She was already feeling patronised and snubbed by the Royal Aero Club whose Secretary, as he took her subscription fee, had omitted to point out what she was to discover the first time she 'used' her Club: all Club rooms – except for one chairless, passage-like room – were out of bounds, even on Club business, to female members or visitors, alike.

Registering as much withering hauteur as her tiny stature allowed, Billy had stalked out of the Brooklands interview to seek sympathy and equal indignation from Blondeau; he, somewhat to her chagrin, counselled calm. The two of them would *make them see*, no doubt meaning the R.Ae.C.[2] as well as the Brooklands' committee. He would undertake to fly at the next meeting at Brooklands, thus qualifying for a month's free rental of a hangar. He would win first prize; that prize money would then go towards future rent and leave enough over for him to attain their next goal, to compete at the Lanark International Flying Meeting. It was as simple as that. It needed to be. Their funds were sadly depleted by the cost of transporting the packing cases to Brooklands, and they had to live and eat until the fateful August Bank Holiday weekend, when their future in flying would be decided. They found some *dud lodgings in Weybridge* and, to eke out the little money they had, took whatever was left over from their breakfast to sustain them for the rest of the day, when they went to the track.

Over the ten days of hard, lonely work to rig and set up the plane, the camaraderie of Mourmelon was sorely missed. The Brooklands' flying community, established in some seventeen hangars, viewed the latest lunatics – a Frenchman and a woman (!) – with cautious reserve. Billy, although not surprised by the reception of her fellow countrymen, felt as dismayed as Gustave, who grew ever more determined that 'they' should see. Their activities did not go unreported. The *Aero* noted: 'A Farman is being erected by Mrs Bird who intends to drive it under the tutorship of M. Blondeau.' Quite how long Mrs Bird thought her alias would hold is not clear, but it did not promise to be for long, given *The Aero*'s interest: 'Mrs Bird (who is, we understand, the wife of a well-known novelist) intends to learn to fly...'

The day came to wheel the Farman out of the hangar; the small crowd that gathered was an opinionated one. '*Brooklands is a death trap for flying, what with the river and the sewage farm.*' '*The Gnome engine is not the one for here, it hates the damp air.*' '*Look, the machine does not look right, no one knows how to tune up a Farman, it's a secret.*' Gustave worked methodically and without haste. Billy, whose *inside felt very wobbly*, asked him in French – they only ever spoke French to each other – how he felt. '*Do not worry,*' was all he would say. The smoke from a lit cigarette rose unwaveringly upwards; the weather was fine. It was time to start the engine. Billy sat on the machine and two men standing by were asked to hold the tail while Gustave swung the propeller. The Gnome gave its own peculiar trumpet call on the first swing and the onlookers, robbed of the spectacle of Gustave wrestling for at least an hour to get it going, watched as he took Billy's place, waved the men to let go and very gently taxied along the grass before rising effortlessly into the air. Oh, sweet reward! Billy *watched with gulps of relief* and when Gustave returned to earth shook his hand in delight. Gustave blew a kiss on two fingers to their beautiful craft and said, '*You see!*'

A small and disproportionately satisfying success. Now everything hung on Gustave's performance on the Bank Holiday Monday, August 1st. Come the day, only two other planes took to the air, a Hanriot flown by Cordonnier, which also took to the River Wey, nosediving into the bank, and a Sommer, flown by a Mr Gibbs, who failed to complete the course. 'At six o'clock, however, the improved conditions brought out Blondeau on Mrs Grace Bird's Farman biplane, and he successfully completed 15 rounds of the course in 36 mins 47 secs, the distance covered being about 25 miles.' Gustave had won the £60 first prize.

Assured of their place in the aviation village, the partners happily set about dismantling the Farman ready for loading into scenery vans for transportation by rail from Weybridge to Lanark Racecourse for the international meeting the following Saturday. The journey took from five o'clock in the evening until seven o'clock the following morning and they and their craft arrived safely. Unluckily for the Peruvian, Chavez, and the Dutchman, Kuller, their's were set alight by burning cinders from the engine of the train and the North-Western Railway had also distinguished itself by burning A.V. Roe's plane. Once they had reached Lanark racecourse, Gustave and a couple of helpers off-loaded the plane into the appointed hangar, while Billy went to look for lodgings. The town was packed with visitors and the only rooms still available were exorbitantly expensive. Hunger and exhaustion finally drove her to the desperate measure of accosting passers-by, but her risky strategy paid off and, taken home to meet the wife by one who took pity on her, Billy and her charm secured a room for herself, and a sofabed for Gustave.

Back at the flying field and after a large and sustaining Scottish breakfast, courtesy of Maggie, a waitress in the racecourse restaurant and a friend to be cultivated, Billy was ready to give Gustave a hand rigging the machine. They had allocated to them a cheerfully, resourceful young man, Guy, who was to be their guide and nurse for the duration of the meeting and, subsequently, friend for life. He rustled up hot cocoa and sandwiches, when they had to work through the night, and lent his sweater to Billy as she shivered and sewed the damaged fabric of the plane. He watched Gustave tuning up the engine with the aid of Billy's hand mirror and teased the local girls that every Gnome engine had a brush, hand mirror, towels and face grease. When the studiedly eccentric Chavez[3] *used to tie a bit of wood to a string and pull it along, admonishing it* as Toto, *his pet dog,* saying (in French): '*Dirty beast, don't pee on the aeroplane, you will have some Scotch cake later, you know,*' for Guy, as for all the people of Lanark, it was clear that the aviators were exotic creatures to be fêted, photographed and fussed over.

Seven nations were represented at Lanark and among the competitors were many old friends from Mourmelon, which added to the pleasure of taking part in what was generally considered a well-organised meeting. Selective in her recollections, Billy was able to overlook what must have been an expensive disappointment: Blondeau's poor showing. His bid to enhance his reputation and to earn good prize money began promisingly. On the first day, he elected to fly at dusk, when the wind had dropped; round and round the course he went and descended at nine o'clock into third place in the first heat of the long distance prize. In the second heat, on the Monday, disaster struck: the lever jammed and the Farman dropped thirty feet to the ground and flipped over. Blondeau jumped clear, but the lower plane was wrecked, the propeller in splinters and the stays broken and twisted: the engine wasn't too well either. Despite the team's best efforts, the Farman was out of commission until the final day of the competition, when Blondeau attempted to fly the fastest mile and the fastest kilometre. His reward: ten pounds for being the second fastest biplane over a measured mile. Ten pounds put him among the prize winners but, at the bottom of the list, he was a long way from the nearly two thousand pounds won by the most successful participant of the week.

The meeting closed with what was a very jolly dinner in the Meeting's HQ in the Clydesdale Hotel, while an enthusiastic crowd 'stood in the street and cheered lustily as the names of the prize winners were heard through the open windows.' Finally, the aircraft were packed and loaded on to great long wood-carts drawn by huge N.W.R. horses ready to be transported to the nearby railway station. With their cart loaded, the cords pulled tight, the horses patiently awaited their absent drivers. Billy, less patient, and confident that it would be no more difficult than leading a pony and trap, persuaded the team by clicks and tugs to start. A big mistake. The horses, used to shifting tree trunks, pulled so strongly that the lightweight load positively floated behind them and they were, as she put it, straight into third gear from a standing start. Grabbing a rope, Billy hung on, making woah, woah noises, but she and the cart were dragged inexorably down the road. Rescued by a very angry driver, who wanted to know just exactly what she thought she was doing with his horses, she so successfully mollified and amused him, he turned instructor. As the teams once more set off, this time under control, he proceeded to teach her the right inflection for horse language in Lanarkshire.

At Brooklands, Blondeau's reputation as a Gnome expert, as well as a knowledgeable mechanic and flyer, had grown. Maurice Ducrocq, a French business man living in England, heard of how he 'had started the Gnome, that capricious spinning monster, at the first turn of the propeller, and made a fine flight,' and keen to learn and ready to pay, sought him out. On 21 October, after twenty-one lessons, Monsieur Ducrocq became the first Frenchman to learn to fly in Britain, as well as the first pupil of any aviation school in the country to qualify for the Royal Aero Club certificate. He could not praise Blondeau – quiet, sympathetic, lucid, patient, efficient and totally lacking in fus – highly enough. Gustave's technique of first taking his pupil up to a considerable height as a passenger, so that any fear or wild and distracting exhilaration might be mastered before instruction began, obviously paid off.

Ducrocq's article, 'How I Learnt to Fly' in *Flight* blew Billy's cover, which was in tatters anyway. Grace Bird had had her final squawk two weeks earlier: 'Would you kindly correct an error in *Flight* which has appeared more than once. M. Blondeau is my partner, and therefore it is not representing things as they actually are to say he flew on Mrs Grace Bird's biplane. The error arose by my signing the entry for the Neill Cup[4] when M. Blondeau was not in England, and consequently he had to fly in my name.' Ducrocq, in his article, had written of the partnership of Mrs Hewlett and M. Blondeau. A fortnight later that partnership was made official in *Flight*, when the Hewlett and Blondeau Aviation School trumpeted its arrival, announcing two firsts to their credit: the first Pilot's Certificate for a pupil in England (Ducrocq licence no. 23) and the first English Army officer, Lt. Snowden-Smith (pilot's licence no. 29).

A year from the moment when she had first fallen in love with the idea of flying and had thought only of being able to acquire a machine on which to do so, the incredible had happened. Not only had she the machine, but she, a middle-aged, married English woman was in partnership, in aviation, with a Frenchman ten years her junior. But far greater than that, she was part of a movement and an active participant rather than a member by association. A lone woman accepted by her fellow pioneers, united in boundless enthusiasm and courage in a thrilling cause – the exploration and advancement of man-made flight. Life was physically tough, money was short, conditions were primitive, and Billy was in her element. True, she had yet to realise her one great desire: to fly her own plane. But achieving this ambition and thus refunding her initial investment was still some way off. Compensation for this frustration was to be seen as one of a band of pioneers and, besides, the partners needed to earn their living. Going into the business of teaching others to fly was unorthodox for a middle-class Edwardian woman but, given the circumstances, the logical thing to do. A dab here and a dab there of 'pioneering spirit' soon dispelled the faintest taint of trade, if there was any, not that that would have concerned the grand-daughter of tradesmen made good. As it happened, by the time the adventure of the new had been subsumed by the emphasis of business, the world was a different place and Billy had a new cause that made acceptable her engagement in anything so unladylike as manufacturing: the defence of her country.

As flying could begin as early as five in the morning and finish as late as nine at night, the partners took a *very suitable and amusing workman's cottage with four rooms, just finished at Byfleet,* close to the Track. Named The Limit by Billy – her friend the artist Graham Robertson[5] painted its name on the gate – and furnished with *a table, two camp beds and some pots and pans and, most important of all, two primus stoves,* which she took from home, it became her base for the next eighteen months. Pupils and fellow aviators were as impoverished as Hewlett and Blondeau and The Limit offered hospitality of sorts to all-comers. Everyone mucked in doing, whatever was required, cooking, washing up, and the cleaning. The Limit's absolute luxury was the bath: those who could only afford to live in large packing cases in their hangars,[6] in summer used the river Wey. Meals were *extremely primitive.* Billy's most favoured vegetable, as it required no cooking, were the lettuces that she planted in the tiny garden. Gardening was chiefly done after morning flying, while waiting for breakfast or a turn in the bath, consequently pyjamas and dressing gowns were the usual garb; an iron spoon and a jug were the tools. With such a relaxed dress code, Billy thought nothing of answering the stones flung at her window by an eager pupil, opening the door clad in *scanty attire* for after all, he had walked the five miles from his home for a flying lesson at four in the morning. Seen as a tomboy elder sister or an indulgent favourite aunt, Billy encouraged the legendary enthusiasm of the Hewlett and Blondeau pupils.

Billy boasted that she never encouraged her daughter to leave her life in London but, as Pia was only fifteen years old and continued her education at a school in Baker Street, saddling herself with motherly responsibilities was hardly a practical or attractive option for Billy. Maurice, a kind of widower as he described himself to Newbolt, didn't like to leave his daughter, who was as good as gold and much dearer to him, stranded in London while her mother 'ploughs the air and scatters – caster oil!' He and Pia kept each other company at Northwick Terrace. Not that Pia did not visit Brooklands: she was a regular enough passenger on the Farman to be dubbed 'the youngest aeronaut in the world' in a fulsome article about 'Mrs Maurice Hewlett. Airwoman' in *The Sketch*. To Pia, of course, life at Brooklands was wildly romantic and she adored staying at The Limit. The dedication and daring of all those who rarely wore ties and mended their clothes with whatever came to hand, who chiefly relied on cigarettes, apart from tea, bread and butter and the odd can of food for sustenance, and who toiled hour upon hour with scant regard for their own welfare, was intoxicating. *'After once tasting the excitements of your life it's not easy to forget them. I hope I shall marry a poor man, so as to live on nothing in a dud little cottage. It's much nicer than sweltering on crimson velvet*, wrote Pia to Billy. Happily, thus far, Pia had been spared the horrors of sweltering on crimson velvet, nor was it anything she was fated to suffer in the future.

There was now considerable kudos for Maurice, having a wife who was not only in the forefront of the newest and most exciting development, but ran one of the first flying schools. Glamorous young pilots and the weekly increase in duration and distance of flights patently demonstrated flying was no longer a ridiculous idea. Marie Belloc Lowndes was avid to see life in the aviation village of Brooklands and Maurice introduced her to Billy. The 'sight of the bird-like flying machines in the huge hangars adjoining The Limit' filled her with awe and she thoroughly enjoyed the delicious luncheon cooked by her compatriot, Gustave. This highly intelligent mechanic, Mrs Lowndes asserted, drew her aside and earnestly begged her to try and persuade 'the good lady' to be more businesslike. If, as she claimed in her book of memories published in 1946, Blondeau's one wish was to save money quickly, return to France, marry his fiancée, and start a flying school near Paris, then, in my view, Blondeau was going about it in a very roundabout way. Perhaps a desire on Mrs Belloc Lowndes' part to protect the reputation of Mrs Hewlett and thus, by association, that of her dear friend Maurie, required a little embroidery of the facts. It must have been obvious to her that Billy and Gustave shared the same house.

Although their simple living conditions were infinitely preferable to those at Mourmelon, financially life was precarious for Hewlett and Blondeau. Aside from the cost of renting a hangar, there was the expense of petrol and oil. Running a profitable school with a steady income was made all the more difficult by the peculiarly inconvenient wind conditions prevalent at Brooklands that frequently disrupted flying and, in winter, daylight flying hours were greatly reduced. Added to which, it was a nerve-wracking experience watching all their assets take to the skies in the hands of a pupil flying solo. A smashed machine would either have to be replaced, or repaired: either way it meant expense and loss of income.

Get a plane, learn to fly, was as formal as the plan had ever been. Now, if the nascent partnership was to have a future, it was imperative to have a plan and to obtain another Farman was as good as any. Without any capital, finding the necessary funds meant scrimping and saving and working even harder. Constructing the body themselves would cut costs, but there could be no saving on a new Gnome engine. With Farman's licence to construct, Blondeau, who had ideas for a lighter machine with less wing surface, chalked out his modified plans as he crawled to and fro over the sitting-room floor.

It was necessary to take on a carpenter and a handy man, once construction began, but the partners' investment in an acetylene welding plant, the first of its kind in England, with which they provided a welding service to members of the expanding Brooklands Flying Village and motorists from beyond, paid splendid dividends. Another lucrative sideline was the sale of accessories imported from France: the smaller of the two packing cases, that had first housed The Blue Bird, became the Store. In order to save the profit-eating cost of the carriage of goods from the railway station to the hangar, Billy decided to buy back her old De

Dietrich from her sister Veena. It was heavy and dilapidated; it preferred to go fast and made enough noise to wake the dead; but it was solid and strong. It was also open. The night Gustave and a pupil, who had volunteered to accompany him, collected it from Chester, it snowed; they arrived stiff with cold and covered with frost. Their reward: Billy's joy at being reunited with her old friend.

By March 1911, the new Farman was built and Billy had sewn and fitted all the canvas to the framework and then *doped it with a kind of white-ash.*[7] In the damp and very early morning mist of the first day of Spring, as it was wheeled out of the hangar for its maiden flight, the plane looked pure and beautiful and rather small. Billy sat on a petrol can, waiting in the chill air for visibility to improve, and reflected on how important this moment was for the partnership. So far, no machine constructed at Brooklands had flown at its first trial and she mentally prepared words of comfort for Gustave, should the craft of their hopes and hard work fail. She shivered with apprehension, more for the machine's safety than for anything else and when the ribbons of mist had drifted clear moved over to help fasten down the tail of the plane and then climbed on board. Gustave started the new Gnome engine, Billy throttled and let it out as he directed and then climbed down for Gustave to take her place. She freed the tail and with a roar the Farman sped along the ground. A few sleepy men emerged from their hangars and in tactful silence kept Billy company as she watched as Gustave took to the air and disappeared into the last lightly lingering mist. On the ground, they listened intently to the engine. Presently, with a returning roar, Gustave flew sweetly in to land. *"Not even (showing half a finger nail) that to change.'* He cried jubilantly. *That was his day and he deserved it,* wrote Billy. The all-British Blondeau-Farman reflected great credit upon its constructor, wrote *Flight* magazine. Lt Snowden-Smith, who had bought the Gnome engine and so had the majority share in the machine, *was simply mad with delight: The lightness and ease of control* made it the machine Billy loved to fly. For her *it felt like being on a sheet of writing paper in the air.*

Lieut. R.T. Snowden-Smith, Army Service Corps, was Blondeau's favourite pupil and one of his best. Sufficiently wealthy to have learnt to fly as a hobby, before there was any official policy of the armed forces paying for their staff to learn aviation, Snowden-Smith was always keen to acquire as much flying experience as possible and would often take up passengers, or pupils, on behalf of the Hewlett and Blondeau school. He also decided to try cross-country flying and, before he had acquired his own nippier little Farman, he had flown to Aldershot. Blondeau, torn between equal concern for his machine and his pupil, had accompanied him by road. When Snowden-Smith landed on the Queen's Parade that cold November morning, it caused no end of a bustle, but the discovery that it was a 'military' pilot who had played such a jape, turned prankster into hero. In celebration of the impromptu and successful demonstration of the potential of aircraft for military purposes, the Hewlett and Blondeau Flying School and its star pupil[8] partook of a hearty breakfast at the Queen's Hotel in Aldershot, before returning to Weybridge. A year later and in his own machine, Snowden-Smith was to cause consternation in Aldershot once again. Shortly after taking-off from the parade ground, a faulty plug in the engine forced him to land on the rifle range, which happened to be in use at the time. Happily, the first known British military aviator to be under fire was left unscathed, as was his machine, which, because the field was unsuitably small for safe take-off, had to be dismantled and returned, ignominiously, to Brooklands by road.

At Brooklands, motor race meeting days – those days for which the Track had been constructed – meant that many spectators parked their cars outside the hangars, much to the irritation and inconvenience of the aviators. Concern was voiced regularly in the aviation press that both motor-racing and flying enthusiasts should park so close to the sheds and that spectators should wander freely onto the flying field. In addition to the obvious danger from planes and public coming into unhealthily close contact, there was also the considerable inconvenience of manoeuvring the aircraft on the ground in the mêlée. The flyers, therefore, took mischevious delight in making sport of their pet hate – smart young motorists.

On one particular afternoon, two young men, dressed to the nines in *Dunhill's latest motorieties*, had parked their racy number with its canary-coloured body directly in front of a hangar and swaggered off, well pleased with the dash they had cut. An aviation mechanic who had the tools, and the whole afternoon in which to fashion it, secretly made a wooden plug to stuff into their exhaust pipe. On their return, the swells put on their goggles and coats and wound up the car. They wound and they wound. They took off their goggles and coats. They wound. They looked under the bonnet. The crowd that had collected offered advice. The carburettor was taken to pieces. The magneto was checked. The plugs were cleaned. Red-faced, dirty and defeated, they seriously spoke of walking! At this point, the scruffy-looking mechanic stepped up, swung the starting handle once and the engine began to run as sweet as an angel: he had loosened the plug when all heads had been under the bonnet.

The friction between the two communities had much to do with the flyers feeling aggrieved by their perceived second-class treatment. Being an aviation pioneer did not pay: taking on pupils, giving joy rides, or winning the small prizes from the race meetings held three or four times a year did not allow for much in the development and testing of new machines. Paying rent for the use of the hangars and the aviation ground was reasonable, but what did not seem reasonable was the charge levied for haulage of all goods' deliveries from the main entrance, which lay at farthest end of the circuit from the hangars; nor did it seem reasonable that any visitors to the Flying Village, whether on a business or social call, were required to pay the standard entrance fee to Brooklands of one shilling. However, the aviators' grievance that truly irked them was that they were used as an attraction for Brooklands. 'Flying daily at Brooklands' was advertised all over London, with a 1/- entrance charge, and of that they saw not a penny.

At a meeting of aviators and constructors, it was agreed to a man (and one woman) that all suffered similar financial constraints and that they resented being used as an attraction to the Club's sole benefit. A letter, with sixteen signatories, was sent to the management committee. This is what Billy claims the letter said and, as no copy of it or any correspondence relating to the strike exists today at Brooklands, who is to gainsay her?

Dear Sirs,

We the undersigned, rent hangars with the use of the aviation ground at Brooklands. For the hangars and use of the aviation ground we pay £100 per annum. Our object is to store our aeroplanes, construct them and learn to fly. When the ground is full of people we are unable to use it for experimental purposes. We do not pay rent for the advantage of giving exhibition flights for Brooklands Club and the general public.

Brooklands advertises that flying takes place daily, and it charges entrance money to view the same. On Race days flying is advertised more than motor races. We are exhibits on those days, and we ask for 25 per cent of all the gate money taken on week days and race days. Such money to be divided amongst those aviators who contribute to the exhibition advertised.

In addition, our goods must be delivered to or near our hangars and not left at the lodges.

Unless these conditions are accepted before the next Race Meeting, we, the undersigned, have decided that no flights take place, all our hangars will be closed between the hours of 11 a.m. and 6 p.m.

This list is dispatched to give Brooklands a fair warning of our intentions.

The Club arranged a meeting. In the blue corner, the aviators ready for a good scrap; in the red corner, the Committee. *They thought they had us easily. We were certainly underdogs, very poor, of no account, being only adventurers, we had no friends in high places.* Well, that's coming over a bit strong given the influential circle the Hewletts had moved in! Billy, in her own way, clearly had as romantic a streak as Maurice. Convention decreed ladies first and, as the sole woman present, battling Billy came out punching. This for the underdog! That for authority! Her father might not have viewed the efforts of man struggling to achieve something as unnatural as flight as a cause worthy of support, but he would have recognised and approved of his daughter's spirit in pursuit of her truth, which, on this occasion, she pursued with more force than politeness. *Most rudely I called the great Brooklands officials by their names without rank or prefix. I was reproved for this, but quoted, 'On ne dit pas Monsieur Caesar.' We were dismissed like naughty schoolboys.* Round one to a slightly battered committee: Mrs Hewlett, they realised, was no lady, she was one of the boys.

For the next Motor-racing Meeting, three small prizes were offered to tempt the aviators, and flying was to begin early afternoon. The 'naughty schoolboys' agreed that one machine (Hewlett and Blondeau's) flown by another pilot should fly punctually at 3.00 p.m. and when he had gained all three prizes in the one flight, he was to retire from the aviation ground and lock up his hangar. The prize monies would be divided between all who could have been competitors. Come the day, 'Strike of Aviators at Brooklands' was printed on large placards and hung on all the shuttered hangars. The disreputable aviators (Billy's description), in their even more disgraceful cars, stationed themselves in choice positions to watch the fun. Desperate officials tore down the placards and offered bribes to one or two pilots to fly, but without success. On the dot of 3 o'clock, before the majority of the spectators had had time to move from the stands down to the flying field, the lone pilot took to the air. He had soon completed all the manœuvres eligible for the three prizes on offer and was tucked up snug in his hangar, to the fury of the officials.

Well no – it wasn't quite like that! According to *The Aero*, the Brooklands management committee had refused to be blackmailed into any concessions and had already proposed allocating five per cent of the gate money to the aviators but, until the offending letter was withdrawn, were unprepared to enter into negotiations. Evidently, the strikers withdrew their letter the Wednesday before the Race Meeting on the Saturday (13 May, 1911) but warned they would still stick to their demands and would fly only enough to qualify for the prizes (a measly five percent of the gate was hardly an incentive to do otherwise). While the motor racing was on, Gilmour and Pixton flew for 17 mins and 21 mins 29 secs respectively in a very nasty puffy wind, after which all the sheds were shut up. Later that afternoon, the well-known Mr Cody, who had accepted a last minute invitation from the committee to fly his vast 'Flying Cathedral' from Farnborough to give a demonstration on the day of the strike, glided magnificently to earth from a height of something like three thousand feet to a rapturous welcome by the strikers: the sturdy navvies hired in case such strike-breaking should provoke trouble could only amuse by their gaping astonishment 'at the method of peaceful picketing adopted by the aviators.' Cody, after some very pretty flying, beat Pixton's time by twelve seconds and was declared the winner, but, as neither Cody nor Pixton had been aware that Cody was supposed to be a competitor, there was nothing for it but for Pixton to go up again. With just minutes to spare before seven o'clock, the official time limit, he took off and flew for a few minutes longer than the required minimum of fifteen for his flight to count, thus making his aggregate for the afternoon forty minutes. Pixton won first prize. Round two to the aviators.

Another matter on which the aviatiors and the Brooklands Committee clashed was crossing the one hundred foot wide motor racing track. For safety reasons the Committee had forbidden anyone to walk across it, at any time. This was not an order which affected the motorists, as their facilities were based close to the main entrance, but those members of The Flying Village, who could afford to live off the track, lived in Byfleet, and the most direct route from their hangars was a short walk across the track, through an opening they had made in the boundary railings and out on to the Byfleet road. To enter and exit by the main entrance on the Weybridge Road, one and a half miles away, seemed nonsensical. One and a half miles up to the main entrance from within the circuit, one and a half miles outside the circuit back down to Byfleet, made for a six mile round trip for a meal. Even for the minority who owned cars, the drive to and from the Flying Village for their breakfast or lunch was an unwanted added expense, hence the short cut.

Billy's account, whether or not strictly accurate, does give the essence of the little community, inventive, good-humoured and determined in the face of little funding and little support: visionaries all, who dared to risk life and limb, they disdained to obey petty rules. According to her, the management blocked off the 'illegal' footpath with a barrier of barbed wire: the aviators cleared it with wire-cutters. The management secured the unofficial opening in the tall iron railings with rivets; the aviators made a new opening with nuts and bolts to hold the panel in place and went in and out with the aid of a spanner. Notices went up to the effect that they would be charged with trespass and damage to company property; the aviators wrote a letter to Mr Locke King, the overall landlord of Brooklands, explaining the situation from their point of view and suggesting that a footbridge for their use might solve the problem. A half mile length of boundary railings opposite Byfleet was riveted; mysteriously, overnight, a double gate appeared marked Exit and Entrance. It was dismantled and the local constabulary were requested to guard a mile of the fence but, as they were not on duty at early morning flying time, instructors, pupils and mechanics slid unhindered over the spikes of the fence with the aid of a board; if a bobby was at his post, then a volunteer undertook to distract him when necessary. After a week without incident, the police guard was removed. Once again, under cover of a foggy evening, the inhabitants of the aviation village remade their secret gate.

Shortly after this, it happened that Billy and Snowden-Smith were spotted crossing the track on their way to no. 32, the Hewlett and Blondeau hangar. The carpenter, fortuitiously aware of this, signalled furiously to them to climb in through the window and, with seconds to spare before the officials arrived, the two hid in the large packing case stores cupboard. Pinching themselves to keep from laughing, the miscreants listened as the officials demanded to speak to them, confident this time in the evidence of their own eyes. Previously, they had made the mistake of accusing Billy of crossing the track on the one day she could prove she had not been at Brooklands. She had taken gleeful delight in roasting them for picking on her, a woman and a soft target, while admitting that, indeed, she regularly crossed the track at least four times a day. At last, weary of waiting, the officials left the hangar, allowing the giggling pair to erupt from their hiding place.

The management did build the long-desired footbridge and they also ordered fencing to mark off the ground on the west side of the track, to ensure greater security for flyers and spectators alike. *The Autocar* approved. 'It will be a great convenience to the members of the aviation colony living in Byfleet and also for the large and growing number of visitors from that direction who come in on foot.'[9]

The day George V was crowned king, 22 June, 1911, saw antics which would have done nothing to disabuse the Brooklands Committee of their opinion that the aviators were an unruly lot. Billy was a passing witness; she had gone to the Track to beg a lift to Weybridge station as she was due to meet up with her family to watch the Coronation procession from the Automobile Club. The *Aeroplane*, a rather more gossipy, lighthearted journal than *Flight*, the official organ for the R.Ae.C., described what Billy saw: 'a procession around Aeropolis, headed by a motor lawn-mower, as bandwagon, with half a dozen aviators on board.' The lawn-mower, according to Billy, was an eight horse-power, tiller-steered Daimler of prehistoric origins; when not in use, its blades were removed for safety reasons and *for fear of interfering aviators, the starting handle was removed and hidden.* On this occasion, however, the 'interfering aviators' had push-started it in first gear and, as the toothless mower gathered speed to a mighty two and a half miles per hour, it 'came into contact with hitherto immovable body, i.e. doors of Flanders[10] shed. Procession entered over remains of doors, shouldered two aeroplanes aside without damage, and ceased at a work-bench at back of shed. (Proprietor in middle of vehicle).' One man literally rolled on the ground with laughter, but Flanders used language which Billy was moved to record was the worst she had ever heard.

Safe in London, she missed the spectacular shootout and finale to that Coronation day in Aeropolis. Again this was reported in the *Aeroplane* in the same staccato style. 'In evening great pyrotechnic display. Searchlight from S.W. of track v. effective on cottages and main block of sheds. Final *jeu de foie* by assembled aviators with maroons and crackers, punctuated by revolver shots, enough to shatter glass for miles. Total damage done surprisingly small. Chiefly attributable to assiduous care of performers and consideration for feelings of others.' Billy had a different, less circumspect version of events, in which the male occupant of a tiny house called The Birdcage was spotlit by the huge acetylene headlight, as he undressed, as was his wont, before the open window. He fetched his pistol and aimed for the light, but the light shone on, as answering shots came from out of the darkness; only when there was not an unbroken pane of glass left in The Birdcage[11] and his hysterical lady friend had *very wisely left the house where she had no moral right to be and did not wish to be found*, did they cease.

Nine months had passed since the inception of Hewlett and Blondeau, but still Billy had not taken to the sky as a fully qualified pilot, despite having the plane, the place, and the instructor. Her lesson in patience had been infinitely longer than she could have imagined. Her faith in Blondeau as an instructor was absolute. Due to his meticulous attention to safety and maintenance,[12] his remarkable patience and perceptive response to each pupil as an individual, the school suffered not one accident when a pupil flew solo for the first time. Billy, nevertheless, had always stood down in favour of fee-paying pupils; her concern that she might be the one to damage their chief source of income had had a very damping effect. A little rolling practice (taxiing the plane along the ground), or riding passenger with Blondeau, watching over his shoulder as he worked the control lever, was as far as she had got. Also, a badly wrenched knee after a fall from her bicycle and aggravated by having to mind the store, another important source of income, had incapacitated her for weeks. But, in the summer of 1911, Billy knew that if she did not try for her ticket, she would be overtaken in the race to be the first woman in England to gain her licence. There was already talk of a rival, a pupil at Claude Grahame White's hugely successful Hendon school, the dashing Mrs de Beauvoir Stokes.

Mid-July and the diarists of *Flight* and the *Aeroplane* scrutinised and reported on Mrs Hewlett's progress. 'Mrs Hewlett, as a passenger pupil under Mr. Blondeau, made a number of circuits, Mrs Hewlett controlling the lever.' 'The energetic Blondeau out at dawn giving lessons to Mrs Hewlett and Brown of U.S.A. Gale blowing rest of day.' 'Mrs Hewlett flying well on Blondeau-Farman driving machine herself with Blondeau in passenger seat merely in case of mistaken manoeuvre.' 'The Blondeau-Hewlett school machine out with Mrs Hewlett and Brown at 4 a.m. practising *brevet* flights.' 'Mrs Hewlett doing hops on the recovered Farman all by herself.' 'Mrs Hewlett on Blondeau biplane doing circuits all alone on the machine. First time in England an English woman has made a circular flight.' Mrs Hewlett took out the Blondeau-Farman and was doing banked circuits at about 3ft.' 'Mrs Hewlett up alone on Blondeau-Farman, again doing right hand turns. Certainly the first woman to do a right hand turn in England.'

"Whatever you do, don't go near those lumps where the house is pulled down, nor to the sewage farm," Gustave had urged before she made her first solo flight. Billy obediently avoided the infamous sewage farm, but found herself horridly attracted to the lumps, where her taxiing plane was brought to a halt before she could take-off. With manly manual help she was extricated from the lumps, never to return to them. Over the countryside, parched and bleached in the heatwave that engulfed Britain that summer, she practised flying circuits and figures of eight until, at last, it was time to to set a date for when a representative of the Royal Aero Club should judge her worthy, or not, of a pilot's certificate.

In the blessedly cool, early morning light of Friday, 18 August, 1911, Billy was a mixture of nervous happiness as she walked across the dewy grass and climbed on to the Snowden-Smith Farman. The moment had arrived, the moment to confound all the doubters and detractors, the moment to make worthwhile the privations endured during the past eighteen months. Buoyed up by the goodwill of Blondeau, the pupils and all her comrades, Mrs Hewlett taxied across the grass and rose confidently into the air. She flew at over one hundred feet, successfully executed five figures of eight, landed within fifty yards of the judges, took to the air again, repeated the figures, landed even closer to the judges and passed her flying test to the cheers and applause of all on the flying ground, inspectors included.

So unreserved was the general joy, so great was Billy's excitement, even breakfast, that meal of meals to hungry fliers, was forgotten. However, school business could not be neglected, nor good flying conditions wasted. Billy handed over the machine to a pupil, Graham Wood,[13] who went up with Blondeau; after him another pupil, Lt. Longstaffe, took off on his first solo flight, shortly to return to earth in an unrehearsed glide: a cylinder had blown out of the Gnome engine taking part of the propeller with it. Truly, it had been Billy's lucky day.

Showered with telegrams of congratulation, letters and presents from admirers, Billy, in the game of fleeting fame, submitted to a new coiffure and make-up and allowed herself to be photographed looking uncharacteristically glamorous and quite unrecognisable for the front cover of *The Car* magazine. Featured more demurely as a Flight Pioneer in *Flight* magazine, her regular flying gear, which was a variation on her ski-ing outfit in which a form of cycling bloomers, a ribbed jersey and/or an old leather jacket and a knitted balaclava hat featured, had been replaced by a smart new leather version. What Mrs Hewlett was wearing on her head in the small inset portrait of 'Mrs Hewlett in ordinary life' is hard to guess, for it looked like a cross between a busby and half an ostrich. Interviewed and praised, the "tiresome little woman", whom the Brooklands Committee had accused of leading the young men of the Flying Village astray by her defiance, was suddenly someone to know and to flatter. Billy was greatly amused, but what she found sweetest of all was that the original *scoffers* took back *their words generously and fully*. She also had the greatest pleasure, now that she was an accredited pilot, secure with her R.Ae.C. certificate no.122, in resigning from that unwelcoming Club. Showing considerably more chivalry than the club afforded women, she agreed not to reveal her reasons for so doing.

Aviation had a first to be exploited, but Billy found it easy to refuse to *show off at Exhibitions* and *to swagger*. Particularly so, after the fiasco of the Hewlett and Blondeau exhibition of flying at the first Plymouth Aero Meeting in September, an embarrassment that she conveniently wiped from her memory! Contracted to appear on the Saturday, Monday and Tuesday of the meeting, the partners first had urgently to replace the Farman's damaged engine. Blondeau travelled to France to purchase a new one directly from the manufacturers, but it proved troublesome and he was left with little time in which to fit and test it before the meeting. A last minute hitch in acquiring suitable transport for the plane resulted in the partners arriving in Plymouth a day late, and when, on the Monday afternoon, the 'remous', or wully-wa, as their friend Graham Gilmour called the air eddies, were very treacherous, Blondeau declined to risk his machine for the fast dwindling crowd. He did go up for the second contracted session between 5.30 and 7.00 p.m., but problems with the throttle caused the Farman to overshoot on landing, puncturing both tyres on some woodwork outside the hangar. Come the Tuesday the air 'was in a very troubled state in the early afternoon', too troubled for Blondeau. He waited for a more propitious moment, but, when he did start, a cylinder was found to be knocking and needed re-adjustment. At this point, the management lost all patience and, despite Blondeau estimating he needed but a quarter of an hour before he could fly again, bade the clamorously impatient crowd go home. In true form, 'Mrs Hewlett intervened with a slight argument' and handed back their cheque. Later that evening, Blondeau took a 'lady friend of Mrs Hewlett' up as a passenger and demonstrated his machine and his flying skill more than adequately in the opinion of the patient correspondent to *Flight* magazine. Hewlett and Blondeau returned to Brooklands ruffled and considerably out of pocket.

Neither of them had the right temperament for exhibition or competitive flying. Blondeau was too safety conscious and his preferred style of flying close to the ground was hardly spectacular, even if it was considered by some to be 'far more difficult than flying really high.' How he had once been persuaded into racing a motorbike, as an attraction at Brooklands on a motor cyle racing day, is a mystery. The *Aero*, quite rightly, described it as a farce, as the fastest motorbikes had a speed of 80 m.p.h., the fastest aeroplanes a maximum speed of 70 m.p.h. and Blondeau's Farman could only manage 40 m.p.h. Billy did take part in 'quick get-off' competitions among friends and colleagues at Brooklands, which was much more her style, and once beat Sopwith, Petre and Fisher into first place to become the first aviatress to win an open competition. Her ambition had originally been straightforward: to fly her own aeroplane. Living *amongst men, young and old, who lived with one aim, fearing not death, caring not for other things, respecting not overmuch law and regulation that stood in their way*, as she did at Brooklands, was an additional and unforeseen reward. She had found her world, she was happy. When Cecco wired: *'Can you teach me to fly in 14 days?'* she felt her cup of happiness would surely overflow. *'Yes, intelligence and weather permitting,'* she replied.

M was so broadminded about my flying that I promised him not to encourage or interest our son in it: he said one in the family was enough. Whatever hope Maurice might have expressed, he was realistic enough to know it was a forlorn one. What young man, who rode a motorbike, whose mother had taught him to drive a car and who now ran a flying school, would not be interested in learning to fly? *I never invited him to see me at Brooklands.* As Cecco was serving at sea when Billy first went to Brooklands, he had had little opportunity to visit her. *He only came down twice for the day and was then mostly out with me in a car.* A photograph in *Flight*, 14 January, 1911, clearly shows a very happy Naval Lieut. F.E.T. Hewlett (*Flight* promoted him from Midshipman nine months early) sitting as a passenger behind Lieut. Snowden-Smith, after a ten mile flight at Brooklands! *Nor told him anything about the life.* If Billy had not, then Cecco had a sister, a father, and motoring and aviation journals, who could. Hardly surprising, therefore, when in March, 1911, the Royal Navy signalled its intention of exploring the tactical possibilities of flying by setting up officer training courses at Eastchurch, that an already interested junior officer decided to advance his service career along lines far more exciting than hitherto available.

Cecco proved to be an able pupil – 'Lieut Hewlett, R.N., making astonishingly quick progress, doing straight flights and circuits alone' – but his hopes of squeezing his training into two weeks' was thwarted by foul weather and the Gnome misbehaving, which contrived to scatter the eleven days on which he was able to train throughout a month. With a twenty-four hour extension to his leave before he should join his ship, HMS *Inflexible*, and a clear morning, at last, the thirteenth pupil of the Hewlett and Blondeau school to pass without a breakage gained certificate no. 156 on Monday, 9 November. 'Excellent work, and a credit to Mrs Hewlett, the first British aviatress,' enthused the *Aeroplane*, much taken by the fact that Cecco had only flown solo seven times. Mrs Hewlett, in no way dismayed that her son thought Blondeau landed better than she, hugged and hugged Cecco. *All-pervading, intoxicating delight,* greater than anything she experienced when she passed her aviator's certificate, suffused her. Everyone she met had to be told of her pride and her joy. *Before I used to feel a bit out of my family, now I shared my biggest interest with the one I loved best. I only remember being foolish all day, even after Cecco had gone. We were both aviators – hurrah!*[14]

The Aeropolis (unpopular with the locals for the racket of its little planes' engines, and an irritant to the Brooklands Committee) was a bohemia of early aviation. The privileged and the impecunious, the serviceman and the civilian, the engineer and the designer, the mechanic and the pilot, the thrill seeker and the serious, the eccentric, they were all there. A certain Mr Hewitt preferred to live in the trailer he towed behind his car, both hung about with pots and pans; in the trailer was his bed, in his bed, head on the pillow, was a crocodile, stuffed, on the bed sat his dog, alive. Jack Humphrey, whose monoplane once 'rolled solemnly into the Blondeau-Hewlett machine, removing top and bottom planes and sundry other parts,' was known for some reason as The Mad Dentist. 'Better,' the *Aeroplane* had scolded, 'for those unable to control machines if they would confine their peripatetics to the more open portions of ground rather than endeavour to do their tricks of artillery drivers among school machines pursuing their lawful vocations.'

Tommy Sopwith fell into the wealthy category rather than the eccentric, even if he did keep a small brown bear as a mascot. According to Billy, Poley was a fairly tame bear, entertaining to watch when he lay on his back and licked a honey jar clean, troublesome only in his pursuit of other treats. A stripped down Gnome engine, every part covered with the best quality castor oil and laid out neatly, in order, on clean white paper, was too good a feast for the little bear from the adjacent hangar to ignore. Discovered licking the no. 4 cylinder inside and out, he had to be lured away with a jar of honey and chased off with ash struts. On another rather more serious occasion, he had been found hanging upside down, picking juicy knots of wood from the Hewlett and Blondeau shed roof, which he licked and then discarded. Regretting the loss of one particularly tasty knot, he climbed down on to their plane below and hunted for his lost tit-bit all along the top of the fabric-covered wing. Eventually, the day came when Poley[15] grew too insistent and naughty and, after he badly clawed one of Hewlett and Blondeau's visitors, he was packed off to a zoo.

On the other side of no. 32, the Hewlett-Blondeau shed, was the one owned by Howard Flanders that had suffered such an invasion on Coronation day. Here Flanders designed and assembled monoplanes, but in 1912 he moved to shed no. 12 and set up a flying school, with E.V.B. Fisher as one of the instructors. Fisher, a very good-looking, well-educated young man of immense charm in his early twenties, lived and breathed aviation. He wore *fewer and older clothes than any tramp; his trousers were mended with bits of copper wire and he wore no socks inside his evening pumps* and he used to give Billy *silly and darling little presents* such as a mushroom, a bird's egg, a tool found on the track, or a single wild flower and she loved him, as did everyone else.

The day Fisher crashed Flanders' latest monoplane and died with his passenger, all flying ceased for the day. A distraught Flanders was not seen for a week. *We all cried openly as for a dear one of our own. He was buried in a small church not far off. All Brooklands came to the funeral in everyday clothes and overalls, in our dud old cars, just as we used them, unwashed and uncleaned. His own pals lowered him into the grave, most of us had some small token to offer. An old woman limped up with a bunch of violets, written in pencil on the bit of paper was, 'From one he was always kind to.' I do not remember noticing his family or friends, it seemed to all of us aviators that it was our loss, our aims he had died for, and our own funeral might be any day.* [16]

It was a funeral that mirrored in some way the one prescribed for himself by another friend, Graham Gilmour. Coolly aware of the dangers of his profession, Gilmour had left written instructions. 'There was to be no tolling of bells, no mourning, no moaning, and if any flowers were to be sent they were to be coloured. His hearse was to be a four-wheeled farmer's cart or a motor lorry – not one of those dreadful things, hearses.' [17] He died one icy February in 1912, when with more skating than flying at Brooklands, he crashed into the Deer Park in Richmond on a cross-country flight testing a Martin Handasyde Dragonfly with a more powerful engine. Two hours earlier Billy and Pia had waved him off as he chaffed with his mechanics, *accepting everyone's invitation to tea at the Blue Bird café that afternoon.*

Her dear friend, Baroness de Knoop, had once pleaded on her knees and with tears in her eyes for Billy to abandon her folly, the dangers were too great. Shaken by the urgent sincerity of her friend's appeal, Billy had seriously questioned her own motives in refusing to do as she was begged, but apart from feeling horribly selfish and saddened that they should part, each as distressed as the other, Billy knew that she wanted nothing else but to be involved in the single most exciting happening of the time: aviation. Now, nearly two years after she and Blondeau had first wheeled out their new Farman, the time had come to move on from their hand to mouth existence. The flying school had been a creditable success, but had never generated much income. New designs and more powerful motors were evolving rapidly. As the more extreme of the anything-might-fly examples of the early days were weeded out and development, rather than experimentation, became the norm, the construction of accepted models looked a more promising option than teaching others to fly them, certainly, it was less hazardous. Gustave had already shown that his strength lay less in creativity and more in fine workmanship, so when in the Spring of 1912, he received an order to build a two-seater Hanriot, the decision to clear the hangar of the school planes in order to carry out the commission made sense.[18] It soon became clear, however, that with the demands of the new, makeshift was no longer good enough; their hangar had no water, light or power; Hewlett and Blondeau had outgrown the resources available at Brooklands. It was time to go.

The partnership had survived where pilots more talented and daring had died, but with some luck, great determination and dogged hard work, they had achieved a great deal for a couple of underfunded enthusiasts. However, their momentous decision to move on and expand had a price. No longer would Billy[19] have the freedom to walk out to her own aeroplane and, as the sky lightened, climb on to the Farman to take to the air. No longer would she feel the exhilaration of skimming effortlessly through that quiet, peculiar to the early morning, accompanied only by her shadow as the sun warmed the earth.

CHAPTER 18

MESSRS HEWLETT and BLONDEAU

In business in Battersea

By the end of July, suitable premises had been found in Battersea and the former roller-skating rink[1] converted by the car firm, Mulliners, who had flirted briefly with aircraft manufacture, became Hewlett and Blondeau's new works. The site, 2-16 Vardens Road, had an added benefit, its proximity to Clapham Junction station (misleadingly so named despite its being situated in Battersea). Blondeau, with past experience in manufacture, drew up the necessary plans to make for greater efficiency in the grandly named Omnia Works and workmen were engaged, through the local Labour Exchange: *two were really good, two were passable carpenters, the others simply rotters*, whose wages were fixed *according to their ability and industry*. With this settled, or so the partners thought, Blondeau went to France on business and Mrs Hewlett remained in charge. The tyro company directors were about to receive their first lesson in labour relations.

Two union officials came to call. They wished to point out that carpenters should be paid union wages. Once enlightened, Mrs Hewlett was happy to assure them that some union men might be paid more than the union rate, if considered better workers. That, evidently, would not do, all men of whatever competence were to be paid the same (lower) wages as prescribed by the union. She forbore to voice her opinion that that was incomprehensibly ridiculous and offered, instead, to dismiss the inferior workers and keep only the good ones. Their consequent threat to withdraw all labour and close the Works she considered a *great cheek* and she assured them the Works would be run her way and if anyone was to close them, it would be herself. *'Then it is war between us,'* the officials declared, *'we will see who wins.'* Having no intention of giving in, before she had started, Billy assured them that she always found a scrap exciting. Gustave returning from France, loaded with rolls of drawings, wood and metal parts, eager to begin construction, found the beleagured Works at a standstill. Hewlett and Blondeau had discovered too late that Battersea and its environs was *a hotbed of Unions.*

The partners decided to advertise in the north and Scotland, as well as locally. 'Wanted, a few intelligent boys as apprentices; also improvers for aeronautical engineering – Omnia Works, Vardens Road.' Any applicant who was a union man was politely declined, all others were given a trial, on union wages and by mid-August every post was filled. The pickets at the gates pressed the new employees to join the union and prophesied the inevitable failure of the company.[2] The local bobby, whom Billy had been careful to befriend with *a short sermon on flying, its future use, the advantage to men to get training,* merely laughed when she asked if he *couldn't move on those loafers outside? "They won't stay long now you've cooked their goose pretty well."* When the pickets were ready to slope off in defeat, Billy shook hands with *her sporting opponents*; she also explained that she had already gone to a great deal of trouble to overcome many obstacles in order to be involved in flying and she would continue to struggle for a future she passionately believed in. Nothing was going to stop her.

By December 1912 the Omnia Works was in full production. Three Hanriot machines had been built and then dismantled – conveniently, early aeroplanes were relatively simple constructions – packed and dispatched to Rheims for reassembling, flight testing and eventual handover to the French government. *Flight* magazine decided to feature the company.[3] They were impressed, particularly with the fact that no fewer than ten men had been on probation before the right one had been selected to be in charge of the oxy-acetylene welding work. It found the workmen responsible and experienced, the stores stocked with everything that could possibly be required for aeroplane construction and that, except for a special type of wire strainer that could only be obtained in France, the machines entirely British built. The future of Messrs Hewlett and Blondeau looked bright.

Financially, the firm was still struggling and there was little money available for management, or administrative staff. Gustave was manager, draughtsman, foreman, errand boy and chauffeur. Billy was secretary, typist, accountant, sewing woman and chauffeur. Her office skills were negligible, her letters unbusinesslike and frequently not copied, and her accounts incomprehensible to all but herself. Sewing the canvas for the wings was her one natural skill, although her confidence was once severely shaken when the Admiralty returned a newly delivered Caudron: the canvas was loose on the wing. Panic and dismay dissolved into laughter when it was discovered that a mouse had nibbled the string stitches and used them to furbish a snug little nest in the wing tip. On another occasion, the terrifying rattling in the wings of a naval plane was revealed to be hundreds of dried earwigs bouncing about: it was decided to leave them be.

The double life of running the house and servants as well as the works, the early and late hours, soon made me feel shattered and cross about small matters that went wrong. It was hard on both lives, so I gave up home, took a flat in the Prince of Wales' Mansions,[4] put in the Byfleet scraps of furniture and found it a saving of time and energy. Coverage of what was effectively the end of Billy's marriage gets no more succinct than that. As well as which, even if Northwick Terrace had for the previous two years been a convenient bolt-hole rather than a home to be run, this version of events neatly side-steps the issue of the exact nature of her relationship with Blondeau. He, from her account of life in Battersea, would also appear to have lived in the flat in Prince of Wales Mansions, although Billy does not write as clearly of house-sharing as she did in The Limit at Weybridge. Had she deliberately, or through careless unconcern, decided to allow the impression to stand? Once again, it is hard to guess Billy's motives, if indeed she had any. As family (Pia regularly, Cecco occasionally, stayed at the flat) and close friends would have known the truth of whatever the situation was, Billy might have considered her relationship with Gustave – be it a discreet affair, a close platonic friendship, or a practical business arrangement – an irrelevancy in her public account of her life in aviation. At the time, sharing a flat might well have been a financial expediency; equally, the management of a small hands-on business could not have afforded to appear anything less than correct. The Mansions' smarter location and distance from Omnia Works promised greater privacy and either Mrs Hewlett and M. Blondeau kept their private life very private, or there was nothing in it to be private about.

Kroschka, the Great Dane, would have known. He shared the flat too. He had been passed on to Billy by a great favourite of hers at Brooklands, the charming, stammering Gordon Bell.[5] It had been love at first sight for Billy and it had taken a week of determination to win over Kroshka but once he had graciously accepted Billy and Gustave as his devoted companions for life, his loyalty was absolute, extreme even. Before Billy had found the Battersea flat, she once needed to leave Kroshka in the care of one of her sisters in Eccleston Square. Desolate, the Great Dane slipped from the house and headed for Victoria Station. Hatless, coatless and panting, Billy's sister caught up with him, by then a mortified captive of a railway porter; Kroshka had been chasing down the platform after his mistress's departing train. Once established in Prince of Wales Road, Billy walked Kroshka to and from the Omnia Works for a few days, after which she took the omnibus, while he followed, keeping to the pavement. Eventually, Kroshka chose his own route to work.

In the small, non-union Works, the mixed nationality workforce was as ready as the bosses to work irregular hours, should an urgent order require it. M. Blondeau would roll up his sleeves and work alongside the men; Mrs Hewlett would sleep on a car cushion in the office until she was needed to sew and dope the wings. Handily, an all-night tea stall which parked not far from the factory acted as an unofficial works canteen. *'Les Anglais doivent bien aimer leur thé, s'ils le promenent dans des petits chariots au milieu de la nuit,'* (The English must be very fond of their tea, if they transport it in little carts in the middle of the night), a Frenchman remarked on the explanation of the puzzling disappearance and reappearance of men with steaming mugs of tea at three o'clock in the morning. Above all, the men were very conscious of the shop's motto: 'Remember you have a man's life depending on how you do your work.' Mr Fox, the rigger, once, of his own volition, worked till dawn, replacing every bit of cable on a naval plane because he considered some of it inadequate.

Visitors were entertained at the Omnia Works private club – a table kept exclusively for her friends by Mrs Stiff, who ran the bakery opposite. There, *cakes and buns were filling and wholesome, the tea nice and strong* and Kroshka was assured of a constant supply of gingerbread nuts. More welcome even than clients, were pilots, former pupils, Cecco and his fellow officers, anyone who could talk of developments in aviation, or their experiences in flying, even their experiences in crashing. A stunt flyer for the cinema (regrettably, neither the identity of the handsome American nor the titles of the films in which he flew are available) was also a regular. He liked to supervise all necessary repairs to his aeroplane and would frequently appear, due more to the jealousy of his wife than the hazards of his job, looking more wrecked than his machine. When asked what he did on the occasion his wife ran a hatpin into his leg, while they watched a film together in which he had a love scene with the heroine, he said: *'I sat still and let her get through – she's such a good woman.'* Another day he arrived at Vardens Road with sticking plasters all over his face; his wife *had punished him with her comb and brush* that morning for arriving home late for supper by some twelve hours. Eventually he left his 'good woman', but Billy never heard whether he found a more forgiving one.

A caller not favoured with a tea at Mrs Stiff's was *Six-footer, broad of shoulder, self-confident manner, top-hat, buttonhole, shiny boots complete;* patently, a cad. Unexpected and unannounced, this salesman had waylaid Mrs Hewlett in her office. He had a complaint. He had lost a client because M. Blondeau had insisted that only castor oil was to be used in his Gnome engine. Mrs Hewlett hastened to assure *Six Foot Oil* that, unlike himself, Mr Blondeau knew all there was to know about the Gnome engine; any other oil but castor would be too thick for it. Furthermore, his staggering enquiry as to what it would take for Hewlett and Blondeau to recommend and sell his oil for all the engines they installed, needed clarification. *Did he mean to pay her for using something which she knew might cause an accident, or death to men who flew?* As *Six Foot Oil* was shown the door, with Mrs Hewlett's vow to inform all the aviators she could of his perfidy ringing in his ears,[6] he no doubt reflected on her excess of sentiment and lack of business acumen.

Knuckling down to a working day and a working week meant that Billy had to adapt to the customs of another class. *We had a workman's hour for lunch, it was a very scratch and hurried meal* and a badge of her proud new status. Sometimes, if time was pressing, she and Gustave ate at a small restaurant; Kroshka, who knew a good thing when he was on to it, would sit quietly under the table until the end of the meal, when he would leave his masters to return to work, while he paid a brief but satisfactory visit to the kitchen. Without a servant to shop, let alone cook for her, Billy would buy supplies for lunch or supper on her way home. As the working week was six full days, Saturday evening was for the *grand shopping effort.* Billy loved to join in the general chaff and chatter as she and Gustave, sometimes accompanied by Cecco and Pia, and always by Kroshka, shopped in the market at Clapham Junction. After the West End and Weybridge, she thought housekeeping dirt cheap: *such things as quails, prawns, new-laid eggs, grapes, etc. were about half the price.* Some scratch meals!

On Sunday [7] *morning at 11 o'clock,* wrote Pia in her delightful account entitled 'The Aviators' Holiday', *this car* (she was referring to the De Dietrich) *was standing in the road outside our flat. We live at the top of all, and all the tins of food, cooking utensils and rugs had to be brought down five flights of stairs We dropped everything on the pavement in front of Gustave, who stood by the car, vainly trying to pack all we brought him into the two boxes at the back, which were already more than half filled with the numerous tools which are needed when we go on an expedition on the De Dietrich. There were also supplies of paraffin, oil, and carbide.* [8] *However we tied all the rugs, including the old cover of an aeroplane which had been treated to make it waterproof, on to the spare tyre brackets: we carried no spare tyres for the simple reason that we hadn't got any. We took about twenty minutes to pack up and at last Mama came downstairs bringing all we had forgotten, Cecco's toothbrush, a tin jug and a pot of honey. Her last words before starting were; "Cecco, are you taking a razor?" "Yes." "Then I don't think Gustave need take his." "It's his I am taking," was Cecco's reply, shewing the dreadful effect aviation has had on his morals.*

A lively discussion now ensued as to which of the three certified aviators should drive the car. Mama was knocked out at once, because she hasn't renewed her licence for at least two years, [9] *and though Cecco didn't know the road, Gustave kindly let him have the privilege of taking the wheel. Then came the question, who should sit with Kroshka in the front one of the two boxes behind? I struck, as I hate his fidgeting, and so Mama got in, calling him after her. With a good deal of pushing he got in and sat down between the tyre levers and the tin boxes, in a space that was really only big enough for one of his feet. Where Mama put her's no one knows, but then they are very small.*

Cecco sat proudly in the driving seat, and Gustave started up the car, which set up its usual cheery roar and rattle at the first turn of the starting handle. Gustave then took his place by Cecco, and I sat at his feet on the step, where I got all the oil from the engine (she needs a good deal) and all the grit and stones from the road.

We enjoyed the beauties of the road to St Leonard's Forest very much and found not only a lovely place, but two pools of water which is very necessary for us, as Kroshka must drink and we must wash. Gustave and Cecco at once began making a clearing in the bracken for the famous tent, which the former had been planning all the way along. When it was finished it looked splendid. The Wright biplane canvas made an excellent tent, and was all the more suitable for us as it still bore the marks of oil and shewed the places where the ribs of the wings had been. While we arranged our beds, each after his own idea, we put the rugs and blankets into the tent. Kroshka went straight there, planted himself in the middle of the wraps and so all we could do was to take all the rugs he wasn't using, and make our beds as best we could.

We went and fetched some milk from a nearby farm and then got some water from the drinking pool to make tea and sat down to supper, being careful not to eat too much bread, and then sat squatting round a candle stuck on to the lid of the bread tin, playing Coon Can[10] on three biscuit boxes. We soon got too sleepy to go on, and retired to our little nests in the bracken, leaving the tent with its mathematically correct poles and pegs to the luxurious Kroshka. During the night, whenever the coldness of the bracken or the lumpiness of the ground woke us up we heard this snoring going on uninterrupted and so could comfort ourselves with the thought that at least one of our party was having a good night.

We slept late the next morning, and at 8 Cecco, with an overcoat covering any eccentricities in his dress, took the car in to the village for some bread. We had a splendid breakfast – even Cecco thought so, as he was at last allowed to make his much desired fire, and Gustave spiked a kipper on the end of a bit of aeroplane wire and cooked it over the blaze, holding it with a pair of pincers. Its tail burned a little, but was quickly extinguished by being trodden on, and Gustave said it was very good, and as a French man he ought to know. As we sat round, for a wonder not talking about aeroplanes, Gustave said he wished he had a sketch book. Cecco asked if he could draw, and he said in his odd, but expressive English, "Yes, I was drawing very much once, but now I don't done it any more. 'Orses, lions, mouse, elephants, anything." This remark was greeted with shouts of laughter on account of the pronounciation, but he didn't care a bit, and simply waited till we had done. The weather cut short our jolly party *by becoming rainy and we knew that if the ground got very wet we shouldn't be able to get the car along the soft track back to the main road, so we began to pack up at breakneck speed. Cecco started up the faithful De Dietrich: the car was missing a bit, but as Cecco says, with the De D. it isn't on how many cylinders she goes, but whether she goes at all that matters. She got bravely up the hills, and met by smiles and cheers at our quaint appearance we got back to town and the flat. We all, including Kroshka, agreed that we couldn't have had a better time. And it was so cheap. Aviators are proverbially hard up, and so this is very important for us to consider. Not counting food, which we should have needed at home just the same, our trip only cost us 7/- for petrol.*[11]

Kroshka threatens to appropriate this chapter for himself, he features so prominently, but rightly so, as he was a dog of great character and sagacity. One Saturday afternoon, when Billy was going *on a family outing* and Gustave had *his private affairs*, Kroshka had been locked in the flat, with a generous dinner of raw meat and the best cushions at his disposal. *Gustave returned first to find the front door wide open, but no Kroshka.* The porter had seen and heard nothing, so Gustave, utterly mystified, set out slowly through the Saturday crowd for the Works. Suddenly, coming towards him was Kroshka who, to the surprise of all around, placed his forepaws on Gustave's shoulders and warmly licked his face in greeting. Kroshka, it was known, could open doors with knobs that turned, but how he had managed the Yale lock of the front door of the flat remained a mystery for ever.

Kroshka was also the equal of his mistress for persistence and dedicated to his motto, 'Never Be Left Behind'. It made a shopping trip 'up west' with Pia rather more expensive than Billy could have wished. *We tried hard to persuade Kroshka to go to the works as usual. He refused over and over again. He waited in the street till we came out, then he followed us.* Ignoring him, mother and daughter decided to catch their bus for Piccadilly, but then watched in dismay as Kroshka followed the bus out of his home territory and across Chelsea Bridge, where they lost sight of him. Concerned, they alighted and reported his loss at the nearest police station, with the intention of checking for news on their return; they then continued their journey. As they descended from the top of their bus, they were torn between rage and relief to see *Kroshka quietly smelling everyone who got off all the buses at the Circus.* And the cost to Billy? A taxi home. *Too many parcels plus an outsize in dogs* left no other option.

In 1913, Messrs Hewlett and Blondeau took a stand at the Aero exhibition at Olympia. In addition to their acetylene welding equipment, the popularity of which, according to *The Aeroplane*, was 'too well known to require emphasis,' they exhibited inclinometers, revolution counters, cables, wires and petrol tanks fitted with Securitas fireproof tubes. King George V, to the disappointment of the aviation press, was shown round the exhibition' by sundry notabilities of the motor trade.' However, the following year, when the king opened the Exhibition of Aeroplanes and Aero Engines, the motor trade was scarce to be seen. Again, Hewlett and Blondeau were one of the exhibitors[12] and Billy contrived to make their small stall as distinctive and attractive as her limited budget allowed. There was a slight hiccup when their own carpenter, who was building the stand, nearly came to blows with a couple of squiffy men who objected to him being non-union labour, but it was the measures employed, in the interests of the King's security, that blighted the event for one indignant half of Hewlett and Blondeau. As a woman, Billy was an object of distrust and suspicion to the police, made wary by the kicks and bites suffered in the Suffragettes' campaign. Every time she entered Olympia to work on the stand, they would question her closely; they even, on the day of the opening ceremony, tried to prevent her reaching her own stall. Failing to do so, despite their very best efforts, they then posted a couple of coppers to make sure she did not leave it until the King had left the building. *My son in the Naval Flying corps, most of our pupils in either the Army or Navy, our work mostly on Government contracts – I own,* wrote Billy, *to feeling very hurt.*

And angry. *I had never believed in the Suffragettes' way of trying to get the vote, as I am much too feminine – I simply could not kick or bite. But I never spoke against them, as I took no interest in their aims or methods. I had more responsibility than I could conveniently cope with as a woman, I was quite incapable of taking on any more. I had gone through quite as much privation and hard work as they had in prison and had gained my objective. Now my reward was suspicion, disgust and hatred. I was looked upon as dangerous. I knew perfectly well that Aviation had helped England, I was doing a bit to further that help, yet I was prevented from looking at the King of England who came to encourage those who were in it and of it. I was far from included amongst pioneers, I was worse than Pemberton Billing* [13] *who kept his hat on as the King passed. It was knocked off for him, but he was still worthy to stand with all the rest of the pioneers.*[14] *However, I sat in the darkest corner with Kroshka and thought of flying the cut-down Farman at dawn, dipping to meet my shadow aeroplane on the wet grass, the river all gold, partridges and rabbits just waking up, frightened at the noise. I had my reward, I was happy in my work, and happy in my friends. What did I care for glory or what people thought? I forgave the Suffragettes, the police and public opinion. I drove back to Vardens Road and tea at Mrs. Stiff's.*

CHAPTER 19

NEITHER A SPORT NOR A SIDESHOW

Aviation prepares for war

Ladies, Mrs Hewlett, celebrity aviatrix, was addressing a women's group, *I've been assured that I am only to tell you of a few personal feelings of how Aviation strikes me – as a woman. I can't help feeling they may bore you, and as I hate nothing so much as being bored, I beg you will hastily leave the room directly you feel it coming on.* Disarmed, her audience could only sit tight. *We don't yet know how far this new science will alter the world, it must rub boundaries off the earth, nations cannot help getting mixed, and what effect it will have on laws, character and trade are mere speculations,* Billy admitted, but, as she had said a year earlier, *flying will revolutionise war.*

That had been in 1911 and, shortly afterwards, in November of the same year, Billy had written a letter from The Limit, which reflected the frustration felt by all fervent, cash-strapped pioneers. *There can scarcely be a patriot left blind enough to deny that England is behind other nations in the science of Aeronautics. ... Nearly every European country has been before us in realising that to use the air as a highway is not merely a sport for the rich dare-devil, nor a side-show for fairs in the summer months. It has been accepted, we may say, as a new force. International Congresses have already met and passed laws regulating aerial traffic in such matters as frontier-regulations and customs duties. Foreign Governments, in fact, are treating aviation as the greatest science of the century and the triumph of rapid motion ... England is asleep where this new science is concerned, and surely she ought to wake up.*[1] *It is disgraceful that we are doing nothing to equip ourselves against a new danger. Our supremacy on the sea will be useless unless we defend the air above our ships and around our coasts. We are an island no longer* ... Mrs Hewlett then had much to say to *Dear Sir* about rich financiers fattening themselves on the genius of the impoverished, and the need for investment and reiumbursement for those who had already done so much pioneering work. She closed, as his *obedient servant, CERTIFICATED PILOT,* with the advice that the British Government should follow the example of the French.

The French army by the end of 1910 had boasted thirty-nine pilots and twenty-nine military aeroplanes: at the British Army manoeuvres of 1910, there had been only three planes, all privately owned, two of which had been flown by Dickson and Loraine, fellow pupils of Blondeau at Mourmelon. Robert Loraine, an actor appearing in *The Man from the Sea* in the West End, had, on a whim, offered his immediate and amateur services after reading a report in the *Daily Mail* of how the 'Red' Army had successfully used Captain Bertram Dickson[2] for reconnaissance. Loraine arranged for a Morse-key radio transmitter for air-to-ground operations to be fitted into his own Bristol Boxkite, and drove down after his evening performance, ready to fly the following day for the 'Blue' Army.

Billy drafted her impassioned letter some six months after the Air Battalion had been established by the War Office at Larkhill – on April Fool's Day, 1911. This military flying school, which superseded the Balloon School at Farnborough, began life cluttered with a certain amount of baggage in the way of assorted airships, balloons and kites, but, among the first six officers attached for immediate duties, was one former Hewlett and Blondeau pupil, Lieut. R.T. Snowden-Smith, Army Service Corps. Only officers with good eyesight, immunity from seasickness, a knowledge of foreign languages, as well as an ability to read maps and make field sketches were accepted: bachelors under eleven and a half stone and thirty years of age being given preference. A further two officers, twenty three NCOs and one hundred and fifty three men, plus two buglers, four biplanes (a Wright, Farman, Paulhan, and de Havilland), one Bleriot monoplane, four riding horses and thirty-two draught horses took the Air Battalion to full strength.

The Royal Navy's foray into military aviation was modest and a month earlier thanks to the eclipse of the sun over the Fiji Islands. Francis

McClean, a renowned amateur astronomer, due to travel in a government expedition to witness the eclipse, had placed his own new Short S.27 [3] at Eastchurch at Admiral Sir E.H. Seymour's disposal. As a result, on March 1st, four naval officers interested in learning to fly and with paid leave of absence in which to do so, arrived at Eastchurch. One of their number, Lieut C.R. Samson, was later to take off in his S.27 from special staging erected on the foredeck of the battleship HMS *Africa*, straight into British aviation history books.[4]

Eventually, prodded by the Press and poked by enthusiastic advocates, civilian and military, the Admiralty and the War Office lumbered into action. In April, 1912, the Royal Flying Corps, made up of five sections, the Military Wing, the Naval Wing, the Reserve, the Central Flying School (near Upavon on Salisbury Plain) and the Army Aircraft Factory at Farnborough, renamed the Royal Aircraft Factory, was formed. Successful applicants for commissions in the RFC, whether civilians or officers from the Services, had first to acquire their RAeC certificates privately; if accepted for advanced training at the Central Flying School they would be reimbursed the £75 private tuition fee. This arrangement, ostensibly to protect the many civilian flying schools from the loss of fee-paying pupils, was also a neat way of leaving the schools to bear the cost of maintenance of the machines for tuition. Three courses a year were planned at the Central Flying School, twenty-five training aeroplanes were ordered and provision was made for between 140-150 pilots to be trained each year. However, the Senior Service with its quota of just forty pilots a year, insisted on retaining Eastchurch as its elementary Flying Training School; a decision influenced, no doubt, by the active experimentation already taking place into adapting existing planes and designing new ones for taking off and landing on water.

The civilian market alone would not have sustained Hewlett and Blondeau. Orders from the Services, both Royal Navy and Army, were vital and extra funding for aviation development was a welcome boost to good construction companies such as themselves. Almost before they had settled into the new premises, Hewlett and Blondeau found themselves, thanks to their first pupil, Ducrocq, who worked for Hanriot, involved in the first British Trial to select an official military aircraft. Two Hanriot machines, built by the parent company in France, were entered in the Trials to be held on Salisbury Plain[5] and spare parts were urgently needed for them.

All was not complete till five in the afternoon, when Ducrocq blew in breathless and laden with engine parts, anxious to start off. (Billy, with such larks to relate, overlooked details such as occasion or date). *We packed the car carefully and drove away for the Plain about 5 p.m. The pace was limited by the fragile parts which we protected as much as possible from friction and dust. At Andover a storm of such force dropped upon us that we used everything to protect our spare parts and actually dared not drive through it. When it was over, a thick fog hung over the road, so thick that neither hedge could be seen. We had to push on, but we took a wrong turning in the mist and went out of our way.* It was August, 1912. *We had to buy petrol, so fed ourselves and the car at the same time at an inn. By then it was black night, we saw no one to ask, and were fairly lost on Salisbury Plain.* At long last, they reached the sleeping camp at Larkhill. They found the Hanriot hangar (a large tent) and drove in, the headlights picking out the waiting machines. The men disappeared leaving Billy, in the care of Kroshka, to an uncomfortable night.

Billy, who had shared the backseat with Kroshka – a dismal failure as a pillow as his legs would keep sliding off the seat – awoke at dawn to the slang of the French mechanics and their frankly expressed views of life in general and the Hanriot and her own company in particular. Her appearance, together with the spare parts, astonished the mechanics, as did her fluent French; then with a tin mug of good French coffee in her hand and Kroshka at her heels, Billy wandered out to relish her second startling appearance of the morning, when a number of old friends and colleagues,[6] including Gordon Bell, hailed her with delight. Kroshka, too, was received with flattering warmth.

In all, thirty-one planes were taking part in the Military Aeroplane Competition; some were all British; some all foreign; some of British design but with foreign engines; and some of foreign design but built in Britain. The pilots were either French or British, including the charismatic American, Samuel Franklin Cody, a British citizen since the 1909 Doncaster Flying meeting . Cody was flying a rebuilt version of his Flying Cathedral rather than his original entry, a monoplane which had come off second best in an encounter, while landing, with a stray cow. That cow did Cody a favour, for luck and an accumulation of not very compelling reasons in themselves were to see him the winner of the Trials.[7]

Much to Mrs Hewlett's delight, it was not long before she was commissioned as general petrol carrier and with the car loaded with full cans she drove to appointed filling locations, and returned with the empties. *Oh! what a glorious sight. The hollows were filled with pink mist, the sky all red, and pink-tinted machines dipped into pink baths of mist to re-appear a mile or so away.* It must have been one of the better days, generally the weather was atrocious – like the food, until the Army was called in to do the catering – throughout the two and a half weeks of the Trials.[8] *The Trials went on till nine o'clock, some came down, some engines misbehaved and made horrid vulgar noises. Everyone was excited and very busy.* Come breakfast and Mrs Hewlett was *taken into the mess tent and waited on by so many kind men that the breakfast (she) ate (was) a shocking record.* Kroshka, too, did his fair share of appreciating the generous hospitality, before the partners began the return journey to Battersea. Their efforts had not been entirely wasted as the two French Hanriot machines came a respectable third and fourth in the competition.

The following year, 1913, the *Daily Mail*, a consistent and enthusiastic promotor of aviation, offered a prize of £5,000 for their Waterplane Circuit of Great Britain. The circuit was to be completed within 72 hours, all competitors and their craft were to be British and taking off and landing was only to be on water. The starting and finishing line for the competition was Calshot and as Lt. Spenser Grey R.N., was C.O. of the naval air station and a Caudron hydro-biplane was under construction at the Omnia Works, it was unthinkable that Hewlett and Blondeau should not take advantage of their former pupil's posting. Furthermore, Sub-Lieutenant F.E.T. Hewlett, currently serving on the aircraft carrier HMS *Hermes*, would be free to accompany them. Cecco, much to Billy's fierce pride and delight, had already experienced *hard flying* when he was based at the Isle of Grain naval air station and on a visit to the station she had, to her son's consternation, made sure to thank the dashing Commander Samson[9] *for his splendid example of bravery and his way of training pilots.* In the face of such flattery, the famously difficult and plain-spoken Samson could do nothing less than to ask Mrs Hewlett to fly with him – which she did at once – and then to invite her to the Mess. By Billy's benchmark – the quality and quantity of breakfast or tea, plus high-spirited fun with a group, all male and young, that included wrestling with recalcitrant cars – her weekend in Sheerness with Cecco had been one of the very best.

The need for economy, plus a touching faith in the August weather being kinder than the previous year, meant that the old De Dietrich was once again packed to overflowing. The advertised start of the race was scheduled for six a.m., Saturday 16th, which meant a late night drive to Southampton.[10] It was a jaunt to remember and it only seems fair to allow Blondeau to interject his centime's worth; the capital letters below represent his heavily accented English.

The 'round England sea-plane race' was starting at Southampton and we wanted badly to see it. We worked hard all day, at night Cecco and Pia came to the flat. A ROYAUME OF UNION OF ENGLAND COMPETION FOR THE FLIGHT. I WAS NOT IN IT. *We all, with Kroshka, got into our old two-seater, furnished with a searchlight tied on with string in front of the radiator, and set off for Southampton about 11 p.m. We got to the downs above Winchester about 2 a.m., tired, very hungry, cramped, blinded with dust, deaf with the rattle of the car. There in the dark we voted for rest and refreshment. We sat in a row by the roadside in the glare of the searchlight, fed, drank, then all five fell asleep. Suddenly we started up, awakened by a strange noise. We found a Royal Mail van had stopped and was wondering at the strange sight. It was dawn, the searchlight still burning showed a primus stove in the roadway, four people and a dog peacefully sleeping. When we shewed signs of life, the Mail van went on. Much refreshed by our rest, we resumed our journey, arriving at the Hamble river sea-plane station at 8 a.m.* WHERE THERE WERE SOME OF ENGLISH NAVY MEN AT AN HOTEL THERE, COMING THERE TO FLY. WE ARRIVE VERY EARLY – TRAVEL ALL NIGHT. ARRIVE AT THAT PLACE EARLY IN THE MORNING. THERE WAS NOT A THING AND WE BLEW THE HORN OF THE CAR. *One of our former pupils was C.O.*[11] SPENSER GREY WHICH WAS IN THE NAVY LIKE CECCO. *He came out in pyjamas, rubbing his eyes. We all shouted at once. He said, 'Just stop that awful car' – (it had stopped some time) – 'now come in to breakfast.' We came in, had baths, got rid of some dust,* BECAUSE WE WERE INVITED MRS HEWLETT AND ME TO HAVE BREAKFAST AT THE TABLE OF ADMIRAL MARK KERR[12] WITH ALL THESE MEN, OFFICERS ETC. *We filled up with heavenly coffee in company with an Admiral, a journalist, many aviators and beautiful ladies* AND THEY WERE FRENCH. THEY ASK ME,

DO YOU KNOW WHERE THEY COME FROM? CAME FROM A PLACE IN PARIS. I DID WELL KNOW, IT WAS A – WITH A VERY BAD REPUTATION – STREET FULL OF … SORT OF WOMEN. IT WAS ONE OF THOSE WOMEN, IT WAS ABOUT RUNNING SOME PLACES LIKE THAT, WITH GIRLS.

Discretion, however, sealed Blondeau's lips and, after breakfast, the motley party boarded the Air Station tender for transfer to the motor launch, *Enchantress*. C.G. Grey, editor of the *Aeroplane* and a loyal and supportive chronicler of Hewlett and Blondeau, their Works and deeds, was as vastly amused as themselves by *a well-known, vulgar millionaire got up in full yacht rig.* He was much tickled to note that Sir Thomas Lipton, 'whose interest in aviation hitherto (was) believed to be solely ocular,' was, in the company of 'sundry gentlemen in irreproachable white caps, violently cinematographed on the stern of the *Enchantress*.' That the camera operator 'thought it necessary to don a khaki costume, apparently borrowed from a mounted infantry-man of smaller size, complete with Stohwasser leggings and a khaki cycling cap and goggles' only made Grey rather more savagely hope that 'some of the well-to-do people who at present waste their money on entirely useless racing yachts may be tempted to spend something on the development of waterplanes.'[13]

Due to a number of factors including the late arrival, followed by swift take-off of the one participating pilot, *there was nothing to see*[14] and *after a spread tea on shore* the disappointed five set off for London. That night, two company directors, one naval officer and a young woman, chaperoned by one Great Dane, slept in the New Forest on beds improvised from fir branches, a stream their *en suite* bathroom, a picnic breakfast their room service. The 'waterplanes' might have failed them, but Billy had only praise for their faithful servant. *We did the whole journey there and back without a single stop for car repairs, one tyre burst with a loud report as we drove back into the works. We most religiously thanked and blessed that old De Dietrich for giving us such a joy ride. We even washed her – our utmost mark of gratitude.*

The whispers of war grew louder, the pace of production of military aircraft quickened. Omnia Works supplied aircraft to the French and Russian governments and, after an inspection by draughtsmen from the Royal Aircraft Factory at Farnborough, was contracted to construct two

BE2a, a biplane developed for reconnaissance work (one, BE2a no. 50, was to become one of the most famous machines in the R.N.A.S., serving in the U.K., France, Flanders and the Dardanelles). During their visit, the government draughtsmen had also expressed an interest in acquiring some patterns that Gustave had developed for use in the Works. Evidently, despite their request being refused, they made drawings of the patterns and later got the credit for inventing them. Practised at being the superior underdog, Billy commented: *It is a great asset to be capable of using other people's ideas and getting all the credit as well.*

In April 1914, the partnership of Hewlett and Blondeau became a registered limited company. Mrs H.B. Hewlett held 2001 ordinary shares, as did Monsieur G.Blondeau. Mr Maurice Hewlett held 1,000 preferential shares, a significant gesture for a man who had lectured some 5,000 working men in Leicester on war prevention in the month Billy left him for France.[15] Then he had said: 'If the Labour parties of Europe agreed that upon any Declaration of War in Europe there should be a simultaneous General Strike, not only that war, but all war, would cease.' Maurice's socialism – more idealistic tendency than deep-rooted, heart and soul belief – and his pacificism were both effectively compromised by his patriotism and his love for the two members of his family preparing for the fight. Now, faced with a bleak prospect as an author – sales no longer earnt him the income he had once enjoyed – Maurice was prepared to provide more capital than he could really afford and stand guarantor to the bank for over a thousand pound overdraft for the sake of Billy and her company.

Hewlett and Blondeau was at the limit of its capacity at Vardens Road. Without space in which to expand, new premises had to be found. All points north, east, south, and west of London accessible by car and train, from Kent to Essex, Hampshire to East Anglia, yielded nothing suitable. At last, a London agent came up with a promising site, which a deposit, as a gesture of goodwill until the title deeds had been located, would secure. Billy was all for paying, but Gustave counselled caution; no deeds, no deposit, but, yes, a meeting the following Monday. What happened next, as extraordinary as it sounds, was, according to Billy, true. Saturday mid-day, an unsigned telegram dispatched from the Regent Street post office was delivered to the Works. It read: *The Duke d'Orleans wishes to meet you Sunday morning at (address given quite close to the projected ground).*

Billy would have returned the wire to the delivery boy as 'opened by mistake', but Gustave accepted the telegram, as he had an idea that it was one of their flying friends using the Omnia Works as a lover's post box.

By Sunday morning, the missive was still uncollected and, for fun, the two of them decided to take a picnic, drive out to the address and await events. They found a small house with a long drive and stables and fields beyond. After a wait in the car, when nothing happened, Billy took the telegram and herself up the drive. The owner of the house, a large, elderly man clad in very sporting clothes, assured her that, if her partner was a Frenchman, the telegram had not been sent in error. As he showed them around his grounds, he explained that he was a horse breeder and, more relevantly for them, a Francophile. He knew from his own tenancy agreement that there was a clause in the title deeds that precluded the building of a factory on the land they were interested in. Not wishing to jeopardise his own tenancy by openly warning them, he had hit upon the plan of sending a telegram, in the hope that mention of the Duke of Orleans – someone whom he knew well and was indeed expecting as a house guest – would be intriguing enough for them to follow it up. The sporting gentleman's horses much admired, their picnic enjoyed in his garden and every protestation of thanks given, the grateful partners departed. That night, they fired off a curt letter of dismissal to the agents.

Our lease had only two weeks to expire, we had contracts and orders for six months. It seemed we were faced with disaster. Once again, out of the blue, rescue appeared; an offer of one acre of land, free, on condition that Hewlett and Blondeau built a factory on it. Deciding it *was just another trap to catch idiots and not worth a penny stamp,* they ignored it; but the Luton businessman telephoned the company and his persistence persuaded the partners to visit the site, part of a very large, very uneven cornfield, and very unsuitable. However, there were three level acres in the middle of the field for which they were prepared to pay. Their benefactor, a businessman and developer, who had conceived the idea of promoting local labour opportunities and thus the demand for housing, accepted their offer. The *Luton News and Bedfordshire Chronicle* reported on 21 May, 1914, that building work for an 'Aeroplane Works for Leagrave' was to commence in readiness for occupation in July. On 24

June, 1914, Hewlett and Blondeau Limited paid Henry Abraham, Plait Merchant, £600 for a parcel of land situated in Backside Field on the west side of Oak Road in the Parish of Leagrave, Bedfordshire. Leagrave, then a small and attractive village, was known as 'the blockers' seaside', as the source of the River Lea at Leagrave Marsh was popular with the workers in the Luton hat trade. It had neither mains electricity – that was not laid on until 1916 after persistent badgering of the Luton Town Council – nor main sewage, so diptheria and cholera were constant and serious health hazards – but, crucially, it did have a main line station, necessary for the transport of finished and crated planes.

Moving the entire contents of an aircraft factory, its machinery, materials, and stores was not a task for the fainthearted. Rehousing it under canvas surrounded by standing corn in the middle of a field, until the main block could be built, added another dimension to the task. The precious machinery was covered by truck tarpaulins hired from the railway, and the stock and stores were housed under canvas. And as a good number of experienced hands chose to exchange the order of Battersea for the alfresco uncertainties of Leagrave, the completion of an Admiralty contract was effected in the temporary shelter of half a barn, 'loaned' to Hewlett and Blondeau Ltd by Mr Abraham's tenants, who farmed the land.

Sad to relate, the matter of the so-called loan became so contentious it ended up being heard in the Luton County Court the following year. The plaintiff, Mr Fensome, was represented by a Mr Lathom; Mrs Maurice Hewlett represented Hewlett and Blondeau Ltd. 'Bright and amusing passages marked the hearing …'[16] and His Honour was moved to exclaim, at the mention of a Lieut. Hewlett, RNAS, who had had his moment of fame some months previously: 'You are not the mother of this aerial man? I didn't know how you could be. You look much too young.' The plaintiff's claim for £4 10s rent outstanding on a portion of his barn was dismissed – Mrs Hewlett, by then a more efficient business woman, had the correspondence to prove their case – and the thirty shillings damages for the corn trodden down by the factory workmen was reduced to ten shillings. His Honour felt Mrs Hewlett had done very well. 'Well, sir, I don't,' said the lady, miffed that they had not been awarded costs.

Within a few weeks of Hewlett and Blondeau settling like crows in the corn field, the main services of gas and water had been laid on, the first workshop had been put up, and a telephone installed. But, before the 50 h.p. gas engine to provide power and lighting had been delivered, war, the threat of which had been grumbling like distant thunder, broke over their heads.

CHAPTER 20

A CHANCE OF SOMETHING DARING TO DO

The Cuxhaven Raid

Perversely, the very event that would ensure the continued expansion of the company, also threatened the new works with imminent closure. The declaration of war had the forty-three year old Blondeau hurrying to the French Consulate with his military papers; there was a serious possibility that he might be called up. He was instructed, however, to continue as he was for the time being. Relieved, Billy turned from the contemplation of an alternative career as a nurse, chauffeur, or pilot and concentrated on the business, but it was not until after a meeting at the Admiralty at which the Omnia Works received further contracts for twelve and six BE2c's respectively, that the uncertainty concerning Gustave's status as a French citizen and possible call-up was resolved. His value to the aircraft industry and the war effort on behalf of the French and British allies lay solely in running the company.

Those early weeks were a nightmare of begging, wheedling, and bribery to build, stock, and staff the new factory and, in the midst of all the madness, Billy, in her *utter ignorance of what war meant*, was to have her first glimpse of the anguish and suffering it was to bring. Among the old hands from Battersea days were several Frenchmen. When their 'appelle' came from the French Consulate, Gustave suggested that he and Billy should accompany one young boy, whose sister, Marie, Billy had promised to care for, to Victoria station. Throughout the achingly silent journey, Marie sat holding her brother's hand, occasionally stroking his arm, as her tears dropped, soundless and unheeded. The silence was broken but twice; the first time the boy begged Mrs Hewlett's pardon for wearing his work overalls, but he wished to keep his one suit clean; the second time he thanked Blondeau for being so good to him. *The tremendous force,* wrote Billy, *the organisation necessary to get at each man, wherever he might be, to take away his will, make him leave his trade, family and life was there before my eyes, and filled them with tears and my heart with sorrow.*

'Cecco is at Westgate with a hydroplane waiting for a chance of something daring to do.' Olga Milne Watson, wrote to her little daughter, Gabriel. 'Poor Auntie Billy is very anxious, but she has so much work to do.' 'I do my best to persuade his mother that he will remain there. God knows! The strain of waiting for sea-news is one of the hardest things to bear.' Maurice wrote, at the same time, to Henry Newbolt. Invasion via the east coast was a serious threat. Maurice holidaying near Aldeburgh in the summer had written: 'A Zeppelin wouldn't at all surprise *me*, and I hope not the defending force.'

Germany, it was believed, had fleets of Zeppelins, whose size and shape magnified their menace to an island hitherto reliant on its fleet and the sea to save it from invasion. Bold action was required to tackle this quietly sinister horror and it was decided the most damage could be done by attacking the sheds in which the Zeppelins were housed and, as they were inaccessible by sea, they should be bombed from the air. Again an impossibility, as there was no plane capable of reaching the Heligoland, let alone making the return journey. However, the Royal Navy, with the *Ark Royal* not yet in commission and the old *Hermes*, on which Cecco had served, inadequate for its needs, had already acquired HMS *Riviera*,[1] a cross-channel passenger packet for the South-Eastern and Chatham Railway Company, and her sister ship, HMS *Engadine*, as well as a slightly older and slower ship, the *Empress,* for conversion into seaplane carriers. With canvas screens on the forecastle and quarterdeck to provide shelter for the seaplanes and long handling booms installed to lift the flimsy craft on and off the ship, the three converted ships and their arsenal had been intended for reconnaissance with the Grand Fleet based at Scapa Flow. Instead, they were attached to the Harwich Force and the world's first carrier strike was planned. Thus, Cecco, an experienced seaplane pilot, was whisked from kicking his heels in Westgate to take part in what became known as the Cuxhaven Raid.

The first sortie with the Harwich Force[2] on 24 October, when it sailed overnight for the Heligoland Bight, was a washout; fog and rain in the morning made take-off for the seaplanes out of the question. The fleet had no option but to turn for home. Frustrated, Commodore Tyrwhitt, commander of the Harwich Force, declared himself 'sick to death of everything connected with aviation.' A touch impatient, perhaps. It was the first seaborne aerial attack attempted and launching it successfully very much depended on the weather. Winter and the North Sea was a stormy combination, although flat calm, so favourable for off-loading the aircraft from the carriers, had its own peculiar drawback. It could take up to four minutes to break the suction between the plane's floats and the sea: a nerve-wrackingly long time if enemy craft were in the vicinity.

A second attempt was aborted in November, and with administrative delays and bad weather, it was not until the end of December that another sortie to bomb the Zeppelin sheds was launched. By then, Commodore Tyrwhitt had modified his attitude to aviation, or pilots and their safety, at least. Mindful of the superiority of the German naval forces and the very real possibility of attack by German aircraft, he ordered that, if the carriers were not in a position to go to the aid of their returning planes, the destroyers of his fleet should do so, albeit with some caution; a destroyer's wash could easily swamp the tiny aircraft. In addition, the line of submarines to be stationed south of Heligoland, were to be ready to attack any enemy vessels and act as supplementary rescue vessels for any ditched airmen. Finally, to lighten the planes to facilitate take-off, they were only to carry petrol for three hours flying time: it would mean less time for the pilots to find their target and return to the fleet, but it would also mean less time for the Germans to locate and attack the British force. On the evening of 23 December, 1914, the seaplanes were shipped aboard their carriers and by five o'clock in the morning of Christmas Eve the Harwich force was underway, while more than a hundred ships of the Grand Fleet were steaming to take up their positions in the mid-North Sea. In all, some one hundred and fifty vessels, directly or indirectly, were to be involved. The mission of the nine aircraft, carrying three bombs each, was to hit the target that the fire power of the Grand Fleet could not reach.

The weather was calm and cold and the journey uneventful until ninety minutes from the launching point, when the British squadron encountered four German trawlers; Tyrwhitt agonised over whether he should abort yet another attempt but, despite the British picking up a flurry of urgent sounding German radio messages, decided to carry on. At six a.m. on Christmas Day the three aircraft carriers stopped, line abreast, twelve miles north-east of Heligoland. Within half an hour all nine Shorts[3] were bobbing gently on the sea as the mechanics, balancing on the floats, unfolded the wings of the Admiralty Folders and Type 135s, and prepared to turn over the engines ready for take-off. The pilots, kitted out with lifebelts, flares, flashlights, matches, maps and charts, provisions for forty-eight hours, first aid dressings, a long list of essential tools and a revolver with six packets of ammunition, climbed down into their cockpits. The three pilots from the *Empress* opted to follow the practice of taking a mechanic in their second cockpit. From the *Riviera*, Flight Cdr Kilner had a passenger, one Lt Robert Erskine Childers RNVR, author of *The Riddle of the Sands* and a keen sailor, whose intimate knowledge of the Frisian coast and German estuaries had proved invaluable in his preparation of the maps and charts used for the raid. All three pilots aboard the *Engadine* favoured keeping their aircraft as light as possible over the dubious benefits of a passenger neither trained as a pilot, nor an observer.

In tactical command of the seaplanes and commanding officer of the three carriers, Squadron Commander Cecil J L'Estrange Malone judged when it was light enough for flying. Tension mounted as the take-off operation, plagued by engine problems and difficulty in lift-off from the calm sea, took far longer than planned. Eventually, Flight Cdr Francis E.T. Hewlett took to the air in his Short No. 135 at 6.56 a.m., followed within the next twenty-five minutes by six others, but engine failure robbed two of the nine pilots[4] of their chance for glory. The weather, however, so calm and clear was soon to turn treacherous: mist, then fog rolled in as the planes flew south-east. Lack of visibility, engine problems, and minimum fuel eventually required that every pilot turn and head for his pick-up point just north of the island of Norderney, his mission a failure; nor was there much hope of retrieving the situation by making useful observations. At the best of times, flying with one hand while jotting down notes with the other was never easy and with fog and enemy fire from either the large German Imperial High Seas Fleet defending the coast, or the land-based batteries, it was impossible.

Meanwhile, the course southwards had not been without event for the British squadron. The slowest carrier, the *Empress*, had had to be rescued from attack when she fell behind before she could creep to her appointed place at the agreed rendezvous. The raiding force began to straggle back; the first to be picked up was Flight Cdr Ross in Short No 119, but as his fuel was so low, he was forced to land near the destroyer *Lurcher*, which then delivered him and his seaplane to the *Engadine*, an hour's tow away. Short No. 136, with Kilner and Childers aboard, spluttered in with a failing engine but enough fuel to reach their carrier *Riviera*; Edmond's No. 811 followed shortly. These two were the only planes to reach their carrier, thanks to the commander of the *Riviera*, Lieut. E.D.M. Robertson, insisting on their carrying fuel for four hours flying time rather than three. Two German seaplanes now livened things up by bombing the squadron, but retreated in the face of lively, if inaccurate, British fire. With four planes overdue and the three-hour deadline up, Commodore Tyrwhitt hung on. Ten men had taken to the air, six had not returned. After a wait of five hours and several skirmishes in which German submarines were repulsed, the Commodore reluctantly ordered the squadron home.

Five of the six missing men, unbeknownst to the fleet up top, were safe and enjoying Christmas dinner, courtesy of Lieut. Commander Martin Nasmith in submarine E11 as it sat on the seabed and their three flimsy craft bobbed to their fate in the waves. Each had been forced to come down some twenty-five miles short of the squadron, luckily, within the vicinity of the E11. Nasmith, with sublime cool daring, rescued the men, who were not without courage themselves, but as the last pilot scrambled into the conning tower hatch and bombs from an overhead German airship made it imperative to crash dive, Nasmith had no time to radio the Fleet.[5] Later, when it was safe to surface and head for home, the good news was passed on to the support destroyer, *Lurcher*, the last of the Harwich Force to leave the area. Now there was only one who had not returned: Cecco.

Billy was cooking breakfast when Pia walked in. Pia, who should have been in London spending Christmas with her father, was walking through the back door on Boxing Morning. She looked *very ill and quite bloodless.*

She just said, "Cecco is lost." Billy gripped the back of the kitchen chair. *"I would much rather be told at once – he's dead."* But no, the Admiralty had told Maurice no more than that Cecco was missing. He had been sighted, standing on the floats of his machine,[6] as two German destroyers headed in his direction: there was a chance he had been spotted and taken prisoner of war. It was to be hoped so, for now terrible gales raged across the North Sea and, although mercifully Billy was not to know it at the time, they were so fierce, four sailors had been swept overboard and three destroyers severely damaged as the Grand Fleet returned to its base in Scapa Flow.

Numb, Billy finished cooking breakfast. Like automatons, she and Pia ate it. Both outwardly calm they travelled to London. Finding *it impossible to realize that the one being (she) loved more than any other was in the utmost danger, might even be dead*, Billy with *M. suffered, each in (their) way* and *tried hard to keep the hope in the other alive*, over that Saturday and Sunday. But the waiting for news became too much and Billy decided to return to Leagrave and the distraction of work. On the Monday, the raid was headline news. In the hands of some elements of the press, the Admiralty statement became a story with a capital S. The fate of the 'daring and skilful pilot' was made all the more piquant by whose son he was and, depending on which newspaper you read, he was either the son of the famous novelist, Maurice Hewlett, or the son of the famous airwoman, Mrs Maurice Hewlett, who had taught him to fly. Letters of condolence flooded in from friends, acquaintances and even members of the public. Maurice filled his days with writing letters. 'I have seen or heard from almost all his companions in the attack. They all say that he came down unhurt, that he was seen standing on the float ... (of his seaplane). He had on a floating jacket and is a wonderful swimmer. All we can do now is to wait with patience and courage. My wife is awfully brave about it, down at Leagrave working hard. Pia is with me – very quiet and even-minded. I simply wait for the telephone or a telegram, because I can't afford that either of them should get it unprepared. It's pretty bad. But the kindness of people of every sort and kind, known and unknown, is perfectly extraordinary. It *does* console; I never thought it would – but it does. And it humiliates me too, to feel how ungracious I have often been, and how arrogant.'[7]

'We all feel the loss of your son very keenly both for his personal charm which endeared him to all and for his professional ability which was exceeded by very few if any in the Naval air service.' So wrote the Captain of the *Riviera*, E.D. Maxwell Robertson. 'Always cheery, and quite regardless of his personal safety he was always as keen as possible when there was a chance of doing anything. In justice to him though I must say that he always took any obvious precautions and did not make the mistake of confusing foolhardiness with boldness … As long as I knew that he was prisoner of war I should quite reconcile myself to his temporary loss, much as we should all miss him both personally and professionally.' Comforting words. 'With regard to his clothes etc. an inventory has been made and they will be dispatched to you shortly. Most of his things however are at Grain Island including his motor bicycle and I have written to the Commanding Officer there informing him of the course I have taken.'[8] Not such comforting words.

Six days after his disappearance, there was still no news of Cecco. In Leagrave, Billy was touched beyond measure by the unspoken sympathy of the work force expressed in helpful tiny ways, or by waiting at doors and corners just to say good-morning or good-night. At home, where the portraits of 'Mrs Bird', pen and ink pictures of every kind of bird from chicken to eagle executed by her irreverent but affectionate offspring, flapped damply in the draughts, the waiting was all the harder to bear. Hope began to slip from her grasp. On New Year's Eve, the night for resolutions, she forced herself to accept what she believed lay ahead: life without her beloved son. As she did so – and exactly as it should always be – there was a thunderous knocking at the front door There, panting and with barely breath to speak, stood one of her employees. How he came to be the messenger is not clear, but it had something to do with the lateness of the hour, the Works telephone, Billy's lack of one, and the determination of Maurice and the Admiralty that she should get the news immediately. *"He's safe"* – *a gasp for breath* – *"your son."*

It was too late to travel to London that night, the last train had long gone, so Billy had to wait for the next morning to hasten to Northwick Terrace. There she found Maurie in the bath and they *both made more bath water with tears of joy.* The fates had been kind and the Hewletts were spared the heartache of the deaths, crippling wounds, illnesses and breakdowns suffered by those within and without their circle. Cecco was safe and well in neutral Holland and would be returned home as soon as diplomatic measures would allow. Throughout all that New Year's Day and over the weekend, they were joyful and humble in the light of the great goodwill and kindess expressed by the hundreds of letters now sent in celebration. As Henry James put it in his loquacious and emotional letter: 'No one can be possibly surer of your utterly overwhelmed postal state than yours and your wife's.'

Most reactions, however, were brief. 'Hearty congratulations on splendid news in todays' papers. Ripping!' from their old friend, the artist Walter Cadby. 'Hurrah! AHH' wrote Anthony H Hawkins, who had earlier written with a message of sympathy and hope. 'Do come and see us some Friday evening and bring daughter,' commanded Angela Thirkell. 'I was with the Sutros last night when the message came, and rejoiced with them' – William Archer. 'I have been going about all day happy for your sake. Yours ever, Q.' – Quiller Couch. Barrie, Belloc, and Binyon, Colvin, Gosse, Harrison and Newbolt and many, many more by their kindness 'humbled' Maurice 'to the dust'. W.B. Yeats's friend, Dunsany expressed the appeal of Cecco's safe return from the daring (albeit unsuccessful) raid: 'Dear Mr. Hewlett, A line to congratulate you on the exploit of your son which is so in keeping with the heroic age that your spirit seems to reside in. That he should have come safe out of it is the final novelist's touch, showing him to be the descendant of your dreams, for I notice that the hero is never killed even in such desperate ventures. You never I think wrote quite such a thrilling tale as the fortunate journalists who had the Cuxhaven raid to describe. Yours sincerely, Dunsany. P.S. I go out next month.'[9]

Edward Marsh, private secretary to Winston Churchill,[10] the then Lord of the Admiralty, wrote to Maurice: 'My dear Hewlett, I hasten to send you this thrilling and magnificent story, envying your feelings when you read it! Don't show it except to your wife and daughter (from whom I had a charming visit this morning) till you see it in the papers, as perhaps the Air Department may have cut out some details. Yours ever, E.M.' The 'magnificent story' was Cecco's official report. For the informal and even more interesting report, the Hewletts had to wait until the evening of 3 January, when Cecco came home.

The hero of the moment was as astonished by all the fuss, as he had been to receive a telegram of congratulation from his king. In fact, he had

had to seek enlightenment as to his unknown well-wisher, George R.I., was. As Cecco saw it, he had taken part in an action and failed and his safe return was thanks to two Dutch guardian angels, the captain of a fishing trawler and the British Vice-Consul in Ijmuiden; without the first he would have died, without the second he would have been imprisoned.

Like his fellow pilots, Cecco had been hampered by the mist and cloud. Forced to glide down to 200 feet in order to see the water and to check he was on course, an enemy cruiser spotted him. Enemy fire and evasive action, combined with the poor visibility, meant he had to judge whether or not he was over his target by his flying time. When he dropped to about 150 feet and saw nothing but open country, he realised it would be useless to drop his bombs and that he must turn back. Flying through the mist he was cheered when it suddenly cleared, but rifle fire from a Zeppelin that silently appeared from a cloud above him required that he temporarily alter course out of range. After three and a half hours flying and still with not a speck of the flotilla in sight, the Short's engine began to missfire; spotting what looked like a fishing vessel he circled it, ascertained it was Dutch, landed and secured astern. The captain, regrettably, had no oil for the overheated engine, so all Cecco could do was to wait for it to cool and hope to restart it for what he thought would be a quick dash to find the British fleet. Two hours later and an engine stubbornly resistant to any useful activity, there was not a lot more to be done. With hopes of spotting a ship fading fast, as darkness and the wind increased and Captain Konijen grew increasingly concerned that he should not be discovered by the Germans assisting an enemy, Cecco saw nothing for it but to scuttle his craft.[11] He punched holes in both main floats' tail compartments and, with his revolver, shot holes in the tail float: nose first the plane sank, leaving the tail plane and rudder tossing on the sea. Grateful for the offer of sanctuary aboard the *Maria van Hattem*, Cecco took, as a memento of his murdered Short no.135, the clock from its dashboard.

As hospitable as his hosts were, Cecco found the next six days pretty tough. The primitive and cramped conditions on board were made worse by the need to batten everything down as the trawler rode out the storm. Thrown so often out of the berth, which the captain had kindly found for him, Cecco chose to sleep on the floor. When his emergency rations were finished, he ate the same food as the crew – fish, gutted on a board, fried and placed back on the same board for every man to grab his share. None too keen on herring at the best of times, Cecco was grateful to the captain for some garlic sausage and dark rye bread, even though it was cut with the one fishy knife. When the weather allowed for fishing, he helped with the nets and navigational duties. Ironically, communication between the Englishman and the captain was in German: the German tutor with his cylindrical hat of Cecco's childhood had had his uses after all.

Satisfied with his catch, the Captain at last made for Ijmuiden. There the Port Authority ordered the trawler's unexpected guest to follow them ashore; he, however, refused to move anywhere until he had seen the British Consul. After some altercation and much grumbling, Mr Reygers-Bergen, the British Vice Consul, was found and fetched. He took Cecco to his residence and, over the next couple of days, allowed his charge the luxury of the use of a bath, good food, and a change of clothes that did not reek of fish. More importantly, he successfully argued that Flight Cdr Hewlett had not been engaged in an act of war at the moment he was picked up by the neutral fishing vessel outside the three mile limit, whereby he should be treated as a shipwrecked mariner, not a prisoner of war.

Captain Cornelis Konijn and his crew were given a £100 reward by the British Government – the only material benefit of the Cuxhaven raid for anyone. However, the benefits in terms of morale for the RNAS, in particular, and the public, in general, were beyond price. The courage and daring of all the airmen who, for well over three hours, flew in open cockpits in the fearful cold and wet of winter weather and who cocked a snook at the German High Seas Fleet, made the technical failure of the Cuxhaven Raid seem like a victory.[12]

CHAPTER 21

A CONTROLLED ESTABLISHMENT

A mixed blessing

One day at home with his *'nervy'* family, then it was time for Cecco to report back for duty, but on the way he made a diversion and the Omnia Works made sure to show its appreciation. The men banged hammers, files and other suitably robust and noisy tools in accompaniment to their cheers and Cecco, for whom the failure of his mission and the destruction of his plane had made the Press attention unwarranted and tiresome, was touched by the spontaneous outbreak of such rough music. Needless to say, one half of the directorship of the company positively blazed with pride and joy!

As a company working in munitions, Hewlett and Blondeau Ltd qualified for an armed guard supplied by the Leagrave Detachment 2nd Supernumerary Company, 5th Battalion Bedfordshire Regiment. An habitual practice of economy alerted Billy and Gustave to any opportunity they might exploit and cheap labour from the regiment, or the recruits from the near-by training camp (Luton had thousands of servicemen quartered in and around the town), was one of them. The workshops needed to be extended and rather than use the previous unsatisfactory builder, Blondeau drew up the plans and appointed a foreman. Mrs Hewlett with her assurances that it was to everyone's benefit – the men's because the work toughened them up physically, the commanding officer's because it kept his men out of the public house – charmed him into turning a blind eye to such an irregular arrangement. Hewlett and Blondeau benefited, because the men were paid mere pocket money: but that went unsaid. They hesitated, however, before accepting the Reverend Rust's offer of his services. The only work available was in the erecting shop, under a foreman – not quite the place for a vicar – but, by his example and comradely behaviour, the Vicar of Ridgmount proved to be a *saint in overalls* and *worth a year of sermons.*

Not so the local vicar. His first mistake had been to ask Mrs Hewlett never to make a repeat spectacle of herself, such as the one that had so greatly shocked his Sunday morning flock. The spectacle? The Fiat all strung about with saucepans, colanders, clothes and shoes, with a grubby Gustave behind the wheel, next to him a bulky looking Billy, with her overalls over her coat, holding a jug full of milk and a loaf of bread and, in the back, an equally bulky looking Pia embracing a dressmaker's dummy with a red bust and wire skirts. It was a cold October day in 1915 and they were moving out of the jerry-built house that had revealed itself to possess but one redeeming feature, its proximity to the factory. Although new, it had been so badly built it leaked on all sides. The windows either let in the rain, or the wind blew them into the garden. Door handles came away in the hand thus enforcing departure via the window. Fires refused to draw or to use the chimneys for smoke extraction and earwigs crawled round and round the cornices, or into boots, sponges and clothes. Beds had to be placed as far from the damp walls as possible and aired, if the sun allowed, in the garden. *Four good curses from four suffering victims, some in English, some in expressive French, were the daily portion of the builder.* Having profited by her share in her mother's estate – Mrs Herbert had died earlier in the year – Billy was able to afford a well-built, well-designed bungalow (it is now divided into two) with a large garden and a large cart-shed, which she used as a temporary store for whatever furniture she and Maurice no longer had a use for. Much of it came from the Old Rectory in Broad Chalke, a family extravagance given up in 1912.

The vicar's second mistake – to reprove Mrs Hewlett for her irreverent Sabbath behaviour – was made the greater by his doing so during her lunch hour. Mrs Hewlett, a working woman with time neither to pay nor to receive calls, as the vicar must surely understand, had but one day in the week in which she and her family were not engaged in war work:

Sunday. And, as she utterly disagreed with the vicar that the war was a punishment for everyone's sins and only to be won by prayer, she would continue to see it as an engineers' war which she would help win by making aeroplanes. The vicar got the hint and did not call again.

Billy's working day began at seven in the morning, which she hated, but once she had established a routine of always having her alarm clock ten minutes fast, bathing at night, leaving her clothes ready to jump into and her bike ready to leap on to, she managed very well. After she had done the rounds of every shop and checked that her particular concerns, namely the wing room, the dope room, the painting shop and the wing-wiring gang lacked for nothing, she would hastily pedal home for breakfast, after which she returned to her office in a more seemly management mode.

Blondeau, on the other hand, preferred to arrive later and stay later, when the offices were quieter after 6.30 p.m. Undisturbed, he could then better interpret the drawings of the planes to be constructed, draw up working plans for each of the shops, calculate materials and parts required, and set in motion the manufacture of the requisite components. He lived in constant dread of the arrival of blueprints for modifications, as they might arrive any time throughout the weeks of preparation for production. On one occasion, the first machine was off the line and awaiting packing for dispatch when revised blueprints arrived.

Under the Munitions Act of June 1915, Hewlett and Blondeau Ltd was classified as a Controlled Establishment, which gave the newly created Ministry of Munitions – responsible for all aspects of munitions production – temporary government control over factories such as theirs. The Ministry also had the power to set limits on munitions firms' profits and to control wage rises, and it had negotiated with the engineering unions for the standard workshop practices of limitation of production and the ban on female labour to be lifted. No longer could Hewlett and Blondeau refuse to take on union men, although the allocation of skilled Australian engineers, union men to a man and towers of strength and productivity who turned out the metal components[1] as though they were toys, sweetened that bitter pill a trifle

Another aspect of the Ministry's governance which M. Blondeau and Mrs Hewlett, justifiably proud of their reputation for good workmanship, found deeply galling was the imposition of Government inspectors.

These men, who were evidently unfit for active duty or employment in the manufacture of supplies, were also bereft of knowledge of aviation and lacking in common sense. One inspector examined and passed five thousand small nuts. As he used an iron tool and a hammer to stamp each one of them with his inspector's mark, every nut was flattened and rendered useless. *Another, with a seal for preventing fraud, broke into small pieces twelve ash longerons,*[2] *all planed wood. By merely cutting out the knots several hundred feet of good ash could have been used for small struts. Wood was rare and very precious.* In order to teach a lesson to one, *who thought he was very clever, discovering faults and bad work,* Gustave ordered a finished machine, *smothered with stamps, lead blobs on all cable, rubber stamps on the wings etc.,* ready for dispatch, to be dismantled. Aghast, Billy and the men in the shop watched. Gustave waited for a specific part to be checked by the company inspector and when it was pronounced faulty, called for the government inspector. *He came, he saw, he said nothing, his ignorance glared him in the face before all the people he had bullied. I own,* wrote Billy, *I was fearfully pleased and did not feel ashamed of being so.*

Billy was naturally predisposed to question officialdom. *Meek, cringing and subservient,* which she perceived to be the necessary requirement of a supplier, she never was. Any pretension, or misplaced attitude of superiority from any official whom she felt to be her inferior, had her ready to appeal to her friends in high places:[3] *the underlings disliking their ways being brought out into the light.* For Billy, a stern moralist, but not of the sex and religion school, something was either right, or it was wrong, and those that trespassed by her lights were ascribed the worst motivation for doing so. A former member of the Stock Exchange, sent as Assistant Supply and Production officer, *his ignorance only surpassed by his laziness and his "side",* she particularly disliked as he did her. It is to be hoped that Mr Ashley Pope, imposed upon the company as a manager in 1916, was not that gentleman. Mr Pope's task was to regulate working practices that had been suitable for a small, hands-on business with a staff of twenty-five, but which were counter-productive for a staff of three-hundred. He found the two partners 'with their minds in the air', but charitably credited Mrs Hewlett with industry, careless as she was of hours and meals; the workers, he noted, were doing any jobs they thought needed doing; tea was made too often; and smoking was rife throughout the factory, including the highly inflammable doping area.

His concern over smoking is understandable. There had been a fire in the wood store one night. Luckily there had been little damage and Mrs H. on night duty – a duty that she hated – had thoroughly enjoyed presenting herself as an easy target for the hoses. Rather to her disappointment she remained dry: she was sure there were a few who would have been tempted to soak her. The blackout warden, on the other hand, would have been relieved the flames lighting up the night sky were quickly doused; being bombed by a Zeppelin was a genuine fear.

I quite forget what the strike was about now, something to do with Lloyd-George and trades unions and higher wages generally. Anyhow 73 men out of 300 'went out' in accordance with their unions' instructions. It dislocated the entire organisation at a moment of great importance in our output. A guess that Billy was referring to the May Strikes of 1917 was confirmed by the *Luton News*. Its coverage, however, lacked the drama of Billy's account in which she and Gustave, righteously indignant, held out against the scurrilous union men. Genuinely concerned for their staff's welfare, but distrustful of unions, whose practices they considered dishonest or unnecessary, Messrs Hewlett and Blondeau were never going to be sympathetic to a strike, official or unofficial.

Discontent had been growing steadily among the working class. War had brought high prices, poor housing and shortages of coal and bread, all made worse by the stepping up of conscription. As more and more skilled men, such as engineers, were called up, the Government, contrary to their earlier agreement with the Amalgamated Society of Engineers, planned to allow the use of skilled female labour in private factories, that is, factories that were neither nationalised, nor Controlled Establishments ,under the jurisdiction of the Ministry of Munitions. A movement of protest began in Rochdale and spread to other engineering centres and, on Friday, 11 May, although unauthorised by the Executive Council of the A.S.E., the Luton Shop Stewards called a strike.

Almost at once a deputation of foremen, without coats, and sleeves rolled up (a token of their readiness), many girls from the offices, several from the machine shop, waited outside our office and begged an interview. Gustave and I were really terrified as we bid them enter. An old hand from Clapham Junction spoke for them all. They were ready there and then to work as ordered so that the twenty-odd machines, in construction, would be delivered on time. *Struck dumb with the brave spirit of co-operation and the simple way they stood ready for orders*, the partners hastily re-organised the work as well as they could and sent telegrams to those who were indispensable to the running of certain shops, asking them to come to the office. A *long rigmarole about their fellow workers at the front who would return to find their wages lowered, their places taken by women, and no work* cut no ice with Mrs Hewlett. For her the *obvious answer was that they* (the men at the front) *wanted help now, so as to be kept alive to return at all*. The promise that those who did not return to work immediately would never work for Hewlett and Blondeau again persuaded four strikers to change their mind.

The next *ten days and nights were a nightmare of struggle and superhuman effort. Gustave was a wonder, he could put his hand and brain to any work and do it better and quicker than an ordinary workman. He was so quick, never flurried, but just got it done.* The men were awed by his expertise and energy. At the end of the *lurid ten days* and with the order successfully completed, Mrs Hewlett and Mr Blondeau, still in their working clothes, waited on their workers during a thank you tea.[4]

In fact, the tea was two days after the strike was called. 'Quite an unexpected and interesting little event took place at the works of the well-known aeroplane manufacturers, Messrs. Hewlett and Blondeau Ltd., on Sunday last … The piece in the local paper sounding more like a publicity handout than a piece of reportage continued, quoting Mrs Hewlett: 'Mr Blondeau and I have asked you to tea so as to have a few minutes in which to tell you how glad we are that we have the same aims and the same way of expressing them. They are: We all want to give our friends and relations at the Front the aircraft they ask for. … I have written to Mr. Forbes, of the Ministry of Munitions, and told him that the majority of workers in Hewlett and Blondeau's have behaved like soldiers, and that the Ministry should be proud of them, as the output will not suffer because of the strike. All here can meet the soldiers when they return and say, "I have never struck work while you were fighting," but I also want you to add to this one great virtue, generosity. Don't show any grudge. "Judge not, that ye be not judged," says the Bible, and very good advice, too. Do not spoil a good deed by even a little bad word. The men on strike are in the minority here, make allowance for their different way of looking at life… We recommend you for distinction in munitions work for saving output. A propeller should be your medal (loud applause).'

The following Sunday, 20 May, the strike was called off after the direct intervention of the Prime Minister, Lloyd George. Issues raised would be resolved between the Executive Council and the Government; charges against strike leaders under the Defence of the Realm Act would be dropped and men returning to work should do so without fear of victimisation.[5]

On the Monday morning, on the entrance gates to the Omnia Works for all to see, two telegrams were pinned; one was from the Ministry of Munitions; the other from the Queen, who thanked the workforce and congratulated them on their loyalty. *You can imagine they were appreciated and read by all, gloated over and copied for keeps.* If they were, it is a pity no copy remains today.

After our joy came tribulation at its heels. Five Union representatives demanded that all who had been on strike should be reinstated, same work, same pay. Two directors pointed out that the disruption to routine and the concerted effort to complete the contract in hand had displaced preparation for the next order, which meant an enforced *lull in production,* so no work, no pay. Victimisation, cried the men; practical truth said Blondeau and showed them the order books. *'We leave it to you,'* weasled the Ministry of Munitions, when Mrs Hewlett phoned for advice. Losing her patience and telling *one man that he was too ignorant to argue with,* was not a good way of trying to make the men see reason. *"You oughtn't to speak to our leader like that, "* one said. *"You have a poor leader if he can't answer a woman with sense,"* she said. And the consequence was? A threat: if the men's demands were not met *the whole of England would be called out on strike.*

"A threat is the last weapon to make me give in, from now on I'll fight without considering the issue, you shall be responsible for your own deeds," was Billy's ringing return, as she once again left Blondeau to fight his corner, while she *slipped out to the telephone.* Mrs Hewlett brought the Ministry of Munitions up to date. They, a trifle rashly given the Prime Minister's placatory intervention, evidently thought *a strike would do harm for the moment, but they were prepared for it if necessary.* If that indeed had been their attitude, Mrs Hewlett returned to the fray, armed with plenty of cigarettes: they all smoked furiously, while the men talked *the hind leg off any dog (even Kroshka's).* In the end, Blondeau offered them the only job available, cleaning old iron, but on full pay. The men refused such

degrading work. And there, Blondeau had them, they had turned down an offer of re-employment. The men were paid off with ten days back pay. As they left they vowed to show the cheating war time amateurs, a woman and a Frenchman at that, whose Sunday tea had been pure bribery, that they could not treat labour the way they had, trying to run an engineering works by filling it with women. Billy disdained to shake their hands and *advised them to have some food and beer, as both their manners and tempers were offensive*. 'At a firm outside Luton there has been some little trouble,' reported the Luton newspaper, 'but the men were confident that the firm, which it was stated had refused to reinstate men who had come out, would give way, and everything would be amicably settled by this weekend.'

'War time amateurs' was in many ways a fair criticism. In describing her on-going battle with the union men, which Billy thought *great fun, but very silly,* she wrote of when there was a *real Works Manager*, or *a real General Manager*. It was as if she recognised that she had never aspired to run a 'real' business. Her motivation, almost from the beginning, had been patriotism. Without any preconceived ideas as to how a business should be run and a readiness that matched Blondeau's to muck in when necessary made her an even more unusual director than she already was. However, she knew there was one area where she should not even try to muck in: running the canteen. To her relief two angels came to her rescue; one in the guise of a cheery cook, who even did a little singing and dancing on the side; the second, an efficient manager, the mother of a pilot whom Billy met when visiting her Squadron Commander son in charge of seaplane stations Dover and Dunkirk. As the canteen was in a converted garage with a corrugated iron roof and an earth floor, their talent to transform wartime rations into imaginative meals was remarkable. When at last a well-appointed canteen and entertainment room was built, suitable for a staff of three-hundred, it was too late, the war had ended.

An equally felicitous outcome of Billy's chance meeting with Mrs Whitehouse was the arrival of two more dogs, Mac and Hero. Mac, an Aberdeen terrier, belonged to Cecco. A fussy passenger – his preference was for a Short seaplane for the crossing from Dover – Mac showed an unfortunate tendency to collect too many fleas and ticks in the sand dunes of Dunkirk for his own, as well as Cecco's comfort. Denied his flying trips,

Mac took to wandering about the town in search of his master and the day he was picked up as a stray was the day it was decided he should live with Kroshka until Cecco had a posting suited to them both. The Airedale Hero, on the other hand, was too large and heavy to fly and generally spent his time around the plane sheds, or watching Whitehouse, his master, taking off and landing in Dover harbour. Alone one day, he went down to the harbour and boarded a destroyer. For his master, their meeting in Dunkirk was serendipitous, for Hero it was what he expected; they returned to Dover, each by their original mode of transport. Rather pleased with himself, Hero tried the same trick once again, but this time the destroyer went to Felixstowe, where he stayed. It was by sheer chance that he and Whitehouse, grounded after a flying accident and on a temporary posting, were briefly reunited two months later. Transferred to guard duty at the Omnia Works on Mrs Whitehouse's special pleading, Hero *took his war work in the same spirit of devotion to duty as the rest of the firm.*

Gentle Kroshka was the guard dog for the babies of the workers. Once fortnightly there was either a social or a concert, often followed by dancing, in one of the big workshops or the hall of the local school in Norton Road. During the dancing, the babies would be put with Kroshka on the platform. Bored, but patient, he would suffer them to pull him about and sit on him. He treated Mac the same way, often rescuing him from other dogs that Mac had goaded into ferocity. Mac lived to chase rats and cats.

Cats and sparrows! They were war time pests for us, wrote Billy. No door could be left open or window left uncovered by a wirescreen, otherwise one or other were in the house eating whatever food was left out. One evening, Billy had finished her share of supper, one kidney, and left Gustave his, plus a pat of butter as large as a filbert nut, and some milk in a jug on the kitchen table. Suddenly Gustave, Mac and Kroshka burst into the sitting room with the news that a cat was in the house. Billy rushed to the kitchen; the jug lying broken on the floor was all that remained of supper. Sitting, spitting at the excited dogs from the top of the gas meter, was the cat. With the dogs shut in another room and protected by a pair of fur gauntlet flying gloves, Gustave advanced on the thief, cooing "*Poosi, poosi, come along, poosi.*" The end was swift. *Forgive him, he was a hungry and tired man, he had no supper*: Together they buried the cat in the garden by torchlight.

Billy was at a loss to understand why the cats did not live off the huge numbers of sparrows that ate the dogs' food, the chickens' food, pecked holes in the bread, ate and soiled the butter, blocked the gutters and nested in the chimneys. *Perfect curses*, the sly, wily, cheeky sparrows woke her with their piercing cheeping when she slept out on the porch. She hated them and rated them worse pests than rats and mice. The local council, in their drive against vermin, advertised in the Luton paper of 24 May, 1917: two shillings a dozen for dead rats; threepence a dozen for fully fledged house sparrows, tuppence a dozen unfledged, and a penny a dozen for their eggs. What price sparrows these days?

The last of the animals to feature in life at Leagrave were the pigs. The ultimate in efficient recycling, they were to process canteen leavings into future canteen meat. Housed in a makeshift pen on a bit of rough grass between two work shops, they proved to be expert escapologists, and chasing a speeding pig through the machine shop, or rescuing one from drowning in a large tank of water, after it had taken a wrong turn in its dash for freedom, was splendid sport. They had their own column, The Aeropiggeries, in the house magazine, *Aeromnia*. Avro and A.W, the first in a succession of piglets, were reported to be a trifle disgruntled on hearing their high-flying names, but were swelling visibly. Come the fell day, a butcher and his assistant were found among the packers to dispatch the pigs.

CHAPTER 22

HEWLETT and BLONDEAU'S WAR BABIES

Ministry of Munitions Training School

Dilution of the work force with female labour, as necessary as it was, was a hot rivet of an issue throughout the war, particularly in munitions and engineering, fields traditionally exclusive to men. Under the National Registration Act of August 1915, all women between 16-65 years of age had been required to apply for a Registration Certificate indicating their availability for war work in whatever form it might take. With men being trained up in schemes co-ordinated by the new Ministry of Munitions to replace those skilled men who had volunteered, women were needed to take over the repetitive and unskilled tasks. By the time conscription was made law in 1916, there were some 256,000 women working in the munitions industry. To meet the increased demand for skilled workers, once conscription had thinned their ranks, it was then necessary to train women in skilled work. The government's aim was to double the number of women working in munitions.

The debate about women and work wrangled and broiled throughout the nation. Men feared the loss of their jobs. The craft unions feared that, once it was discovered that women could work as well as men, employers would prefer to use them as cheaper labour. The middle-class establishment feared that women might not willingly return to their roles of child-bearing and home-making, once they had tasted the fruits of good money, some of which, oh heavens, they might even spend on themselves.

The Suffrage movement found it difficult to reconcile their belief that women had the right to equal pay for equal work with the need for women to maintain their biological and traditional role of mother and home provider. It was generally understood that women were needed to do the work for which there was a shortage of men. They were also needed to produce and bring up the next generation and were expected to provide a home for the men, when they returned from the war. However, if women worked outside the home, or away from home, they could be exposed to a range of unwelcome and potentially immoral influences; for example, young girls who worked alongside married women could be corrupted by the married women's talk of sex and childbirth. Further dangers threatened the young working class girls, the majority of whom, prior to the war, would only have found jobs in service; with more freetime and extra spending money to spend on clothes and entertainment, the evils of drink could not be far behind. The weaker sex needed to be protected from themselves. Licensing hours had been imposed, but laws were also introduced to prevent women from drinking in pubs, for if the women spent more and drank more, then they were bound to be so corrupted, and there would be more illegitimate babies.

The 'war baby' scare, whipped up by the press, the church and the pious, did unfathomable harm in Billy's view; far better the Church and the press had done something useful and in silence. The female reporter, who called at the factory to enquire about the company's experience with war babies, was lucky in that Mrs Hewlett was out and she met the General Manager instead, otherwise her reception might have been even frostier. *Brazenly* the reporter asked: *"How many war babies have you had in this firm?" "I only know of one, madam." "Oh, now I'm sure that's not true, surely you suspect more if you don't actually know?" "No," insisted the manager, "our girls have been most disloyal to their country in not increasing our decimated population."* Exit frustrated reporter.

Blondeau, displaying an illogical degree of prejudice, as his argument could well have applied to an untrained man, felt that a woman who had never worked in a factory and had no idea of its rules and conventions would get in the way, good material would be spoilt and a skilled man would be hindered in his work. Billy, while impatient with much of Gustave's argument, nevertheless appreciated that a skilled worker, of any gender, would be reluctant to work alongside an unskilled one. She, therefore, gave a lot of thought as to how to facilitate the integration of women into the workforce and came up with what would now be called an induction course. Serious and heated discussion eventually extracted from Blondeau his consent for a large room to be set aside for the girls, who would become accustomed to factory life while receiving preliminary training in woodwork preparation, glueing and sandpapering.

Once her enterprise was up and running, Mrs Hewlett was greatly surprised to be sent for by the Ministry of Munitions Training Department, which had come to hear of their small-scale, but independent, effort. She was further surprised to learn that the Ministry wanted the school to be expanded to train women and girls for other firms, not just her own, and they wanted her to run it. The supply of teachers and pupils and all costs would be born by the Ministry and a delighted Billy decided the school would be her personal contribution to the war effort, as opposed to her salaried work in the company. She had found a duty, both pleasing and as wonderfully remote from her mother's vision of a woman's duty as the moon from the earth.

The *great, resourceful, broadminded* – you can tell she liked him – Sir James Currie, head of the training department at the Ministry, was a man *who inspired hope, joy in work and who could smooth away every difficulty.* With the task ahead of her, Mrs Hewlett was going to need help and the Munitions Training Department, who were *just splendid to deal with,* arranged for her *to visit their centres, to learn from bigger and better firms how to organise mixed labour.* Billy admitted that she would have been a fool if she had not profited *by their knowledge, organisation and strength.* Blondeau, too, who had come to share her vision of the training school within the company as part of the war effort, agreed to support her all he could in ensuring the existing staff accepted the trainees as just that, not cheap labour.

Finding enough billets for the girls, who arrived ten or twelve at a time, from as far afield as Scotland and Ireland and London, was a headache; accommodation was at a premium with S.K.F. and Vauxhall in Luton, and the munitions factory where the canary girls made shells, bombs and grenades, down the road from Leagrave, at Chaul End. Matching *outlook, manners and sympathy* of landlady and lodger was not always possible, but the talents of one young girl, who was *not very refined and spoke with a cockney accent*, recommended her as an ideal lodger to the wife of a naval captain. Apart from being a professional dancer and very entertaining, she also received a joint of meat from her butcher father, once a week. It was in that cottage that Mrs H. and the Boss enjoyed the most original and lively hospitality of the war. *The dining table for six was a card table, the dishes were each an effort of one of our hostesses. Each one named her own creation, illustrating it on a menu – quite a work of art. Each lady took turns at service, rapidly covering her pretty dress with an overall, she then became Mary Ann, spoke and behaved as a maid as she adopted the part. I wanted to take a turn and put on 'the overall', but they declared they had taken all the jokes, prepared all the 'faux pas' and would not have them interfered with. It was such a success that they did it again. At the bottom of the menu was:*

0000 000 00 00
Add six strokes.

It resolved into – 'good god do go'.

Ever willing to give praise where she thought praise was due, Billy credited the success of the Training school to her quiet, disciplined and orderly secretary, whom she poached from the General Manager's office. However, without her own sense of humour and perceptive concern for the welfare of female staff, the Ministry Training school and the integration of women into the workforce would not have been the success it was. As there was no mention of the dreaded Welfare Supervisor being appointed at Hewlett and Blondeau – all Controlled Establishments qualified for one – it is to be assumed that Mrs H. also filled that office. When the women, after a long, long day, groaned that corruption had surely to have been easier on the feet – a trainee caught recruiting for the oldest profession among her young and not so green fellow pupils had recently been sacked – Mrs H. would probably have grinned. A Welfare Supervisor, on the other hand, might have felt it her right to enquire further into the private and moral lives of the married women and single girls in her care. Too many Welfare Supervisors had been known to stray beyond their worthy workplace duty, which was bitterly resented and led to the suspicion that they were there more for the benefit of management than the workers.

As much as she might roar with laughter when she heard that girls at the Chaul End factory had stripped a man, painted him black and locked him out, Billy, nevertheless, was careful not to employ such potential troublemakers. And, if troublemakers were discovered in the firm, Mrs H. was ruthless in dismissing them. Sometimes, however, if they were among those girls sent by mothers, guardians or friends in the belief that Billy could be relied on to take care of them, they had to be dealt with differently, like the motherless, pretty and vain girl who had run away from the convent of her upbringing. Greeted early one morning by a concerned instructor, Monsieur Toutet, Mrs Hewlett had listened in mounting amusement to his tale of the young Miss, her blouse and its descending neckline. The first week it had been on a level equivalent to four inches below Monsieur Toutet's collar; the second week it had crept two inches lower, about level with the top button of his waistcoat; now, and he had paused dramatically, it was as low as his fourth waistcoat button. What was he to do? Billy, struggling to repress her *most unseemly fits of laughter*, asked the perplexed man to send the young lady to see her.

Rather than reproving the girl, she praised her work and admired her hairstyle. She then asked to see whether a khaki shirt, with a collar and tie of the girl's choosing, to go with her khaki uniform skirt, might not make the girl even prettier. Magically, it did and from thereon the girl expressed her feminity in an impressive variety of ties! Kept *till the end safe from tragedy, the poor child* even starred as the heroine in a short propaganda film in which a munitions worker falls in love with her brawny fellow worker and rescuer from a fire. The amateur prize fighter, picked from the wood machining shop, proved a faint-hearted hero; he utterly refused to pluck the heroine, handsome if a tad heavy, from the window of the burning top floor and demanded a replacement of his own choosing. The now demure young lady, the lightest of the girls – he had checked – played her part to perfection. Not so the workforce. Bent double with laughter they were quite unable to simulate horror and fear as they dashed about, but judicious use of smoke disguised this. By the end of the day, a great number of holes had been made in finished wings, a great deal of fresh paint had been watered and great deal of time had been lost.

Another success for Billy was a deaf girl who applied for training.

When she watched the girl as she read her note, *I'll take you*, it was if she saw the girl's soul. *Some stronger influence behind and beyond me made me take her*, wrote Billy who, in that moment of practical sympathy, had given the girl the means by which to escape her harsh and lonely life. The girl worked in the wood shop for the duration of the war (the foreman regularly asked for more deaf girls – they concentrated and never quarrelled) and then married one of the nicest and steadiest of the men.

But out of all the women and girls from every class, Billy found the most adaptable to be those who, often with a look of mute appeal, admitted to domestic service; theirs, she was able to assure them, had been the most useful training for war work. It was instinct, therefore, that made Billy assign a cook of forbidding mien and a chin of obstinate proportions to intensive instruction from one man, a splicer. After three days, she went to check how the cook was getting on and found her working steadily at her station, an untidy bench in a workshop open to the elements down one side, twisting high tension cable into splices. The latest of the cook's splices Mrs Hewlett took to the government inspector, who passed it and stamped it there and then. *"You are the first woman to make a splice. Up till now it has been done only by men, and chiefly naval men,"* Mrs Hewlett told the cook. *"You have already made one important step in showing that women can do this work and set a whole trade of men free to do other things."* And she arranged for the woman to have her own bench, a vice, a set of tools and a supply of the finest cable.

Three days later, she went to see how the cook was getting on, but found the woman's eyes full of tears and her chin more determined than ever, for every piece of her work had been rejected. Unable to prove it, the ex-cook suspected that the men changed her splices for their rejects. In private, Mrs Hewlett handed the cook some red cotton and instructed her to hide a tiny piece deep inside each splice. A couple of days later, she again visited the woman at her work station. Seeing the rejected splices lying on the bench, she summoned a man, working close by, to cut them all in half: there was not one scrap of red cotton to be seen. Mrs Hewlett told the men exactly what she thought of them, but refrained from sacking them until the cook had personally trained up three female replacements.

Word got round that Hewlett and Blondeau were using girls as splicers. Other companies needed splicers and, as fast as the cook trained them, they were snapped up. The Ministry of Munitions wanted the cook to go and train up women for a company that was splicer-less, but even an offer of £5 a week to work in a firm of great size and modernity would not tempt her to leave a 'place' after so short time; after all she had been seven years in her previous employ, she was earning quite good money, thank you, and she didn't wish to better herself. Eventually, a compromise was reached. The redoubtable cook agreed to be 'lent' to the other company, but only on the clear understanding that it was for no longer than three months.

Mrs H. was devoted to her girls, her *dear friends*, she was proud of their individual and collective achievements and appreciated their stamina and hard work, but the women who touched her most were those who had been used to working in the mills in the north. No strangers to long hours and hard work, they had to cope with the oil, the smell, the noise and monotony of the machine shop during a 13-hour working day from seven in the morning until eight at night, which they did without grumbling. One of them, she loved. Her *devil girl, ugly as a toad but like that animal she had beautiful eyes. A fierce worker* full of boundless energy, no foreman wished to get rid of her, but she was for ever in mischief and Mrs Hewlett was *always being sent word of her latest sin. When I approached her machine to scold or reprove, she gave me a look of such joy, her eyes told me plainly that she knew I loved her, and she really did not care what I said as long as I talked to her. I weakly ended by having a friendly conversation, begging her to try and behave for one week – she promised, kept it to the exact date, when she began again, and I began again.*

So very different to the *small young girl with a lot of fluffy fair hair, very gentle manners, a lady in dress, speech and bearing, who one wonderful day came and asked to do war work.* In that diminutive girl, proficient in higher mathematics, who had worked with her brother in a small engineering works and could file straight and scrape bearings, Billy saw the thin end of a very small wedge for diluting the fitting shop, the last all-male bastion. There had been no training for the shop, as neither the foreman nor Blondeau had wanted any woman messing it about, but as more men were called away and more work came in, the shop struggled to cope without enough skilled staff. *It seemed a cruel way of using such a darling, refined, clever girl,* but who was Billy to refuse such a valuable sacrificial lamb? She detailed the attitude of the Unions to female engineers and the antipathy she would experience from the men and, in the interests of her plan working, Billy warned the girl neither to expect, nor to seek help. Understandably dismayed, the girl meekly agreed to try to do what Mrs Hewlett asked. She was engaged to start at seven o'clock the following Monday morning, lodgings were found and Mrs Hewlett went off to tackle the foreman of the fitters, Mr. Arthur, a nice man and an old hand in the firm.

"Mr Arthur we must get help in your shop, and as we can't get boys, I have found a girl, and I want you to try her."

"But, Mrs H., I don't think it will do, the men will swear sometimes, and that's not nice for a girl to hear."

"I'm always about and I never hear any worse swearing than I use myself, and if I did, I should pretend I didn't hear them."

"But, Mrs. H., the men won't like a woman to be paid like a man."

"Certainly not, not even as a boy. This girl will work one week, and you shall tell me what she's worth – just a shop boy, or improver, or no good at all, and I'll take her away if your report is to that end."

With bad grace Mr Arthur agreed.

The following Friday, Mrs Hewlett asked Mr Arthur, in the most casual way possible, at what rate the girl should be paid. *"She was equal to an improver,"* he enthused, *"and she was most helpful to the Belgians."* He even hinted that her calculations were rapid and exact. Billy credited Hewlett and Blondeau's record of being the only aviation firm to employ equal numbers of men and women to that girl's courage, tact and cleverness. Not every apple in the female barrel, however, was good; the *woman who called herself a lady who applied to run the Red Cross room*, but who felt it beneath her dignity to clean the room herself, was one. And Billy, who had her own very clear idea of how a real lady, titled or otherwise, should act, had great pleasure in dismissing her.

Perhaps if *a lady of great importance*, who made an official visit to Omnia Works, had disarmed the bristling prejudice of one of its directors, there might have been more about Hewlett and Blondeau Ltd than a couple of letters of regret in the archives of the Imperial War Museum. Generally, Billy loathed taking visitors around the Works, *as if it was a show*, but, on this occasion, she believed it would mean good publicity for her training school. She, therefore, ordered the instructors to have their best work on show, forbade anyone to be missing between three and four o'clock, checked that all overalls were clean and mended, and that all floors were thoroughly swept and then laughed at herself for *acting the proud mother showing off her ducklings, hoping they were swans.*

The visitor arrived *supported by a title, a secretary with a notebook and two other ladies* and was greeted by *a small, grubby person,* hatless and in very old clothes; too late did Billy remember her own appearance. She asked if the *grand lady* would like to see the Works first, in order to get an idea of what the girls were doing, and was loftily informed, as the party swept off on their round of inspection, that that was what they had come for. They watched the dear little Irish girl, *the quietest, brownest bit of beauty in the erecting shop,* with her mass of very dark brown curly hair, liquid brown eyes, brown trousers, and brown working coat, who had been trained intensively to wire all the aeroplanes (for a man, a job more suitable for a contortionist). They watched a large hefty girl as she assembled an undercarriage, and others as they doped, sewed, and painted an Avro 504K. They watched the wing-wiring girls in their many coloured overalls and the lady asked for a photograph to be taken of them, despite Mrs Hewlett protesting that they were no longer part of the training school. Finally, they visited *the tin shop, the very worst shop for behaviour, but a wonder for work. They had a place to themselves for their stinks and smoking messes. They were given to singing songs in parts, when the foreman complained that some of the last verses were forbidden, they burst into such a roar of 'Onward Christian Soldiers', he could not be heard.* Mrs Hewlett gave the women a very stern eye on entering and the Lady was duly impressed by these grubby 'angels' and wanted a photograph of them too, with the soldering iron and baths of smoking solder and the rack of cables in sets along the wall.

At last, they reached the school, nicknamed the *War Babies*. Billy swelled with pride, for their school was the only one in which girls were trained as aeroplane mechanics in a place devoted to aeroplane construction alone. Now her visitor would be impressed by how their excellent results were achieved. *Horror of a woman. She just walked through, said "Very nice" and did not ask for any photograph or information.* The Lady then praised Mrs Hewlett's most interesting work and assured her that she would be given *due and adequate recognition* in the piece she was going to write. Robbed by surprise of an adequate reply, and clutching the list of photographs requested by the lady's secretary, Mrs Hewlett wondered irritably, as she waved off the party of visitors, how it was that her guest could get petrol, when she could not?

That night, Billy *thought the visit out with calm and reason* and concluded that it was *one of those put-up shows of lauding women's work, rewarded with a title or medal which everyone laughed at.* Whipped to a fury by her own calm reasoning, she then paced her bedroom for half the night. In the morning she wrote the letter that now resides in the War Museum and identifies her visitor.[1]

March 7th, 1918

Dear Lady Norman,

I afraid (sic) I formed an incorrect idea of the object of your visit here yesterday. I understood it was to further the work of the training section of the Ministry of Munitions. Much as I am honoured by your appreciation of what I have done for Aviation and for women, I am unable to comply with your request to form part of an Exhibit for the War Museum. I have a great dislike to be put in a glass case and labelled till I am dead.

My work has always been my pleasure, it is part of myself, I prefer working entirely on my own, and in my own way, therefore it is not representative but individual.

I prefer to remain unknown, as the public eye bores me and also hampers my freedom in many ways. Occasional good results are my reward. I am truly sorry not to help you in any way but I assure you it is not a loss to your exhibition, many women have done more extraordinary things than taking a pilot's certificate and running a firm. I have had so much help from others that I take no credit to myself.

Thank you again for your kind sympathy and appreciation which I much value.

Lady Norman had visited Hewlett & Blondeau Ltd on behalf of the Women's Work Sub-Committee of the Imperial War Museum (a forward-thinking group!). Billy's misunderstanding of the purpose of the visit may have arisen from the fact that the sub-committee was working closely with the Ministry of Munitions and her anger at the lack of interest in the Training School might have had something to do with her hoping that the outcome of the visit would mean more pupils and, consequently, more income.[2] The firm employed three hundred men and three hundred women; the only deterrent to taking on another three hundred women in the shops was the shortage of accommodation. However, Billy was not to know that the Ministry of Munitions was discouraging further migration of labour, refusing to allow hostels to be built and generally reducing the numbers of women being trained for munitions work. Also, finished aeroplane bodies outnumbered aeroplane engines. Hewlett and Blondeau neither made engines nor propellers.

If Lady Norman had been a plain Miss or Mrs and had arrived all the way from London alone – and on a bicycle – might things have been different? Unlikely. There was more than enough of the Reverend Herbert in his daughter for her to write *no motive is entirely pure if you receive pay, either in money or glory for what you do. My work was paid work (all except the School), therefore it paid to run the works efficiently to their utmost capacity. A great deal of the help I had was not paid for, just given. That was what deserved reward and recognition, not me. I laughed when I thought of using my dear friends to blow my own trumpet, photographing them for my glory!! What glory? To be on show in a War Museum!!*

A whispered 'horror of a woman' could apply to Mrs Hewlett. If it had not been for her principles, contemporary documentation of the Omnia Works would be available today. Whose to say 'her dear friends' whom she did not want to use to blow her own trumpet, might not have enjoyed sharing a little bit of that glory themselves; seeing their place of work and, possibly, themselves featured in an exhibiton would have been something to have been proud of, particularly for those who, after the war, would slip into the background again. And being 'put in a glass case and labelled till (she was) dead' – all those years of trailing round museums with Maurice clearly had had a depressing effect – hardly rates as the public eye that 'bores and hampers'. Little, if anything, had hampered Billy once she had set her mind to it. However, once the war ended so would the need for training schools and, without the purpose and drama of war, it is hard to imagine Billy being content to continue with the day to day business of running a factory in peacetime: it would be as tedious to her as running a domestic household. Perhaps, subconsciously, she knew she would be seeking something new with which to occupy herself, hence her reluctance to be defined by a label at the age of fifty-four.

In a supplement to the *Aeroplane*, the author of a piece entitled The British Aircraft Industry had already written of the uniqueness of Hewlett and Blondeau in that 'the senior partner of Hewlett and Blondeau is a woman – Mrs. Maurice Hewlett to wit – and one who has long since proved her business capacity as well as other remarkable qualities.' Small wonder then that the poor Women's Work sub-committee should have thought that in, Mrs Hewlett, they had found a prime candidate for their project. There were plenty of women doing war work – bus conductors, lorry drivers, post(wo)men, coal heavers, farm workers, shell fillers, fuse makers, millers, grinders and lathe workers – but for a woman, made glamorous by a romantic career in flying and her marriage to a well-known author, to be a co-director of an aeroplane factory, was something else. Mrs Hewlett was remarkable, but not, as she would be the first to point out, because she had set out to be remarkable. She had responded to the moment and landed where the moment had taken her. She had never actively promoted feminist causes. Her faith had been in aviation, never in what the suffragist movement might achieve for women. Her relationship with her female staff had been too personal, almost maternalistic, for her to be able to put her work into a wider context. 'I think perhaps though you do not realise,' wrote a Miss Monkhouse, on behalf of the sub-committee, 'that we are collecting for future generations more than for the present generation, and any records you might feel you could give us would be under lock and key until we all of us are probably in our graves.'[3]

Regrettably, Billy had not shared that vision.

CHAPTER 23

CHRISTMAS LEAVE

A glimpse of the Front

Surrounded by staff with fathers, brothers, husbands and sons at the front, as well as being the mother of a young man serving in machines similar to her factory's output, Billy's experience of war was very different to that of her sisters. They, like the majority of women of a similar age and class, were one step removed, carrying out tasks that were an extension of their womanly role – billeting refugees, or caring for wounded servicemen. Temperamentally, Billy was better suited to the challenges and demands of running the factory, than the mopping up and stopping up of voluntary work, but a strong sense of patriotic duty made any requests for her charity hard to refuse. At the time an old flying friend approached her on behalf of a wounded Anzac, she had a badly wounded Canadian helping as best he could in the office and the flambuoyant George Dyott staying while he oversaw the production of his latest design, the Dyott Battleplane. An extra soul to consider was the last thing she wanted. So, when a six foot, walking-stick thin young man with fair hair, golden moustache, and the bluest of eyes, strode into her office one morning, it is not surprising that Billy did not recognise the young New Zealander as the herald of a new and final stage in her life.

It was not unusual for service men, bored with the tedium of recuperation, to find their way to somewhere as open and friendly as the Omnia Works, where they might find light but useful work. So it was that Dobson, with his left hand gloved and permanently in his pocket after it had been smashed by a Turkish picric bomb at Gallipoli, arrived determined to learn what he could of the construction and maintenance of aeroplanes. All went well until the Easter break, but when the factory reopened, there was no sign of Dobson, nor was there to be until he turned up more dead than alive eleven days later. After falling in with an officer acquaintance from Gallipoli and accepting a machine gun and an invitation to join in clearing Dublin of the rebels, his family visit became five days of fighting. He had joined the Easter Rising of 24-29 April, 1916. Once he was fit enough to leave hospital – he had been found senseless in the street – he limped back to Leagrave.

In his long and unplanned absence Dobson's lodgings had been relet, so Billy felt she had no other recourse but to take him in on a temporary basis. She put him to bed in the one small, unoccupied room of her bungalow and nursed him as best she could. The first night she was awoken by *incoherent, furious words that sounded like a man fighting and yet suffocating;* after she had woken him and *the horrid look went out of his face,* he begged her to stay for a minute. From then on, whenever he was haunted by the horrors of Gallipoli and, sweat-soaked, fought the terrors of the night, she would *talk of any stupid frivolous subject, tell a funny story, and when the fit was over, sit in the light and hold his hand till he fell asleep.* Dobson, ashamed of being unwell and of burdening her further, nevertheless, allowed her bit by bit to see into his life. *Never openly shocked,* and certain that *no one else had ever seen into his inmost conscience, and no one had ever been able to see the good for the evil that covered it up,* Billy *dug out the good he had, the brilliant possibilities he had never used, held out an object to aim for besides mere adventure.* Months went by until Dobson, finally declared unfit for further active duty, was repatriated. As she waved him off on the boat train from London, Billy knew he was still an ill man and never expected to see him again.

In her little book for propaganda, *Our Flying Men,* Mrs Maurice Hewlett celebrated the pilots and their courage and skills. Her anecdotes might read like boys' adventure stories, but all that she wrote came from the men themselves; she knew what it meant 'to be of value to our artillery' – gun-spotting and artillery directing – and what was involved in bombing raids, dog-fights and aerial photography; she knew that submarine spotting seaplane patrols risked being 'archied' (Royal Flying Corps vernacular for German anti-aircraft fire coined from George Robey's monologue of 1915, 'Archibald? Certainly Not'). Everything interested her, from the merits of safety belts to flying by instruments (a concept alien to her experience), the loneliness of night flying, and how it felt to land with lights as a guide. She heard of dangerous secret missions – but the censor had other ideas about her sharing them – and she knew that, despite the hazards they faced, all pilots would rather be in the air than suffer on the ground in the trenches. And the Christmas after the Royal Flying Corps had flown relays of F.E.'s (nicknamed the Flying Piano) over the German positions to disguise the din of the British tanks positioning themselves for their first terrifying appearance, Billy was to glimpse the grim heroism of that most unglamorous war in the trenches.

She had been to spend too short a break with Maurice and Pia in Maurice's new home in West Wittering and she was returning on Christmas Day to relieve Gustave at the works; the very real fear of Zeppelin raids required they should take it in turns to be on duty over the holiday. After a very slow and a very cold journey, she was settled in a corner seat of a third class smoker for the last leg of her journey. The carriage began to fill up. A young soldier got in with an older one, both were dirty, unshaven and tired. Mud clung to their clothes and boots and gear hung from every strap and button of their uniform. The young soldier, before attending to his own gear, carefully unloaded his friend, put his enormous pack in the rack, disposed of his mess tin and trench hat under the seat, and settled him in the corner seat opposite Billy, who wondered what it was that was wrong with the older man. *'I've a little woman up there, and I want to send her word that I'm coming,'* he said suddenly, at a pitch as though he was hard of hearing and his expression changed and his eyes softened and were full of fun. *'Well, old chap, we'll see what can be done about a wire,'* half shouted his young friend, but the older man was deaf to all but his thoughts.

Two young girls got in. Billy had eaten one of her two apples she had brought for her journey, but she passed that and what biscuits she had to her fellow passengers and wished hard for the miracle of the loaves and fishes to repeat itself. Two more soldiers pressed into the carriage, one of them without luggage and bubbling over with happiness. *'I've had a jolly good dinner, apples, oranges, nuts, bananas, Christmas pudding and roast pork and apple sauce. I like the roast pork. It was at the Y.M.C.A. hut. I just walked in and asked if I could have a bit of food, they gave me all that. When*

I'd done, I just said, how much? They said it was all given me free and for nothing! Yes, all for nothing. I told them I was a lucky devil, and then they gave me – yes – gave me, mind you, this box of cigarettes – they're the right sort, too – have one – (here everyone was offered a 'teoofa', and all accepted except one of the young ladies). They gave me this, too. (Here he stood up and took a leather case out of a deep pocket, containing paper, envelopes and a pencil.) I've made use of it already, all my important papers in this side pocket. My permit from Rouen, all signed and in order. You'd think it was precious if you knew the trouble I've had to get it. Just for ten days leave I had to wait three weeks. I thought they'd forgotten all about me, so I asked the officer three times every day for a week, like that it saved wearing out his memory. I could not leave a thing like that to chance, could I? It don't look much now, but it's worth a lot to me. Here a small, grubby piece of paper was shown round and put back in the leather case and let down into the deep pocket inside his coat.'

He was interrupted by the arrival of a young Belgian soldier, so clean and so neat that Billy thought he could never have come from any front. A lady in black kissed him before he got in and she said to everyone in the carriage *'Vil you put in out at Lycester, please.'* One of the young ladies said she would. The lady in black waved her hand in a perfunctory manner, said goodbye in Flemish and walked away. With a shy smile and a tiny gesture of a salute the Belgian accepted a cigarette from the Y.M.C.A. soldier, as he sat down. Billy, who asked in French where he came from – he had come from the front and was in England for the first time and off to visit his wounded brother convalescing at Leicester – was then asked to act as interpreter by the soldier she nicknamed Y.M.C.A. and was hard put to keep up with the fusillade of his questions and the Belgian's replies. Soon the carriage was full, six soldiers on leave, three ladies and an elderly civilian. As the train moved off through the cold Christmas afternoon, the carriage filled with cigarette smoke and the windows steamed up, and the servicemen seemed as happy as schoolboys having a beano, one soldier was lost in his private world.

Billy was appalled by the stories of the trenches, but when Y.M.C.A. talked of the new and awesome tanks, she began to ask questions about their speed and horse-power. Suddenly, as though the word tank had flicked a switch, the shell-shocked soldier began to talk, intelligently at first, but soon he was lost behind his vacant stare in the depths of which mingled fear and horror. Then, equally suddenly, he stood up in the centre

The senior partner with sleeping partner, Omnia Works

Exhibition of Aeroplanes and Aero Engines, Olympia, 1914

Zeppelin, possibly off the Kent coast, 1914. Cecco Hewlett was stationed on coastal defence at the RNAS base, Westgate on Sea

All that survives of Short no. 135

Short Type 135, no.136.
Cecco Hewlett flew no. 135 in the Cuxhaven Raid

AW FK3 in construction at Leagrave

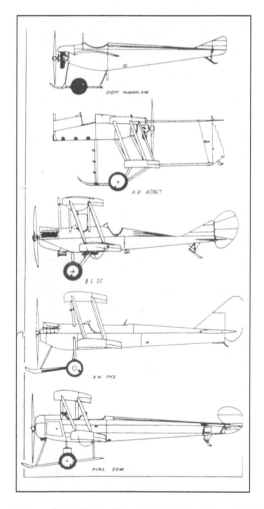

Aircraft built by Hewlett & Blondeau Ltd

Fantasy

Mrs Hewlett showing how it is really done

Kroshka and his mistress in 'Peggy' the old De Dietrich at Leagrave.

*Canteen crockery and
War Work badges*

Pia Richards

Maurice Hewlett

On Gurston Down above Broad Chalke.
Inscription carved by Eric Gill

Portrait of Maurice Hewlett by
John Collier, now in the Broad
Chalke Village Hall

HOTEL DES INDES
WELTEVREDEN
JAVA — NED. OOST-INDIË

Codes: { MERCUUR 5e ED.
A. B. C. 5e en 6e ED.
BENTLEY
TOURISTENVERKEER

Telegram-Adres:
„INDES" WELTEVREDEN
Telefoon Wl. 1468 tot 1474

Weltevreden, 18ᵃ Sept. 1931.

Dear Crew of the Ooievaar, I'm feeling
very lonely & lost without you, I hated
flying away & leaving you - on the way
I dropped tears, more than one for
each of you - also I can not laughed
to-day.

I shall not forget you, & shall follow your
journeys as near as I can -

You all made my flight a series of delights
your happy ways, kindness, & unselfishness
made me I love you all

I shall treasure your picture -
I shall not love the people on the Boat -
Oh! NO - I shall not love the crew -
Certainly NOT - I shall dream of the 11 days
with you -
                    Hilda B. Hewlett

Draft of letter of thanks to the crew of The Stork

Old Bird and her catch, Tauranga, New Zealand

Old Bird possibly wearing the 'three foxes for B.'
that Maurice Hewlett bought his wife in Greece in 1914

of the carriage and drawing himself upright, intoned: *'I had a pal – we did everything side by side. He was a Frenchman, his name was Jean Jacobs.'* He faltered and the look was there again that saw what they did not. The silent carriage watched his face. *'He stopped one and I cut the cross myself and wrote Jean Jacobs on it.'* As he spoke, he folded back his bulky overcoat to show them a long, thin French bayonet in its leather case tied to his belt by a thick piece of string. *'I sent all his things to his people, but I kept this, and I'll never part with it till I part with my life. They wouldn't want this, would they?'* In the hushed carriage, someone murmured *'No'*: the soldier once again retreated to his corner.

The train pulled into her station and Billy longed to tell the carriageful of the love and gratitude in her heart for them all. She wanted to thank them for their bravery, sacrifice and cheerful giving. She wanted to kneel and kiss their brave hands that had fought for her. *'I'm English,'* she managed. *'A happy leave and a good New Year to you all.'*

CHAPTER 24

MANY TEARFUL GOODBYES

The Armistice

As the problem of acquiring essential raw materials grew more acute, the Government stepped in and took over their distribution. For aeroplane construction, good quality wood had to be imported from Canada and America, with the usual wartime risk of being lost in transit to enemy action. It was unfortunate, therefore, that the Omnia Works were awaiting delivery of a large consignment of silver spruce from the docks, when they were suddenly required to re-apply through official channels for what essentially was their undelivered order. It was even more unfortunate when a replacement for their original consignment of seasoned wood turned out to be far too green to use and had to be returned. *We were promised our share of our own spruce every week, but we never got an inch of it. We received letter after letter asking why we were late in delivery of machines. We told the Air Department. Then came officials who raged and cursed. We showed them our empty wood shop and our slack wood workers. Still they cursed us for not delivering our promised machines. Still no wood came.*

Summoned to the Air Board in London, the directors of Hewlett and Blondeau *sat like criminals in the dock before General Alexander and many lesser lights in spotless khaki.* Whatever they said or demonstrated with correspondence and papers *were wiped away as useless detail – they savoured of excuses.* 'Mrs Hewlett,' General Alexander eventually said, '*this is a very serious matter, have you any explanation to offer why your machines are not delivered?*' Mrs Hewlett, hitherto uncharacteristically silent, felt justified into venturing into male territory. She agreed that their receipted invoice, which the Ministry held, confirmed the delivery of the spruce, but acceptance of delivery did not automatically preclude the return of substandard goods. Nor, as she pointed out with some asperity, did it record that her company still awaited a replacement for the unusable consignment, as had been requested. And, yes indeed, there were fifteen finished fuselages in the factory, but they were made of ash, which had been acquired before the Government commandeered all supplies; to keep their men from being too idle, while awaiting good quality spruce for the wings, they had ordered them to go ahead with the construction of the fuselages.

General Alexander called for a man, the bullying official who now stood sheepishly and meekly behind the General's chair. The General said 'Why have I not been informed that the spruce delivered on this invoice had to be dried?' The bully (just another underling who thought contractors could be stamped on and not turn!) did not answer, and got very red. In parting, General Alexander congratulated the triumphant partners: *'You have done all you could under the circumstances. Whenever you have any difficulties, please come direct to me, I will assist you in every way.'*

The problem over the wood was rather more complicated than Billy's indignant memory allows and affected many more than just Hewlett and Blondeau. In November 1917, the then Lt. Col. Alexander, Controller of Supplies Department, Aircraft Production, Ministry of Munitions of War, Air Board Office, had advised, at a meeting with aircraft manufacturers, that Red Louisiana cypress should be purchased as a substitute for the near depleted stocks of silver spruce. Three months later, in February 1918, he sent an official memo from his office, listing all the approved substitutes for silver spruce, among which was the Louisiana Cypress.[1]

Two months later, the now Brigadier General Alexander had to issue a directive to all aircraft manufacturers stressing that the cypress was of such poor quality that it could no longer be allowed for main spars, longerons, engine bearers and struts: only such supplies that were sufficiently dry and complied with A.B. Specification V.1 to the satisfaction of the Director of Inspection could be used for structural parts not subject to stress. There was to be no delay in complying with these instructions and if any was anticipated, his department was to be advised at once, in order that supplies of necessary alternative timber could be arranged. The aircraft manufacturers were to acknowledge receipt of his letter and give the attached duplicate to their resident inspector. Did Messrs Hewlett and Blondeau Ltd do so? And if they had, would it have made much difference? Perhaps not, given the Ministry of Munitions ability to shuffle paper. Eight government departments[2] over eight months, from February to September 1918, batted to and fro the problem of responsibility for implementation of the directive, and compensation for and storage of the undesirable timber, while the aircraft manufacturers and timber merchants fumed and fretted.

In the summer of 1918, not so many months after Lady Norman's visit, the first building application for a new canteen was submitted.[3] Extra land had been bought from Mr. Abraham in 1917, the workforce was the largest it had ever been, but with room for more, and the existing canteen was stretched to its limit. Under the heading The War or National Interest to be Served by the Building on the application for the building licence, the large numbers and difficult logistics of employees and trainees were explained. The Ministry of National Service recognised the need for proper cooking and feeding facilities and granted a licence to build the new canteen at a cost of £4,565. Four months later, and eighteen days after the men hammered on their benches in a drum roll of celebration as the Armistice was declared, when the future of the Works was in jeopardy, the forms for the provision of wood necessary for building work on the canteen to begin were sent to the Controller of Timber Supplies.

Before the Works closed for the first Christmas of the new peace, Billy gave a speech, the text of which she kept, poorly typed on flimsy paper, much folded and worn. Heartfelt and grateful as it was, her speech also warned of the inevitable and radical changes ahead. It was hard to be upbeat when the future was so uncertain.

I appreciate more than I can express the cooperation you have given Mr Blondeau and me during the War. I am very sorry I was not in the Works when the news of the Armistice came. 'Tho late in the day I wish to tell you that it is with pleasure we give you the wages for the hours you celebrated the great event. We propose to include them in the last pay before Xmas.

You have answered to every appeal we have made to you to give more and more time and energy and I hope you can say of us, that, on our side we have answered every reasonable appeal for more money and for any help we could give to lighten the work or to make your life easier.

This has united us in a common bond during those four years. For my part I do not want my respect and real friendship for you to die out. And if you want to keep it also on your side, we can carry it on, in the future.

This is a small firm, you all know its history how it has been built up from a very few pounds by hard work, by good work, to quite a respectable size, and unrivaled reputation.

Mr Blondeau and I have never taken any money out of profits, all profit allowed to us has been spent in buildings and machinery and better tools. Excess profits are to be paid for some time to come.

Our Contracts for War work will not end in less than 3 months, and possibly longer. We have to find new work, invent new methods to do it, change over from aeroplanes to something wanted for re-construction. I want your help and sympathy while we are making a new start on some new work. Help us by being patient, believe in our continued intention to treat you as fellow workers and give you good wages.

You know other firms are dismissing workers, much bigger firms than this and richer, but we believe we can keep all our workers, men and women, and revert to peace work without any serious break. Give us your cooperation again. I feel we have only to tell you its for your good and the good of the firm to carry on as we have done before, as a happy family with one aim.

You must see that not being a rich firm we must suit our cloth to our coat we cannot pay a heavy wage bill every month with very small returns. Trust us as we trust you, we have always paid good money for good work and we mean to continue to do so.

In order to give you time to arrange for our holidays I will end by saying that we shall close on Sat. 21 at 12 p.m. and open on Monday 30 at 7 a.m.

Good intentions do not make for an assured future. The seeds, for what Hewlett and Blondeau became because of the War, had been sown in the early days at Brooklands. Lack of capital and creative energy had left but one option – good quality construction of the designs of others. However, even firms which had developed and built more than one successful design, such as the Sopwith's Pup, Camel and Triplane, found themselves struggling after the Armistice. It is unlikely, therefore, that the story would have been any different for the Omnia Works. The Blackburn Aeroplane and Motor Company (1916) did survive to make aeroplanes for the next world war. They managed this, though, by initially making bread tins for the local Jackson's Bakery. For Hewlett and Blondeau the three month minimum winding down period requested by the government was an opportunity in which to cast about for an alternative to aeroplane manufacture. *We were in perfect accord,* wrote Billy. *As we had made money out of the war, we felt we could not profit by it, unless we shared it with those who had worked, suffered or fought. Gustave and I decided that we would carry on till we had spent all our profit.* However, such altruism was not to be taken to the point of excess. If debt threatened, the company would go into liquidation. The longed-for peace with victory meant joy and uncertainty in equal measure.

As the women drifted back to their former lives and the animating urgency of fulfilling orders died away, Billy, who had made the running of the Training School her voluntary unpaid war work, found herself redundant. Aimless and drained by the four years of unremitting effort, the opportunity to get away from it all was as unexpected as it was welcome. But, with her going, the working partnership of Hewlett and Blondeau effectively came to an end, as her farewell party at the Omnia Works acknowledged. *After a concert we had speeches in which everyone said the nicest things of each other. I made a speech and said that I had been very happy all the years I had worked with them, I should never forget the friends I had found, no friends had been with me so long, day by day for years, I could never think of those years without thinking of them, etc.*

Then one of our Clapham Junction men spoke for all present. They had felt the same towards us, and they wished to give me a parting gift. I could hardly believe it. They presented me with a gold wristwatch, inscribed:

> *Presented to*
> *Mrs. Maurice Hewlett*
> *as a token of regard from*
> *Omnia Works*
> *Leagrave*
> *4.3.19*

and a cigarette case with my name on it also. I was quite unable to say anything. I stood up and said I should like to hug them all. I could not say any more. We had very many tearful goodbyes, danced, ate and drank.

CHAPTER 25

IN THE SERVICE OF HODGE

Maurice finds a cause

The end of the war marked a complete reversal of status for Billy and Maurice. Where Billy found herself redundant and rudderless, after four years of ceaseless effort in a worthy cause, Maurice found himself, after four years of a relatively aimless existence, with a role to play. He might be dished as a novelist and he might be poor, but he was active with a sense of purpose.

In the April before war broke out, Maurice had revisited Greece. His companion had been Pia – for whom, once in a fit of depression, he had thanked the Heavens that he had one who still loved him. Their trip, uncertain to the last because of the ongoing unrest in the Balkans, had, not unnaturally, been of a less ecstatic nature than when Maurice had paced 'with Heart bared beside Gay, Virgin and Huntress of the Wild, Sister and Sovran of the Graces.' Then, he and Gay had spent seven weeks in the spring of 1912 exploring the land whose myths and legends had so informed his writing. The so-called *Diary in Greece, 1914* are his letters home to her, judiciously edited and collated and included in *The Letters of Maurice Hewlett*. They are a delight, detailed, humorous, and observant of people as much as of locations. The train through France was enlivened by competition with 'two funny old women' for occupation of the lavatory; the boat trip from Italy to Greece was enlivened by the presence of a Russian Grand Duke and his entourage and a rendezvous with the Kaiser's yacht for its replenishment. What was not commented on were international politics. However, one puzzling and incomprehensible reference, to which only wide reading and wild conjecture provided a possible solution, indicated that Maurice was not entirely ignorant of Britain's vested interest in what was happening in the Aegean. 'I've seen K. who lives in a very grand house ….. and is waited on by innumerable Greek sailors with very white teeth and curly heads. We are to dine there to-night, and I hope to clinch C.'s affair. He won't have to become a Greek – which was all he jibbed at.' The K. in question could very well have been Rear Admiral Mark Kerr,[1] the C. could only have been Cecco. Kerr was Head of the British Naval Mission to Greece and Commander-in-Chief of the Greek Navy (1913-15) and very interested in the use of aircraft in naval warfare; Cecco was an experienced pilot of seaplanes who had been under Kerr's command in the Royal Navy. If WWI had not broken out when it did, it is quite possible Cecco might have been in charge of training pilots for the Greek navy.

Maurice, although fearing that his confounded physical frailty might cause him to crack up, was a doughty traveller. Ponies were 'much easier to ride than mules. Not so shockingly abrupt in their movements.' But, the effects of fourteen hours in the saddle, one day, nearly finished him and aspirin and tea had to be administered in generous quantitites. Accommodation in the mountain villages ranged from simple to primitive and worse; the room which he and Pia shared in a once thriving and well-endowed monastery was the filthiest Maurice had ever slept in. 'It was quite comic, the shifts we were at to put anything down on anything. We spent nearly two tins of Keatings and laid various booby traps of jugs of water, etc., to put off hermaphrodites appearing out of trap-doors in the night. There were many such in the room you must know.' Trapdoors he meant, not the novices, with their smooth faces and long hair whom he likened to hermaphrodites: the monks he thought wild beasts. After a month, with heaven knows how many varieties of seeds and bulbs dug up and stashed in their luggage, plus a fine carpet for Gay, and three fox furs (very cheap at eleven shillings each) for Billy, who loved 'to be selling furs with the best', Maurice, worn by the rigours of the trip, was weary of Greece and longed to be home.

Acknowledging the dreadful inevitability of war left Maurice sickened: 'It's all very hateful, and makes one despair of mankind; surely the most inferior order of creation. Consider the trees! I take off my hat when I pass them.' Infected, however, by the need to do something for his country, he produced, at his own expense, a chapbook, *Singsongs of the War*, but their lack of fervent up-beat patriotism failed to appeal to the very people Maurice hoped to reach. Philosophical and out of pocket to the tune of £20, Maurice reflected ruefully that only a wealthy man could afford to set up as a balladmonger. But there was one ballad, 'In the Trenches', that did earn him, if not the status of War Poet as is now accepted, at least a modest entry in *A Treasury of War Poetry. British and American Poems of the World War 1914-1917* now rolling, with many thousand other shades, over that mighty ghostly plain, the internet.[2]

His hopes of finding regular useful employment where wit, intelligence and penmanship counted for something were dashed after attending a meeting called to discuss the setting up of a clearing house for articles and interviews. His services as a propogandist in what was to become the Ministry of Information were not required. Downbeat war poetry and his speech in 1910 alerting the workers of Leicester to the potential of strike action as a formidable tool for world peace had, no doubt, militated against him. And, although he believed with every fibre of his being that Britain and her allies were fighting for something sacred and divine in its origin – freedom of the individual man, freedom of the individual race – he did hesitate slightly before joining Sir Francis Younghusband's Fight for Right campaign. Letting slip his fiercely held, if mildly expressed, belief that war was about the most sickening fuss anyone could make would have certainly undermined his credibility as a speaker in the cause. Another minor horror of war, hard to refuse but harder to comply, had been to take part in a Poet's Reading organised in aid of the Star and Garter Fund, twice, once in 1916 and once the following year. Self-acknowledged as a poor reader of verse, Maurice considered it a silly entertainment, where most of the poets read badly. Regrettably, Cynthia Asquith[3] thought him tedious, but he was not the only one she criticised.

Having already relinquished many of his official ties with the Royal Literary Fund,[4] the Society of Authors and the controversial Academic Committee of the Royal Society of Literature,[5] the establishment of which had caused so much bad feeling during his tenure as Chairman of the Management Committee of the Society of Authors, it was clear there was little to keep him in London. Besides, rattling around alone in a large family home that needed more staff than he could afford, or find, to run it, made little sense. As the second year of the war got into its stride and *after 15 years of prosperity, so called,* Maurice retreated to the quiet of an old farm house a mile from the Sussex coast in West Wittering. What furniture he did not need Billy took or stored in the outhouse of her comfortable new bungalow in Leagrave; conveniently, they each moved in the same month.

As a writer, Maurice had but one occupation to follow, but his desire to write the sort of novel that had made his name and fortune had long dried up. Inspiration came to him in the Icelandic sagas. Of all the classics, they were the most unapproachable in their naked strength. 'Their frugality freezes the soul; they are laconic to baldness.' In the circumstances, they seemed the most appropriate. Having 'soused himself' (to use a favourite expression) in them, Maurice decided that if he 'humanised a tale of endurance, and clothed demigods and shadows in flesh and blood,' he would have done useful work, for heroism abounded on all sides, throughout the dreadful years of war, on a scale equal to that of the long gone heroes of Iceland. Regrettably, the reading public found the stories grim and the style of writing wooden. The farmworkers and their families of West Wittering, however, lapped them up. In addition to making available to them much of his garden as allotments for local food production, Maurice also held weekly readings, open to anyone who wished to attend. A cynic might point out that being read to for an hour, in a desert of entertainment, made a welcome change, but then a cynic would not be aware that Maurice's concern for the welfare of those less well off than himself – 'he helped many a poor boy and girl with their education' – cost him more than he could afford.

Friends that he could persuade to stay with him made welcome breaks in Maurice's remote and solitary existence. Gay, whose regular letters were keenly awaited, arrived with her noisy, healthy young family to enjoy the beach and the 'double bathing-house on the shore, so that mixed bathing could be had in comfort.' Robert Bridges came whose long and *delightful visit* had Maurice celebrating *a great advance in friendship with him*; the Binyon family also – Maurice had thought Binyon's 'Fetching the Wounded' very beautiful and envied his power of 'being indignant without being angry'; and Nellie and Edmund Gosse. Their reunion, after he and Gosse had drifted apart in 'the superficial cross-currents of life' in that 'beastly town', made him extremely happy. And Gosse's generous encouragement about the piece that preoccupied Maurice heart and soul, had him able not only to face inevitable poverty, but to welcome it. As poetry, the unfinished Hodgiad, or English Chronicle, was not going to put many pounds in Maurice's pockets. Nevertheless, because of his unforced and deep respect for the English peasant (a term used with the noblest and most poetic intent for the hard-working, poorly paid man of the land), his intense patriotism and his theory that England was made up of two classes, a governing class and a governed class, he wrote what he must. But the title was not easy to come by. 'Pregiatissimo,' he wrote to Gosse, 'I think that I have a title for the Hodgiad. Es ist ein Korker. The Hind's Epick.' But he was quick to appreciate the superior merit of Gosse's return: 'The Song of the Plow: being The English Chronicle. Ripping. How fond not to have got that before. NO more Epix for me.'[6]

The Song of the Plow began with the year 1066. The history chronicled, 'misty and full of dim rumours, with occasional flashes of things in the doing,' was less the fighting and junketing of kings and more the laws – such as the Enclosures, Corn Law, Poor Law, to name a few – that impacted directly on the life of the hero, Hodge, whose status remained essentially unchanged throughout. (Hodge means agricultural labourer, the significance of which was lost on some readers). Only with the coming of the Great War, when the Peasantry rose unbidden (conscription did not come in until nearly two years into the war) to fight the menace of German despotry, did it cast off its shackles to become the equal of its masters.

"See there the poacher of the game,
And there the master of men and pheasants,
And there the man who makes them tame
And drives them over guns for presents -
Who shall care now such blood to class
And docket men as lords or peasants?"

When the reviewer in the *Times Literary Supplement* declared the poem a failure, Maurice felt hurt, as he was sure was intended, but more for his symbolic hero than for himself: that Hodge should be dismissed as an 'elemental hog', outraged him. The dyspeptic reviewer had clearly been unable to see the poetry for the history, which he found violently obnoxious. Binyon, though conscious of the faults of the poem, nevertheless felt indignant enough to protest in *The Times* at the shabby treatment of a 'finely sustained effort of impassioned narrative, on a most difficult theme, sown with passages of great power and beauty.' Enormously cheered, Maurice was further made happy by a letter – almost the jolliest thing he had ever had – from his new friend, Jack Squire.[7] Squire, a sharp young man, was then Literary Editor on the *New Statesman* and wrote under the pseudonym Solomon Eagle; loathed by Lytton Strachey and later mocked by the Bloomsbury set, Squire was liked by the old guard of Gosse and his circle. Initially, Squire had thought Hewlett 'rather a brute', but acquaintanceship and time redressed this impression and Squire felt able to call his third son, Maurice: Maurice repaid the friendship by making Squire his literary executor, although it is hard to know quite what Squire's contribution amounted to, as there is nothing to suggest that it was anyone other than a family member who dealt with Maurice's work after his death.

Maurice found himself 'quite homesick' once his English Chronicle was done. 'Tremendously in earnest' over Hodge – he sincerely hoped that in some way it might further the cause of the agricultural worker – he had found writing his story fun from first to last. He had never been bored, nor had he struggled to finish it. But despite his epic selling well for poetry, there was still a need to review his sickly finances. If he was to escape 'the degrading occupation of writing bad novels,' he needed to let Elm-Tree Farm for a couple of years and move into a cottage with one woman to do for him; which is not at all what he did. Instead, in a move more likely to repair his lonely woes than the growing hole in his pocket, he retook the Old Rectory, which he had had to give up in 1912 shortly before he and Gay went to Greece; overseas travel with lovers, platonic or otherwise, was costly. Whether on a whim, or by design, he and Pia had visited Broad Chalke one August day. The neglected garden and the old building glowed familiar and beautiful in the sun. It was vacant. It was irresistible. Maurice took it on the spot. Six weeks later, and Elm Tree Cottage, his residence for a mere 21 months, sold to the as yet unknighted Henry Royce,[8] Maurice was home, home in his beloved Wiltshire. Before a fortnight was out, just briefly, he was joined by Billy, Cecco and Pia, *together again for the first time since Cuxhaven.*

Galvanised by his move and as joyful as a repatriated exile, he suddenly found in Mrs Warman, his housekeeper, the voice for his threnody, *A Village Wife's Lament*; a voice that had eluded him for weeks. He put into words what he believed lay in her heart 'too deep for utterance but that of tears.' Defensive war was a pious duty; aggressive war was a madness and criminal folly. Maurice longed to reach with his poetry just such a person as his housekeeper, but feared he was not in the same league as 'the cracks – Burns and the balladists.' However, what he had had to say in his English chronicle did speak to an interested party: namely, the Board of Agriculture. His appointment to undertake on their behalf an investigation into rural labour conditions was made, Maurice was proud to claim, for the first time in history on the strength of a poem, *The Song of the Plow*. And, 'for the sake of Poetry' as well as for all the Hodges who worked the land, Maurice determined to do the job well. His schedule was gruelling, the time of year the least clement for travel, accommodation made the starker by food rationing, but throughout January and on into April, 1918, he scoured Northumberland, Cumberland and Westmorland from Durham to Barrow-in-Furness seeking out good and genuine peasants so that he might report back to the Wages Board on their hours of work, wages, chances of promotion and living costs. 'I am up to the neck – literally snowed up with the bloody forms (no, bloodless) of the B. of A.' Maurice wrote to Squire at one point. 'They would draw the heart out of any reformer – except me, I keep going by steadily pursuing my own aim.'

The job brought in on time, Maurice returned to the heart of the village. A serious bicycle smash, which left him looking like a tattooed cannibal chief and feeling like a boiled cabbage, could not dim his spirits, even though it left him ill for a week. The final, short phase of his life was beginning, blessed by a year of bounty at the Old Rectory. In September, the garden produced, as Maurice wrote to Cecco, who had just been posted to Mudros, 'the finest crop of apples in England' and Mrs Warman, with the aid of Billy's sugar ration, had made 150 lbs of jam and was 'still RUNNING.' The same lady had, in the nick of time, his father was happy to report, been prevented from ordering 500 PARTRIDGES, rather than the 500 cartridges requested by Cecco. How Cecco's fellow officer and bearer of said partridges would have liked them by the time they had reached Mudros, he could not imagine! Peaches, nectarines and pears were in such abundance they were dispatched to relatives daily and such was the reputation of the garden, a gentleman, unknown to Maurice, wished to 'work in it, for his keep.' No man, not even Shakespeare, would have been bearable as a housemate to Maurice, whereas he could have imagined 'being happy with almost any woman who wasn't (a) very ugly, (b) a great talker.'

Mid-October and the war was nearly over. 'Haig will be made a marquis, and Lloyd George, perhaps a Duke. But greater, infinitely greater than all these people seems to me Private or Lance-Corporal Atkins. He and his folk at home – whether in pastoral Wiltshire or suburban Anerley – oh, what a people! So many virtues, so few graces! Such a golden core and such an unlikely husk! He will be at his worst soon, when he is making London hideous with his uncouth rejoicings – but remember him in 1915-16, when things were at their worst.' And it was for the sake of that golden core that, five days into the peace, Maurice found himself unable to deny the Sarum Labour Party their desire that he should be their candidate for South Wiltshire in the coming General Election. With absolute clarity he knew he did not want to accept, but reluctant to forsake 'the poor chaps' he delayed making his decision until after he had attended a meeting at the Labour Party office in London. There, it would appear he was let off the hook and by the end of December, with the return of Lloyd George to power, he was rejoicing that neither would he be required to spend money that he did not have, nor would he be threatened with the purgatory of living in London.

Maurice had been excited by the new policy of the Labour Party, in which membership would no longer be exclusive to workers with the 'horny hand' of tradition, and had asked Sidney Webb to put him up for the Fabian Society. An idealist, he wished to work towards the realisation of the dream at the end of the Hodgiad.

> Thus Hodge shall win at last his land –
> You, Earl of forty thousand acres,
> Give your four thousand; you who stand
> Master of five, for the new takers
> Give your two roods, to avoid the shame
> That England scorn her Empire-makers; –

It was a pipedream. For a start, Maurice was a contradictory socialist and however much he liked to think himself a profound anarchist with the avowed intent of breaking down as many British Institutions as possible, temperamentally he was unsuited to playing the kind of politics that could smash a window, let alone a whole institution. He was diverted by the Labourers' Union chaps addressing each other as 'Dear Sir and Bro.' and wondered if they wrote 'Dear Madam and Sis.' to the women and, when he wasn't being flippant, genuinely found politics interesting. He had campaigned hard in 1910 on behalf of the Labour movement and had written an impassioned two-column letter to the *Daily Chronicle*, which was printed on its front page on 4 January, 1910, under the headlines: **DUTY OF WORKING MEN**, STIRRING APPEAL BY FAMOUS NOVELIST, **"HODGE IS KING"**, LORDS A DANGER TO THE STATE, **CLEAR THE PASS.**[9]

The phrase 'Pink Wash', which he used to describe the 'vapouring and blustering about Empire and All-Red Maps,' by the Conservatives, acquired a charm of its own for one little girl. Audrey Lucas, the only daughter of E.V. Lucas, loved Maurice as the favourite of all the visitors to her parents' home, despite, or perhaps because of, his diabolical habit of teasing her. Frequently reduced to inarticulate and purple-faced fury, she was delighted to discover how amused her father had been at Maurice's use of the term 'Pink Wash'. Ignorant of its meaning or origin, she took to using it as her final word against her dear tormentor.

That same terrible month, when Mrs Grace Bird had entered his life and Billy had left it, was when Maurice had also addressed 5,000 working men in Leicester, as a direct result of his approaching Ramsay McDonald asking to be allowed to speak to one of his Trades' Union Congresses on War-Prevention and other topics he held dear. However, Maurice's post-war resurgence of interest in and commitment to socialism and the Labour Party was not to survive the Railway Strike of September 1919. 'The L.P. has no hold on the Trade Unions, the Unions none over their members. They are a rabble, not a party.'

'I am quite reconciled to being old and perfectly ready to clear out, when directed. So long as they don't bury me alive, I don't care what happens. Perhaps you think they have done that to me already.' E.V. Lucas, to whom this was addressed, might well have thought that Maurice had done it to himself by abandoning the literary life in London:

not for Lucas the duties of local affairs for which Maurice found himself more and more in demand.

'I am getting to be the fashion here,' he wrote to Cecco. 'They are sticking me in every local office they can, and many which they can't. 1) Parliament. I refused. 2) County Council. I refused. 3) Wages Board, Accepted. 4) Rural District Council, Accepted. 5) Parish Committee, Chairman, alright. 6) Magistrate, of course. 7) Vice-President of the Boy Scouts, golly! They will want me to be Sheriff next, and then I shall have to see men hanged.'

Of them all, the District Council was to be the most demanding of his time and energy, the blame for which can be attributed to its Housing Committee established to implement the Government's ambitious post-war Housing Act of 1919. If he had doubted the viability of the scheme, Maurice, nevertheless, threw himself heart and soul into what he believed was a valid and important project. He had seen too many villagers living with dirt floors, crumbling walls and no sanitation. Inspecting land for new homes, cottages for purchase and repair, or condemnation and replacement, engaging architects sensitive to the existing Wiltshire villages, submitting plans for approval – more than once – were the lot of the Committee. His disgust and anger when the Government reneged on what had been an unrealistic and financially unsound scheme after two and a half years, Maurice could only vent in a blistering letter to *The Times* on 12 July, 1921. Most acutely he felt the stigma of bad faith. He had pledged his honour to the architects of the new houses and to their future tenants and was unable to redeem it. Additionally, his council, like all rural district councils in England, was left with land it did not want, and liability it could not afford and a housing problem that had been aggravated rather than eased.[10]

The District Council had been left in debt, for Maurice the outcome had not been so drastic, but it had been costly. Unable to drive himself, he had had to hire a car – the driver of which so resembled Swinburne's friend that Maurice nicknamed him Watts-Dunton – and pay for the petrol for the tours of inspection round the county. Given that, shortly after the war, he had written, rather cheerily: 'Incidentally, I am ruined – but blame the Germans for that, not me,' the imperative to earn more money had grown more urgent. But age and committees sap the energy, original creative work becomes harder and harder. Before he finally found a medium that suited him perfectly and which allowed him to be most himself, he gave a passing thought to two possible methods of capitalising on his reputation and earlier work.

Pre-war there had been talk of a three-month lecture tour to the States, a lucrative and welcoming country for a number of Maurice's friends. Tempting as £250 a week with all expenses paid was, he only briefly toyed with the idea of resurrecting the plan. He suspected he had come to be regarded as something of 'an extinct volcano', read only in a few American university circles. Next he considered the cinema as a new medium in which to re-cycle some of his work, but for that he needed Pia's collaboration. Together they egged each other to wilder and wilder flights of fancy, but motherhood now had a greater call on her time. However, his books – too many words for too little action – had little appeal for the film agencies. As solving the problem of getting literary quality into a thing which was all visual presentation defeated him, it is fair to say that Maurice hadn't quite grasped the essentials of the moving pictures. He did sell the rights to *The Forest Lovers*, but whether or not it appeared on screen remains a mystery and although *The Spanish Jade* was made into a film (Alfred Hitchcock was credited with the Intertitle card design[11]), it is doubtful that Maurice reaped the benefit.[12]

Oddly, he was once under the impression that Douglas Fairbanks wished him to direct rehearsals of a film he was making on Richard Coeur de Lion. As Fairbanks had already covered the Lionheart's career in his film of Robin Hood, it is a puzzle to know why Maurice understood his services were needed; possibly he and Fairbanks had met socially in London and the subject had come up in small talk. As it was, he never even got close to experiencing the horrors of Hollywood, but Billy did.

CHAPTER 26

A SOUTH SEAS IDYLL

Raratonga

When Billy went to Hollywood, she was entertained by Douglas Fairbanks. However, that was not to be until years later, when she was *en route* for home after she had visited New Zealand for the second time. Her first trip to New Zealand had been in direct response to an appeal from the mother of Dobson, the terribly wounded young Anzac she had befriended during the war. Dobson had been ill and had once again turned to the bottle for comfort and pleasure. Was there any way in which the kind Mrs Hewlett, who had done so much for him once before, could help now? Out of the blue and in the opening of an envelope, Billy had a new cause. With the war ended and the Omnia Works limping along while Blondeau explored post-war engineering and alternatives to manufacturing aeroplanes, she was, in effect, redundant. Here was a worthy mission with the added spice of possible adventure. Counsel in dull correspondence would not do. She would go and help Dobson in person.

On March 13, 1919, one among the many thousands criss-crossing the world to return to distant homelands, Mrs Maurice Hewlett set sail from Liverpool on a single ticket for St John's Brunswick, the first leg of her journey to New Zealand. *It was a mixed class boat, very mixed indeed, soldiers returning to Canada, many with families, munition girls, men and women who had been in England for war work. Democracy reigned supreme. The stewards were a scratch lot, the Captain and officers were afraid of them and let them be as rude as they liked to passengers, drink in the cabins without reproof, and order people about in the roughest way.* If only they could have measured up to the paragons of domestic virtue, the Canadian fathers, who *nursed the babies, gave them bottles, amused the children and waited on their wifes, in the most natural and cheerful way.*

Seated at table next to an old Lancashire woman, who wore a *bonnet with strings, shawl, old black cloak and elastic-side boots* and had an appetite that told *its own tale of privation,* Billy encouraged her companion to tuck in to all that she fancied. Billy found mealtimes *a liberal entertainment* and was highly amused at one dinner when a G.I., on her other hand, rose to the challenge of oysters and assured her after swallowing them that they were *'down now anyhow.'* She listened avidly to the tales of peril and hardship suffered by her cabinmate, a refined Scottish governess on her way to a post in Montreal, who had escaped from Kiev via Moscow under the noses of the Bolsheviks, but it was the munitions girls for whom she cared the most. Once she had seen how they were shunned by the other women on board, she promenaded round the deck with them, listened to their stories and joined in their games. Appointed their unofficial leader, Billy *was able to prevent a good deal of rough play and eliminate some of the most offensive language, songs and rough behaviour. Needless to say the other 'ladies'* bedecked in furs, *'the wages of sin',* cold-shouldered the leather-coated Billy, that is until they recognised her intentions. Then Billy, rather than accept the invitation of Lady X to join her for tea, *took the occasion to take tea with the munition crowd, skipped and danced with them, and organised races and sports under Lady X's nose.* Naturally.

After ten days of cold, discomfort, overcrowding and unruly stewards, they landed at St John's, where the interior of the disembarkation hall felt as though it *was heated to hell temperature* and the welcome and care of the 1,500 passengers was as warm, if not as demonic, as the heating. Billy was kissed several times in farewell by her old Lancashire friend and, after feigning womanly helplessness, managed to wheedle a sleeper bound for Montreal. There she changed trains for Chicago and, although she liked the Pullman cars, *well furnished with spittoons under or by every seat in the smoking saloon,* Billy preferred the observation car in spite of the dust and smell of oil. American heating, once again, was too much for her. When her dining companion, on the final stage of her trans-American journey to San Francisco, alighted at Odgen, Billy wished she too could have taken the thirty-mile sleigh ride through soft snow to her ranch of four hundred head of cattle. She would so have enjoyed witnessing how the fashionably dressed young woman *with a most unusually beautiful figure, not the full American stiff kind, but with the grace and souplesse of a Greek athlete*, could use a lasso, break horses, plough with a full team, make butter, all the while ensuring her ranch hands did not spit in her presence.

In San Francisco, Billy found herself treated like a celebrity thanks to Maurice's American agent, who had been alerted to her achievements by Maurice and requested by him to look after her. 'Mrs Hewlett, Britain's First Aviatrix Here' was the headline of the article on the front page of the Sunday edition of the *San Francisco Chronicle*. 'On Way to New Zealand Where She Will Establish Flying School,' the paper proclaimed over a picture of her in her most fetching flying gear. Either it was imaginative reporting, or Mrs Hewlett had had an agenda of which, subsequently, she made no mention. Dinners and teas were arranged for her benefit, including the delightful novelty of a barbecue picnic and, when it came time to board the cargo boat bound for New Zealand, she found her cabin filled with flowers, fruit, sweets and *heaps of papers and amusing literature*. She loved the fuss, but did not for a moment feel that she deserved it.

Billy credited the captain of the *Paloona*, with whom she took tea daily, with her *initiation to the Islands and the particular atmosphere of the Pacific*. She was, however, already conditioned to potential enchantment by her reading, notably *A Vagabond's Odyssey*, in which New Zealand and Pacific islands emerge from a confusion of fact and fiction.[1] The chief engineer, a rugged Scot, who *greatly approved of modern dress for women, as he appreciated the economy of using the minimum amount of material*, instructed her in the myriad varieties of tropical fish. Disappointed by the local population of Papeete, their first landfall – she thought them *degenerate and of poor physique*,[2] Billy was charmed by the natives of Raratonga,[3] a *fine race, extremely happy and delighted to see visitors*, and much admired the skilful way in which they paddled their outrigger canoes through the narrow gap in the reef. But, as the ship neared Wellington, horrid doubts cast their shadow. Would she find Dobson alive, or too ill to recover? What would she do if he was dead? Her relief at spotting his tall, khaki-clad figure on the dockside was tempered by her dismay at how gaunt he looked. Dobon's greeting and the realisation that barely out of his sick-bed he needed rest, made the thousand miles she had travelled a matter of insignificance. A scheme, no doubt incubated on the journey from Raratonga, hatched instantly into simple proposal. The two of them should go to the Islands and do nothing. As suggestions go, it was hard to fault. Lunch eaten, they booked their passage on the Paloona for the following week.

As neither Wellington nor *the select week-end settlement for Wellingtonians, rotten little sheds on grass* at Ryan Bay impressed Billy, she left for Auckland without regret. Once again, reporters tracked her down; they did not ask her silly questions, but neither did they amuse her, as a Wellington reporter had, by enquiring after her *somewhat respected husband* by his Christian name. Invited to visit the flying school at Kohimarama, where Dobson had been stationed on his return from Europe, Billy was surprised and very much flattered to see that one of the photographs, pinned up on the office wall, was of herself flying at Brooklands. Evidently the Walsh brothers, Leo, the managing director and Vivian, the chief pilot and superintendent, whose business it was, had both become aviation enthusiasts at the same time as herself and had followed the progress of the early pioneers with great interest, Hewlett and Blondeau among them.[4] Impressed by the New Zealand Flying School and the quality of its aircraft, Billy enjoyed a thrilling flight over Auckland harbour in one of its seaplanes piloted by a most able, but blushing pupil. She also met J.W.H. Scotland, who had ordered a Caudron from the Omnia Works when they were still in Clapham.[5] As she lay, unable to sleep that night for thinking of the school in Kohimarama, she marveled that her *first efforts had reached so much further than anyone could have imagined.*

An awful dot-and-go-one train returned them to Wellington, a city that did nothing to improve its standing in Billy's eyes. It was mid-day Saturday and everything was shut. She had little money, her passport needed to be stamped and the boat was due to leave at eleven o'clock that night. Eventually, surely one of the most obliging passport officials ever was tracked down and a deal was struck. If Mrs Hewlett would be so kind as to collect Mr Twiss and his wife – they had no car and lived some distance from the centre of Wellington and were going to the theatre that night – then they could call by his office and he would deal with the matter, in time for curtain-up. With mission accomplished and time in hand before the *Paloona* sailed, Billy and Dobson then sought dinner, but there was none to be had. It was after eight o'clock and the hour for serving dinner had passed. As they ate their way through as many ham sandwiches as they could decently order in a café, Billy tried to imagine her pet bugbear, the Trade Unions, having similar power over restaurants and hotels in London and Paris, but failed.

The trip to Raratonga began with a terrible storm, which Billy did not only survive without being sick, but enjoyed; magnaminously, her stricken fellow passengers forgave her. Disembarked at Raratonga, Billy and Dobson were ferried from the ship to the capital, Avarua, on the northern shore of the island, where they put their gear in the Whare, the Government hotel, and, armed with a card of introduction from the kindly Mr Twiss, went to call on the Resident Commissioner, Cook Islands, F. W. Platts[6]. He promised to help them find accommodation and introduced them to a Mr. Kohoa, a Raratongan who owned *three houses, a very superior motor car, plantations of coconut, bananas, tomatoes, pineapples, taro, a fat wife and five children.*

After viewing Mr Kohoa's first offering, Billy was not optimistic about his next, particularly when she learnt that there was no water laid on and that *other conveniences were lacking which he named without beating about the bush, and in very plain language.* Made of louvre boarding, with an unpainted corrugated iron roof and roughly cemented floors, it had just two rooms and a verandah front and back, but it was set in a clearing among coconut palms fifty feet high. *A stream ran close by and in the immediate foreground was a large kennel, built of sticks stuck into the ground, held together with native string, the overhanging roof made of woven palm leaves. From the kennel a very, very old man slowly emerged.* Something about this *six foot two inch brown skeleton, clothed only in short pants* reminded Billy of Joe Pennell and she christened him Joseph on the spot, *Joe being far too familiar for such a veteran.* While Mr Kohoa explained that the veteran would do all that they required in the way of fetching water, coconuts and fruit, Joseph *screwed himself into the kennel again and returned with a dingy cardigan jacket on his lean shoulders. He had evidently not been expecting a lady visitor.* After discussing the shack's deficiences with the Platts and enjoying *quite the best tea* that she had had for years, she agreed to take it.

A shopping expedition to the Cook Island Trading Company provided the necessities of housekeeping, and they were ready to move in. On the larger of the two tables a *very common wooden clock ticked loudly*; there were four chairs, two beds made up of *large cases of kapok, as were the pillows with one sheet apiece and no blankets,* cooking was to be done outside. Mr Kohoa, with Mrs Kohoa clad in a dress *the hooks or buttons of which had gone on strike,* showed Billy how to make a fire from dried banana leaves, split coconuts and wood. After their supper of a tin of sausages heated up, bread and butter, bananas, oranges and tea, the four of them sat and talked in the brilliant moonlight as *now and then a coconut fell with a crash, flying foxes flew across from palm to palm, and the wind played with the long waving leaves, making quite a new sort of dry swish, different to the rustling leaves of home.*

So began Billy's most perfect dream. In the morning, she rose from her bed on the front verandah and walked the short distance to the shore. The sandy bed of a dried stream, *out of the wind and out of view,* made a choice dressing room and *after a swim, an air and sun bath* on the deserted beach, she returned to the house. Joseph had lit the fire in the grandly named cook-house, a few posts supporting a palm roof, and fetched the water from the spring; Lottie, the cook, a cheerful half-caste with one visible tooth and a black dress, had begun to prepare porridge, eggs and bacon and coffee for breakfast. Billy tightly hugged her happiness to herself.

Raratonga, a roundish island, is set in a lagoon, ringed by coral, which shows red-brown in the turquoise blue of the water that laps the sharp white sand. Billy and Dobson were staying on the southern shore, somewhere near Titikaveka, and the breakers, a quarter of a mile out, beckoned so imperatively on their first day, Billy just had to wade out to the reef at low tide. Luckily she wore shoes for, when the water was up to her neck, she could not see where to place her feet, her hands and knees were slashed by the coral when she fell and the black sea slugs were nasty things to tread on. At last, *wounded fit for Blighty* and groggy with the beauty and wonders of the coral world, she limped back to camp. Dobson was unscathed, he had been out fishing in the outrigger canoe discovered on the beach that morning. A couple of duckings had graphically demonstrated that it was a single-seater and after Billy had failed to control it – she felt it was akin to driving a car she did not know *down Bond Street on a May afternoon* – it had been left to Dobson to master. His catch was cooked by Lottie for their supper and, as the moon came up, Peaira, Lottie's amiable and thoughtful husband, joined them for what became a regular evening gossip on the front verandah, where Billy's bed had been converted into a divan by a rug and the pillows in scarlet and white cotton covers.

Later, a bigger and better outrigger washed up on their beach, which, if they positioned themselves exactly right, would take the two of them. In a Robinson combination – Heath and Crusoe – paddles were fashioned out of some handles, lids of tomato boxes, string and nails; a sail was made with the tablecoth and two flour bags; and half a coconut shell, if used frequently and energetically, did as a baler. With the tide running and the wind up, Billy thought it *quite the most amusing craft* she had ever been in and she *wished Cecco could have been with them*. Together she and Dobson used it to explore the reef; they sailed along the coast to visit the Platts at their beach house, pulling into land a couple of times to caulk the rapidly filling body of the canoe; they fished from it; in the moonlight they paddled through the shimmering phosphorescence; sometimes they even got out and pushed it.

Many passages in Billy's chapters on her South Sea adventures are dated and read like diary entries. Her journey from wartime England had swept her from cool monochrome to a hot riot of colour and every detail was important. She described daily meals, picnics, planned or impromptu, feasts and the cooking and distribution of roast sucking pig. She wrote of the ocean, its reefs, their favourite playground the lagoon, and the colours, shapes and feel of its myriad tropical fish. Equipment used, clothes worn, the lack of any sanitary arrangements, the numberless mice and mosquitoes, the necessity of acquiring the skill of lighting a fire by rubbing two pieces of wood together – *a most exhausting process* – had all to be recorded in this world of novelty and delight.

Billy had introduced Dobson to the islanders as a son, badly wounded in the war, whom she had temporarily adopted, but for the emotionally and physically damaged Dobson she would have been both mother and tomboy sister. Just as she had once soothed away the horrors of his nightmares and sought out and affirmed the good in him, so she did yet again. With her encouragement and readiness for any adventure or expedition, she kept him sober and helped Dobson pull himself out of the savage self-destructive behaviour he had once again fallen into after nearly dying of the 'flu that had killed so many in the pandemic of 1918-19.

Billy's great quality, the ability to have fun, was a tonic remedy for Dobson's ills. With the force of her energetic enthusiasm and the willingness of Peaira to be their friend and guide, the two of them, no doubt, gave cause for the white administrative community to fear they had gone native, such as when they joined Peaira *'rummying'* in the silken lagoon. It was night and Peaira had turned up dressed in patched trousers stained with octopus ink and a brown woollen cardigan, carrying a torch made of *a long water pipe, over four foot long, stuffed with rags and paraffin poured down it* and *six bits of thick wire barbed and fastened into a handle* to form a spear. In bathing clothes and shoes, Billy stood beside Peaira as his torch flared over the reef and she marvelled at how he saw where to strike. Anything poisonous or dangerous, he scraped from his spear into the canoe; when an eel twisted round his spear shaft and bit into the side of the canoe, it first had to be beaten to death before it could be scraped off. Anything safe to handle, Billy carried with pride. Only when the moon clouded over and a cat's paw of a wind ruffled the waters of the still lagoon did they return home.

As happy to study the pools and coral at low tide as to go fishing, inquisitive Billy found herself hastening, one day, towards a native with goggles on his head and spear in his hand hunting along the reef. Realising, as she drew near, that he had no seat to his trousers and anxious that *the sudden encounter with a white woman might greatly embarrass him,* she made sure to approach him from the front, but he was either *quite unconscious of his unconventional back view,* or consciously unconcerned, as he instructed her for the next hour or two in the exotic inhabitants of the reef. Only the eel with its *horrid jaw and jagged teeth* and the octopus wih its *horrid sucking feelers* really gave her the shivers. She and Dobson once dared to hunt down a venemous sea-snake in their lagoon; it escaped twice but *with fearful energy it was chased and for the last time got bagged.*

Inland, *the thick, fat, green vegetation that piled itself up the steep mountain* begged to be explored. The stream they followed, and the ferns that grew towered over it, and sprouted from trees, moss and rocks had Billy in raptures. No less picturesque was the young man with *quantities of black curling hair, round which he had woven a halo of fern leaves to keep the flies off his face,* whom they met in the clearing where the taro and bananas were cultivated. After a cigarette and a drink of fresh coconut milk, Billy, ignorant of what she was letting herself in for, blithely set off with Peaira to see the view from a nearby ridge. Now she learnt what that fat green vegetation was made of, fallen trees, holes hidden by vegetation that reached her waist, and creepers as strong as cords which made her grateful to Peaira and his sharp sickle. Nevertheless, as they returned home, Dobson having bagged one flying squirrel despite chronically damp cartridges, she reflected it had been a good day. She would try to preserve the squirrel skin, even if it did stink, and they would climb the island's highest peak another day for the view would surely be even more spectacular.

It was a better prepared Billy, with thick boots and well-oiled stockings, who tackled *the mountain*. Not so Dobson, he wore sandshoes with half the right sole missing. Peaira, as usual, was barefoot. After five hours struggle over, under and through, they reached the summit and the splendid view made the terror of squirming round trees on sheer-sided spurs worth it. All around, the island was bound by the snow-white surf, which separated the blue of the coral lagoon from the dark, full blue of the Pacific. Contemplating the descent, as they enjoyed their picnic of eggs, bread and delicious cool green coconut milk, they realised it would be as hazardous, if not more, than the ascent. Deceptively sound-looking surfaces were often decayed and the risk to ankles and limbs had been acute. Once on the lower slopes, they each picked a couple of oranges to suck and from the banana plantations they ate more than they could keep count of. Twelve hours after they had set off, they straggled home and Billy, with gasps of relief, discarded her boots and stockings, *two months of going barefoot had made any kind of footwear abominably hot.*

On the day in June, when the arrival of the mail coincided with that of the Governor General of New Zealand, Lord Liverpool, Billy had no difficulty in knowing which event to celebrate. Desperate for her first news from home, she borrowed *two buckled wheels and some old bits of iron tubing, no remains of brakes at all, and only excuses for pedals* and cycled the ten miles to Avarua, but as the single main road that encircled Raratonga was sandy and she had set off in the pouring rain, it was difficult to tell what was sweat and what was rain by the time she reached the capital. Mr Platts, taken aback by such prodigious energy, insisted that she recover from her exertions at his house in the calming care of his wife. Tea and supper later and a hasty acknowledgment of her letters' safe arrival posted back, Billy was impatient to devour her mail in private, but *the dear, kind Platts* refused to let her cycle at night alone and found a cart going her way. Their thoughtfulness was to no avail. Bored by the cart's slow pace, Billy was soon pedalling home, the moon more effective than any headlamp. Dobson was abed, but awake and waiting, and it was long past two in the morning before the two of them put their letters aside for sleep. But Billy grieved. Kroshka had died the day after she had left. She had loved him so very much.

A real fat thunder storm broke at seven the following morning, the start of Lord Liverpool's official visit. Bidden for the ten o'clock opening reception, Billy, clad in her best clothes, had set out by taxi in plenty of time. When the engine suddenly cut out, she knew without a doubt that it was magneto trouble, but the driver could not, or would not understand what his passenger, a woman, was telling him, a scenario all too familiar to Billy. Instead, he stood in the torrential rain cranking and cranking the starter handle, until tired and dispirited, he enlisted the help of passers-by to push the car under nearby cover. There, in readiness to really get down to business, he proceeded to undress, until Billy anxious that he should go no further than his vest and trousers, begged a bit of rag from an interested spectator and wiped the magneto dry. Then she made the driver crank up, as she tested the spark with a screwdriver and Hey Presto! Too dirty, too wet and too late for Lord Liverpool's reception, but voted the most wonderful mechanic on Raratonga, Billy returned home.

The following day, the Platts hosted a luncheon at the residency in Avarua for His Excellency and entourage. Poor Mrs Platts. Not only would her freezer not open, but food had gone astray and her suppliers, being *en fête*, were too busy to replenish her stocks. To cap it all, the two guests, who were to be seated next to Lord and Lady Liverpool, arrived horribly late. It was not their fault, they had ordered a car in plenty of time, but punctuality was a concept foreign to their driver. When Billy and Dobson walked in, it was into a stiff and silent company. Despite being as cheerful as she could, Billy thought *it was a sticky party and Lord Liverpool a fat and very heavy man to entertain.*[7] Tea on board the *Tutainikai* was hardly any better, but what was *quite worth the boredom* was watching the more stout-hearted of the elite of Raratonga, both white and brown, bedecked in their best, *trying to make the gangway as the tug heaved up and down alongside the steamer.*

The following reciprocal entertainment by the Raratongans put Billy in mind of how once the islanders' captives must have felt, as they watched the dancing, impressive and very barbaric, before they became the feast's main dish, Long Pig.[8] On the second day's entertainment hosted by a king of another village (it had been a queen the day before), she rather pitied Lord Liverpool as he sweated in his uniform of office, seated on a carved wooden stool. Beside him his host's decorously cool take on formality consisted of *a very old top hat, blue trousers and a dark blue waistcoat, bare feet, and just nothing else.*

The overnight disappearance of their outrigger was as mysterious as its sudden appearance nearly three months earlier. *We sorrowed for the good sails we had made and the many fish we had landed in her,* but it was time for Billy to cast-off for home. The spirits that had watched over them had reclaimed their toy. But first, she and Dobson, whose fame, or notoriety, depending on ones' point of view, were to attend a 'Tutuka', a now obsolete ceremony, instituted by the first Christian missionaries, in which six native houses in each village would win a prize for being the cleanest and best kept. Like so many events for the islanders, *birth, death, marriage, returning home, going away,* it was an excuse for a celebration, in which *orange wine, which attacks the walking powers chiefly,* was an obligatory constituent. One hundred suckling pigs were slaughtered, wrapped in banana leaves and roasted overnight in pits covered by red-hot stones. *The sight was scarcely appetising, the fat ran out through the leaves, the bigger pigs were raw inside and though most of them were very small sucking pigs, no one could think 100 roast pigs a charming sight.* Billy prayed she would not be invited to the feast. Being a member of the inspection party was trying enough; ennui threatened to overwhelm her after ten houses *with exactly the same furniture or lack of furniture,* but she did covet the woven mats, and bedcovers and cushions of local and bold design and rather regretted that it was no longer the accepted custom to put your hand on something you would like as a gift.

A picnic on the beach – she had managed to avoid the native feast – and the long day came to an end. Deadly tired and laden with shells and wreaths, Billy and Dobson headed home in Peaira's buggy, but sleep did not come easily that night. Driven off her verandah and indoors by the wet and blowy weather, she was driven out again by the rats that nibbled her hair, but two horses, noisily protesting their entanglement in the ropes tethering them to a nearby tree, had her up once again. After sorting them out, she made for the shore, where she found a *dry patch of sand under a bank, scraped a hole for hip and shoulder, and slept till dawn with no rats or horses, only hermit crabs who were silent.* She saw the dawn from her bed, *bathed and had a sun and wind bath.*

Her pareo (sarong) packed, and the little house cleared, it was time to leave Raratonga.

CHAPTER 27

LIQUIDATION

The end of a partnership

'The decorations were very smart, wide bands of scarlet bunting being used to represent a frieze and alternately round the walls were true lovers' knots of black crinkly paper and quaint little bouquets of red japonica.' The Canterbury Club Ball was lavish in its honour of the visit of HMS *New Zealand* and Viscount Jellicoe of Scapa, a future Governor General Of New Zealand (1920-1924). Among the guests was 'Mrs Maurice Hewlett (London)', wearing a 'floral tunic frock of pink shiny satin' – a frock, one fears, in a class of its own, as all the others described by *The Lyttleton Times* were prefaced with 'very lovely', 'elegant' or 'beautiful'.

Billy and Dobson had arrived in the second week of September to find Christchurch (*a sort of imitation Salisbury and very English cathedral town*) full of *gaiety and great rejoicing*: the Admiral was to present a flag of the *New Zealand* to the city. A nice hotel, a good dinner and a trip to the cinema marked their return to civilisation. A couple of days later and Billy, thanks to a Mrs Anderson, was enjoying meeting a number of interesting people, watching the *universally good* dancing and partaking of a *swagger supper* at that Canterbury Club Ball.

Billy's knack of acquiring friends and contacts wherever she went, no doubt enhanced by her reputation as Mrs Maurice Hewlett, was a useful talent that allowed her, in the couple of weeks before she sailed for home, to learn enough of New Zealand for it to affect her powerfully. First off, Mrs Wigram, wife to the founder of The Canterbury (NZ) Aviation Co., organised permission for her to be taken up in the latest Bristol fighter.

Full of buck at the thought of going in so fast a machine, Billy had strapped on cap, goggles and belt with keen anticipation but, although overwhelmed by *the beauty of the scape – land, sea, mountains, snow, distant mist, where light and shade all united to create a wonderland of colour, form and distance*, she had been a touch disappointed when her pilot had declined to loop the loop. Flying with Sopwith, she reflected, had been far more exciting. However, she spoke enthusiastically to the *Lyttleton Times* of the uphill pioneering work undertaken by the Canterbury (NZ) Aviation Company at Sockburn and the suitability of the Canterbury Plains for training pilots. In her view, the mountainous terrain of a great part of the country made seaplanes an essential for New Zealand and she sketched her vision of little seaplanes, with wings folded, nestling in sheltered points all round the coast, 'ready for defensive patrol work, or carrying between seaport towns.' She could not emphasise enough the part that flying would take in opening up so sparsely populated a country, where the ships were slow 'and the trains were not everything that could be desired,' the last being a remark of unparalleled diplomacy on Billy's part. A fellow passenger, recipient of her eloquence on the extraordinarily obstructive system of booking railway tickets and the agonies of travel, made worse by strikes or lack of coal, had been moved to remind her that New Zealand was 'God's own country', to which she agreed, with the exception of its trains. *'The trains are certainly so,'* he answered. *'For He loveth all creeping and crawling things.'*

A renewal of her acquaintanceship with the witty and entertaining Dr Pomare,[1] the well-known Maori doctor and health reformer, who had been part of Lord Liverpool's entourage visiting Raratonga, allowed her to learn more about a people in whom she detected a *touch of poetry in their nature and turns of expression*. And what she saw of New Zealand women made her admire the way they coped with life's trials, big and small. She was thinking most particularly about housework here, for even wealthy housewives generally did their own, as servants were hard to come by. When she had joined Dr Daisy Platts-Mills,[2] a prominent and pioneering woman doctor, and dampened and folded the clothes while her friend ironed them in the kitchen, Billy had been charmed by the naturalness of it all. Alternately delighted and exhausted by the freedom and democracy of the country – she found it disconcerting to be discussing cooking with a fellow guest, a fat and vulgar cook housekeeper one minute, and books and art with her hostess the next – she knew without doubt that she wished to return to New Zealand.

Good lord! What a ship. The old loafing 'Athenic' took nearly two months to reach England. The Panama Canal, *a modern wonder of the world,* opened just five years earlier, and Washington, a congenial overnight stop away from the slow and dirty coaling of the ship at Baltimore, went some way to relieve the tedium of the journey, but a*fter the burst of Washington,* it was a matter of endurance and Billy survived *by writing all the morning, not talking before teatime,* and joining Colonel B.[3] in being *the leaders and clowns* of their *very family first class circle. Really English and really old,* she was, along with the Colonel B., the only other English person *not afraid of being natural!* 'If only some of these good people knew what fun it was to be natural, – and not to care whether one is *outre* or not, the world would be a very different place. As it is, what precious few people *dare* enjoy themselves!' Thus had Maurice written to his fiancée in 1887. So, dared by the Colonel, Billy did walk down the centre of the tea-table, she did wear her nightgown to dinner and she did pour iced water down a man's shirt front, which is perhaps not quite what Maurice had had in mind thirty years earlier. She even let the Colonel cut her hair with nail scissors on deck, but for whose amusement it is hard to guess.

Billy had *left a great big lump of love behind, for (she) had learnt enough of the Southern Ocean to love her skies by day and stars by night,* but the achingly slow sea voyage home worked like a kindly buffer between a dream made real and the reality of a post-war England. Boarding the ship at Liverpool had been as Billy wrote: *the practical end to my aviation period. I left everything that had overbrimmed my life since 1910, and was glad in one way for the change.* But what, one might ask, of poor Blondeau? Had he felt abandoned when his fellow director left him to run the factory on his own for eight months? Poor and abandon are emotive words and imply that theirs had been more than a working partnership, but had it? Insisting that it had been purely a comradely partnership would unfairly deny our heroine personal sex appeal and the chance of a late-flowering romance – she had been forty-six and seven years older than Blondeau when they first met. On the other hand, extrapolating that theirs had been an intimate relationship, because they shared abodes, would be too simplistic as the imperative to husband their meagre funds would have been sufficient reason for sharing accommodation. Also, for Mrs Maurice

Hewlett to have gone to France under a pseudonym to save her husband embarrassment, only then to indulge in an adulterous relationship in so public a place as Brooklands, is beyond credibility. Her honesty and dislike of hypocrisy could have made her happy to carry on an affair in public, but her disapproval of one member of the 'track' sharing a house with a lady who, *very wisely left the house where she had no moral right to be and did not wish to be found*, would suggest otherwise. Machinery, and machinery of a particular kind, had brought Hewlett and Blondeau together. If there had been no war, might they have stayed together as long as they did? It is hard to say. Billy concluded her memoir with her farewell party at the Omnia Works; a handwritten postscript, entitled *Interval after 1919 N.Z.*, mentions Blondeau one last time *The works were very piano, Gustave was trying with superhuman efforts to galvanise them into new activities.* As he had arrived in her life, without remark, so he left.

It had been very much in his own interest that Blondeau should find an alternative to the manufacture of aircraft. He had money invested in the firm, and at forty-eight, was too young to retire and too old easily to find employment elsewhere, whether in England or France. Finding a product to manufacture and sell in sufficient quantity to keep the reduced company afloat was a challenge, so there was something symbolically charming about his decision, as a flyer and engineer who had turned farmland into a factory, to make stationary machines for farmers. *The Implement and Machinery Review* were impressed by his stationary engine Omnia; it was economical on fuel, simple to understand and easy to run, making it, in their view, greatly appealing to farmers. Intended to drive anything from a circular saw to cream separators at £40 a go, the Omnia stationary engine sounded a bargain. Sadly, there were not enough farmers requiring Omnia threshing machines, straw elevators, or stationary engines to save the company and, in the same year that the giant Sopwith Aviation company closed, so did the Omnia Works.[4] Hewlett and Blondeau Ltd went into liquidation. On October 19, 1920, Messrs Fuller, Horsey, Sons and Cassell began the six day auction of the Works and its contents. No one opened the bidding for the eight acre site, with 110,000 square feet floor space, at £100,000, nor indeed at the reserve of £50,000 – Electrolux acquired it in 1926 for £27,000 – but machinery and equipment of every conceivable shape, size and sort, from every shop, store, and office, even from the first aid room and the canteen, were sold at bargain prices in what the local paper called a 'big event'.

Gustave had been a wonder in Billy's eyes – after Maurice's nervy inadequacies concerning anything mechanical, Gustave was positively heroic. He was also a *born teacher*, whose *patience knew no bounds*. Such a model of steady virtues should not, therefore, be allowed to vanish so completely; particularly, when he had encouraged the more giddy Billy in an adventure that cocked a snook at convention, put her husband's reputation in jeopardy, risked her own, and gave her what she wanted: an aeroplane she could fly.

Blondeau was an enigma and a serious-looking one at that, although his fledgling co-director looked no less serious when photographed in the Omnia Works, Vardens Road. He was a Frenchman who chose to live in a country whose language he never really mastered; a fine engineer; a greatly respected boss, and, according to Mark, Pia's eldest son, sinister. There is nothing to support this thrilling observation, other, perhaps, than his strangling the cat that stole his supper, which does show a certain ruthless streak. However, there is something a touch unsettling in how Blondeau arranged to live out his retirement, clues to which were only disclosed with the discovery of his will. Uncertainty as to whether Gustave had remained in England combined with a false assumption that, if he had, he would have died, at the latest, aged eighty-five, had meant that searches through the Registries of marriages and deaths had thrown up a surprising number of Blondeaus (or should it be Blondeaux?), but never the right one. Gustave, retrieved from the obscurity of the past by his will, defied all expectations by dying, aged ninety-four, in March 1965; not only that but he had died in Luton and the chief beneficiary of his estate had been a woman understood to have been his one-time landlady. As her son had been the recipient of a modest legacy, a hunch that he might still live in Luton, when acted upon, unearthed modest treasure. Eric Pedder had photographs, souvenirs that his mother had saved from the factory, and his own memories of Mr Blondeau, as he unfailingly called him. He knew Oak, now Oakley Road, where the Omnia Works had been built; the Electrolux factory, with one original block, all now demolished; Hewlett Road and Hewlett Path,[5] a ghostly echo of Hewlett and Blondeau Ltd; the site of the wet fish shop that belonged to Mr Choppard, the firm's driver; and the bungalow (now semi-detached) where Billy had lived in The Avenue close to the junction with Grange Road and conveniently situated for Leagrave station. Here, at the junction, Blondeau claimed, was where Kroshka would wait to greet him whenever he returned home from a trip to London.

In a portrait photograph taken in the Thirties, a dapper and by then moustacheless Gustave looked much more the type to invest in a cinema in Clacton than the serious engineer of before, but that venture was short-lived and Gustave was left to indulge his love of the silver screen as a patron instead. After a spell in London he returned to Luton but, rather than returning to his house, 'Maymore' in Marsh Road, he moved to 176 Old Bedford Road and it is here that the slightly unsettling image of a sleek, grey cuckoo will intrude. His former secretary, a milliner who had joined Omnia Works at the start of the Great War and who had helped Blondeau clear up the business and clear out the factory when it went into liquidation, became his housekeeper. When Blondeau made over the house to her in 1940, Olive Pedder became his landlady, but, to some, including her daughter-in-law, her husband appeared more lodger-like than Mr. Blondeau. Certainly, it was only ever Mrs Pedder who was Blondeau's companion on his annual holiday, when they would travel on the Golden Arrow to visit his family in France. Mrs Pedder's son, Eric, had the warmest memories of Blondeau helping him with maths and science homework; he also had, thanks to his amateur enthusiasm for recording, a reel-to-reel tape of Blondeau reminiscing. It was a breathtaking moment when Blondeau's rapid, heavily accented and broken English, filled the room. Transported by this modest time machine, as Blondeau laughed heartily, or paused, no doubt to allow for elaborate hand gestures, the listener was there, touching aviation history. Regrettably, the recording's painful associations for the widow of her gentle Eric sealed its fate. It went missing.

CHAPTER 28

ESSAYIST

A writer to the end

In his essays, the final medium by which he earnt his living, it was as though Maurice had finally lit upon his perfect conveyance, an elegant, well-balanced carriage, drawn by a matching pair of bloods, Well Read and Well Written, in which to bowl along, at a spanking pace, the roads of his own choosing. Certain byways might be visited more than once, but each time a different aspect of the view was presented and, when the going got a little heavy under the weight of erudition and Latin phrases, there was always a breather to be enjoyed, gathering wild raspberries on the Wiltshire downs, glimpsing a moment of domestic intimacy in the lamp-lit cottage windows, or reflecting on the potency of mead.

Balaam[1] is English slang for trumpery paragraphs used to fill out the columns of a magazine or newspaper and, typical of the man, Maurice chose to label his ventures into journalism as such. However, the one hundred and thirty-seven pieces, re-published in four volumes of collected essays, give the lie direct to the trumpery charge. Erudite, with a lively interest in men and the world and possessed of decided views, Maurice, rather than elaborating on a theme in a novel, which had a tendency to give birth to characters such as 'the rotten panting poet in *Mrs Lancelot*' who had so irritated the New York representative of Maurice's agent,[2] was able to express himself directly and succinctly. Of course, there was the anxious search for a home for his essays, but once he was given a monthly slot with the *London Mercury* courtesy of Squire, its editor, and once he had delegated the distasteful task of chasing fees to the Society of Authors, his feelings of insecurity abated somewhat. The subjects of his essays ranged through history, literature, nature and reflection on contemporary issues, even his duties as a local councillor and magistrate. But, however earnest he might sometimes be, he still wrote with a lightness of touch. 'Parenthood is one thing, and marriage is another, one a good deal the older relation. In my belief, happiness consists in the two – but who am I to say that either without the other is not in itself a good? A child is a child, however begotten, and its mother a mother however made so.' So he wrote of a quietly dignified single mother who required him, in his capacity as a magistrate, to attest her vaccination-paper, so that her child 'with three romantic forenames and its mother's surname, was laid out to be the battleground of Providence and the small-pox, those inveterate foes.'

Nourished by dwelling in a beautiful river valley, influenced by his neighbours who lived 'close to the heart of their great Mother Earth' and who had 'an insight for many things hidden from wiser folk,' he brewed his pet nostrums for the healthy recovery of his country from the sickness of war. He wanted men to be gentlemen and women to be modest. He wanted what he called the 'Laws of Being' to be obeyed; men to have work and women to have children. Where now the animality, the slippery subversiveness of his earlier "fleshly" authorship? Extremes had always appealed to him from the 'combination of shocking barbarism with delicate sentiment' of the Middle Ages to the starkness of the Norse sagas; the soft centre had always been his romances. But now Maurice, mellowed by age, the war and reduced circumstances, had fashioned a new ideal to promote. Poverty, Love and England and through the first two, he believed the third would thrive. He also found himself increasingly drawn to the Quaker religion and he undertook a week-long tour to Manchester, Liverpool, Sheffield, Scarborough and Darlington speaking on the Peace for the Society of Friends in the first month of 1921. He was accommodated in Quaker households and was utterly charmed by the Friends' way of life, but despite finding in the Quaker Faith a credo that matched his own, he did not feel the need to seek formal membership. Gregariousness afforded him no strength, but the feeling that what he believed was shared by the gentlest and noblest community of people he had ever mixed with, did. He had returned home, extremely tired, but stimulated.

As industrious as he was, firing off essays when Committee meetings, Petty Sessions and the like allowed, going 'a bust on b.f.t.'s'[3] as Maurice confessed to Lotta Leaf, another extravagant acquirer of plants, proved a rude awakening for him. The overall cost of running the Old Rectory, plus what he spent on the garden, outstripped his income some threefold. He might preach poverty, but he drew the line at penury. He would have to move. 'I leave this old house at Michaelmas for a smaller one – possibly en route for the much larger one which waits yawning for the needy,' he wrote to Squire.

Mascalls, its pseudonym in an essay and the name by which it is known today, bore no resemblance to the hermitage he had once, tongue in cheek, envisioned for his latter years. It was neither built of puddled chalk and straw and thatched with reeds, nor was it thirty-foot long with a gallery at each end, with a bed in one for himself and for a co-hermit or hermitess in the other. It was a damp-ridden, rat-gnawed stone cottage in Broad Chalke, with 'parting walls, sagging ceilings, gaping floor-boards, dry-rotten joists.'

'Yet what a pleasant seat for an old house, on a ridge above the eddying chalk-stream, full in the sun, with a view over the valley into the heart of the West! What a shady orchard of cider-apples, what a sheltered, ripe old walled-garden, what a green water-meadow edging the brook!' Maurice might exclaim at how the family, tenants for generations, had uncomplainingly allowed time, hard times and disrepair to make it uninhabitable, but he wondered with heartfelt sympathy what it must be like 'to be driven from it, if you have lived there all your life, and laboured its earth, and gone out and in; brought your bride there, got your children there, seen your old father die and borne him thence to the churchyard, returning then to know that you are Mascall of Mascalls.' Similarly, the irony, that he had benefitted from a landlord's termination of an agricultural worker's tenancy would not have been lost on him. Much of his work had been taken up by inspecting just such cottages which, if they were not purchased and repaired by the Housing Committee, would have been condemned for habitation.

Billy inspected his future home and gave it her approval. As work began on Mascalls, Maurice started to empty the Old Rectory. Furniture, surplus to his needs, Billy undertook to use or store in an outhouse at her bungalow in Leagrave. Paintings and books by the ton (many of them rare and valuable collectors' items) were sold, or packed. Leaving his garden, the one creation that had never disappointed him, was a wrench, but there was a new garden to plan and plant. The yield from his vines had been bottled and corked, November was hurrying into December, when, and as if for old time's sake in the old house, Maurice suffered his winter 'flu (his failure to succumb in the terrible pandemic of 1918-19 is a mystery), but, by mid-December, he was installed in his little cottage. He might be tired and feeling his age and every chimney might smoke in one wind, some in all winds, and one in no wind, but, as he wrote against Christmas Day, 1921, he was quietly happy. Gone were all the trappings begot by his past success and affluence. Long gone was the angst of his love for Gay and rare were his visits to her court at Gosberton, now frequented more by those of his introduction than himself.[4]

To Maurice's surprise two American writers sought him out in his final retreat. Hamlin Garland, with daughter, an equally ardent fan, particularly of *Richard Yea and Nay*,[5] was most disconcerted to discover its author living in so humble a home. However, the spirits of both were wonderfully restored by permission to visit the Old Rectory, the true and fitting setting for an author of medieval romances. Charitably, they deemed the quaint and dainty cottage sadly lacking in modern conveniences to be a haven of a scholar grown elderly. In contrast, Walter Tuttle was entirely satisfied by the charming stone cottage; it was the sort of retreat that every artisan of the arts yearned for. Happily for all concerned, their visits had been expected, otherwise finding Maurice gardening, as Squire once had, in a brown dressing-gown and sandals, with bare feet, gray and cadaverous, might have seemed an eccentric step too far for his American admirers. As it was both parties found Maurice a charming host, neither remote nor austere and with a glance candid and friendly, although he had seemed rather small and sad to Garland, for Tuttle, as he sketched him, Maurice had been a beguiling raconteur.

Maurice's birthday, 62 – *God bless us all* – *Board Meeting. Dined and slept at Netherhampton,* where Lady Newbolt – her husband, Henry, was on his way to Canada – was charming and let Maurice talk into the small hours. It was 1923 and with crocuses, plants of symbolic and magical properties often used as imagery in both Maurice's poetry and prose, appearing in mid-January, daffodils before the end of February, and grape hyacinths and three sorts of anemones by the first of March, Maurice rated it an *annus mirabilis* in the garden. 'I have been writing,' he wrote to Lotta, 'about flowers for *Country Life* – twaddle, but they seem to like it. I don't know anything about them really.' The last a typically deprecatory fib ,for his four flower essays are an exuberant tour of his garden.

Careful only to write for publication on subjects which he had researched, or knew well, Maurice leaves an impression of a man with limited and rarefied tastes. He never touched upon contemporary music or art, which is a shame as it gives a false impression of a man deaf and blind to what was happening beyond literature in the arts. That he was not is hinted at among *The Letters* and unpublished correspondence. He had been 'much edified and amused' by the Italian Teatro dei Piccoli at the Scala Theatre which, with better dressing and decor generally, he thought could have rivalled the Russian Ballet. And he saw *L'Apres Midi d'une Faune* in Paris; he enjoyed the operas of Wagner and Strauss; he invited Ezra Pound for Christmas; he made sure to read *Blast*, the Vorticist magazine. He also loved to go the Music Hall and was moved by Paul Nash's *Menin Road*. Contemptuous of men who, as they grew old, grew intellectually and emotionally fat or feeble, Maurice, in company, was effortlessly the contemporary of any younger man. If he had attended university rather than moving, as the eldest son, into the family business of law, might he have then been in a position to follow a career in anything other than the church or law? And, if he had, would Academe have tempted him? A brilliant talker, opinionated, passionate to learn as well as to impart knowledge, a lover of language – English and foreign - interested in philosophy, religion and politics, and ready to box the compass in any discussion on any subject, it is not hard to imagine him as a stimulating and provocative don.

May 2: *Home.* May 15: *County Council all day.* May 16: *Revising Immortality.* May 25: *Finished Oxford Lecture I draft.* May 26: *Assizes Grand jury. Lunched with the judge.* May 30: *Finished draft Lecture II. Fine. East wind.*

Two weeks later Pia wrote to inform Maurice's literary agent, the Authors Syndicate, that Mr. Hewlett was very dangerously ill and would not be able to attend to business for weeks. The following day, Billy sat in the bay window of the sunny little sitting room of the cottage and wrote to Edmund Gosse. It was Friday 15 June.

'Dear Mr Gosse, I feel I must tell you myself about Maurice, for we have known you as one of our oldest friends, and whatever has happened you are always a real friend.

Maurice was ill about 10 days, he had a relapse after 'flu and got pneumonia. His heart couldn't stand the long strain, and tho' he fought well, his heart gave out at 7.30 am. this morning. He said many funny things, even up to last night, & on Wednesday he told me "he was quite happy & enjoying it all," which I take to mean that he then knew he couldn't get well.

His brain was still full of ideas, and he had many projects, but I would rather him go before he got less brilliant, as he was the most severe critic of himself. Tell dear Mrs. Gosse and your family I feel you are all helping me somehow.

Yours. affecly.

Hilda B. Hewlett [6]

'We announce with much regret that Mr. Maurice Hewlett, poet, novelist, critic, and essayist, died yesterday at his residence at Broadchalke, near Salisbury, of pneumonia following influenza. He was sixty-two. The funeral service will be at Broadchalke on Monday at 1.30. He requested that there should be no flowers and no mourning.'

Billy had been there with Pia to nurse him, once again, when his life hung in the balance. But all their care could not help pull him through, when diligent smoking and nervous intensity and years of unstinting labour took their toll. His death, shocking and dismaying to his friends, was sincerely regretted in generous obituaries in journals and newspapers.

' … One remembers him, apart from his achievements in literature, as a man of singular charm and friendliness, an artist to his finger-tips, a man who touched life closely at many points, and whose whole soul was filled with an intense and creative love of beauty.'

The Times, Saturday, June 16, 1923.

' … To those who were his friends – and to be his friend was to be devoted to him without reservation – his death means more than the end of a full and varied artistic career. It comes as the death of a young man comes. Physically, with his sparse white hairs and seamed dark face, he showed his age. But when he was talking, it was impossible to remember it, so great was his zest for life, so unimpaired his curiosity, so hearty his hatreds and loves, so frank and impetuous his speech.'

The Observer, Sunday, June 17, 1923.

'… Hewlett's unwearied intellectual curiosity gave his readers many diversified pleasures. The true way of gratitude to such an artist is to remember the ample scope of his own enjoyment.'

New York Times, Monday, June 18, 1923

' … Maurice Hewlett did many things, and did them well. He has to his credit the romances of his earlier days, of which *The Forest Lovers* is the most conspicuous; some of the most vivid historical novels in the language; modern novels of considerable invention; short stories of distinction; poems and dramas that have not received the attention and praise they deserve; and a great deal of miscellaneous work which shows him to be a graceful essayist, a discriminating critic and a politician with generous sympathies.'

The Manchester Guardian, Friday, June 22, 1923.

' … As a literary career, his seems exceptionally interesting, and very much of its time. And when one reflects that his life was only sixty-two years and that he was thirty-six when success first came to him, one is surprised. But not more surprised at this than regretful over the thought at a generation hence, probably not more than a tiny remnant of his own countrymen will read or remember any portion of his various and accomplished writing.'

The New Statesman, Saturday, June 23, 1923

' … It must be said also that he was a splendid friend, fiery in his loyalty, indulgent in his patience, and a great open-air companion.'

Hugh Walpole: D.N.B. 1922-1930

' … He died a disappointed man, I fear, and I doubt if his books will find many new readers. They were vigorous and full of brio, but they were derivative, and derivative work seldom has a second innings. But books are not all; he was a most tonic personality: I find myself missing him continually; he always made me feel fifty per cent better.'

E.V. Lucas: *Reading, Writing and Remembering*

'… I admired the bravery with which he refused to follow the blind admirers of H.G. Wells, and his courage in chiding Hardy for the 'Apologia' with which he unwisely prefaced his last poem. And he never hit "below the belt".'

Letter of condolence from Edward Clodd

'As it was not possible for me to attend the service at the Temple, I feel I must just say a word to you. Maurice and I had practically no opportunities of cultivating our acquaintance into a fully expressed friendship; and for all I know he may have thought me quite indifferent to him; but I really had a sort of affectionate regard for him which was very sensibly touched by the quite unexpected news of his death.

'Of course I have no idea what manner of adventure it was to be married to him – authors should not be marriageable: they should be boarded out in asylums with relays of adoring disciples to look after them – but now that all the bother of him is over, and nothing left but the glory, you will not mind my intruding with my little handshake. I expect we are both glad we knew him.'[7]

G.B.S. in a letter to Billy after the Memorial Service on Wednesday, 13 July, 1923

Everyone talks of Maurice, and they all say nice things about him.

All very well to say 'too much of a Pilgrim' but that was his nature. I don't see that Literary Immortality is the only, or the prime, object of life. I wish I could have my Maurice back. He was difficult with his lifelong scrapes and his wild opinions but it was so easy to love him.

Sir Henry Newbolt[8]

And the most fitting tribute of all: -

'I never knew before that there were such kind people in the world.'

An old shepherd.

CHAPTER 29

WHAT TO DO NEXT?

And where?

According to Maurice's will, Billy was 'otherwise provided for' and, therefore, not a beneficiary beyond having the right to select whatever she wished from his personal belongings and effects. Cecco and Pia were the chief beneficiaries – of very little, in the end. As his final will was drawn up mid-November 1919, round about the time Billy returned from the South Pacific, it is most likely that Maurice had discussed his intentions with her. Billy, as a joint partner in a company in which her husband had invested, would have thought the will perfectly fair, besides it is pretty certain that Maurice had put more than £1,000 into the company, he had hinted to Macmillan that aviation had taken a good deal of his money. Billy also stood to benefit from the realisation of the company's assets, although it is clear that, when it came to it, she had rated the value of the Omnia Works land and premises greater than it proved. She, no doubt, also approved of her husband leaving his posthumous reputation in Gay's hands. Even if she had felt adequate to the task, she would soon have become bored of dealing effectively with all his papers. Besides, there was the delicate matter of Maurice's and Gay's affair and its legacy of many years of correspondence.

Although they had not lived together for more than ten years before his death, Maurice and Billy had exchanged news and seen each other as much as good friends, who live at a distance to each other, do. Thus, once the company had gone into liquidation, Billy, with time on her hands and a garden big enough, was inspired to emulate Maurice; she too would grow vines. But, after taking herself off to France to learn in conditions, which even by her own stoical standards were grim, Billy discovered winemaking was not for her. Her next venture shortly before Maurice's death had been much more to her liking, three months travelling in Yugoslavia. An interesting choice for a woman on her own, but as the Hewletts had had friends, including Mabel Dearmer, who had served and died in Serbia during the war, it is likely she had a contact there. Maurice had also been commissioned to write a memorial poem dedicated to Elsie Inglis, a Scottish doctor regarded as a veritable saint in Serbia. Certainly, when Billy was in *the comic opera city of Belgrade,* she visited the hospital established by another remarkable Scottish doctor, the *very shy, young and quite good-looking* Katherine Macphail. Indeed, she found herself compelled to visit that children's hospital every day of the week she was in Belgrade, she was so moved by *the sadness and the beauty* of it.

Impervious to travel sickness, fearless whether in a storm at sea or being driven round precipitous mountain roads; uncowed by officials – they were always petty in her book; and with a knack of cultivating influential friends, as well as making new ones, travelling alone gave Billy every opportunity to seize the best of every moment and endure the worst with humour, or daring. Her seemingly reckless attitude to strangers and their invitations were only ever to her advantage and she reached parts of the country no other tourist reached. She met Italians, impoverished White Russians, Poles, Montenegrins (armed), Serbs, Americans, artists and a Miss Dickinson, nicknamed'The Dick', who ran an orphanage in the mountains above Sarajevo and was as adventurous a companion as Billy could have hoped for in a country that was slowly recovering from the brutal effects of war and the terrible ravages of typhus.

When it came time to leave, there was not a sleeper to be had on the Orient Express for a week. *So just to buck them up I said in a lordly way, "I think I'll fly to Paris,"* and with that Billy bethought herself of a conversation she had enjoyed with a *Roumanian lady at a traditional wedding party in a Serbian club.* She, it had transpired, was married to the director of a French-Romanian company which had just opened up a new air route from Belgrade to Paris. Enterprise and persistence – Billy had no idea of the woman's name, nor the address of the company – eventually led her to the temporary Belgrade office of the French-Romanian Company of Air Navigation.[1] Its sole occupant, a laconic Frenchman, accepted her fare and

Monday for her suggested day of departure, but left Billy with the ever vexatious matter of her luggage, now overburdened with the addition of five traditional overcoats, several smaller items of national dress and four perfectly matched Stone Martin skins from the Trebinje market. The extreme gallantry of a friend of a friend, an impeccable English gentleman of stately manners, rescued her from her plight: her luggage would be included with his, when he took the Orient Express.

At Pancevo[2] (now the airport for Belgrade), she met up with the French pilot and his wife and spent a *joyous afternoon with pilots, mechanics and dogs on the ground*; so reminiscent of Mourmelon days. Take-off was the following morning. With her ears stuffed with cottonwool against the noise and chill of the air, all was perfect bliss for Billy until rain and a steady head wind forced her to crouch *behind the bit of talc* (windshield), the only form of shelter there was. Some four hours later, they landed at Budapest, where a kind office girl gave her a cup of black tea, which washed down the two small rolls she had grabbed from her morning coffee, and then she and her pilot set off in a different plane. Some five years out of the business, Billy was no longer *au fait* with the makes and class of aircraft.[3] As the weather grew even more vile, the promised rest and food in Vienna loomed large in her thoughts, but when the pilot showed every intention of stopping the night in Vienna, Billy expressed her preference for continuing with the journey, if another pilot and machine could be found. Indeed, they could, but it meant no time for any such luxury as eating. Her stomach growling with hunger, the by now bone cold Billy could do nothing but endure the bucketing and bumping of the faster craft; at Prague, she decided, she would positively insist on food. But no, the next machine in the relay was warmed up with the pilot already at the controls. *'Mais depechez-vous, madame,'* someone called, as she tottered stiffly to the ladies room. Hypothermic and ravenously hungry, but now supplied with a pair of goggles, so she could use her eyes *which before had been impossible, for the wind blew them to,* Billy rather enjoyed the final leg of the journey. It was remarked of passenger transport at the time, that many could barely stand the conditions for two hours. By the time they reached Strasbourg, Billy had been flying in an open plane for over ten hours. *Deaf, stiff and feeling like an empty portmanteau,* she had to be dragged out of her seat and lifted to earth. *'N'importe ou,'* she managed to croak, when asked where she wished to stay. Whisked through the city in a car hooting all the while, taking corners on two wheels, and full of men volubly and understandably concerned for her welfare, Billy felt fear for the first time that day. At last, a big hotel, a comfortable room, a French maid standing by ready for orders and a head waiter who begged her not ... But that, sadly, we will never know! The last page of her typescript was lost too long ago.

Once the sale of the Omnia Works site to Electrolux had gone through in 1927, Billy, with a tidy sum banked in her name, at last had the means to return to New Zealand. As unconventional as ever – Veena had noted in her engagement diary against a dinner date with Olga: 'Billy there style boy!' – her chosen mode of transport part way to paradise, nevertheless, concerned her family and friends. *'You'll be sorry when you hear the boat is too decayed and old to start. Eaten up by rats and cockroaches of course.'* Should it prove so, Billy had every intention of keeping it to herself. But she didn't need to, although there was one small drawback to the sumptious accommodation she enjoyed on the cargo boat, the *Santos* of the Johnson Line, namely her cabin mate, an *old, dowdy and proper* American spinster. The Swedish Christmas, celebrated soon after they had passed through the Panama Canal, was *a milestone, a bizarre mixture of North and South*; the Swedish crew the happiest and most democratic she had ever encountered; and the multi-lingual captain the most kind-hearted and unselfish of her experience. It was he who had gone to Billy's rescue when the ship was struck by a tornado. She had taken to sleeping on deck, once they were in warmer waters, and pinioned by the wind, had been unable to do anything but hang on to her rug and mattress in her corner and keep her head down. Suddenly, above the din, she heard his voice apologising for disturbing her, but he thought she had better get inside and, somehow, he bundled her into his *deck cabin*, where he made the bed, waited till she was in it, turned out the light and left. The American spinster, shocked by Billy laughing at being put to bed by the Captain, thought it her punishment for wanting to sleep in odd places. The miscreant could only think it was her reward.

From San Francisco to New Zealand, Billy travelled on the *Makura* and had the added pleasure of discovering that it was captained by her old friend from the *Paloona*. On a one-day stop at Raratonga, she politely excused herself from joining the shore party of a fellow passenger, the Prime Minister of New Zealand. Instead, she and Dobson, looking fit and every inch a soldier and who had been in charge of the returned servicemen lined up to greet their honoured guest (not Billy), visited their old lagooon. *'To hell with all men and their conventions!'* she had cried, as she raced for the sea. *'This is what I've lived for!'*

In New Zealand, she caught up with old friends; she tried the best of trout fishing on Lake Taupo, and was highly amused the day *the Duke of York drove by, and all the fishing men and women stood by the roadside in full rig, holding up their rods as a polite welcome;* and in Tauranga she explored what else the town had to offer when the weather completely scuppered her week of sea-fishing.

En route for home and once more in Raratonga, she indulged herself in *'mat fever'*, i.e. *lying about watching the lagoon and talking to old friends,* but after a week she was restless. Dire warnings of dirt, cockroaches, a diet of bully beef and an over-powering smell of copra, bearable only to white women if they were either a *nurse on duty or somebody's wife who had to accompany her husband as Agent or Resident Commissioner,* made signing on as a passenger on a schooner of 150 tons that traded between the southern Cook Islands quite irresistible. As one of the last to board the tender of the *Tagua,* she joined in the laughter when a bystander was heard to sigh deeply and say, *"Poor devils."*

The native crew, some of whom were accompanied by their wives of amazing girth, squeezed into what space was not taken up by their cargo of copra, cotton, food stuffs and kerosine. Of the three male passengers, one shared the Captain's bunk, one slept by the dining table in the cabin and one slept on deck. Billy had the luxury of *a very hard bunk, one pillow, one sheet and plenty of air.* The ship's three cats fitted in where they could. The contrast between cruising on a liner, First Class, and sailing in the gloriously untidy, but business-like schooner could not have been greater, nor Billy's pleasure; the calm and peace, after the vibration and noise of a steamship, was a revelation. The dress code, bare feet and, for the men, *vest and shorts, the former holey, the latter very short,* was sensible; the early morning slosh with seawater adequate; and the locally grown and roasted coffee delicious. *No one to worry, no care taken of one's comfort or wants, just a contented happy crew to whom time, efficiency, and hurry were words of distant places.* When they were becalmed, they fished. When they had to shoot the reefs in the native canoes, that came out to greet and unload the *Tagua* at each island, Billy *just loved* it.

At their first stop, Mangaia, *like two green biscuits, the smaller on on top of the larger one with cream round the edge spilled on the sea*, the island's Resident Commissioner, a Mr McGruther, part-Scot, part-Maori and a fellow passenger, disembarked, repaired to his official residence, and returned formally attired to greet the Captain and his passengers and invite them to his cool and imposing Mission House. Meeting *one of the old style of white men, who drank like a fish, had untold numbers of children and claimed that it was not his fault that they all had different mothers*, made Billy feel very sad and ashamed of her race.

On the island of Mitiaro, they bathed in the lagoon, had cold tea and ship's biscuit for their supper and were eaten in turn by the mosquitoes, as they slept out overnight on the beach; they, by this time, were the remaining two passengers, Billy and an anonymous Englishman. In the morning, on their walk back to where their boat was anchored, they met up with a Catholic priest, who had briefly taken passage on the boat. Billy pitied the *dear man, looking so dreadful in a very long, dirty, black cassock, unshaven and under-washed*, proximity to which latter state had more than once propelled her on deck to seek fresh air.

Off Atiu, Billy caught her first big fish, a five foot, forty pound paara, not bad for a little dot of sixty-three years and five foot two inches. The captain, possibly in the mood for celebration, agreed to indulge her when she suddenly took a fancy to being the *first white woman to land on the deserted island of Tukatea.*[4] The ship's boat with a crew of five was put at her disposal, but once they had negotiated the reef of uncharted waters, there was not a lot, to see besides a great number of birds, a coconut grove and hundreds of huge dried shells of lobster. The landing party shot the reef once again and, not a moment too soon. A storm of such ferocity broke over their heads as they climbed aboard the *Tagua, all hands, including passengers and the Captain, hauled on ropes, let down sails, and worked in the lashing rain for dear life. I stood by, realising it was a toss up if we capsized or not, and I was not going to be below and die in a trap. It was a jolly good fight. I stood by and admired the Captain.* Billy was ever ready to worship a hero. *He yelled his orders, took a gigantic part in helping to carry them out; saw the essentials at a glance, kept his brains, used his sinews, and saved the situation. I had only one tailor-made cigarette left; I smoked it, as it would have been a pity to leave it if we had to be shipwrecked and drowned.*

Safely at Manuae, then owned and cultivated by a Mr Bunting, now uninhabited and a marine park, Billy *nearly cried for sheer joy in the beauty* of the sunset over the ravishing coral island. Then on to Aitutaki, the fat, rolling trader's last port of call. By this time, Billy's trip had taken on an element of a royal progress – the blend of stranger, white and woman was potent – and she was transferred ashore, much to her chagrin, by the Resident Commissioner's own boat, the *Lady Alice*, rather than atop the cargo: *no one had made any fuss when (she) sat perched on the chest of drawers at Aitu.* Immediate and lavish use of carbolic soap and fresh water in a *real bathroom* [5] soon restored her to good humour and after a hot and stuffy night in a comfortable bed with mosquito net in the house of the local schoolmaster and his wife – the Residency was a bachelor establishment, the anonymous Englishman slept there – she was ready for a day's picnicing under coconut palms in the lagoon of a tiny local island. She watched the eight-strong crew of the *Lady Alice* as they fished with spears and *glasses with rubber rims, which enabled them to see clearly,* and admired the *brown naked bodies and well developed muscles of the natives as they rowed with all their might, a rare and beautiful sight.* And as they returned once more to the *Tagua* which, with a fair wind and a little help from her engine, would reach Raratonga with two days to spare before she embarked on her return to civilisation, she *was sad to think those three weeks were ended.* She had loved them more than any other adventure. *They had been the real thing.*

It was the opening night of Grauman's Chinese Theatre and the premiere of Cecil B. de Mille's spectacular, *The King of Kings*[6] and Billy's hotel was just round the corner. As she lay, unable to sleep for all the noise of the razzmatazz, she vowed that if Hell, which had sounded preferable in its more entertaining way to the insufferably dull Heaven, was anything like Hollywood, then she would strive to get to Heaven. She had just spent five wonderful days in the Yosemite in the happy company of a Dr Winslow[7] and his family, which had gone some way to compensate for the regret she felt at leaving the South Seas. Now, the shock of modern city life was searing and matters did not improve. Hollywood, on further acquaintance, made *Sodom and Gomorrah childish in sin.* In Hollywood, *science, literature, religion and all the arts and industries, were used to lure the soul and intellect into degradation – not in the place itself alone, but over the whole world to the masses. Shoddy swindling, sham, extravagant graft –* her indignation was unbounded – *the end and aim of all was to make MONEY.* Worse still, she was *invited to look at the footling fakes and paper toys* of the sets, she, who had stood *dumb and reverently before real works of art.* But her righteous indignation and intemperate description of the Jews, the money men, as she *waited with the poor in pocket, and with the rich in brains, and saw producers, told a few lies, tried to be as nice as possible, and hurried away a wise and a sadder woman,* masked her grievous disappointment. Unconfessed, but revealed in a letter from J.M. Barrie, was her real motive for visiting Hollywood. 'Dear Mrs Hewlett, Here are some letters of introduction which I hope are the sort of thing you mean and that they may be of service to you. Chaplin and Fairbanks I think produce 'on their own'. Mrs Fairbanks is Miss Mary Pickford. I dont know their Holywood (sic) address, and of course they are likely enough to be elsewhere. I should think you would in any case have an interesting time and can see from your letter that it might also prove worthwhile in a business way. All good wishes to your journey and its object.' She and Pia, whose husband Robin had written a treatment of one of Maurice's books, had hoped to profit from them in the cinema. But the Hollywood readers – *the most common, ignorant, vain, empty girls of twenty years old, chosen because what appeals to them will appeal to the vast uneducated masses, pander to their love of vulgarity and excite their lowest passions* – did not share that hope.

The hospitality of Douglas Fairbanks and his wife was balm to the sores of indifference suffered by Mrs Maurice Hewlett, particularly acute after years of flattering attention. A Rolls Royce coupé (it was a matter of importance always to document the make of every car), driven by a Huxley-quoting chauffeur, took her to tea at the Fairbanks's beach house; instruction in film-making as an *Art with a big A* from the screen idol himself; a visit to a couple of houses along the beach, matchless for their taste, convenience, comfort and unthought of luxury and Mrs Hewlett, Disgusted of Righteous City, was prepared to think more favourably of film and the film world. In fact, after a most amusing dinner party *with wit and beauty equally divided in the guests,* she was ready to express the belief that *God might save Hollywood because of one just man and woman: Mr and Mrs Fairbanks.*

Within a couple of years, Billy and the Richards family had left England and settled in Tauranga. The siren call of the Islands had been resisted, not without regret, although judging by a letter from the writer Eden Phillpots to the widow of his old friend, Maurice, Billy had been close to being conned into buying something in the South Sea Islands by a dodgy dealer. However, taking all things into consideration and certainly with regard to the children, Tauranga promised a freer and more rewarding life than had been open to them in the ten years since the war in England. Billy bought a property large enough for her to enjoy creating a garden and the Richards became citrus farmers, six miles from the centre of town and close to the sea. Life on the farm was hard work, but the children ran barefoot, rode bareback (Robin had insisted they learnt to ride without saddles) and were in or on the water most of the summer. Pia created a setting for a childhood that, perhaps, she might have liked herself, and was happy. She never wanted to go back to England and, when she had to give up milking the Jersey cows and other farmerly tasks in order to tutor her daughters, Ann and Elizabeth, she found she enjoyed herself even more. Sadly, the idyll had to come to an end: the financial climate of the time and Robin's ill health, the result of his wounds sustained during the war, made running the farm no longer feasible, and Pia and her family moved to Auckland. No doubt, distance between herself and her mother would have added to the appeal of that city for Pia. Billy had very definite ideas and she had little sympathy or time for Robin.

CHAPTER 30

ONE LAST ADVENTURE

Long distance flight

On her doorstep, figuratively speaking, Billy had all that she could wish for, acres of unspoilt countryside in which to camp, teeming rivers and lakes to be fished and, if all that was too tame, the sea. Clad in an alarming and unique outfit, undoubtedly of her own design, and looking like a cross between a Victorian sea-bather and an elderly member of the chorus in a twenties' pierrot show, she would go deep sea fishing in her thrilling new playground. But it was not all play. Shortly after the end of the war, Billy had spoken on the opportunities, or rather lack of them, for women to become pilots, but her forecast for their future had been along the lines that women would one day *pilot their air car as they now do their land car.* Subsequently, she was able to appreciate the broader potential of aviation (with or without women) and believed sincerely that it was crucial to the development of New Zealand, so together with a Mr H.T. Morris she bought Southern Cross Airways Ltd,[1] a company with ambitions, but only one aeroplane. It was a short-lived venture and the company folded without a single flight being recorded. Rather more successful was her active promotion, as founder member and first president of the Tauranga Aero and Gliding Club (1932), of the search for an alternative site for the Tauranga airfield, whose limitations were glaringly obvious, situated as it was on the tidal flats of the Waikareao estuary, where landing and taking off were restricted to one hour either side of low tide.

Once very much attuned to the use of aircraft for military purposes,

Billy was not slow to perceive the potential in aviation for civilian transport; witness her maiden international flight from Belgrade. Prone to action over reflection, it was very much in her character to investigate the benefits of intercontinental air travel. How much better it would be if she did not have to spend weeks and weeks at sea in order to visit her son, her family and her many dear friends back home. When the gushing *Sydney Sun* reporter interviewed 'England's First Airwoman', who addressed the English-speaking Union of that city in March 1931, she would have been surprised to learn what it was that the 'frail-looking,' – appearances can be so deceptive – 'white-haired soul' with eyes that had not lost 'one atom of their spark and intelligence,' had in mind for her return journey.

One of the friends Billy hoped to meet, his health permitting, was Dr Winslow, who wrote to her: 'I'll leave Giant Despair behind and you will do the same with Doubting Castle.' That she ever inhabited Doubting Castle seems uncharacteristic, as does her confession of doubt. And where did this doubt lie? She had escaped from the 3 C's (crowds, convention and civilisation) of Europe; now she planned to spend four months revisiting them. Was she uncertain in her choice of Tauranga as a permanent home? Or did she hope, in fact, to persuade her beloved son, when she visited him at RAF Leuchars where he was now in command, that he should emigrate to New Zealand? Or were her doubts of a more immediate concern; i.e. the wisdom of her intended route home to God's Own?

The Cassandras among Cecco's fellow officers certainly saw nothing to recommend flying from London to Batavia, as Jakarta was then called, before completing the journey to New Zealand by sea. He, knowing his mother once she had set her mind on something, merely remarked that it was 'a dull way to travel, just to be a passenger, with no responsibility, shut into a machine and sent through the air at 120 m.p.h.' Thus, on Wednesday, 2nd September, 1931, at Croydon airport, Mrs Maurice Hewlett, K.L.M.'s first all-through passenger from Amsterdam to Batavia – another first to add to her personal list – posed with a suitably 'simpering smile' and three other passengers for a photograph, prior to take-off on her complimentary flight to Amsterdam. As she did so, she wistfully reflected that it seemed very tame compared to the start of her journey some eight years earlier; no walking out to the waiting plane over wet grass with her one small bag in her hand; no picking her perilous way over the wings and through the wires into a cramped and open hole. Instead, her luggage was stowed aboard ahead of her; the wicker of her chair was softened by two large cushions; cottonwool for ear plugs, chewing gum and stout sick bags (Billy was also a good sailor of the skies, not even turbulence over the desert made her sick), were all supplied; and food, so lacking on that previous exhausting flight, was guaranteed, prepacked, for each stage. When her overnight hotel in Amsterdam, a city as clean as if it was scrubbed with soap every morning, proved to be equal to any in Europe, Billy felt a flicker of anxiety that the whole journey might be just a little too luxurious and well-organised for adventure. However, a good pilot was essential for her adventure and she took to Soer, the Chief Pilot of the *Ooievaar* (*The Stork*) at once. His infectious smile and *carry it all before manner*, which reminded her of the heroes of the Norse sagas – Maurice's work had not gone unread by his wife – filled her with confidence in his abilitiy to pilot the triple-engined (Bristol engines, Billy was pleased to note) Fokker[2] from Amsterdam to Indonesia.

Take-off was slightly delayed by the late appearance of one passenger. Rather than being annoying this was reassuring – oversleeping and being left in the middle of nowhere was not the sort of adventure Billy had in mind – but as she was the sole passenger from Budapest onwards and as she soon grew accustomed to the pre-dawn starts, she had little to fear. The capacity of the fuel tanks was sufficient for nine hours flying, but refuelling was carried out, on average, after four hour's flying, when crew and passenger grabbed the opportunity to stretch their legs and enjoy a smoke. A system of pre-paid vouchers meant that there was no requirement to change money from Amsterdam to Batavia; all lodgings, cars, meals, even tips, were accounted for in the book of different coloured tickets; lunch and thermos flasks of hot and cold drinks for the following day were supplied at each overnight stop. In her comfortable corner seat, by a window 'to open or shut' as she liked, Billy had little to do but write up her notes, or gaze down at the world not so far below.

The further they travelled east, Belgrade, Athens, Cairo – a city which invoked nostalgia for the Cairo of her youth – the more spartan the overnight accommodation became. She had hoped to meet her nephew, Claud Pelly, in Baghdad, but he was out of town. What with a cholera epidemic and the searing heat, Billy was glad of the company of the crew, as they joked of what was safe to eat in their dirty, stifling hotel, just as she was glad to join them on the roof to sleep; this a cooler place, if marginally less private than her bedroom with its flapping blue blind for a door. Bushire (Bushehr), the first stop in Persia (Iran) was followed by Jask, also on the coast and important for its relay wireless station, which happened to be run by an Englishman and their host for the night. Karachi, Billy decided, was *the Clapham Junction in making for flying*, for K.L.M. was one of three airlines that stopped over there. Just as at Mersa Matruh (Matruh, on the Egyptian coast northwest of Cairo), when Billy had marvelled at the sudden materialisation out of the desert of an English woman, who ran a nearby camp for artists and writers and others seeking rest or refuge from the world, so was she also surprised to be pounced upon by two smartly dressed English women at Jodhpur. They, it transpired were governesses to the children of the local Maharaja and were keen to learn all they could before flying home the following week for a holiday. The sound of the Fokker flying in was like the once-weekly chime of a clock summoning all within earshot to an exchange of news and information.

Soft conditions after recent rain made the stopover at Allahabad a two-night, rather than a one-night, stop. Soer's landing had been *just a masterpiece, only to be appeciated by those who knew the difficulties*, but, once down, the wheels sank into the soft ground. Taxiing to reach the petrol pumps let alone taxiing for take-off was impossible. Cars pulled and locals pushed, but the draft from the three roaring Bristol engines blew their clothes and turbans into streamers, *leaving them naked or nearly so, and they fell down like ninepins holding to the hem of their clothes*. Until its wheels were dug out and the sun had dried the too long grass sufficiently, *The Stork* was stuck. As the hotel was squalid and the town offered no diversions, the crew and Billy spent the day sitting in the shade of the wings, telling stories, improvising sports with a ladder, a spade and a propellor starter, and acting out dramatic scenes, which they photographed for fun. Calcutta, four hours flying distance, provided Soer with a different challenge for there he had to land his plane 'with much circumspection', as a cow with a broken leg had been killed the previous evening and the spot was still black with vultures, 'hopping, fighting, flapping and gorging on the carcase.' And, in Burma, although the rainy season was nearly at an end, conditions at Akyab were still dangerously soft. Before taking-off the following day, Soer and his co-pilot had had to recce the airstrip by car, in order to mark with a red flag the soft spots to be avoided. Billy too had her fair share of excitement in Akyab. Carried off from the airport, 'for want of better game,' by two jovial members of a wedding party, who had just waved off the bride and groom, she persuaded her friendly kidnappers, the English Chief of Police and someone to do with forestry, that in the interests of all their safety she should take the wheel of their car. Happy to comply, they treated her to a brief tour of the sights and a royal tea, before returning her to the K.L.M. Agent's Dak house for the night. *The cook was a chinaman, the food good, everything else primitive but clean. The mosquitos were small, silent and active.* In self-defence, Billy and the crew dined with towels round their ankles and necks.

The cold, as they crossed the mountains *en route* for Bangkok at a height of 10,000 feet, forced Billy into her warm coat, but as they dropped lower and lower and Soer circled the city, so that she might see the temples from the air, the coat was returned to the hook by her chair where it had hung since London. There was to be one more overnight stop at Medan, followed by a gruelling day's flying to their destination. The first leg to Palembang took six hours over nearly unbroken forest. With little in the way of visible landmarks to help navigation, Soer had to rely on the compass and the drift register; the wireless operator, whose duty it was to take the drift readings through a trap door in the floor of the aircraft, saw a tiger disappear under the trees and the Chief Pilot saw a large monkey in the jungle crown: disappointingly, Old Bird, as she now was to her grandchildren, saw only her namesakes. With the tank once again filled to capacity, they pressed on to Jakarta, a mere three hours away. There, Miss Obertop, the editor of a newspaper, welcomed the celebrity passenger with a bouquet of orchids and *was helpful and kind and didn't bother (her) with any questions*, but Mrs Hewlett could hardly bear to say goodbye to her dear crew in so soulless a place as an aerodrome. When they begged her to go with them to the cool of the mountains, where they would begin their much needed three week rest and recuperation – Soer had lost eight pounds in eleven days, standard for such a gruelling flight – she was only too happy to climb aboard The Stork for one last time. A short hop, half an hour, and they were in Bandung and a hotel so spread out, they required taxis from reception to their rooms. *I've been so feted and so spoiled, that I cant yet sift all my thoughts,* Billy wrote to a friend from Jakarta, shortly before her departure home. *As to the Dutch crew they have been quite devoted and I'm quite in love with them.* To her *Dear Crew of the Ooievaar,* Mrs Hewlett wrote: *I'm feeling very lonely and lost without you, I hated flying away and leaving you – on the way I dropped tears, more than one for each of you – also I cannot laugh today. I shall not forget you, and shall follow your journeys as nearly as I can. You all made my flight a series of delights, your happy ways, kindness, and unselfishness made me love you all. I shall not love the people on the Boat. Oh! NO. I shall not love the crew. Certainly NOT – I shall dream of the 11 days with you.*

Few, if any, air passengers today would be moved to write so, just as few would be prepared to pay over £8,000 (the approximate equivalent of £185, the all-inclusive fare from Amsterdam to Bandung in 1931) for eleven days flying with some very dodgy overnight accommodation. However, it is worth remembering that Billy was the sole passenger with a crew of four to herself. Admittedly the risks were more numerous, if on a smaller scale; when the wireless fused and began to smoke at 7,000 feet over the Balkans, they *suddenly had five minutes thrilling adventure.* Also the journey took longer than a liner would today and every time they landed *stacks of papers had to be passed every time by heaps of officials,* but for Old Bird there were novel and thrilling wonders to enjoy. *Most scenery,* she wrote in a letter to her sister Olga, *is of no account from the air, but cloud effects, shaking storms and sunrise and sunset are far more beautiful and immense.* Other advantages? Check-in time; half an hour. In-flight meals; arguably no worse than today, with perhaps the exception of one of dry bread, very tough meat and very salt fish out of a tin. Jet lag? None.

Flying for Billy had always been an intense, physical and intimate experience; the communication with the pilot, the sight of the earth beneath her, the feel of the weather on her skin. Because of her daring and passion she had experienced the sweet thrill of flying solo in the flimsy of wood and wires of her Farman, at dawn, over a sleeping countryside. Twenty years later, she had been flown into different dawns over a wide world in a way denied to all but a tiny minority of today's beneficiaries of those early pioneers in aviation. Twice she had been in at the start of a hazy, promising future in air travel. But the air travel of today, unimaginable to Grace Bird, Old Bird, or Billy, is not something any of her personas would have enjoyed.

CHAPTER 31

THE OLD BIRD

In 1934, Mrs Maurice Hewlett hosted a triumphant reception in Tauranga for Hine-O-Te-Rangi, Daughter of the Skies. Twenty-five years after she had been moved almost to tears by the sight of Paulhan flying at the Blackpool meeting, Billy met New Zealand's beautiful record-breaker, Jean Batten.[1] It was truly fitting that the Old Bird should greet the young woman; a young woman who had believed from early childhood that her destiny was to fly and who had been born within a month of the day that turned Billy from the wife of a famous novelist into an aspiring aviation pioneer.

Comparison of Billy flying solo over Brooklands with Batten smashing the woman's solo record from U.K. to Australia neatly demonstrates the advances made in aviation over a quarter of a century; advances unmatched in attitudes towards women in aviation. When asked if she thought women would become pilots, Billy had replied with a question. Women had eyes, ears, hands, nerves and courage, so what more could they need? Another world war and the ATA (Air Transport Auxiliary), the least discriminatory employer ever, was formed. Never mind if you were one-armed, one-eyed, one-legged, or a woman – but, perhaps, not all at once – if it meant that RAF pilots were freed-up for combat duty. One in every eight were women pilots. For those ferrying new, repaired and damaged aircraft throughout the dark – often literally – of WWII from factory to delivery point, pay was equal to that of any other pilot of equal rank in the organisation. That would have pleased Billy, as would the fact that there are now female military and civilian pilots, even if her own career in aviation had had more to do with her pleasure than in a cause on behalf of women.

At her side, also to welcome the Garbo of the Skies, was a Group Captain in the RNZAF Reserve of officers, Billy's 'Darling Sonny'.[2] Cecco, as keen to break free of the constraints of the English climate and society as his mother and sister had been, had resigned from the Royal Air Force in March 1934 and sailed for Tauranga and a new career. On a site purchased by his mother, on the corner of Devonport Road and First Avenue, he opened a new garage and service station, Hewlett & Co. Ltd (NZ). Harold Tufnell, a former employee of the Omnia Works, Leagrave, was the Fitter. Once, Maurice had wished to leave The Old Rectory to Cecco; shades of 'Knowing you leave your lands/The better for your son/Thankful he stands/To reap what you have won.' But patrimony had been extinguished in a reversal of fortune and Cecco and Pia's living inheritance had been matriarchal. From the unsought and unforseen wealth, the wages of Billy's irrational desire to own and fly an aeroplane, they had been given land and fresh horizons in a new country.

As President of the Tauranga Aero Club, Billy wasted no time in engaging Cecco in the urgent hunt for a suitable replacement site for the Club's flying field. The eventual expansion of the Club's new flying field at Whareroa, Mt. Mauganui, to fully-fledged Tauranga airport is proof that Cecco's expertise, acquired while in the R.A.F., was put to good use.[3]

Unexpectedly, what had initially promised well as a change of course, given both his and his mother's early interest in motoring, grew steadily less attractive to Cecco. Instead, the temptation to emulate his father, who had produced his own wine in Wiltshire, grew stronger. The location and climate of Tauranga was promising for viticulture. Cecco began modestly, close to his house, but the problems of marsh-like land and the consequent abundance of weeds dictated that he and his new wife, Dorothy[4], should move a few miles out of the rapidly expanding Tauranga to Maungatapu, then a rural area where the population was still predominantly Maori. A move no doubt welcome to Dorothy. Billy, with the confidence of one rarely prey to self-doubt, was generous with her advice as to how things should be done; a quality trying for any daughter-in-law. Equally trying – before the new Hewlett family had moved out of her range – was the way that she would decide, if she chanced upon their son napping in his pram, that he would benefit from a walk, or that the location of his nap site was open to improvement. A certain carelessness over the brake once accounted for the pram being discovered upended at the bottom of a grassy bank, its erstwhile occupant, mercifully, unhurt and sleeping sweetly.

Brisk, bracing, intelligent, impatient, intrepid – excellent qualities in a friend, or travelling companion; hardy, energetic and fun-loving – frivolous she would call it; determined and single-minded, more than a little self-centred; not at all prudish, except in matters governed by her own strong moral code and brand of snobbery; warmly affectionate, coldly intolerant, Billy to Old Bird endeared or alienated herself in equal measure. With increasing age, her attitudes and habits acquired a rather more eccentric quality. Her lectures on diet would have had nutritionists of today cheering, although she did insist that it was essential to avoid _all_, yes all, pre-cooked, tinned and concentrated foods. Officially blind, she would, nevertheless, drive her car with her gardener-cum-handyman crouching on the running board shouting directions; the clothes she habitually altered to her own particular taste were even more unconventional; the economies, learnt in her childhood, such as saving string, smoothing brown paper for re-use, storing fruit – too often until it rotted – became compulsions. It was, also, not unknown for her to sit on the kerb and empty the contents of her handbag onto the road, rather than rootle around in it to find what she wanted. Independent, but watched over by loyal staff, two of whom had followed her out from England, Billy lived on her own and did things her way.

Like her M, she had always been true to herself, but Maurice had shaped his life by his intellect, his ambition as a writer and, ultimately, his philosophical acceptance of what that dealt him. In four stages of Billy's life four men, Father Herbert, Maurice Hewlett, Gustave Blondeau and the near-anonymous Dobson, had been a pivotal influence. She had profited from what they offered her, whether it was the security of home and marriage, or the key to independence and new adventure. But, from Victorian vicarage to small New Zealand seaside town, via Edwardian London and the pioneering world of aviation – a progress in which she acquired and practised a variety of skills – she was to remain essentially the same at 79 as the young woman she had been at 21, one who lived for the moment.

How it was that she and Maurice had ever married seemed at first a riddle without answer. He found inspiration in the past, she in the future. He was cerebral, she was practical; he was more inclined to introspection, she to action. Once the ramifications of their parents' connections through friendship and marriage had been sorted out, their meeting and mutual attraction then became less of an extraordinary and unlikely event. Each to the other, in that social circle, must have appeared glamorously different, willing and ready to dare and dream beyond the roles in which they found themselves. That M pledged to strive to produce something beautiful and true, however vague its form, made him heroically worthy of devoted support. That Billy was eager to learn and to explore new worlds with him was tonic to Maurice. With a mutual interest in art and a readiness for laughter, how joyously promising life together must have seemed. Appreciative of the qualities in the other that they themselves lacked, they could not have foreseen that those different attributes would, one day, lead to their separation. In fact, Billy had once been incensed when an unidentified *cruelly clever authoress kindly spread the scandal that M could not stand his awful wife so had gone off indefinitely.* When they parted, it had been with grace and without recrimination on either side: respect, and love turned to affection, ensuring their loyalty and friendship to the end. And, as Maurice had, when the end came, Billy faced it with pragmatism.

It was the New Zealand winter of August 1943; her son, recalled to serve in the war, this time with the New Zealand Air Force, was stationed in Wellington; her daughter and family were in Auckland. Never one to linger over farewells, the realist and keen fisherman one night penned a note: 'Dump me in the sea.' The following morning, she was found in her bed, with the note pinned to her pillow. Typically, her final demand proved to be a lot less simple than her intent, but it was a good death for one who had never been faint-hearted. When news reached England, Veena wrote in her diary against Saturday, 21 August. 'Old Bird – Darling Billy died.'

ENDNOTES

All unpublished quotes from the private writing of Hilda and Maurice Hewlett have been written in *italics* in the text.

All quotes from the correspondence of Maurice Hewlett are from *The Letters of Maurice Hewlett*, Metheun & Co Ltd, 1926 (ed. Laurence Binyon) UNLESS otherwise indexed.

Chapter 2

1   In 1834, William Herbert (1792-1863) bought the lease of Cavendish House from Thomas Cubitt; Cubitt built himself a new house as part of his development of 200 acres in Clapham.

2   'St. Peter's Church Vauxhall, with St Anselm (Kennington Cross), and Lambeth Mission and St Mary is now part of the North Lambeth parish. A Heritage Centre incorporated into the building in the 1980s continues the tradition of reaching out to the community by hosting festivals, concerts, exhibitions and local activities. Sung Eucharist is celebrated every Sunday in St Peter's.

3   Robert Gregory: Vicar St Mary the Less 1843-1873. As Canon of St Paul's Cathedral (appointed 1868) caused a rumpus when he instituted a system of fines for non-attendance and unpunctuality by the choir. Appointed Dean of St Paul's in 1890, died in office 1911.

4   Tothill Fields belonged to the Dean and Chapter of Westminster and was developed in first half of 19th century.

5   Bought for £600 and donated for the vicarage by a Mr R. Foster, a liberal churchman. (*The Community of the Mission Sisters of the Holy Name of Jesus*) (CHN).

6   History of CHN

7   LMA: P85/PET 1/20/1

8   George W. Herbert (GWH) spent Michaelmas term at Oxford, 1854, in preparation for ordination as deacon (1854) and priest (1855) in Worcester Cathedral: his first curacy was at Pershore.

9   GWH's allowance cut to 'almost to real poverty' but bowing to the inevitable his parents re-instated it after a short period. William Herbert was too kindly and generous a man to do otherwise.

10   GWH and his fellow curate, Dr Frederick Wickenden, were publicly credited with being instrumental in uncovering the medieval frescoes of the Pinvin chapel. Louisa Herbert (displaying unexpected qualities and considerable agility, given Victorian dress) spent 'weeks on tressels and a few boards repainting the diapers in the chancel of the tiny chapel while the Scripture subjects in the nave were traced and reproduced by the South Kensington Museum.' [In Memoriam. LMA, P85/PET/1/24/4].

11   Six cities, set aside by law (Old Testament: Num. xxxv, 6) to which both Israelites and strangers might flee for safety when they had killed anyone without premeditation.

12   Mrs Herbert spotted talent in a chorister, Alfred Eyre: he became assistant organist at St. Peter's but was dismissed for playing Shove Ha'penny. Organist at Crystal Palace and not a man to bear a grudge, he assisted at GWH's funeral and played at Mrs Herbert's funeral - at her family's request.

13   The Home of the Good Shepherd in Ranelagh Road, Malvern Link was another.

14   LMA: P85/PET/1/24/4

15   A female Penitentiary was a particularly Victorian charitable organisation for the rehabilitation of "fallen women". A penitent was chiefly trained in domestic service skills.

16   After his death a Herbert Memorial Fund was opened to provide a stipend for a permanent curate to help carry on his work.

17   WHM Aitken, *The Record* 1894

18   Among the Guilds were the Comrades of the Cross (for young men), The Pierced Side and The Pure Offering (for women), The Children of Divine Grace (for young women in service or business) and The Ward of St Peter (for poor boys working in the potteries who attended St. Peter's Mission School).

19   Unattributed obituary held by CHN

20   CHN II/1/25e

21 In the list of guests, plus their gifts, it was recorded Mr & Mrs Maurice Hewlett gave a sewing machine, sister Pat a Colt six-chamber revolver, sister Gay a knife for the veldt, and Mrs Herbert a Broadwood piano. The newly-weds were to travel to South Africa for Douglas Pelly to resume his missionary work.

Chapter Three

1 Sir James Knowles KCVO (1831-1908). Initially articled to his father as an architect, Knowles went on to found *The Nineteenth Century* in 1877. Hero of Pia Richards' best-loved anecdote, which she recorded because she could not bear that it should be forgotton. Knowles was dressing to go out to dinner assisted by his valet. After spoiling three evening collars in his attempts to fasten them, he asked his valet for a pair of scissors and calmly cut the last collar in half and, without a word, went on dressing.

2 Henry G. Hewlett reviewed poetry and wrote for *The Academy* on a regular basis and published two slim volumes of his own poetry, *A Sheaf of Verse* and *A Wayfarer's Wallet*.

3 Pia Richards began to write about both sides of her family, the Hewletts and the Herberts but, regrettably, did not get beyond a couple of chapters of 'Family Matters'. She left the reader longing for more.

4 Dick Hewlett used the pseudonym Dick Henty. His song, 'Murders', evidently 'made all London laugh' and was sung by George Grossmith in *To-Night's the Night*.

5 International College at Spring Grove, established 1866, closed 1889. Professor T.H. Huxley, a contributor to *The Nineteenth Century* and friend of Sir James Knowles, was a governor. Arthur, son of Sir James and contemporary of Maurice Hewlett (MH), was also a pupil.

6 The twelfth and youngest child of Dr Thomas Hewlett of Harrow on the Hill.

7 Tickets were not issued to anyone under twenty-one without special permission.

8 Arthur Knowles (b. 1861) and Millicent Knowles (b.1863) were born to Jane (nee Borrodaile) Knowles (1842-1863) who died giving birth to her daughter. Beatrice Knowles (b.1866) was the only child of Isabel (sister of Henry G. Hewlett) James Knowles' second wife.

Chapter 4

1   Preacher's Book, St Peter's, Vauxhall. LMA: P/85/PET 1/21/1

Chapter 5

1   At the end of his life MH was to write: 'I may be a good poet or a bad one – that's not for me to say; but I am a poet of sorts.' *In a Green Shade*

2   FETH, future Air Commodore FET Hewlett, D.S.O., O.B.E.

3   Janet Ross (1842-1927) was a writer and *grande dame* of the Anglo-Florentine colony married to Henry James Ross (1820-1902), an Anglo-Egyptian banker.

Chapter 6

1   Dep. Bridges 110, Bodleian Library, OULS

2   Printed privately in 1914. Only twenty-five copies were printed, five of which MH gave to friends. The remainder were destroyed after his death.

3   Stephen Gwynn (1864-1950), writer, one time Nationalist member of Galway.

Chapter 7

1   GWH left an estate worth £125,000; his widow was to receive £3,000 p.a. from an invested Trust fund; his children were to have equal shares of its annual interest, although George was to receive twice that of his sisters (they, no doubt, were expected to be supported by their husbands).

2   Gay was the maiden name of MH's paternal grandmother. It was also his sister-in-law's first name, who had admired his play *Simonetta*. Was MH playing games here?

3   George Herbert was ordained. Mary Louise (Dora) married a Canon (Edmund McClure); she became good friend of Sir Ninian Comper, anglo-catholic architect and designer, who, with his partner, William Bucknall, once a member of the congregation of St Peter's, was commissioned by GWH for the conventual Church of the Holy Name, Malvern Link in 1893. Verena

married the Revd. Douglas Pelly. Olga (Milne-Watson) had a crucifix tattooed between her breasts. Gay (Welby-Everard) painted the reredos which she donated to her local Church of St Peter and St Paul, Gosberton, Lincs.

Grace Monica (Pat) married twice: 1) Donald McDonald. 2) Comte Paul du Prieux. Throughout WWII, the du Prieux lived in a delightful Moorish house in Rabat. In a curtained alcove half-way up the stairs, Pat, without the knowledge of her pro-Vichy husband, hid British servicemen (primarily airmen) on the run before they were passed home. She was awarded the King's Medal for Service in the Cause of Freedom.

4   The post now carried a fixed salary of £700 p.a. The Keeper of LRRO was to undertake no private business, be in attendance 7 hours a day and have 48 working days leave.

5   Henry G. Hewlett died 25 February, 1897.

6   Knowles' letters to HGH were 'returned to sender'. Knowles kept them: they now reside in City of Westminster Archives Centre (Accession 716). The rift was so serious MH did not attend his uncle's funeral. He was also very scornful of his uncle's knighthood.

7   Milton Bronner discussing *The Forest Lovers* in his critical review of MH, wrote: "He used a language that smacked neither of the Wardour street phase of Morris's career, nor of that later period when Morris was enamoured of Anglo-saxon words to the exclusion of all others." Wardour Street was once renowned for the manufacture of antique and reproduction furniture. MH was alert to his tendency to use pseudo-archaic language attractive to historical novelists.

Chapter Eight

1   Mrs Lucy Clifford, novelist, dramatist and letterwriter, widow of W.K. Clifford (d.1879). Left with two young daughters and inadequate means, Mrs Clifford had been secured a small Civil List pension by her friend, George Eliot. She published her first novel in 1885. She recalled the Hewletts in an article in the *Saturday Review of Literature*, January 5,1926

2   Eight years earlier, Douglas Pelly had sailed for Canada and into danger. He narrowly escaped being murdered by J.R. Burchall. *The Swamp of Death. A True Tale of Victorian Lies and Murder*, 2004.

3   Gwynn met the Hewletts through their close and long-standing friends, Percy and Mabel Dearmer. Percy Dearmer (author *The Parson's Handbook*, an anglo-catholic liturgical manual) in 1892 was curate in South Lambeth to W.A. Morris, a former curate at St Peter's, Vauxhall. Beautiful Mabel Dearmer studied art at Herkomer's School in Bushey. An illustrator and writer of children's books, she also contributed drawings to the Yellow Book: her drawing room became a centre for the *Yellow Book* circle. She died during WWI, when serving as a volunteer nurse in Serbia. *Poems*, the war poetry of their son, Geoffrey Dearmer (1893-1996), who survived Gallipoli, unlike his brother, first appeared in 1918.

4   Stephen Gwynn, *Experiences of a Literary Man*, 1926. In her memoirs HBH wrote of an Irishman *full of poetry and the love of beauty* who, according to her, was *naive, innocent as a child, witty, with a natural command of vivid language*, who eventually became a Member of Parliament. Perhaps she was writing of Stephen Gwynn?

Chapter Nine

1   Frederic Harrison (1831-1923), lawyer, Positivist, political radical, writer.

2   Adela Maddison (reputedly mistress of Fauré) made it into an operetta. *Ippolita of the Hills* had a first (and only?) performance at an audition session in a private house, 10 St Catherine Street, London SW1, on 25 February 1926. Singers: De Neville White, Adelaide Rind, Kathleen Lafla, Francis Russell; pianist: Harold Howell.

3   Alfred Sutro OBE (1863-1933). Playwright, champion and translator of Maeterlink, Sutro amassed a fortune in the city before quitting to follow his real interest, the theatre. Hon. Sec. of William Archer and Elizabeth Robins' shortlived venture, The New Century Theatre.

4   In June 1899, Macmillan agreed to pay MH 25% on all English sales: a marked improvement on his terms for *The Forest Lovers*.

5   MH's father, Henry G. Hewlett, writing on modern poetry in 1874 in the *Contemporary Review* had used Gosse's 'On Viol and flute' in his criticism of a current tendency towards affectation.

6   The Gosse collection, the Brotherton Collection, LUL

7   ibid. Gosse had stayed in Vikingnäss (Ljondestangen) 1898.

8 Pia Richards remembered the Hawkins as fellow passengers on their hideously rough crossing to Norway. For some unfathomable reason, she had taken exception to their daughter's doll and thrown it overboard: there was a frightful row.

9 Based on an historic character, Raschid-ad-din Sinan. Leader of a cult of Assassins in Syria, a branch of the Ismaeliens established in Persia.

Chapter 10

1 In 1903, wealthy Leicestershire ship-owner, Charles Booth, bought the copy of 'The Light of the World' for £1000. From 1905 he spent £5000 exhibiting it throughout Canada, Australia, New Zealand and South Africa, before presenting it to the nation. In June 1908 it was hung in St Paul's cathedral, where it is to this day.

2 Gelet Burgess (1866-1951). Artist, art critic, author, coiner of the word blurb.

3 Loie Fuller (1862-1928). 'Born in America and made in France' Fuller was the personification of Art Nouveau. Famous for her dance, La Danse de Feu, while wearing a costume of voluminous folds of silk which she whirled about, lit to her own innovative directions, Fuller appeared at the Folies Bergeres during the '90's. She was also a promoter of artists (Rodin included) and a co-founder of art museums.

4 Israel Zangwill (1864-1926) Writer and fervent Zionist. Profoundly erudite and the kindest of men, Zangwill, nevertheless, was not a man to weigh his words to avoid giving offence.

5 The Dorset County Museum H.3410

Chapter 11

1 Andrew Lang wrote *A History of Scotland*. MH claimed that the mere hint of what he intended to do with the subject had taken Lang's breath away.

2 A.E.W. Mason (1865-1948), author of *the Four Feathers*. The development of Queen Anne's Mansion, where Mason lived, caused grief and expense to Sir James Knowles, over whose beautiful home it towered.

3 Serialisation had begun in May in *Pall Mall Magazine*. Before publication in

hard back in June 1904, MH gave the Queen of Scots one last, light make-over.

4   Built in the 14th century, an offshoot from Wilton Abbey, originally for monks who served the churches down the Ebble valley. A determined search by the family failed to discover the underground passage that allegedly ran from the rectory to the church.

5   Henry Currie Marillier (1865-1951). Engineer (partner for some years in WAS Benson's Metal Works) and journalist (chiefly on *Pall Mall Gazette*). Managing Director, Morris & Co., 1905-1948.

6   Sir Nestor Tirard (1853-1928) wrote a piece on the Toxic Effects of Cannabis Indica in 1890 for the *Lancet*. He was second author with his wife, Helen Mary, of *Sketches from a Nile Steamer for the Use of Travellers in Egypt*, 1896.

7   Sir Charles Theodore Hagberg Wright (1862-1940). Educated privately in Russia, France, Germany, graduated Trinity College, Dublin. Became Secretary and Librarian, London Library in 1893. During WWI wrote on Russian matters for *The Times*.

Chapter 12

1   AA set up in 1905 initially to alert motorists to speed traps. Charles Jarrot, a founding member and on the committee of the AA, was a car dealer (Charles Jarrott and Letts Ltd, 45 Great Marlborough Street, Regent Street). He sold Panhards (one of the first cars the Hewletts owned was a Panhard): he also dealt in De Dietrich cars (the Hewletts were to own one of those).

2   The *Autocar* regularly published long lists of police traps

3   In 1907 the hunt was on to find new road surfaces. The Spreading Competion, under the auspices of the RAC, Roads Improvement Association and the Motor Union, was held near Staines. A picture of the Gas Light and Coke Company brush and spreader appeared in *Motor*, May 28,1907. HBH's sister Olga, was married to David Milne-Watson of the Gas Light & Coke Co.

4   According to HBH she took her 16-year old son, whom she had taught to drive, on a six-day Reliability Trial the following year, but mechanical failure made them withdraw. However, neither a Hewlett nor a Lagonda tricar are listed among the entrants according to *The Automobile Club Journal*, the official organ of The Royal Automobile Club in any subsequent trial.

5   HBH remembered Teresina being in Bond Street and that she gazed into a crystal ball. According to *Lady Cynthia Asquith's Diaries 1915-1918* (rather more accurate as they were written daily), Teresina was a palmist in Manchester Street, who was a nice obviously shrewd woman possessed of a good vocabulary.

6   James Kerr-Lawson (1865-1939). A Canadian, he continued his art studies in Rome and Paris in 1880/1. In 1884 he returned to Canada, but was back in Europe by 1887 where he was to live for the rest of his life. From 1900 his London home was 4 Turner Studios, Glebe Place. His widow, Cassie (Caterina) lived there until her death in 1952. The house at Corbignano was their second home for forty years. A number of Kerr-Lawson's pictures are in the Queen's Collection.

7   Joseph Pennell wrote *The Adventures of an Illustrator* close to the end of his life when he had been back in the United States for some eight years. His memories, that included inconsequential but engaging titbits such as the goats that roamed the city of Westminster (Pennell had witnessed the Archbishop of Canterbury fly for sanctuary from one into Westminster Abbey), were not always entirely reliable. In Chapter XXX he incorrectly gives the impression that the Hewletts visited Italy in 1901.

8   Despite being used to boarding school life – FETH had been a pupil at Aysgarth School in Yorkshire – the tough Naval discipline that the cadets endured at Osborne might well have made him question his choice of career: aged eleven, he had fancied the Royal Navy for the ho-hoing and dancing the hornpipe possibilities.

9   Prior's Field, then an experimental school for girls (founded in 1902 by the grand-daughter of Thomas Arnold of Rugby, Julia Huxley (d.1908) wife of Leonard Huxley) was an obvious choice for modern and progressive parents such as the Hewletts, who were also acquainted with the Huxley family. Julia, Pia's nanny, accompanied her charge as her maid; it would seem to have been standard procedure in the very early days.

10 Whether it is relevant or significant, but the last of MH's letters to HBH, which she had saved and which were included in *The Letters of Maurice Hewlett*, was written in 1903.

Chapter 13

1 *Spanish Jade*. Louis Vance adapted the novel for the stage from which Josephine Lovett wrote the screenplay for the 1922, B & W, 5-reeler directed by John S. Robertson. The designer of the Intertitle card was Alfred Hitchcock.

2 J.E. Vedrenne and Harley Granville Barker. Harley Granville Barker (playwright) with William Archer (drama critic, translator and promotor of Ibsen's plays) worked tirelessly to establish a national theatre.

3 From this distance in time, the inclusion of what appears an already dated confection in a season promoting new plays by new dramatists is puzzling, although it would seem unlikely that Granville Barker, whose own play *Waste* was to run into trouble with the censor the following year, would have risked putting on *Pan and the Young Shepherd* purely out of his friendship with MH. *Captain Brassbound's Conversion* by George Bernard Shaw followed *Pan*

4 General Joseph Bonus served in the Afghan War of 1878-80 and was Engineer in Chief, Scindia State Railway before retiring in 1886 aged 50. His first wife was distantly related by marriage to Louisa Herbert. His second wife was distantly related by marriage to Billy's good friend from her stay in Egypt, Stanley Lane Poole.

5 A popular place among their social circle: Ellen Terry and Ada Galsworthy had both stayed there.

6 Chairman of the Management Committee of the Society of Authors (1909-1911), Fellow of the Royal Society of Literature, member of the Royal Literary Fund (1901-1914).

Chapter 14

1 Louis Paulhan (1883-1963) flying a Henri Farman. In January 1910 he broke the height record flying in the US. In April 1910 he won the *Daily Mail* London to Manchester air race.

2 The Doncaster meeting opened Friday 15 October and ran with breaks, due to inclement weather, until Tuesday 26 October. Their claim to be the first international aviation meeting in the UK is disputed, as the Committee of the Aero Club did not sanction it, owing to the clash of dates with the Blackpool meeting. The American, Sam Cody, formerly an entertainer in a

Wild West show, had moved into aviation via giant kite flying. From 1902-1909 he had been Chief Kite Instructor at the British Army Balloon Factory, Farnborough. He had first signalled his intent to fly at Blackpool, but changed his mind and flew at Doncaster, where his ceremony of naturalisation was performed in front of the grandstand. Ever the showman, he took the oath of allegiance, used the Town Clerk's back on which to rest the certificate for signing and stood bareheaded while the National Anthem was played. He then immediately entered for the *Daily Mail* £1,000 prize for the first British aviator to fly a circular mile on an all-British machine.

3   Henri, Maurice and Richard (Dick) Farman were sons of an English journalist but brought up in France. Henri considered himself the complete Frenchman, although he had British nationality. *The London Gazette* of September 1909 announced: 'The King has been pleased to give and grant unto Henry Farman, Esquire, His Majesty's royal licence and authority to accept and wear the Cross of Chevalier of the Legion of Honour conferred upon him by the President of the French Republic in recognition of valuable services rendered by him.'

4   HBH first discovered Walter Cadby when she was walking near Campden Hill. Striding along, she was diverted by the sound of music and, looking up, saw a young man in shirtsleeves and with gaitered legs reclining on a heap of oriental cushions in the sunshine in the doorway of a converted hayloft, playing a penny whistle with his white bull terrier at his side. Enchanted by this scene, she was more than willing to accept an invitation to climb the outside wooden steps and meet the artist and his wife in their upstairs studio. Cadby painted a small portrait of HBH with the enigmatic inscription 'To Maurice Hewlett a little token of sympathetic admiration' on wood and now owned by Ann Wilcox, HBH's eldest granddaughter.

5   Henri Farman, who made the first flight at the Blackpool Meeting, had had to borrow Paulhan's plane. His own Farman had been temporarily lost in transit by train from France.

6   Hubert Latham (1993-1912) died, aged 29, while big game hunting in the Congo.

7   AL held privately, one of three (two from Barrie and one from Shaw) that HBH had offered for sale to the Autograph Agency, London in 1927. Advised that they would be useless if she cut out the letter content as 'they would become then *mere signatures* worth not more than 1/- each,' she decided to keep them.

Chapter 15

1   Included among them were Farman, Antoinette, Voisin, Saulnier, Sommer and Bleriot.

2   Perhaps, the baroness of HBH's story is actually one Elise Roche (1885-1919) who adopted the more aristocratic 'Baronne' Raymonde de Laroche as a stage name in order to further her career. However, de Laroche quit the stage to become a balloonist, before Charles Voisin (1888-1912) taught her to fly. On 8 March,1910 she became the first woman in France to be awarded a pilot's certificate. In July 1910 she competed in the Prix des Dames at Rheims, but was seriously injured in a bad crash. She recovered to win further flying glory, but was killed co-piloting an experimental aircraft.

3   Jules Vedrines' (1881-1919) most flamboyant act was to land on the roof of Gallerie Lafayette in Paris to win the prize of 25,000 fr.; he became the first to break the 100 m.p.h. speed barrier in 1912. He died making a forced landing on a Paris-Rome flight in 1919. He was accorded a public funeral by the people of Paris.

4   Privately recorded interview with Gustave Blondeau by Eric Pedder in the 1960's. Tape no longer in existence. Despite living for fifty years in England, Blondau never lost his strong French accent.

5   HBH also credited Efimoff with such a flight. In her version, Farman, his anger dissipated in his admiration of the daring and skill of the Russian, embraced Efimoff on his safe landing

Chapter 16

1   6 June, 1910.

2   Max Beerbohm, benignly amused by MH, had once commented on his persistence in writing up fauns. It is also clear that elements of MH and his mode and subject of writing were inspiration for the character Ladbroke Brown in *'Savonarola' Brown* in Beerbohm's *Seven Men*.

3   The slim volume began as *Letters to Mabilla*. It allowed the recipient of Senhouse's outpourings to be addressed every now and then as Queen Mab

(the faery queen and another mythical female who, besides Artemis, appealed to MH).

4   Rest Harrow was the bane of farmers in the days of horse-drawn ploughs, as its deep, tough roots and matted stems habitually arrested the harrow – hence its name.

5   Sanchia Percival, Senhouse's disciple, had lived with a married man in *Open Country*

6   Stephen Gwynn, *The Edinburgh Review*, January 1924.

7   BM Add Mss 58496, letter dated 17 February, 1921.

8   *Rest Harrow*

9   Lord Gorell had expressed his conviction, when presiding over a divorce case in 1906, that there was a need for reform. The Royal Commission on Divorce and Matrimonial Causes was to all extents and purposes his project.

10 Divorce Reform Act of 1969 finally saw the implementation of MH's views.

11 Mrs Belloc Lowndes, *The Merry Wives of Westminster*, 1946

Chapter 17

1   Francis McClean, a trained civil engineer and a wealthy sporting member of the then plain Aero Club, had, through his friendship with the Short Brothers from the days when they were manufacturing balloons under the arches at Battersea, grown progressively more interested in the future of flying. For a peppercorn rent of £1 a year, he gave flying rights to members of the Aero Club on the land that he owned on the Isle of Sheppey: thus Eastchurch was established.

2   *Flight* 23 July, 1910 listed Gustave Blondeau as a new member of the R.Ae.C. The following week his name was among those approved by the R.Ae.C. for entry into the Lanark Meeting.

3   Jorge Chavez (1887-1910). Peruvian born, raised in Paris, died after his Bleriot dropped 30ft to the ground (structural failure) on coming in to land at Domodossola airfield, after becoming the first to cross the Alps in an aeroplane.

4   In the Neill Cup, Blondeau was just beaten into second place by the charismatic and increasingly popular flyer, Graham Gilmour. *Flight* rated the October 5, 1910, flying meeting at Brooklands the best so far.

5   Graham Walford Robertson (1866-1948). Painter, illustrator, costume designer. Moved in prominent artistic circles. Signed himself as W. Graham Robertson.

6   Lt. Snowden-Smith would motorcycle over from Aldershot in the afternoon for an evening lesson. If he could, he would sleep overnight in the big packing case outside the Hewlett and Blondeau hangar, have another lesson at break of day and return to Aldershot in time for his duties at eight in the morning.

7   The Hewlett and Blondeau school created a sensation by taking their old Farman (still flying well) to pieces in order to replace the fabric; something not normally done until the machine had been damaged.

8   The dashing Snowden-Smith brought credit to Hewlett and Blondeau by coming second in the Brooklands to Brighton race held in May 1911. Unfortunately, although, he came second to the winner and star aviator, Gustav Hamel, he was disqualified for flying *over* Brighton and lost his place to Graham Gilmour.

9   The *Autocar*, May 13, 1911. The contractors undertook to finish the work by the third week in July. The motor racing track only had to be closed for one Sunday.

10 Howard Flanders began as one of A.V. Roe's earliest assistants. He designed the Pup monoplane when working with J.V. Neale at Weybridge, and went on to design and construct a series of monoplanes. In 1912, he opened a flying school at Brooklands.

11 HBH greatly disliked Pemberton Billing: his brother was Eardley Billing who ran the famous Blue Bird Café in the Brooklands flying village. If the cottage was indeed nicknamed The Birdcage, it seems an interesting coincidence that there should have been a picture of Pemberton Billing sitting in his special Brooklands Napier car 'Mercury', which, according to the caption, was familiarly known as the 'Birdcage'. (*Flight*, September 27, 1913)

12 Gustav Hamel, another friend from Mourmelon, and the blond, blue-eyed idol of Hendon and Brooklands, only trusted his namesake, Gustave, to check his machine when he flew at Brooklands. He suffered from pre-flight nerves, and airsickness. Sadly, when he was a serious contender to be the first to cross the Atlantic, Hamel disappeared in May 1914 returning from Paris.

13 An instructor of Workshop Practice and Aeroplane Drawing and Design at the Polytechnic in Regent Street, Wood had cycled from London each weekend, camped out where he could and grabbed as many lessons as he could.

14 FETH took every opportunity he could to fly at Brooklands. He once made a bet that he could motorcycle to Brooklands, fly, and return to Weymouth, where he was posted, in the interval between the end of Sunday mid-day church parade and the start of duty at 7 a.m. on the Monday. He won his bet, despite three punctures and a broken belt.

15 A bear, Poley, was featured in a photograph with Sopwith (*Flight*, December 3,1910). According to Sopwith's biographer, Alan Bramson, a bear, Oonie, was given to Sopwith by his sister in 1913. One and the same bear, or two bears? The timing of Poley's banishment to the zoo would have coincided with the six months Sopwith spent competing in the States in 1911.

16 C.G. Grey wrote in the *Aeroplane*, May 23, 1912. 'His was a simple little funeral, suiting the simple way he lived. Only his near friends from Brooklands came to pay their last respect to one of their own kind.

These are the men who work all the hours that God sends, who, because of their work, do not appear on show days arrayed as young men of fashion, and are accordingly despised by superior persons as 'shed-loungers' and 'mere mechanics' but who are in truth the men who have made British aviation what it is, in spite of neglect from those who should have supported them. While the men with money have spent it on buying foreign machines and paying foreign mechanics to look after them in this country, Fisher and his like have spent their all, their small private incomes, their poor little savings, on their work in their own country, and they have turned out machines, mechanics, and pilots equal to the world's best.'

17 *Thames Valley Times*, February 21, 1912. The funeral was at Mickleham church. A bed at Weybridge Hospital was to be named in his memory.

18 The *Aeroplane*, April 25, 1912. ' Bargains for Builders. The Blondeau-Hewlett school are anxious to sell their two Farmans so as to make room for the building of some machines of more modern type, and as both machines are in splendid condition, as is only to be expected, having been always under the master hand of M. Blondeau, they would be most valuable for school work and passenger carrying.' Vickers bought one machine, Sopwith the other.

19 The last flight by HBH to be recorded was on Saturday, 6 July 1912 (*Flight*, July 13, 1912).

Chapter 18

1   Coincidentally, Tommy Sopwith opened up his first aircraft factory in a disused roller-skating rink in the autumn of the same year in Canbury Park Road, Kingston-upon-Thames. Roller-skating was going out of fashion.

2   Any violence that might have been anticipated did not materialise outside the factory, but inside. One joiner did not take kindly to being given the sack by a Mr Moncrieff and whacked him one with a jack plane. He was fined ten shillings by the Hon. John de Gray at the South Western Police Court.

3   'Where Aeroplanes Are Built', *Flight*, December 7, 1912.

4   In fact, the address was 34 Park Mansions, Prince of Wales Road, Battersea.

5   One of the very first members of The Flying Village at Brooklands, a pupil at the Hanriot School and later in charge of the Deperdussin School.

6   HBH wrote: 'That man got very rich and high in rank, but I stopped his game with the Gnome engine.' Was that man Mr Duckham, or someone from that company? Douglas R. Pelly had had a letter printed in the *Autocar*, January 11, 1908 in which he claimed to have used Duckham's oil satisfactorily for two years. Duckham's Oil had hoped, perhaps, for a similarly enthusiastic endorsement from the Reverend Pelly's sister-in law, HBH.

7   At a guess, Whitsun weekend 1913 seems the most likely date with the Bank Holiday Monday allowing the partners the extra time. Also, FETH had just finished one posting on the HMS *Hercules* and was probably enjoing a spot of leave before joining the aircraft carrier, HMS *Hermes*, in June.

8   Required, most likely, for the car's acetylene headlights.

9   It would appear that she had renewed it by 1914.

'Mrs HILDA BEATRICE HEWLETT, wife of Mr. Maurice Hewlett, the author, herself an airwoman and the mother of Lieutenant M. Hewlett, the airman, was summoned for driving a motor-car in a manner dangerous to the public in the Edgware-road.

According to the evidence given by Police-sergeant Check and Constable Hebborn, a May-Day procession of about 600 people, including a contingent of the National League of the Blind, was crossing the Edgware-road at Church-street, "when Mrs. Hewlett, after waiting for about three minutes, drove into it scattering the processionists in all directions. She stopped after being called to three times, and when her name and address had been taken she remarked, 'Now move them (i.e. the crowd) out of the way or I will drive over them.' Had she driven into the procession a little earlier, it was said, she would have run into the blind people." [Golly! You can hear the hisses in Court!]

Mrs. Hewlett, however, in her evidence claimed she saw a perfectly empty space, after the procession had gone by and at once sounded her hooter and crossed the road. "Immediately a large crowd of very rough people collected round and mounted the car, yelling 'Suffragette! We will teach you how to behave to the working classes.' As a matter of fact, she herself belonged to the working class and was not a suffragette. .... She added that her remark to the police was for the purpose of preventing the crowd being crushed by the car when she was ordered to drive on." [How fortunate for Cecco, her passenger, that he had had to go to the Isle of Grain 'to fly with the First Lord of the Admiralty' and was thus unable to give evidence.]

"Mr. Paul Taylor accepted Mrs. Hewlett's explanation of her remark to the police and fined her 40s. with 2s. costs." *The Times*, Friday, June 5, 1914.

10 Kuhn Khan or Rum: in 1912 Charles Goodall & Sons Ltd brought out a pack costing 6d (*The Family and the Firm 1820-1922*, M.H. Goodall, 2000). Card-game similar to Rummy, originating in Mexico. [With whom in Spanish is *con quien*].

11 Pia Richards, unpublished mss.

12 They did a very good trade in their wire strainers when an elderly gentleman bought several as he had been 'trying for ever so long to find some way of keeping his big pictures level on the walls at home.' One can only agree with the *Aeroplane* March 26, 1914, that, 'One is glad to find that Aviation can assist Art, even in so humble a way.'

13 Pemberton Billing had Stand no. 49 with his Supermarine 'flying boat', one of the most original machines of the show, according to *Flight*, March 21, 1914. Flying boat was a catchier description than the hitherto 'Waterplane'.

14 HBH had described the show as the first big Aero exhibition at Olympia. In fact, it was the Fifth Aero Show in 1914, confirmed by this comment in the *Aeroplane*. 'One noted with extreme regret the flagrant discourtesy of one exhibitor, a member of the Royal Aeronautic Club, who deliberately remained covered while speaking to His Majesty and one hopes that further notice will be taken of this incident.'

Chapter 19

1   By the summer of 1912, the enterprising and patriotic Claude Graham-White had organised a 'Wake Up England' campaign in conjunction with the *Daily Mail* to alert the country to the perils of being unprepared in the air. Two hydro-aeroplanes (a Henri Farman and a Paulhan Curtiss) emblazoned with the slogan flew up and down the South Coast, giving passenger flights from a number of beaches.

2   Captain Bertram Dickson, initially cold-shouldered by his former officer colleagues, succeeded in proving to them the inestimable worth of a plane for reconnoitring in the 1910 Army Manoeuvres.

3   Horace, Eustace and Oswald Short began as airframe manufacturers in 1909 at Eastchurch, Isle of Sheppey. In 1911 they began work on adapting land planes for use on water.

4   January 1912. Samson had not been the first in the world to take off from a ship (an American had done so in November of the previous year, 1911), but his remarkable feat gave a tremendous boost to British design and manufacture.

5   August 1-17, 1912

6   Gustav Hamel, Tommy Sopwith, Howard Pixton, R.L. Charteris, Freddie Raynham, James Valentine, L.F. Macdonald, and H. Petre.

7   His great courage, dogged determination and flamboyant personality won the hearts of the British public and when he was killed in an horrific crash in August 1913 he drew a funeral crowd of 100,000.

8   The Trials were plagued by storms, rain and strong winds. Frustrated pilots and their mechanics resorted to playing cricket, even the French. Cody demonstrated lassoing.

9   Samson and FETH were to be the first to make flights in an adapted Henri Farman and Short tractor plane, respectively, at Carlingnose on the Firth of Forth, October 1912.

10 Saturday, 16 August. Later, the start was altered to the more realistic time of 10 a.m. although it was still not absolutely critical for a participant to set off exactly then: the timing of the circuit began from take-off. Flying on the Sunday was prohibited, but competitors were at liberty to repair their machines, if necessary, on that day.

11 Spenser Grey piloted Winston Churchill when he was the First Lord of the Admiralty.

12 According to HBH, the future Admiral Mark Kerr, had personally arranged for FETH, frustrated not to be flying experimental seaplanes while stationed at the Isle of Grain, to be appointed to Kerr's own ship HMS *Hercules*. FETH was to be given as much leave as possible so that he might get in as much flying practice as possible. Thrilled, HBH wrote and thanked Kerr, who dined with the Hewletts in town; he also invited them to dine with him on board ship.

13 The *Aeroplane*, August 21, 1913.

14 Of the pilots entered for the race, only the Australian and chief pilot for Sopwith, Harry Hawker, eventually took off in his Sopwith 100 hp Tractor Seaplane, and then nearly 6 hours later than the official start time. He never completed the circuit, crashing on his approach to Dublin. Lord Northcliffe awarded him £1000 for his valiant attempt.

15 MH wrote an article for the front page of the *Daily Chronicle* on 4 January 1910: headlined 'Duty of the Working Men. Stirring Appeal by Famous Novelist. "Hodge is King". Lords a Danger to the State. Clear the Pass.' He called for the abolition of the House of Lords; he was pro Free Trade and thought 'vapouring and blustering about Empire and All-Red Maps,' as Pink Wash and mere sentimentalism on behalf of the Conservatives; he was anti-war. Following this, he wrote to Ramsay McDonald on 10 January 1910 asking to address one of his Trades'Union Congresses and delivered his speech on 15 January. *The Fortnightly*, February 1910 printed his speech.

16 *Luton News and Beds Chronicle*, Thursday 27 May, 1915.

Chapter 20

1 *Riviera* was returned to 'civvy street' at the end of the war. In WWII, refashioned and renamed *Lairds Isle* she once again served in the Navy, before returning to civilian duties. In 1957 she was broken up. *Engadine* had a similar but shorter career: as *Corregidor* she was mined and sunk, Manila Bay December 1941. The *Empress* was scrapped 1933

2 The Harwich Force consisted basically of four light cruisers and twenty destoyers.

3   Three Admiralty Folders no. 119, Flight Cdr Robert Ross; no. 120, Flight Lt Arnold Miley; no. 122, Flight Cdr AB Gaskell: assigned to the *Engadine*: two Admiralty Type 135 no. 135, Flight Cdr FET Hewlett; no.136, Flight Cdr Cecil Kilner: assigned to the *Riviera*: four Admiralty Type 74 no. 811, Flight Lt Charles Edmonds: assigned to the *Riviera*: no. 812, Flight Ltd Reginald Bone; no. 814, Flight Sub-Lt Vivian Gaskell Blackburn; no. 815, Flight Cdr Douglas Oliver: assigned to the *Empress*

4   No. 122, Gaskell and No. 812, Bone

5   Flight Lt Arnold Miley, Flight Cdr Douglas Oliver and his mechanic Chief Petty Officer Budds, and Sub-Lt Vivian Gaskell Blackburn and Chief Petty Officer James Bell: the latter had to cast off their flying clothes and dive from their tail-in-the-air Short aeroplane into the sea in order to reach the submarine.

6   Flight Cdr Kilner had mistakenly identified an unknown seaplane as FETH's.

7   Walter Page, US Ambassador to London during WWI, wrote in a letter to Frank N. Doubleday & Others of his admiration for the writing men and women – 'true blue and as thoroughbred as any other class' – and particularly mentioned MH's brave behaviour. 'He's no prig, but a real man.' *The Life & Letters of Walter H. Page* by Burton J. Hendrick, 1923.

8   Hand-written copy of original held by Mark Richards (1922-2009), author and poet, grandson of Maurice Hewlett. All the ALs quoted, unless stated otherwise, privately owned by Mark Richards

9   Reproduced with permission of Curtis Brown Group Ltd, London on behalf of the Trustees of Lord Dunsay Will Trust. Copyright © the Trustees of Lord Dunsany Will Trust 2010.

10 Winston Churchill, the First Lord of the Admiralty, had always shown a keen interest in the potential of aviation. He invited FETH to dine with him when he arrived back in London.

11 FETH began his report to the Director of Air Department, Admiralty: 'I beg to submit that I deeply regret that I should have caused so much trouble and should have necessitated the loss of a seaplane to the Naval Air Service.'

12 A member of a sporting committee, William Sutherland ('parentated to the scotch Sutherlands' but obviously one for whom English was not his first language) wrote from The Hague thanking FETH for his *lovely letter* to himself and his 'countrymen, especially the brave fishermen.' This letter was published in De Revue der Sporten, as well as the Dutch national

newspapers, but Sutherland urged FETH to understand 'that the German's do so many trouble to tell that the Hollanders have more sympathy for huns! *Nothing of that* are the *truth!*' This mysterious correspondent evidently features in a photograph in *Six Weeks at the War* by Millicent, Duchess of Sutherland.

Chapter 21

1   Unusually, for aircraft constructors, Hewlett and Blondeau made all their own parts, bolts, nuts, even turnbuckles. They also supplied spare parts to other firms. What they did not make were the aircraft engines and the electrical instruments.

2   Fore and aft framing member of an airplane fuselage.

3   HBH twice presumed on her personal acquaintance with Arthur J. Balfour to write to him on some matter. Once in 1915, when he was First Lord of the Admiralty, concerning the naval Air Service and the construction and supply of machines: Commodore Sueter (Balfour understood privately) would visit her works and enquire closely into the matters she had brought to his notice. He did not. And again in 1918, when Balfour was Foreign Secretary, about an unspecified scheme for the future, which, he feared, neither warranted public backing, nor had much chance of being self-supporting, although he hoped otherwise.

4   A trick, learnt by HBH from her father's ministry: a tea was always provided for those who attended a mission prayer meeting, or joined a church guild.

5   Extending Dilution, the employment of women in skilled jobs, to privately run factories was abandoned by the Ministry of Munitions in October 1917

Chapter 22

1   The letter HBH included in her typescript addressed to Lady ___ did not differ so very much from the original held by the Imperial War Museum (MUN 15/3). Finding the original material was an unexpectedly wonderful bonus. For a long time it had seemed that proof of the whole episode would never be found and the Lady would forever remain anonymous.

2   In the summer of that year, 1918, there were eighty women being trained.

3   Imperial War Museum, MUN 15/5.

Chapter 24

1   PRO: AIR 2/945, A.S.13554/18

2   Aircraft Supply: Aircraft Contracts: Contracts Claims: Surplus Stores: Timber Controller: Munitions Box Department: Sir John Hunter's Department: CCF (Mr Guedellea)

3   PRO NATS 1/620: L.4.M.N.S.

Chapter 25

1   Admiral Mark Kerr (1864-1944). First flag officer to qualify as a pilot (1914). His career was severely compromised by the controversy over the escape of the German cruisers, *Goeben* and *Breslau*, from Greek waters to Constantinople in 1914. MH wrote a broadside (a sheet of paper printed on one or both sides) on the engagement between HMS *Gloucester* and SMS *Goeben, The Ballad of The Gloster and The Goeben*. He would have been dismayed if he had been privy to the full history, now available, of the *Goeben* and *Breslau* debacle.

2   A number of MH works are to be found on the internet, chief among the publishers being Gutenberg with more than ten titles.

3   Daughter of 11th Earl of Wemyss and Mary Wyndham, married to Herbert Asquith. Was J.M. Barrie's private secretary.

4   MH Member of the Royal Literary Fund (March 1901-October 1914: elected at the same time as his friend Owen Seaman, who flattered him with an exquisite parody of his earliest works in *Borrowed Plumes*.

5   The Academic Committee (a national academy of literature), the establishment of which under the umbrella of the Royal Society of Literature caused controversy and considerable ill-will in the literary world, died a mere stripling of thirty.

6   The Gosse collection, the Brotherton Collection, LUL

7   Sir John Collings Squire (1884-1958)

8 Sir Henry Royce lived in St Margaret's Bay, Dover. Poor health since the death of his partner, Charles Rolls, in a plane crash, meant Royce spent the winter months in the South of France. As the war precluded travel to Le Canadel, and West Wittering made a peaceful alternative to Dover (on a direct Zeppelin route and with a seaplane station nearby), Elm Tree Farm became his English home until his death in 1933.

Associated Royce/Hewlett trivia: (1) Royce's engine powered Britain to victory in the Schneider Trophy in 1929 and 1931 from Calshot when FETH was Station Commander. (2) Eric Gill's father was the vicar of West Wittering. Gill met and was so impressed by Royce, that he incised in stone 'Quidvis Recte Factum Quamvis Humile Praeclarum' (Whatever is rightly done, however humble, is noble) for a mantelpiece in the house now known as Elmstead. Gill carved MH's memorial stone.

9 The briefest of summaries of opinions expressed by MH. House of Lords: 'An out-dated, preposterous, and mischievous assembly, composed almost wholly of one class, the privileged, landowning, capitalist class, which cannot, even if it would, discover, far less sympathise with, the griefs and just claims of any other class.' Pro Free Trade: anti the protectionist Tariff Reform advocated by the conservatives. Land Reform: monopoly in land seemed as wicked to him as 'a corner in bread' Church's monopoly must be removed from schools: 'No church in the world, since the Church has ceased to be universal, can be allowed to interfere with the conscience of parents in the matter of their children's education.' Religion: should be taken out of national schools, but if that could not be, 'then there must be right of access to all denominations in every school.'

10 Under the scheme, fifty cottages were built at Bemerton, now part of Salisbury.

11 Progressive Silent Film List by Carl Bennett. Copyright 200-2001 by Carl Bennet.

12 Louis Vance had acquired the right to make a stage play of *The Spanish Jade* and the scenario by Josephine Lovett was made from that.

Chapter 26

1 Arnold Safroni-Middleton born 1873. Stowaway, stoker, deck hand; bushman, sundowner, busker; pedlar of patent medicines, violin teacher, violinist in a

geisha orchestra in Tokyo. Composed march, Imperial Echoes, (signature tune for BBC's 'Newsreel' during WWII and regimental quick march of the Royal Army Pay Corps). Met Robert Louis Stevenson in Samoa and served on a ship from Sydney to Auckland with a Polish Chief Mate, J.C. Korzeniowski (Joseph Conrad). Wrote *A Vagabond's Odyssey* (1916).

2   Papeete had lost a third of its population in the Influenza Pandemic 1918-19, when the numbers of dead were too great for them to be buried and had instead to be sewn into shrouds to be burnt on great pyres. In New Zealand, the epidemic had officially been declared over in January,1919, but the prohibition on passenger traffic between Australia and New Zealand was not lifted until April of that year.

3   Raratonga is one of the southern Cook Islands, just twenty miles in circumference. Formerly annexed to New Zealand in 1900, in 1965 it became self-governing.

4   Austin Leonard Walsh (1881-1951) and Vivian Claude Walsh (1887-1950). Their parents emigrated to New Zealand in 1883. They first established a mechanical engineering and motor importing business in Auckland. In 1910 they formed the Aero Club of New Zealand and bought the plans for a British Howard Wright biplane, which they built in the grounds of the family home in Orakei Road, Remuera, Auckland: their sisters Veronica and Doreen sewed the wing covers for this first aircraft, named Manurewa No 1. Leo considered a flying boat based on the American Curtiss type would suit New Zealand conditions, the construction of which was completed in November 1914 and was piloted by Vivian on its maiden flight, 1 January 1915. In October 1915 the New Zealand Flying School was established on the foreshore of Mission Bay, in Auckland and in February 1916 the New Zealand Defence Department became involved in the running of the school as the British RFC and RNAS required pilots. After the war, the Walsh brothers were associated with the first airmail flights in New Zealand. In 1924 the government took over the flying school and transferred it to Hobsonville.

5   J.W.H. Scotland, in 1914, made the first long-distance flight in New Zealand: from Invercargill to Gore, 38 miles in 38 minutes.

6   Frederick William Platts, Resident Commissioner, Cook Islands at Raratonga 1916-1921.

7   His avoirdupois matched, perhaps, by the weightiness of his name, Arthur

William de Brito Savile Foljambe, Earl of Liverpool: quite hard to be jolly with all that on your shoulders. Lord Liverpool was New Zealand's first Governor General (previously the title had been simply Governor) from 1917-1920.

8   Long pig: human flesh. At the first known landing of Europeans on Raratonga in 1813, fighting broke out between the sailors from the Endeavour and the locals. Ann Butchers, the Captain's girlfriend, had the dubious honour of being the only known white woman to be eaten.

Chapter 27

1   Dr Maui Wiremu Piti Naera Pomare (1875/6 – 1930). His wife had a white father and a Maori mother.

2   Dr Daisy Platts-Mills (1868-1956) was the mother of John Platts-Mills QC (d.2001), a lifelong socialist and campaigner for trade unions and human rights throughout the Commonwealth. He became Labour MP for Finsbury in 1945.

3   The notion that Colonel B. might be a Colonel A.V. Bettington will persist, despite unsuccessful attempts to confirm it. Colonel Bettington had been sent as an adviser on the future of New Zealand's airforce in 1919 and he and Old Bird met in Christchurch, when she was given the flight in the Bristol. Bettington was associated with Bristols.

4   Other famous firms included Martinsyde, Airco and Nieuport

5   Originally Lea Road, renamed Hewlett Road to avoid confusion with Lea Road in Luton in 1928, the year Leagrave officially became a district of Luton.

Chapter 28

1   A balaam-box or basket. An editor's box or basket for worthless or rejected matter (now "spiked").

2   bMS Eng 985.1 Houghton Library, Harvard University. As described by the much tried WTS, New York contact for Maurice's agent W.M. Colles of the Authors' Syndicate. WTS considered MH to be obsessed with sex and animality. He also had trouble placing MH's work, particularly his poetry.

3   b.f.t stood for beautiful flowering tree, an abbreviation used by nurserymen which greatly took MH's fancy. Lotta, daughter of J.A. Symonds, was married to Walter Leaf, the 'banker poet' as MH called him. A man of formidable intellect, HBH only lost her awe of him when she practised a successful April Fool on him, when she and her little Pia were staying with the Leafs.

4   To name a few: Lascelles Abercrombie and family; J.C. Squire and, through him, the cricket team that Archie MacDonell immortalised in *England Their England*; the Belloc-Lowndes; Edmund Blunden; Clifford Bax; Alec Waugh..

5   *The Life and Death of Richard Yea and Nay* was dramatised for radio and broadcast by the BBC Home service in 1955: cast included Valentine Dyall, Maureen Pryor, Leon Quatermaine and Carleton Hobbs.

6   Gosse collection, Brotherton collection, LUL

7   AL in private hands. Reproduced with permission of The Society of Authors on behalf of the Bernard Shaw Estate.

8   Reproduced with permission of Peter Newbolt.

Chapter 29

1   French-Romanian Company of Air Navigation was set up in 1920 using Romanian capital and French technical equipment. Its financial headquarters was in Bucharest. Nicolae Titulesco initiated the company, so it is possible that the 'Roumanian lady', that HBH met, was his wife.

2   On 2nd September, 1923 (about four months after HBH's trip) the Franco-Romanian company inaugurated a regular night flight service to Bucharest from Pancevo: this marked the beginning of world night air traffic.

3   It is likely that the two craft she was passenger in were a Potez 7 (or 9) and a Salmson 2A2: both have been mentioned on two separate websites, one French and one Romanian, each with their own take on the history of the French-Romanian Company of Air Navigation (Compagnie Franco-Romaine de navigation Aerienne): to become CIDNA (Compagnie Internationale de Navigation Aerienne in 1925

4   Tukatea is still uninhabited and is a bird-life sanctuary, visited with great difficulty twice a year by a conservationist.

5   According to HBH, the Resident Commissioner, Captain Valloneth, was also very proud that his house boasted 'two real lavatories with European fixtures'; also that a former non-white Resident Commissioner had been equally proud of his 'lavatory of white porcelain, with a string to pull'. When Sir Maui Pomare visited the Cook Islands in his capacity of Minister for Native Affairs in New Zealand, he wondered at the lack of a polished wooden seat: "Wait, wait" cried the Ariki and took his guest to the main reception room. There, on the wall, was a large photograph of Sir Maui in full fig – framed by the lavatory seat.

6   May 18, 1927.

7   Dr T.H. Winslow translated from the Swedish Poul Bjerre's *The Remaking of Marriage* which was published by Macmillan, N.Y. in 1931. He had provided HBH with excellent company on the *Makura* on the way to Tahiti.

Chapter 30

1   Company formed in February 1929 by D.C. Cattenach and Associates. Ian Keith was appointed pilot of the Blackburn Bluebird III, which was sold on to Messrs J.E. Tidd and R. Kemp of Hamilton, when the company folded.

2   Fokker F.VIIb/3m.

Chapter 31

1   Jean Batten (1909-1982) born in Rotorua, NZ. Went to England to learn to fly. Broke Amy Johnson's record, on third attempt, by five days and flew solo from London to Darwin (16 stops in 14 days and 22 hrs) in May 1934: she made a six week triumphal aerial tour of her home country in June/July. In 1936, Batten made record-breaking flight from London to Auckland.

2   FETH (assumed to be the 'Darling Sonny' of an unfinished – due to turbulence over the desert – letter from the K.L.M. 'Stork') had travelled out with his first wife and daughter. He and Elsie Baker had become engaged in HBH's absence on her first trip to Raratonga and married after her return in 1919. They had one daughter, Jasmine (b. May 1921). The marriage ended in divorce.

3   In 1939, when the airport was officially opened, the then Minister of Defence, the Hon. F. Jones, declared that the road adjacent to the aerodrome be named Hewletts Road in recognition of the services rendered by Mrs Hewlett and her son in pioneering aviation in Tauranga. "Three cheers for the Empire aviatrix!" As forms of commemoration go, having a road named after herself would have seemed eminently more acceptable to HBH than a display in a museum.

Maurice Hewlett had but one road to his name, compared to HBH's three (two in Leagrave). In the company of Congreve, Fletcher, and Farquhar, he is remembered in Roslindale, Boston, USA.

4   Dorothy G. Hewlett (nee Pitt) was a driving force as director and actor in the Tauranga Repertory Company.

ADDENDUM

HEWLETT AND BLONDEAU

Omnia Works, Battersea

3 Farman biplanes for Vickers flying school, Brooklands, later renamed Vickers Boxkites nos. 19-21. Farman biplane for the Pashley Brothers flying school at Shoreham.
3 Hanriot single-seat monoplanes under contract to the French Hanriot company.
1 Dyott monoplane in which George Dyott gave several demonstrations in America. Caudron types C & G. Customers included W.H. Ewen Ltd, J. Scotland in New Zealand, Sydney Pickles, instructor for the Admiralty (his mother was the first woman to drive a car in Australia).
2 BE2a, nos.49-50, for Royal Navy (CP37126/13)

Omnia Works, Leagrave

12 BE2c	Nos. 976-987	CP57016/14
6 BE2c	Nos.1189-1194	ditto
2 A.D. Scout	Nos.1452-1453	CP38552/15

Also known as Sparrow, designed for anti-zeppelin defence. HBH wrote: *The moment Gustave got the designs he knew they would be no good. They had a veritable network of controls inside, very inaccessible, with lots of small wheels and pulleys. We re-named them "Clapham Junctions".*

1 Dyott Monoplane	No. 1598	CP44330/15
2 Dyott Battleplane	Nos. 3687-3688	CP106447/16
24 BE2c	Nos. 8410-8433	CP63855/15
50 A.W. FK3	Nos. A1461-1510	87A/476
50 A.W. FK3	Nos. A8091-8140	87A/476
300 A.W. FK3	Nos. B9501-9800	AS13073 (03.07.17)
150 Avro 504 J/K	Nos. D7051-7200	AS37764 (10.01.18)
100 Avro 504K	Nos. F9746-9845	35A/1675/C1792 (25.02.18)
150 Avro 504K	Nos. H7413-7562	35A/2054/C2332 (31.08.18)
	(No. H7534 converted to 504N)	
100 Avro 504K	Nos. J3992-4091	Order cancelled.

Maurice Hewlett

NOVELS

1898	*The Forest Lovers*	Macmillan
1900	*The Life and Death of Richard Yea-and-Nay*	Macmillan
1904	*The Queen's Quair*	Macmillan
1905	*Fool Errant*	Heinemann
1907	*The Stooping Lady*	Macmillan
1908	*The Spanish Jade*	Cassell & Co.

	Halfway House	Chapman & Hall
1909	*Open Country*	Macmillan
1910	*Rest Harrow*	Macmillan
1911	*Brazenhead the Great*	Smith, Elder & Co
1912	*Mrs Lancelot*	Macmillan
1913	*Bendish*	Macmillan
1915	*The Little Iliad*	Heinemann
	A Lover's Tale	Ward Lock & Co
1916	*Love and Lucy*	Macmillan
	Frey and His Wife	Ward Lock & Co
1917	*Thorgils of Treadholt*	Ward Lock & Co
1918	*Gudrid the Fair*	Constable & Co
1919	*The Outlaw*	Constable & Co
1920	*The Light Heart*	Chapman & Hall
1921	*Mainwaring*	W. Collins Sons & Co

SHORT STORIES

1899	*Little Novels of Italy*	Chapman & Hall
1901	*New Canterbury Tales*	Constable & Co
1905	*Fond Adventures*	Macmillan

POETRY

1896	*Songs and Meditations*	Constable & Co
1898	*Pan and the Young Shepherd*	John Lane
1909	*Artemision*	Elkin Mathews
1911	*The Agonists*	Macmillan
	The Song of Renny	Macmillan
1913	*Helen Redeemed*	Macmillan
1914	*Singsongs of the War*	Poetry Bookshop
1916	*Gai Saber*	Elkin Mathews
	The Song of the Plow	Heinemann
1917	*Peridore and Paravail*	Heinemann
1918	*The Village Wife's Lament*	Martin Secker
1920	*Flowers in the Grass*	Constable & Co

ESSAYS

1920	*In a Green Shade*	Bell & Sons
1921	*Wiltshire Essays*	Humphrey Milford
1922	*Extemporary Essays*	Humphrey Milford
1924	*Last Essays*	Heinemann

MISCELLANEOUS

1895	*Earthwork Out of Tuscany*	J.M. Dent & Co
	Masque of Dead Florentines	J.M. Dent & Co
1904	*The Road in Tuscany*	Macmillan
1913	*Lore of Proserpine*	Macmillan

SOURCES and BIBLIOGRAPHY

Bodleian Library, Oxford University
British Library, MSS Collections
British Library, Newspapers, Colindale
Brooklands Museum Trust Ltd
Brotherton Library, University of Leeds
Community of the Holy Name, Oakwood, Derby
The Dorset County Museum
Harry Ransom Humanities Resource Center, Austin, Texas
Houghton Library, Harvard University
London Library
London Metropolitan Archives
National Archives, Kew
Westminster Public Library

Asquith, Lady Cynthia, *Diaries 1915-1918*, Alfred A. Knopf, New York 1969
Belloc Lowndes, Marie, *The Merrie Wives of Westminster*, Macmillan 1946
Beerbohm, Max, *Seven Men*, New York Review Book 2000
Beevers, David MA (Cantab) AMA, *St Peter's Church Vauxhall. A History*, St Peter's Heritage Centre and The Vauxhall Society 1991
Binyon, Laurence ed., *The Letters of Maurice Hewlett*, Methuen 1926
Birkin, Andrew, *J.M. Barrie and the Lost Boys*, Constable 1979
Bowley, Arthur L., *Prices and Wages in the UK 1914-1920. Economic and Social History of the World War. British series*, OUP 1921
Bramson, Alan, *Pure Luck. The Authorized Biography of Sir Thomas Sopwith, 1888-1989*, Patrick Stephens Ltd 1990
Braybon, Gail, *Women Workers in the First World War*, Croom Helm 1981
Bronner, Milton, *Maurice Hewlett. Being a critical review of his prose and*

poetry, John W. Luce Boston 1910

Chitty, Susan, *Playing the Game. A Biography of Sir Henry Newbolt*, Quartet Books, 1997

Cooper, Ken, *Luton. Scene Again*, Phillimore 1990

Garland, Hamlin, *My Friendly Contemporaries*, Macmillan (New York) 1932

Goodall, M.H., *Flying Start. Flying Schools and Clubs at Brooklands 1910-1939*, Brooklands Museum Publication 1995

Goodall, Michael H. & Tagg, Albert E., *British Aircraft Before the Great War*, Schiffer Publishing 2001

Gosse, Edmund, *Books on the Table*, Heinemann 1921

Gowers, Rebecca, *The Swamp of Death. A True Tale of Victorian Lies and Murder*, Hamish Hamilton 2004

Green, Roger Lancelyn, *A.E.W.Mason*, Max Parrish 1952

Gwynn, Stephen, *Experiences of a Literary Man*, Thornton Butterworth 1921

Harrison, Frederic, *Memories and Thoughts*, Macmillan 1906

Hart-Davis, Rupert, ed., *Letters of Max Beerbohm, 1892-1956*, Oxford University Press 1989

Hartrick, A.S., *A Painter's Pilgrimage Through Fifty Years*, Cambridge University Press 1939

Hassall, Christopher, *Edward Marsh. A Biography*, Longmans 1959

Hewlett, Mrs Maurice, *Our Flying Men*, printed by T. Beaty Hart, Kettering 1917

Hind, C. Lewis, *Authors and I*, John Lane 1921

Hobhouse, Hermione, *Thomas Cubitt, Master Builder*, Management Books 2000 1995

Holman-Hunt, Diana, *My Grandmothers and I*, Hamish Hamilton 1960

Housman, Laurence, *The Unexpected Years*, Jonathon Cape 1937

Layman, R.D., *The Cuxhaven Raid. The World's First Carrier Air Strike*, Conway Maritime Press 1985

Leaf, Charlotte M., *Walter Leaf*, John Murray 1932

Le Gallienne, Richard, *Attitudes and Avowals*, John Lane 1910

Linklater, Andro, *Compton Mackenzie. A Life*, Chatto & Windus 1987

Lowndes, Susan, ed., *Diaries and Letters of Marie Belloc Lowndes 1911-1947*, Chatto & Windus 1971

Lucas, Audrey, *E.V. Lucas: A Portrait*, Methuen 1939

Lucas, E.F., *Reading, Writing and Remembering. A Literary Record*, Methuen 1932

Mackail, Denis, *The Story of J.M.B.*, Peter Davies 1941

Mackenzie, Compton, *My Life and Times. Octave 2,3 and 4*, Chatto & Windus 1964

Marwick, Arthur, *The Deluge: British Society and the First World War*, Bodley Head 1965

Metcalf, Priscilla, *James Knowles. Victorian Editor and Architect*, Clarendon Press 1980

Miller, Geoffrey, *Superior Force. The Conspiracy behind the Escape of Goeben and Breslau*, The University of Hull Press 1996

Newbolt, Margaret, *The Later Life and Letters of Sir Henry Newbolt*, Faber & Faber 1942

Pakenham, Thomas, *The Scramble for Africa*, Weidenfeld & Nicolson 1991

Pennell, Joseph, *The Adventures of an Illustrator*, T. Fisher Unwin 1925

Seaman, Owen, *Borrowed Plumes*, Archibald & Co 1902

Squire, J.C., *Sunday Mornings*, Heinemann 1930

Sutherland, Bruce, *Maurice Hewlett. Historical Romancer*, Philadelphia 1938

Sutro, Alfred, *Celebrities and Simple Souls*, Duckworth 1933

Travers, E., *Cross Country*, Hothersall & Travers 1989

Wilson J.W. & Perkins R., *Angels in Blue Jackets. The Navy at Messina, 1908*, Picton 1985

Yates, L.K., *The Woman's Part. A Record of Munitions Work.*

Herbert, Louisa, *Women's Responsibilities*. The substance of an address given at the Women's Meeting at the Church Congress, Rhyl, October 9, 1891. Held by Malvern Public Library.

The Community of the Mission Sisters of the Holy Name of Jesus commonly known as the Community of the Holy Name. (Original title: *St Peter's Mission Sisterhood*). Published by The Community of the Holy Name.

ACKNOWLEDGEMENTS

For permission to use original correspondence I am grateful to the following: Trustees of Lord Dunsany Will Trust, The Society of Authors on behalf of the Bernard Shaw Estate, and Ana Lowndes Marques Vicente. Many thanks are owed to members of the Herbert and Hewlett families in both the UK and the Antipodes for sharing their memories and photographs so willingly. They include Richard Agnew, Mollie Haynes, Anthony Hewlett, Richard Hewlett, Richenda Miers, Elizabeth Nurse, Denys Reed, Julian Richards, Mark Richards, Lady Diana Tritton, Mai Welby-Everard, Roger Welby-Everard, Ann Wilcox.

The prince of specialist advice and the generous source of much invaluable research on Hewlett and Blondeau Ltd has been Michael Goodall from start to finish.

And, finally, my family deserve a thousand thanks for their whole-hearted, practical, and long sustained support. It ranged from scanning images, designing the cover, and reading more than one version of the manuscript to plying me with sandwiches, cups of tea and, when necessary, glasses of wine, along with their criticism. It was matchless.

9 781848 763371